Trial by Fire

Recent Titles in
Contributions in Military Studies

Trial by Fire

Command and the British Expeditionary Force in 1914

Nikolas Gardner

Contributions in Military Studies, Number 227

Westport, Connecticut
London

Library of Congress Cataloging-in-Publication Data

Gardner, Nikolas, 1970–
   Trial by fire : command and the British Expeditionary Force in 1914 / Nikolas Gardner.
     p. cm.—(Contributions in military studies, ISSN 0883–6884 ; no. 227)
   Includes bibliographical references and index.
   ISBN 0–313–32473–5 (alk. paper)
    1. Command of troops.   2. Great Britain. Army—History—World War, 1914–1918. 3.
   World War, 1914–1918—Campaigns—Western Front. I. Title. II. Series.
   D546.G37 2003
   940.4′0941—dc21   2002193033

British Library Cataloguing in Publication Data is available.

Library of Congress Catalog Card Number: 2002193033
ISBN: 0–313–32473–5
ISSN: 0883–6884

First published in 2003

Praeger Publishers, 88 Post Road West, Westport, CT 06881
An imprint of Greenwood Publishing Group, Inc.
www.praeger.com

Printed in the United States of America

The paper used in this book complies with the
Permanent Paper Standard issued by the National
Information Standards Organization (Z39.48–1984).

10 9 8 7 6 5 4 3 2 1

Copyright Acknowledgments

The author and publisher gratefully acknowledge permission to quote from the following:

Nikolas Gardner, "Command in Crisis: The British Expeditionary Force and the Forest of Mormal, August 1914." *War & Society*. 16:2 (October 1998), 13–32. First published in *War & Society*. Used with permission.

Liddle Collection, Brotherton Library, University of Leeds, Leeds: A.N. Acland Papers; H.M. Alexander Papers; R.D. Jeune Papers; Transcript of Tapes #225–226, Peter Liddle interview with Sir James Marshall-Cornwall, May 1974; Transcript of Tape #268, Peter Liddle interview with Lieutenant-General Floyer-Acland, August 1974. Used with permission.

Archibald Murray Papers of the Imperial War Museum, London. Used with permission of Alisdair Murray.

Rawlinson Papers of the National Army Museum, London. Used with permission of the National Army Museum.

Rawlinson Papers at Churchill College, Cambridge. Used with permission of Andrew Rawlinson.

Liddell Hart Centre for Military Archives, King's College, London: Edmund Allenby Papers, E.H. Beddington Papers, John Charteris Papers, Sydney Clive Papers, Henry De Lisle Papers, James Edmonds Papers, Basil Liddell Hart Papers, Frederick Maurice Papers, Archie Montgomery-Massingberd Papers, Edward Spears Papers. Used with permission.

Lord Loch Papers of the Imperial War Museum, London. Used with permission of Lavina Loch.

British Library, London: Aylmer Hunter-Weston Papers; Shaw-Sparrow Papers; Oriental and India Office Collection, L/MIL/5/825, "Reports of Chief Censor." Used with permission of Crown Copyright, British Library, London.

Henry Wilson Papers of the Imperial War Museum, London. Used with permission of the Trustees of the Imperial War Museum, London.

For Carina with Love

Contents

Maps

Acknowledgments

Without the support and advice of numerous individuals, this project would never have been completed. Its shortcomings, however, are mine alone. Since the inception of this study as a doctoral dissertation, I have benefited immensely from the guidance of Tim Travers, who has taught me much about the history of the British Army while setting an example of scholarship worthy of emulation. John Ferris, Holger Herwig, James Keeley, and Terry Copp offered perceptive criticisms of my dissertation and advice on how to address them. Terry Terriff introduced me to theoretical perspectives that have helped me better understand command in 1914. Dennis Showalter made valuable suggestions and encouraged me to publish this book, despite knowing that he would probably have to read the manuscript again as a result. I learned much from presenting aspects of this work at various conferences. In particular, participants at the Laurier Centre for Military Strategic and Disarmament Studies Annual Colloquium in 1999, and the Annual Conference of the Society for Military History in 2002, challenged me to rethink my arguments and do more reading. Heather Staines and Terri Jennings provided patient assistance in the publication process.

Research for this book could not have been completed without the help of Chris Doa, who provided accommodation in London, and forgot about the rent when my money ran out. It would have been completed sooner without friends who commented on how slowly my work was progressing, and then proceeded to distract me even further. For these much-needed distractions I am indebted to Sandy McDougall, Lars Juergensen, Val Holtom, Jennifer Pettit, Brad Stevens, Rod Henderson, Steve Mitchell and Matt and Chris Williams, as well as my brothers, Tim and Tobi Gardner. I am particularly grateful to my parents, Jim and Loreen Gardner, for their unwavering support. Most of all, I would like to thank my wife Carina, a historian herself, who has improved the book considerably through her incisive criticisms and constant encouragement.

Introduction

In the annals of British military history, the British Expeditionary Force (BEF) of 1914 retains a reputation for valor that far exceeds its diminutive size. From the beginning of the First World War in August 1914 until the conclusion of the First Battle of Ypres in mid-November, Sir John French's "Old Contemptibles" played an important role in preventing a German victory in 1914. After colliding with the advancing German Army in mid-August, the BEF checked superior enemy forces at Mons and Le Cateau, and maintained its composure throughout the prolonged retreat that followed. As the enemy approached Paris in early September, British soldiers joined their French allies in a counteroffensive which swept the enemy back to the River Aisne. Finally, late October and November 1914 saw the heroic last stand of the battalions of the Regular Army, as they endured debilitating losses to repel heavy and repeated German attacks during the First Battle of Ypres.

This interpretation, emphasizing the gallant sacrifices of British regiments in 1914, has proven to be remarkably durable. It emerged as early as 1916 in accounts by Ernest Hamilton and Sir Arthur Conan-Doyle, and was subsequently reinforced by memoirs of British soldiers who participated in the campaign.[1] Sir James Edmonds's two-volume *Official History* of 1914, published in 1922 and 1925, provided a narrative of the operations of the BEF unmatched in its level of detail. Given the official historian's reluctance to criticize his former colleagues openly, however, he included little analysis of decisions made by British commanders. As a result, like earlier histories of 1914, Edmonds presented the campaign primarily as a series of encounters at the battalion level.[2] The operational context in which these encounters occurred remained largely unexplained.

Accounts published by senior British officers in the 1920s and 1930s offered some insight into the experiences of commanders in 1914. Nevertheless, they did not provide a sustained analysis of operations that placed the achievements of British regiments in a broader perspective.[3] It was only in the 1960s that historians began to examine the conduct of the 1914 campaign by senior commanders. John Terraine's *Mons* chronicled the experiences of the BEF in the opening weeks of the war, criticizing the apparent lack of composure that prevailed at General Headquarters (GHQ) in this period. *Death of an Army*, by Anthony Farrar-Hockley, made similar criticisms of senior British commanders during the First Battle of Ypres.[4] Significantly, however, both books were published when British archival documents from the First World War, such as unit war diaries and the personal papers of senior officers, were only beginning to become available to scholars. Thus, these accounts provide only limited insights into the operations of the BEF in 1914.

Since the early 1980s, there has been a proliferation of scholarship on the British Army in the First World War based on newly available archival materials. Historians such as Robin Prior and Trevor Wilson, Tim Travers, and Shelford Bidwell and Dominick Graham have shed significant light on command in the BEF and its impact on operations.[5] Initially, these studies emphasized the difficulties experienced by the British officer corps in adjusting to the technological and organizational challenges of the First World War. A growing body of literature has emerged in the past decade, however, arguing that officers experienced a significant learning curve that placed the BEF at the forefront of European armies by 1918.[6]

Notably, this recent scholarship has overlooked the opening campaign of the war. Although biographies of Sir John French and John Gough have provided insights into the conduct of the 1914 campaign by individual officers, the operations of the BEF in this period remain poorly understood.[7] Even relatively recent accounts of 1914 have continued to focus on the heroic exploits of the "Old Contemptibles" at the regimental level.[8] This lack of scholarly attention to the dynamics of command in 1914 stems in part from the assumption that British officers, at the bottom of a steep learning curve, were simply incapable of exerting a significant influence on the opening campaign of the war, particularly given the rapid pace of operations during much of this period. According to J.M. Bourne: "[t]he battles of 1914 were 'soldiers' battles.' The key decisions were made 'at the sharp end' among formations of company level or even below. Command and control at the highest level was often irrelevant and sometimes impossible."[9]

Bourne's assertion suggests that an analysis of command would be of little use in illuminating the operations of the BEF in 1914. It seems unlikely, however, that British commanders were entirely irrelevant in this period, and for two reasons. First, an inability to grasp the scale and technological realities of the First World War did not render officers incapable of influencing events on the battlefield. Indeed, the officers who planned the British offensive on the Somme had a detrimental impact on operations on 1 July 1916 largely because they did not wholly comprehend the implications of modern firepower. Second, British officers certainly did not go to war in 1914 intending to be irrelevant. On the contrary, the colonial operations in which most had participated earlier in their careers had shown that individual commanders could be a significant factor on the battlefield, and make their reputations in the process. Thus, while the unprecedented scale and intensity of the First World War may have overwhelmed many officers, it is nonetheless essential to examine their conduct of the 1914 campaign in order to understand the operations of the BEF in this period.

Therefore, this study will examine the exercise of command in the BEF from its mobilization in August 1914 until the end of the First Battle of Ypres in mid-November. In the process, it will address a significant gap in existing scholarship by illuminating the operations of the BEF in the opening months of the First World War. While this study will concentrate primarily upon command at the corps level and at GHQ, leadership at the divisional, brigade, and battalion levels will be discussed in the context of particular battles. Thus, the following two questions will be addressed: First, How did British officers exercise command in 1914? Second, How did their conduct of the 1914 campaign affect the operations of the BEF? In an effort to shed light on the "culture of command" in the BEF in 1914, the first chapter of this study will offer a series of brief biographical sketches of senior British commanders and staff officers. These biographies will provide an acquaintance with key members of the BEF at the beginning of the campaign, and suggest several tendencies and values common to many British officers in this period. Chapter 2 will examine the operations of the BEF in August and early September 1914. In particular, it will concentrate on the functioning of the British command structure between the battles of Mons and Le Cateau, a period largely overlooked by existing accounts of 1914. Chapter 3 will examine the advance of the BEF during the second week of September and the ensuing stalemate that prevailed along the River Aisne, focusing on the operations of the army as well as the response of British officers to the unexpected realities of the 1914 campaign.

The last four chapters will examine the exercise of command from the perspective of four of the corps that participated in the First Battle of Ypres. Chapter 4 will consider the operations of Sir Horace Smith-Dorrien's II Corps in October 1914. Chapter 5 will provide a similar examination of the operations of Sir Henry Rawlinson's IV Corps. Chapter 6 will assess the experiences of Sir James Willcocks's Indian Corps in late October and early November 1914. Finally, Chapter 7 will examine the operations of Sir Douglas Haig's I Corps at the height of the First Battle of Ypres, in late October and early November. The study will conclude by making several arguments regarding the operations of the BEF and the exercise of command by British officers during the 1914 campaign.

It should be emphasized that it is not the intent of this study to diminish the achievements of the BEF in 1914. As numerous accounts have demonstrated, British soldiers displayed extraordinary determination in resisting attacks by superior German forces throughout the opening campaign of the First World War. Given the inexperience of British officers in conducting operations against a well-organized opponent equipped with modern weaponry, however, it is to be expected that the following analysis will uncover shortcomings in their exercise of command in this period. By discussing such problems, its intention is simply to provide a better understanding of the operations of the BEF, thereby illuminating the accomplishments of British soldiers more effectively. It is also important to note that what follows is not a detailed comparison of command in the BEF with other European armies in 1914. Occasional parallels will be drawn between the experiences of British officers and those of their counterparts in other European armies. Nonetheless, only additional archival research on the operations of other armies on the Western Front in 1914 would provide a detailed analysis and comparison. Thus, the focus of this examination will be limited to the exercise of command by British officers in 1914. The initial stages of the First World War exposed these officers to warfare of an unprecedented intensity. In order to understand their response, it is most appropriate to begin by gaining an acquaintance with the officers themselves.

NOTES

1. Ernest Hamilton, *The First Seven Divisions: Being a Detailed Account of the Fighting from Mons to Ypres* (New York: Dutton, 1916); Arthur Conan-Doyle, *The British Campaign in France and Flanders, 1914* (London: Hodder and Stoughton, 1916). For memoirs, see for example: Harry Beaumont, *Old Contemptible* (London: Hutchinson, 1933); F.A. Bolwell, *With a Reservist in France* (London: Routledge, 1916); A. Corbett-Smith, *The Retreat from Mons, by One Who Shared in It* (London: Cassell, 1916); A. Corbett-Smith, *The Marne—And After* (Toronto: Cassell, 1917); J.G.W. Hyndson, *From Mons to the First Battle of Ypres* (London: Wyman, 1933).

2. Sir James Edmonds, *Military Operations: France and Belgium, 1914*, 2 vols. (London: Macmillan, 1922 and 1925). On Edmonds's motives, see David French, "Sir James Edmonds and the Official History: France and Belgium", in Brian Bond, ed., *The First World War and British Military History* (Oxford: Clarendon, 1991).

3. See, for example, John Charteris, *At GHQ* (London: Cassell, 1931); Count Edward Gleichen, *The Doings of the Fifteenth Infantry Brigade, August 1914 to March 1915* (London: Blackwood, 1917); Hubert Gough, *The Fifth Army* (London: Hodder and Stoughton, 1931); R.A.L. Haldane, *A Brigade of the Old Army* (London: 1920); Frederick Maurice, *Forty Days in 1914* (London: Constable, 1921).

4. Anthony Farrar-Hockley, *Death of an Army* (New York: Morrow, 1968); John Terraine, *Mons* (London: Batsford, 1960).

5. Robin Prior and Trevor Wilson, *Passchendaele: The Untold Story* (New Haven: Yale University Press, 1996); Tim Travers, *How the War Was Won: Command and Technology in the British Army on the Western Front, 1917–1918* (London: Routledge, 1992); Prior and Wilson, *Command on the Western Front: The Military Career of Sir Henry Rawlinson, 1914–1918* (Oxford: Blackwell, 1992); Travers, *The Killing Ground: The British Army, the Western Front and the Emergence of Modern Warfare, 1900–1918,* (London: Unwin Hyman, 1987); Shelford Bidwell and Dominick Graham, *Fire-Power: British Army Weapons and Theories of War, 1904–1945* (London: Allen and Unwin, 1982).

6. See, for example, Gary Sheffield, *Forgotten Victory: The First World War—Myths and Realities* (London: Headline, 2001); Albert Palazzo, *Seeking Victory on the Western Front: The British Army and Chemical Warfare in World War One* (Lincoln: Nebraska University Press, 2000); Brian Bond, ed., *'Look to Your Front': Studies in the First World War by the British Commission for Military History* (Kent: Spellmount 1999); Ian Malcolm Brown, *British Logistics on the Western Front: 1914–1919* (Westport, CT: Praeger, 1998); Paddy Griffith, ed., *British Fighting Methods in the Great War* (London: Frank Cass, 1996).

7. Ian F.W. Beckett, *Johnnie Gough, V.C.* (London: Tom Donovan, 1989); Richard Holmes, *The Little Field-Marshal: Sir John French* (London: Jonathan Cape, 1981).

8. See, for example, Lyn Macdonald, *1914* (London: Michael Joseph, 1987); David Ascoli, *The Mons Star* (London: Harrap, 1981).

9. J.M. Bourne, *Britain and the Great War, 1914–1918* (London: Arnold, 1989), 28.

1

The "Hybrid" Officer Goes to War: British Commanders and Staff Officers in 1914

The Edwardian officer corps was hardly an organization lacking in military experience. As J.M. Bourne has observed: "The intensity and range of professional opportunity offered by the prewar British Army was enormous."[1] For the commanders of the British Expeditionary Force (BEF), however, the 1914 campaign proved unprecedented in its scale and intensity. Since the Crimean War, the principal task of the British Army had consisted of suppressing relatively ill-equipped native insurrections in the colonies. While the war in South Africa provided some indication of the capabilities of an enemy armed with modern weaponry, no British officer had faced an adversary comparable in size, organization, or equipment to the German Army of 1914. Nor had any member of the BEF controlled a force larger than a division during active operations. Thus, at the beginning of the First World War, British officers had few established procedures or relevant experiences to guide them in their decisions. In these circumstances, there remained considerable scope for the individual traits, preferences, and proclivities of officers to influence their conduct of operations. In order to understand the exercise of command in the BEF at the beginning of the First World War, it is therefore useful to gain an acquaintance with British commanders and staff officers in this period. The following series of brief biographical sketches of prominent officers will shed light on their personalities, habits, and values.

In addition to demonstrating the quirks of specific commanders, biographical information can provide insights into the nature of the military profession in Britain in the early twentieth century. In *The Soldier and the State*, Samuel Huntington defined a profession as a vocational group possessing the following traits: 1) a collective consciousness of itself as a group separate from the rest of society; 2) a responsibility to perform a task deemed essential to society; and 3) a body of specialized expertise relevant to that task.[2] According to this definition, the British officer corps of 1914 may be defined as a "professional" organization. An examination of prominent commanders and staff officers will identify values and practices common to this organization that determined the level of professional *competence* of its members in the task of conducting military operations against a capable adversary. Thus, this chapter will offer a series of historical snapshots of a representative array of officers of the BEF in the opening months of the war. Included in this group are Sir John French, the commander-in-chief, his four senior staff officers, and a selection of six field commanders at the corps, divisional, and brigade levels. These sketches will both illuminate the idiosyncrasies of particular individuals, and provide raw material for a subsequent analysis of characteristics common to these officers at the beginning of the First World War.

AT GHQ—SIR JOHN FRENCH AND HIS STAFF

Sir John French

The operations of the BEF in 1914 were directed by the commander-in-chief with the support of "G" section of General Headquarters (GHQ). "G" section itself was headed by the chief of the General Staff (CGS), and divided into ostensibly equal Operations and Intelligence subsections. Within this command structure at the beginning of the war there existed a diverse and often contentious mix of personalities and ideas.[3] At the helm of the BEF stood Sir John French. Sixty-one years old in August 1914, French was the senior active officer in the British army in 1914 aside from the Secretary of State for War, Lord Kitchener. He had made his reputation commanding the British Cavalry Division during the South African War. In February 1900, he had directed the celebrated charge at Klip Drift that led to the relief of Kimberley. The renown resulting from this feat propelled French's career forward after his return from South Africa. He was appointed commander-in-chief at Aldershot in 1902, inspector-general of the army in 1907, and chief of the Imperial General Staff (CIGS) in 1913.

In addition to advancing his career, the charge at Klip Drift apparently convinced French of the continued value of traditional cavalry tactics, despite the impact of increased firepower on the battlefield. Throughout this period, Sir John French and his protégé, Sir Douglas Haig, remained staunch defenders of the *arme blanche* against reformers such as Lord Roberts, who placed greater emphasis on dismounted tactics. French's advocacy of the charge was tempered by a respect for firepower. Nevertheless, in the years before 1914, he remained a strong proponent of the cavalry spirit, an intuitive philosophy which, in his own words, emphasized " 'élan', 'dash', [and] a fixed determination always to take the offensive and secure the initiative."[4]

However anachronistic this approach to warfare may appear in retrospect, Sir John French was by no means devoid of merit as a commander. As a cavalry officer, he understood clearly the importance of morale, a factor that would figure prominently in the fate of the BEF during the privations of the retreat from Mons. After the war, W.H. Bartholomew, a staff officer at GHQ in 1914, maintained that it was French who had "inspired them all at darkest moments, like a moral tonic."[5] French's ability to maintain morale was facilitated by his affection for the rank and file of the army, a sentiment apparently reciprocated by the soldiers. Sir William Robertson, quartermaster-general of the BEF in 1914, commented in his memoirs: "Sir John was exceedingly popular with the troops, and I doubt if any other General in the Army could have sustained in them to the same extent the courage and resolution which they displayed under the trying circumstances of the first six months of the war."[6]

Nevertheless, neither Sir John French's seniority nor his ability to hearten demoralized soldiers was sufficient to prepare him for the responsibilities of his position in 1914. His motivational skills notwithstanding, French lacked a similar mastery of the managerial aspects of command. Although he had more command experience than any of his subordinates, French had never controlled a formation larger than a division during active service. Furthermore, the commander-in-chief was one of the few senior officers in the BEF who had not attended the Staff College at Camberley. In more general terms, French lacked the intellectual focus necessary to direct a force as large and complex as the BEF over a prolonged period. One of his biographers, Richard Holmes, has suggested that French's capabilities were "marred by his undisciplined intellect and mercurial personality."[7] In November 1914, while fighting still raged at Ypres, these shortcomings were manifested in a strange episode related by L.A.E. Price-Davies, a liaison officer attached to GHQ:

This morning I went to report before going out & Sir John said he wanted to see me. He was like a child & said he wanted me to take him out somewhere and show him something. He wanted to get away from everyone including his ADCs. "We'll go out and poke about, just you & I" !! "We'll take out a thick stick and go look through some peep hole" !! So now I have to think out what to do with him. He said I was not to let anyone know as the 'Corps commanders might be annoyed.' The difficulty in this flat country is to get any place for him to see from which it is not dangerous. I was all this afternoon looking for places. Isn't it too funny—he talked just like a child who wanted to get away from his nurse, & it is so difficult to make him realise the true state of affairs.[8]

Beyond his lack of experience and apparent intellectual limitations, the commander-in-chief's authority within the officer corps at the outset of the war had been undermined by his involvement in the Curragh "mutiny." The incident occurred in March 1914, when several dozen British officers, led by Hubert and John Gough, threatened to resign their commissions rather than obey orders to enforce Home Rule in Ulster.[9] French, then CIGS, believed that the resignation of these officers would spark further convulsions in the army. Consequently, he became involved in a series of clumsy efforts to induce them to reconsider. French was only successful, however, after pledging without government support that the army would never be used to enforce Home Rule. This guarantee clearly exceeded the bounds of French's authority. As a result, he was compelled to retract his promise and submit his resignation. French's abortive attempts at appeasement won him few friends among the disgruntled officers. Nor did his efforts earn the respect of colleagues who had retained their neutrality throughout the dispute.[10] While Sir John French's career survived the Curragh incident, his performance did nothing to increase his standing within the British officer corps. Thus, the BEF entered the First World War under a commander whose motivational skills were offset by inexperience in a senior command position, significant intellectual limitations, and a potential lack of authority over his subordinates.

Sir Archibald Murray

The officer charged with the task of implementing the decisions of the commander-in-chief was Sir Archibald Murray, the chief of the General Staff (CGS). In many ways, Murray's personality and training seemed to counterbalance that of his commander. In contrast to French, whose career had been built on his battlefield exploits, Murray had gained prominence as an efficient staff officer during the South African War. Between 1902 and 1907 he had served as French's chief of staff at Aldershot, and upon the outbreak of war was a staff officer under Sir Charles Douglas, inspector-general of the army. Throughout his career, Murray displayed a strong sense of loyalty to the officers with whom he served. In the years after the First World War, when gossip and recriminations flowed freely between commanders, the former CGS proved reluctant to reveal potentially damaging information, even regarding officers who had behaved less honorably toward himself. Such was the case when Sir Horace Smith-Dorrien, commander of II Corps in 1914, wrote him in search of ammunition to employ against Sir John French, who had relieved both of them in 1915. Declining Smith-Dorrien's request, Murray explained: "I am at the end of my military career, and I hope to finish it without, to my knowledge, having done anything disloyal to anyone I served with or under." Having served under French at Aldershot, Murray felt a strong sense of allegiance to him even in 1914. As he explained after the war, he had accepted the position of CGS only because he had "wanted to see Sir John through."[11]

Neither Murray's devotion to his commander nor his organizational skills, however, were sufficient to offset Sir John French's shortcomings. It is significant that Murray's reputation as a staff officer was made during a conflict in which the initials "p.s.c." (passed Staff College) after an officer's name were relatively rare. Staff work remained a rather inexact science in the British Army, and as a result, it apparently did not require a great degree of brilliance to impress his commander in South Africa, Sir Arthur Paget. Sir James Edmonds, the official historian of the British Army, provided the following account of Murray's "discovery" in his unpublished memoirs:

The fashionable general [Paget] found that his new acquisition could write an operation order and move troops quite easily by bits of paper; never before had he experienced anything so clever. He immediately told some of his brother fashionable generals what a treasure he had acquired, with the result that in less than no time three of them were applying for the services of Major A. Murray and his reputation was made.[12]

Despite Edmonds's sarcastic description, Murray was undoubtedly at least a competent staff officer. As chief of the General Staff, however, he was required to fulfill functions beyond the composition of operation orders. While Murray did not possess the extensive powers of a German chief of staff in 1914, his position demanded that he have the ability to influence his commander when operational necessities required. Murray's allegiance to French, however, threatened to subvert his critical faculties, reducing his inclination to question the commander-in-chief. In his description of the retreat from Mons, Richard Holmes has observed that the CGS "dwelt too much in the Commander-in-Chief's shadow to chivvy Sir John French into issuing formal orders as often as he might have done."[13]

Even if Murray had been able to muster the assertiveness to challenge French, it is questionable whether he commanded sufficient respect at GHQ to make his influence felt. According to Edmonds, the CGS was "regarded as a complete non-entity" in the prewar army.[14] While the official historian's often caustic private descriptions should be treated with caution, this appears to be a relatively accurate assessment of Murray's social standing within the officer corps. In an organization where careers were built and broken by personal contacts, Murray apparently lacked the close association with a powerful patron possessed by many of his contemporaries. That he was not a particular favorite of the commander-in-chief is evident in the fact that Murray had not been French's first choice as chief of staff in August 1914. Upon mobilization, French had requested the appointment of Henry Wilson, then director of military operations at the War Office. Wilson, however, had incurred the distrust of the Asquith government during the Curragh incident and his appointment was rejected. Murray was chosen as a substitute, despite the fact that he was in poor health in 1914.[15] Thus, the pivotal position of chief of the General Staff was occupied by an officer whose fragile health, lack of assertiveness, and scant personal popularity within the officer corps undermined his ability to influence both Sir John French and his own subordinates.

Henry Wilson

Unfortunately for Murray, foremost among those subordinates was none other than his rival for the position of chief of staff, Henry Wilson. While government opposition had prevented his selection as CGS, Sir John French apparently wielded sufficient influence to secure Wilson's appointment to the newly created position of "sub-chief" of the General Staff at GHQ. In stark contrast to the relatively anonymous Murray, Wilson's considerable intelligence, energy and charisma had a significant impact on the prewar officer corps. As the popular commandant of the Staff College at Camberley between 1907 and 1910, he had been responsible for the creation of a coherent "school of thought," emphasizing a uniform approach to staff work and preparation for war against Germany. Following his departure from Camberley, Wilson served as director of military operations at the War Office until the beginning of the First World War. In this post, he was able to give concrete form to his vision of Britain's role in the coming conflict, formulating detailed plans for the mobilization of the BEF alongside the French Army.[16]

Part of Wilson's appeal stemmed from his unconventional, but nonetheless formidable intellect. Count Edward Gleichen, commander of the 15th Infantry Brigade in 1914, provided an apt description of Wilson's critical capabilities in his memoirs. According to Gleichen: "His mind always struck me as being on a different plane from that of other people; not necessarily higher or lower, but oblique, cutting into accepted or other ideas at an angle and shedding a new and different light on them."[17] This quality was occasionally manifested in a bizarre sense of humor. Tom Bridges, a cavalry officer in 1914, related the following postwar anecdote in his memoirs:

When [Wilson] was Chief of the Imperial General Staff at the War Office he used to take a run in the park before breakfast with a bundle of newspapers, and scan them while he had a breather. For this outing he wore a suit of clothes which he had prided himself on having had as a cadet at Sandhurst, old yachting shoes and a disgraceful cap. He was accosted one morning by a faultless city gent, who said: "Got *The Times* there, my man?" "Yessir" said Henry, springing up from his seat, scenting a joke. "Aha! Give me one. Old soldier, I expect?" "Yessir," said Henry, "Rifle Brigade, sir." "Aha!" said the immaculate one, "good regiment, here's sixpence for you." Then, rather impressed by Henry's height, he said, "Sergeant-Major, perhaps?" "No, sir!" roared Henry with one of his diabolic guffaws, "Field-Marshal!"[18]

Wilson's eccentric manner did not resonate with all of his colleagues. John Charteris, Sir Douglas Haig's intelligence chief, commented derisively in 1915: "His imagination seems to take complete charge of his judgment." Nevertheless, in the years between the South African War and 1914, Wilson amassed substantial influence and popularity due to a combination of his own abilities and magnetism. These qualities captivated Sir John French, among others. Although Henry Wilson was a protégé of the cavalry reformer Lord Roberts, and held similarly heretical ideas regarding the reform of the mounted arm, French nonetheless grew to consider Wilson his "single most trusted adviser" in the years before the war.[19]

Despite the strength of Wilson's intellect and charisma, however, there existed a seamier side to his personality. According to Aylmer Haldane, commander of the 10th Infantry Brigade in 1914: "Wilson was what the French term a *faux bonhomme*; he could be charming in an outward sense, but woe betide whoever might stand between him and his future prospects." Hubert

Gough, a cavalry commander in 1914, provided a rather more blunt assessment at the end of the First World War, calling Wilson "an unscrupulous intriguer."[20] Both Haldane and Gough had reason to be bitter, as they had suffered from Wilson's machinations during the war. Their statements nonetheless reflected the sentiments of a growing number of officers in the wake of the Curragh incident, when Wilson's propensity for intrigue had serious consequences. During the controversy, Wilson, a fervent opponent of Home Rule, had been prepared to resign if the army was ordered to coerce Ulster. More significantly, he had manipulated Hubert and John Gough, the leaders of the "mutiny," in an attempt to extract a binding promise from the government that the army would not be used to intervene. His efforts resulted in the resignation of Sir John French, who had yielded the desired assurance without the proper authority to do so.

Bernard Ash has characterized Henry Wilson as "a marked man" in the aftermath of the Curragh incident. Clearly, in political circles, his intrigues had earned him numerous enemies, as was demonstrated by the government's refusal to appoint him as CGS at the beginning of the war. It is evident, however, that he continued to enjoy considerable popularity in the army. Wilson's role in Sir John French's downfall seems to have been lost on French himself, who continued to trust his judgment. In addition, while at Camberley and the War Office, Wilson had created an extensive network of friends and protégés who remained remarkably loyal to him despite his shadier tendencies. According to Walter Kirke, an intelligence officer at GHQ in 1914, "Practically the whole of the MO [Military Operations] Directorate was ready to support him by resigning their commissions if the government persisted in their avowed intentions" during the Curragh incident. Significantly, it was this same group of officers that comprised the Operations Section at GHQ at the outset of the war. Given their willingness to follow Henry Wilson throughout the tumultuous events of March 1914, it is not entirely surprising that even after hostilities commenced, the operations section "continued to regard him as their chief and look to him for orders."[21] Thus, beneath Archie Murray, the ostensibly subordinate role of sub-chief of staff was filled by an officer who possessed the undivided loyalty of the operations section, the trust of the commander-in-chief, and a penchant for intrigue in order to further his personal interests.

George "Uncle" Harper

The linchpin connecting Henry Wilson to the operations section was its head, or GSO1, Colonel George "Uncle" Harper. A sapper by trade, Harper had served as an instructor at the Staff College at Camberley during Wilson's tenure as commandant. As Brian Bond has noted, the two became closely acquainted in this period. In 1911, Harper followed his former commandant to the War Office, where he remained until the beginning of the war. As deputy director of Military Operations, Harper served as Wilson's right hand during the formulation of plans for the mobilization of the BEF alongside the French. Thus, by the outset of the First World War, Harper was a close associate and friend of the sub-chief of staff. Despite his experience as an instructor at Camberley, Harper was in many ways better suited to a command in the field than to a staff position. Walter Kirke described him as "the beau ideal of a fine fighting soldier," a characterization apparently warranted by the fact that he "had a handsome presence and was a great sportsman with a genial and commanding personality."[22]

By the standards of the time, these traits were more evocative of the aggressive battlefield commander than the staff officer. Ultimately, Harper spent most of the war in the former capacity, at the helm of 51 Highland Division between 1915 and 1918 before assuming command of IV Corps in the final months of the conflict.[23] In 1914, however, Harper's long connection with Henry Wilson apparently resulted in his selection as head of the operations section at GHQ. Significantly, Harper possessed far greater allegiance to Wilson than to the legitimate chief of staff. Moreover, he shared Wilson's tendency to place personal loyalties and interests ahead of professional considerations. After the war, Edward Spears, a British liaison officer attached to the French Fifth Army in 1914, reflected on the machinations of both officers: "I suffered a good deal from Colonel Harper myself, and was later to be very cruelly treated by General Wilson, mainly because Petain found him out and refused to have him as Chief Liaison Officer, saying he did not want to have an intriguer of his kind at Headquarters."[24]

Harper's long experience working alongside Henry Wilson at Camberley and the War Office ought to have rendered him a valuable asset in 1914. His familiarity with the habits of the sub-chief of staff might have prevented costly misunderstandings under the strain of active operations. Given the inclination of both officers to subordinate the requirements of their positions to personal interests, however, "Uncle" Harper's appointment augured poorly for the efficiency of GHQ in the initial stages of the First World War.

George Macdonogh

As GSO1 of the Intelligence Section at GHQ, George Macdonogh held equivalent rank to Harper. Both men had begun their careers as sappers, and both were 49 in 1914. At that point, however, their similarities ended abruptly. In contrast to the amiable Harper, Macdonogh struck his contemporaries as diffident and even aloof. Nor did he exhibit Harper's passion for the more recreational aspects of soldiery. Walter Kirke, who served under Macdonogh at the War Office prior to the war, and at GHQ in 1914, characterized him as follows: "Unlike most officers he never played any games and was completely uninterested in any form of sport. His only hobby appeared to be work, with a capital 'W'."[25]

Macdonogh's dedication to his profession was complemented by a formidable intellect. Indeed, the abilities of the head of the Intelligence Section have been acknowledged widely by historians as well as his own contemporaries. Even Sir James Edmonds, who was prone to furnishing rather harsh descriptions of his colleagues, conceded his intelligence. As the official historian recounted, he and Macdonogh had done so well on their Staff College entrance exams "that there was a delay in publishing the results and a change was made to alphabetical order to try to conceal the gap between these two and the rest." Nor did the curriculum at Camberley pose a significant challenge, as Macdonogh found sufficient spare time to enable him to qualify as a barrister in London. Combined with a strong work ethic, Macdonogh's intellect made him an exceedingly efficient staff officer. According to Kirke, "Uncle" Harper's personality may have epitomized that of a successful battlefield commander, but in the realm of staff work "he was not in the same street as Macdonogh."[26]

Despite these impressive credentials, however, Macdonogh's effectiveness at GHQ was undermined by his awkward relations with both Harper and Henry Wilson. This situation stemmed from several factors. First, the distance between the head of the intelligence section and his colleagues was due at least in part to his own remote personality. Even Kirke, who eventually became a close friend, recalled that on their first meeting Macdonogh was "extremely taciturn and uncommunicative and did not appear to have any desire to establish friendly relations." In addition, the fact that he eschewed sporting activities for more intellectual pursuits underlined his status as an anomaly within the early twentieth-century officer corps. Macdonogh also seems to have suffered because of a disdain toward intelligence work on the part of other officers. According to Kirke, Harper "affected to look down on the doings of M.I.5," the intelligence section at the War Office that Macdonogh headed before the war.[27]

While his personality, work habits, and occupation already set Macdonogh at odds with other senior members of GHQ, specific disagreements with Henry Wilson exacerbated the tensions between these two officers. It is difficult to determine the effect of religious beliefs on their relationship. It warrants mention, however, that while the Protestant Wilson had "an intense dislike and distrust for what he called 'Papists,' " Macdonogh was a convert to Roman Catholicism. The Curragh incident, with its religious undertones, brought this dissimilarity to the forefront of their relationship, as Wilson threatened to resign as director of Military Operations in the event that the army was ordered to enforce Home Rule in Ulster. In taking this extreme position, Wilson implicitly left his subordinates at the War Office with a choice of whether or not to follow him. Macdonogh was apparently unique in his refusal to stand behind his chief, a fact that was not lost on Wilson himself. Macdonogh's decision likely stemmed less from his religious beliefs than from a conviction that it was his duty to obey the orders of the government.[28] Nevertheless, he consequently earned the enmity of an officer who did not necessarily allow professional restraint to interfere with the achievements of his own objectives. This animosity, combined with Macdonogh's personality and interests, managed to marginalize him at GHQ despite his manifest abilities. Overall, at the beginning of the 1914 campaign, there existed a complex and often incendiary combination of ideas and personalities at GHQ. This mixture did not bode well for the efficient conduct of operations in the initial stages of the war.

FIELD COMMANDERS—HAIG, SMITH-DORRIEN, RAWLINSON, CAPPER, HUNTER-WESTON, AND HUBERT GOUGH

Sir Douglas Haig

Given the scale of operations in France and Belgium in 1914, and the inexperience of Sir John French and his staff in controlling a force the size of the BEF, considerable responsibility fell onto the shoulders of commanders of subordinate formations. With smaller staffs consisting of less prominent personalities, these officers enjoyed greater freedom than the commander-in-chief in exercising command during the opening months of the war. They were thus able to exert considerable influence over the operations of the BEF in this period. Throughout the First World War, no individual soldier had a greater impact on the fate of the British Army than Sir Douglas Haig, commander-in-chief of the BEF between 1916 and 1918. While his performance in the latter stages of the war has been studied extensively, Haig's command of I Corps in 1914 has received considerably less attention. His experiences in this period nonetheless had a profound impact on his subsequent performance. It is therefore instructive to examine the ideas that shaped his behavior at the outset of the conflict. Like Sir John French, Sir Douglas Haig was a cavalry commander. He had led a brigade in French's cavalry division during the South African War, and afterward the two were associated in their defense of traditional cavalry tactics. Their ideas were not identical. In some respects, Haig surpassed French in his commitment to the *arme blanche*. When French, as inspector-general of the forces, criticized the dismounted work of the cavalry during maneuvers in 1908, Haig complained that he "gave vent to some terrible heresies such as the chief use of Cavalry Division in battle is their rifle fire: led horses to be moved, and men need not be close to them."[29]

Haig's own view is best illustrated by his justification of the unwieldy size of the British cavalry division in a prewar conversation with James Edmonds. As the official historian related: "I asked Haig in 1913, why there were 4 brigades in the Cav Div, more than any one man could control, as the Germans had discovered. He replied 'but you must have 4' 'Why?' '*For the charge*: 2 brigades—first line, 1 in support & you must have a reserve!!' "[30] Stephen Badsey has questioned the veracity of this conversation, dismissing it as "one of Edmonds' stories." It is evident, however, that Haig was reluctant to abandon cavalry tactics such as the *arme blanche*. According to George Barrow, who served on Haig's staff during prewar cavalry exercises, the maneuvers regularly culminated in a massed charge led by Haig himself. As Barrow remarked in his memoirs: "[t]he four cavalry brigades moving over the plain on a summer's day made up a superb picture that bore no resemblance to war as we came to know war not long afterwards."[31]

Haig's preference for traditional cavalry tactics was hardly a sign of indifference toward his profession. Although like most cavalrymen, he maintained an interest in polo, he also possessed a work ethic rivaled among his contemporaries only by George Macdonogh. According to Brian Bond: "At the Staff College he worked harder than anyone else, kept himself to himself, and was seldom seen in the mess except for meals."[32] Even after leaving Camberley, Haig focused his energies almost wholly on his work. After serving on Haig's staff prior to the First World War, Hubert Gough characterized the I Corps commander as a "profound student of modern war."[33] Haig's work ethic, however, was not complemented by an exceptional intellect. Edmonds, who attended Camberley at the same time as the future commander-in-chief, was unimpressed by Haig's mental agility. Nor was Haig particularly receptive to new ideas. According to Hubert Gough: "He did not change quickly in favour of a new plan, even if the circumstances did not turn out to be exactly as he had originally envisaged. He was a trifle rigid in his ideas, and a trifle prejudiced as regards persons."[34]

These opinions may reflect the strained postwar relationships between their sources and Haig himself. The most recent assessments of Haig's command have generally been more charitable.[35] There is little evidence, however, suggesting that he excelled academically. Moreover, numerous studies have emphasized his tenacity in adhering to dubious tactical and operational concepts before and during the First World War.[36] Nonetheless, it is evident that Haig was exceptionally conscientious in his approach to his studies and, more generally, to his profession. According to Noel Birch, an artillery commander during the war: "Haig's one thought was soldiering and his one idea from the first time I met him when he was a young major was to beat Germany."[37]

Haig's meticulous study habits were paralleled by a very deliberate approach to command. Despite his preference for traditional cavalry tactics, the I Corps commander displayed little of the spontaneity and brashness associated with the cavalry spirit. Although he promoted Haig's career consistently in the years between the end of the South African War and 1914, this circumspection did not escape Sir John French. In 1912, French apparently remarked that Haig was better suited to a staff position than to a command in the field.[38] This may have been a reflection of Haig's personality. It seems likely, however, that his caution stemmed in part from a desire to safeguard his career prospects. As Edmonds related to Liddell Hart after the war: "the keynote of [Haig's] career was unrelenting pursuit of his ambition." This preoccupation may explain many of his command decisions in South Africa and during the First World War. Rather than risking an egregious blunder that might have terminated his upward progress through the ranks of the officer corps, he repeatedly tended toward prudence. Haig's concern for his career is also evident in the grudges he held against officers whom he perceived to be preventing his advancement. Herbert Plumer, commander of the Second Army between 1915 and 1917, apparently incurred Haig's lasting resentment after grading him poorly in an examination at Camberley in the 1890s. Even after the First World War, Haig proved reluctant to acknowledge Plumer's competence as a commander.[39]

The relationship between Sir Douglas Haig and Sir John French also reflected this preoccupation. Although they were acquainted beforehand, the bond between the two officers was cemented in 1898, when Haig loaned French a substantial sum of money. Historians have acknowledged the lack of tangible evidence indicating that Haig's act was inspired by an interest in his own advancement.[40] Significantly, however, Haig was not above using connections with other influential figures to further his career. According to Edmonds, Haig took advantage of his close ties to the royal family to gain admission to the Staff College at Camberley. Similarly, he benefited from his association with French after the infamous loan. In the years between the South African War and 1914, Haig remained firmly attached to French as the latter rose through the ranks of the officer corps. French apparently held Haig's abilities and ideas in high esteem. This respect, however, does not seem to have been reciprocated.[41] Nonetheless, even when French's actions met with his disapproval, as they did during the Curragh incident, the I Corps commander continued to sustain this tie as long as it would further his career. It was only in September 1915, when he stood as the senior commander under Sir John French, that Haig became instrumental in the removal of his patron from the position of commander-in-chief.[42]

Haig's interest in advancing his own career was intertwined with a more general concern for his reputation as a commander. While he undoubtedly aspired to as high a rank as possible in the British Army, Haig also sought the respect of both his contemporaries and subsequent generations of British soldiers. His diary for 1914 demonstrates these combined concerns. Following its release after his death in 1925, officers involved in the campaign of 1914 expressed their suspicions of the I Corps commander's recollections of events. Regarding his account of the hasty retreat of I Corps from Landrecies on 26 August 1914, Charles Deedes, a staff officer at GHQ, commented: "I cannot help thinking that the entry made by Sir Douglas in his diary must have been written some time after the event and may therefore not be as accurate as might have been expected."[43]

It would be unrealistic to expect complete accuracy from any personalized account of events. In his biography of Henry Wilson, Bernard Ash has observed: "People of Wilson's generation confided in their diaries, sometimes let their imaginations run riot in them, certainly recorded in them their fantasies of wishful thinking, seeing the events of the day as they would have had them rather than as they were."[44] It is undoubtedly wise to keep this caveat in mind when examining Haig's diaries. His record of the war is influenced, however, by two additional factors. First, throughout the 1914 campaign, the I Corps commander regularly sent a copy of his diary entries to King George V. Given Haig's ambitions, and the king's ability to influence appointments within the army, it is likely that this account provided a relatively flattering description of his own performance.[45] Second, with the help of his wife, Dorothea, Haig produced a typescript version of his handwritten diary at intervals during and after the First World War. In examining Haig's entries for August 1914 prior to the beginning of active operations, it becomes evident that the typed transcript of his diary, held at the Public Record Office in Kew, contains a variety of prescient comments regarding other British officers that are conspicuously absent from the handwritten diary, located at the National Library of Scotland.

As Gerard DeGroot has suggested, these comments include a critical, but quite accurate assessment of Sir John French that may have been added well after the fact, perhaps in an effort to justify Haig's machinations to replace the commander-in-chief in 1915.[46] In light of its accuracy, the supplementary material included in the typed edition of Haig's diary for August 1914 seems to represent an attempt by the I Corps commander to polish his record for the benefit of future observers. This tendency suggests that the typescript should be used by historians with caution. It also provides further evidence that as the 53-year-old Sir Douglas Haig went to war in 1914, his conscientious approach to his profession existed alongside a profound concern for his own career and reputation.

Sir Horace Smith-Dorrien

Haig's counterpart at the helm of the second of the two original corps of the BEF was Sir Horace Smith-Dorrien. At 56 years of age in August 1914, Smith-Dorrien was the oldest senior officer in the BEF aside from Sir John French. Commencing with the Zulu War of 1879, Smith-Dorrien's military career had been built on the small colonial conflicts that had comprised the primary occupation of the British Army during the nineteenth century. He attended the Staff College in the late 1880s, several years before any of his contemporaries in 1914. Even in comparison to a decade later, the curriculum at Camberley in this period did little to encourage the serious study of warfare. As Smith-Dorrien related: "I enjoyed every minute of my two years there. I do not think we were taught as much as we might have been, but there was plenty of sport and not too much work."[47] Throughout his career, Smith-Dorrien favored an approach to his profession that often emphasized sport at the expense of serious intellectual pursuits. His biographer, A.J. Smithers, relates the following of Smith-Dorrien's days at Camberley: "The legend long persisted that at the end of his first three months he was found wandering the corridors enquiring plaintively the way to the library and it is known that more than once he was up before the commandant for not taking his studies seriously."[48] Smith-Dorrien's affinity for active recreation would manifest itself even in November 1914. Almost immediately after II Corps was placed in reserve early in the month, he and his staff began embarking on a daily pheasant shoot behind the lines.[49]

Whatever his limitations as a military intellectual, Smith-Dorrien had attained a formidable reputation as an infantry commander in the Zulu War, in Egypt in the early 1880s, and in South Africa. Nor was he bewildered by the tactical debates during the years between the end of the South African War and 1914. On the contrary, as commandant at Aldershot between 1907 and 1912, he was responsible for a variety of reforms, most significantly forcing an increase in the dismounted training of the cavalry stationed at the base. These efforts undoubtedly contributed to the tactical superiority of the British cavalry over its

French and British counterparts in 1914.[50] Such innovations, however, did little to endear Smith-Dorrien to proponents of the *arme blanche* such as French and Haig. Nor was his popularity in the officer corps enhanced by his explosive temper. As a result, it is not entirely surprising that in the period between the end of the South African War and 1914, Smith-Dorrien was marginalized from the two principal cliques through which senior officers furthered their careers in this period, the well-established Roberts "ring," and the emerging circle around Sir John French. His reforms at Aldershot, particularly those pertaining to the mounted arm, in fact earned him French's hostility. Consequently, by 1914, the commander-in-chief's antipathy toward Smith-Dorrien was well known within the British Army.[51]

Smith-Dorrien was not entirely without allies in the officer corps. He had served in South Africa under Lord Kitchener, and afterward had supported Kitchener in the establishment of the Staff College at Quetta in 1907. As secretary of state for war in August 1914, Kitchener was in a position to reward his protégé with the command of II Corps upon the untimely death of its original commander, Sir James Grierson, following the arrival of the BEF in France. It is worthy of note that Smith-Dorrien was not Sir John French's choice for the post. The commander-in-chief had in fact requested that Herbert Plumer replace Grierson. Despite his awareness of French's hostility toward Smith-Dorrien, Kitchener nonetheless appointed him to the position.[52] Thus, beyond the unprecedented scale and intensity of the conflict confronting the entire BEF in 1914, Sir Horace Smith-Dorrien faced additional challenges. Haig, his ambitious counterpart in I Corps, viewed him with a healthy measure of professional jealousy, due to the fact that Smith-Dorrien held the senior rank of the two. In addition to the potent grudge that Sir John French held toward the II Corps commander, the commander-in-chief apparently shared Haig's concern over Smith-Dorrien's rank, as French hoped that his own protégé would succeed him in the event that he was replaced.[53] Smith-Dorrien's diaries and letters give no indication that he returned their hostility. Nevertheless, tensions between the three senior commanders in the BEF threatened to undermine cooperation between them under the intense strain of operations in 1914.

Henry Rawlinson

Six years younger than Smith-Dorrien, Henry Rawlinson represented a different generation within the officer corps. Commander of 4 Division and later IV Corps in 1914, Rawlinson had established himself as a capable, popular and influential officer in the years following the South African War. As commandant of the Staff College at Camberley between 1903 and 1906, he introduced a variety of practical innovations that attuned the curriculum more closely to the necessities of modern war. At the same time as these reforms improved the quality of education at Camberley, Rawlinson's reputation as a sportsman and his "youthful debonair spirit" increased its prestige.[54] Rawlinson's outgoing personality resembled that of Henry Wilson, and the two were in fact close friends. Both were protégés of Lord Roberts, and their connection to the former commander-in-chief of the army rankled those who ran in different circles. In the aftermath of the South African War, Sir John French, a descendant of the Wolseley "ring" who headed his own emerging clique, was suspicious of both officers, referring to them in one instance as "R's special 'Pets'."[55] While Wilson eventually won the ear of the future commander-in-chief, French remained suspicious of Rawlinson even at the outset of the First World War. In spite of the fact that he had served as commanding officer of 3 Division since 1910, Rawlinson was not included in the Expeditionary Force in August 1914. He attributed this omission to French's displeasure with his performance on maneuvers the previous year. As he complained in his diary: "To introduce a personal matter into his choice of command was in my opinion petty but I had nothing to do but submit with the best grace I could."[56]

Whatever the reason for French's decision, Rawlinson's self-portrayal as a victim of injustice rings rather hollow. Much like his friend Henry Wilson, Rawlinson's otherwise impressive reputation was blemished by a propensity for intrigue in pursuit of his own ambitions. This tendency earned him Hubert Gough's characterization: "clever but crooked."[57] Much of Rawlinson's behavior as a commander during the First World War can be attributed to this mixture of traits. Examining his career on the Western Front primarily between 1915 and 1918, Robin Prior and Trevor Wilson have observed that early on in the war, Rawlinson showed signs of grasping the tactical and operational conundrums that he faced. Yet they conclude nonetheless that "far from being a steady learner, Rawlinson's conduct of operations revealed no consistent advance in wisdom."[58]

This puzzling pattern can be explained by Rawlinson's combination of intelligence and keen sensitivity to his own career prospects. He may indeed have discerned the implications of firepower more rapidly than his superiors during the war, Sir John French and Sir Douglas Haig. Nonetheless, given that neither French nor Haig was particularly receptive to advice from subordinate commanders, Rawlinson no doubt risked incurring their wrath by questioning dictates from above. Consequently, as Shelford Bidwell and Dominick Graham have observed, "Rawlinson's political sense seems to have overborne his moral courage."[59] The tendency of professional competence to be subordinated to personal interests, present at GHQ, was thus evident in the commander of IV Corps as well.

Thompson "Tommy" Capper

Subordinate to Henry Rawlinson in IV Corps was Thompson "Tommy" Capper, commander of 7 Division. In an officer corps often inhabited by sportsmen and social climbers, Capper stood out in that he treated the study of warfare as an intellectual pursuit. Prior to the First World War, Capper was recognized for his advocacy of the offensive. Though the power of offensive action was virtually an article of faith in the prewar officer corps, Capper believed in its efficacy to such an extent that that he "personified the offensive spirit of the British army."[60] As an instructor at Camberley, and subsequently as commandant of the newly opened Staff College at Quetta between 1906 and 1911, Capper emphasized the supremacy of offensive action, led personally by officers imbued with a sense of self-sacrifice. According to Hubert Gough, a student of Capper at Camberley, "he always inculcated a spirit of self-sacrifice and duty, instead of the idea of playing for safety and seeking only to avoid getting into trouble."[61]

Such a philosophy was easy enough to teach in a classroom. Capper went to excessive lengths, however, to demonstrate it during active operations as well. Maintaining that it was the duty of every staff officer to die in battle as an example to the soldiers, he reputedly entered his staff mess one day during the war and exclaimed: "What! Nobody on the Staff wounded today; that won't do!" He then proceeded to send his staff to the front line on various assignments. While it is impossible to confirm this story, the details of Capper's demise are sufficiently clear. During the battle of Loos in early 1915, he was killed in action after riding his horse openly in front of enemy lines in an effort to inspire the soldiers of 7 Division.[62] Ultimately, he demonstrated his belief in self-sacrifice in no uncertain terms.

Notwithstanding the rather bloody implications of his beliefs and his explicit demonstration of them, Tommy Capper was by no means the proverbial "donkey" so maligned in postwar literature. Certainly, he went to extremes in emphasizing the necessity for officers to lead by example. Nonetheless, Capper's aptitude as a trainer of troops, a commander, and a military intellectual was recognized throughout the officer corps. Describing the efficiency of his own 10th Brigade in his memoirs, Aylmer Haldane boasted that his formation "was regarded by those who inspected it periodically as, together with Capper's brigade, the best-trained of that size in the British Army." In his own memoirs, George Barrow paid tribute to Capper's intellect, commenting: "Capper had within him a little of the spirit called 'genius' that makes the few men who possess it different from all others." Even the acerbic James Edmonds, a classmate of Capper at Camberley, seems to have held the 7 Division commander in even greater esteem than George Macdonogh. As Edmonds related after the war, Capper was the one individual "really fitted to be there as a Staff Officer and future commander."[63]

Brilliant though he may have been, Capper's acclaim was far from universal. As the chief staff officer of 7 Division, Hugo Montgomery, related to Edmonds after the war, Capper could be "most *difficile*" as a commanding officer.[64] In particular, the commander of 7 Division seemed to lack the steady temperament necessary to win the confidence of his subordinates. Sir Douglas Haig, who probably erred to the opposite extreme, commented sourly that Capper "was too full of nerves and too much of a crank to get the best out of officers." L.A.E. Price-Davies, a friend of Capper, expressed similar sentiments more diplomatically, remarking: "He is a man whom the troops must know to appreciate."[65] Thus, Tommy Capper's virtuosity as a commander was diminished by his rather extreme ideas regarding leadership, as well as a lack of the interpersonal skills evident in soldiers of a lesser intellectual caliber.

Aylmer Hunter-Weston

Although he valued many of the same ideals as Capper, Aylmer Hunter-Weston, commander of the 11th Infantry Brigade in 1914, held a rather different conception of command. Hunter-Weston attended the Staff College between 1898 and 1899, at roughly the same time as many of the senior commanders and staff officers of the BEF during the First World War.[66] While his career had not progressed at the same rate as some of his more illustrious colleagues at Camberley, Hunter-Weston also seems to have avoided the often acrimonious tactical debates and political maneuverings of the years before 1914. Marginalized to some extent from the dynamic but often dangerous upper ranks of the officer corps, Hunter-Weston also retained a more traditional and ingenuous approach to his vocation. Much like Tommy Capper, Hunter-Weston placed great value on the qualities of honor, bravery, and self-sacrifice. His high estimation of these attributes is evident in his role in the 1914 court-martial of two lieutenant-colonels of 4 Division, Elkington and Mainwaring. In the darkest hours of the retreat from Mons in August, these two officers had surrendered their battalions to the mayor of a French village on the assumption that they were about to be captured by the Germans. Fortunately for the troops, although considerably less so for Elkington and Mainwaring, they were discovered by the cavalry officer Tom Bridges, who cajoled the two battalions into resuming their retirement. As the soldiers continued to retreat, the two colonels were arrested and later cashiered by Hunter-Weston, who rather reluctantly administered their court-martial. As he related to his wife: "I was very sorry for them but that did not prevent my doing my duty & marking the enormity of their offence from a military point of view."[67]

The saga did not end with the court-martial, however. While Mainwaring retired, Elkington immediately enlisted in the French Foreign Legion, where he was wounded repeatedly and earned a reputation for considerable valor over the next two years. Hunter-Weston evidently remained in correspondence with the disgraced officer, and by mid-1916, he became convinced that Elkington had salvaged his honor. He thus took up the officer's case with the Adjutant-General of the British Army and successfully secured Elkington's reinstatement at his former rank. In a laudatory letter written in August 1916, he informed Elkington of the good news, stating: "I congratulate you very heartily that by your gallant conduct in enlisting into the Foreign Legion, and by your gallant services while in that legion, you have been able to wipe out the stigma on your fair fame which your moment of mental aberration had cast upon it."[68]

Hunter-Weston's high estimation of honor and bravery was accompanied by a strong attachment to his soldiers. Like Sir John French, he professed to care deeply for the troops under his command, and he apparently devoted considerable attention to them in 1914. A recurring theme in letters written to his wife was his paternalistic relationship with the "well-trained and well-disciplined Band of Brothers" that comprised the 11th Brigade. Even after being promoted to the rank of major-general in October 1914, he related: "I hope it won't mean I shall have to leave my Brigade. I don't think so. I love my Brigade and we all run together so well."[69] Hunter-Weston was also willing to lead his troops personally in many situations. At Le Cateau, on 26 August 1914, he and his subordinates repeatedly restored the wavering line of the 1/Hampshires of the 11th Brigade. As he related to his wife: "[o]n three occasions they retired from their positions, but on each occasion by personally leading them forward and explaining to the young soldiers that it was essential that they hold this position we were able to maintain the position without undue cost."[70] Under Hunter-Weston's command, the 11th Brigade was one of the most aggressive in the BEF in 1914, and it achieved several subsequent successes under his command. According to E.K.G. Sixsmith, as the army approached the Aisne in mid-September, only in the front of Hunter-Weston's brigade "was a resolute effort made to seize a crossing place by a surprise coup."[71]

The 11th Brigade's crossing of the Aisne was due in large part to Hunter-Weston's personal leadership. He did not, however, share Tommy Capper's notion that senior officers should sacrifice themselves as an example to their soldiers. Quite the contrary, in the orchestrated battles that followed the advent of trench warfare in the autumn of 1914, Hunter-Weston believed in a clear demarcation of duties between front-line officers, who led the troops, and the brigade commander and his staff, who planned operations. Relating the course of a battle in a letter to his wife in November 1914, he provided the following description of his own role: "I have organised the affair well. I have taken all precautions to ensure success & to minimise defeat. The result is in the hands of destiny. I have done my part."[72]

This depiction was not simply an attempt to alleviate the fears of Mrs. Hunter-Weston. In October 1914, it is evident that the 11th Brigade commander limited his duties to the organization of operations, despite his apparent affection for the troops. Once the battle was underway, he conceived of his duties as completed until it had subsided at the end of the day. In Hunter-Weston's view, this left himself and his staff with actual leisure time. As he related in his diary on 28 October 1914, the 11th Brigade staff and that of 4 Division took an opportunity to shoot game while their troops were engaged in battle nearby. According to Hunter-Weston:

The final bag was 6 pheasants, 7 rabbits & 3 hares. We should have done better if it had not been for the Garde Forestier who saved many rabbits' lives by uttering a scream of "lapin!" whenever he saw one & setting off in hot pursuit. The shoot was made more interesting by the Germans who were shelling the CHATEAU DE LA HUTTE only 150 yards away from one of the stands with extraordinary accuracy. On the E edge of the wood we could hear German shells bursting & our rifle fire; to the N we heard our 60 pounders & to the S a Bde of 18 pounder was firing continuously. Aeroplanes of both sides were being shot at all the time over our heads & siege howitzers were doing steady work in the West end of the wood.[73]

Thus, while Aylmer Hunter-Weston valued notions such as honor and personal bravery, and was willing to lead his troops during mobile operations, he adopted a managerial style of command that emphasized planning and staff work following the advent of trench warfare in the fall of 1914. This paradoxical approach to command reflected the changing nature of the officer corps in 1914.

Hubert Gough

Although the traditional roles of the mounted arm were increasingly marginalized in the First World War, the cavalry spirit figured prominently in the collection of ideas with which many officers entered the conflict. No senior commander personified this philosophy more than Hubert Gough, commander of the 3rd Cavalry Brigade and 2 Cavalry Division in 1914. While Sir John French and Sir Douglas Haig were proponents of the *arme blanche* in the years before the war, Gough's expression of the cavalry spirit transcended tactics. The intuitive philosophy of the mounted arm blended with his personality, resulting in an independence of mind that colored his actions on and off the battlefield. Price-Davies, assigned as a liaison between GHQ and 2 Cavalry Division, reflected on this trait to his wife, remarking: "All the staffs I come across are so nice to me. In some ways Hubert's staff [are] not so nice but they are always rather busy and fussed & Cavalry are always rather independent cusses & don't care much for people from outside & object to superior commanders & staffs & such like."[74]

For Hubert Gough, this suspicion of superior commanders often verged on active disdain. According to E.H. Beddington, who served under Gough before and during 1914: "he had no respect for those above him unless they came up to his own standards, and he frequently told us what he thought of those senior commanders who failed in that respect." Gough attempted to inculcate his own attitude in his subordinates, teaching them to hold matters of discipline in light regard. As Beddington related in his memoirs:

It so happened that I was in command of "A" Squadron one day and brought it on to parade five minutes before time. Goughy appeared at 9.0am and had his trumpeter sound "Squadron leader." We all galloped up and saluted, and he addressed us as follows. "Good morning Gentlemen. I noticed 1 squadron on parade this morning five minutes early. Please remember that it is better to be late rather than early. The former shows a sense of sturdy independence and no undue respect for higher authority, the latter merely shows womanish excitement and nervousness. Go back to your squadrons."[75]

This same lack of regard for higher authority shaped Gough's behavior during the Curragh incident. Not only did he threaten to resign rather than follow orders, but under the influence of Henry Wilson, he had the temerity to prod Sir

John French into exceeding the bounds of his authority in order to secure a solution to the episode satisfactory to himself.

Notwithstanding his often impulsive actions, Gough's embodiment of the cavalry spirit impressed other proponents of the mounted arm. Douglas Haig, whose own advocacy of the *arme blanche* was less often complemented by a corresponding sense of boldness, remained fond of Gough and advanced his career for most of the First World War. Sir John French retained an affection for him even after the Curragh incident, when Gough had played a prominent role in compelling his resignation.[76] Thus, despite the difficulties that it foreshadowed under the strain of operations, Gough's maverick behavior captured the imagination of his superiors. While his approach to discipline would seem to be something of an extreme case, he represented only one of the many and diverse approaches to command in 1914.

TENDENCIES AND TRAITS OF BRITISH OFFICERS IN 1914

Clearly, a diverse group of commanders and staff officers occupied the upper ranks of the BEF in 1914. Beyond providing an acquaintance with these individuals, however, the preceding sketches reveal a variety of common characteristics among British officers that shaped the way they approached their chosen profession. While many officers displayed tendencies that promised to increase their competence in conducting a large-scale campaign against a capable opponent, they also maintained values and practices that were not entirely suitable for this task.

The preceding examination of selected senior officers suggests that they were by no means typical of the British officer corps as a whole. As J.M. Bourne has noted, "[t]he summit of ambition for most pre-war Regular officers was to command the battalion in which they began their careers."[77] Soldiers who sought posts above the regimental level were exceptional in their aspirations. This was particularly true of those who attended Camberley in the 1890s, when many regiments viewed the Staff College with disdain. Thus, in comparison to the rest of the officer corps, those individuals in the upper ranks of the BEF in 1914 appear unusually ambitious. For decades prior to the First World War, ambitious British officers had advanced their careers by coalescing in "rings" or cliques around powerful patrons. It is therefore not surprising that many senior members of the BEF in 1914 belonged to cliques within the officer corps. Henry Wilson and Henry Rawlinson were associated with the circle of officers around Lord Roberts, while Sir John French had enjoyed the patronage of members of the Wolseley "ring." Moreover, certain officers in 1914 headed their own emerging cliques. French, for example, had furthered the careers of Sir Douglas Haig and Hubert Gough, while Henry Wilson's circle of protégés included "Uncle" Harper and members of the Military Operations Directorate at the War Office. These groups were not mutually exclusive. Henry Wilson, for example, enjoyed a close relationship with Sir John French despite having a different patron. Nevertheless, given that they emerged to advance the careers of ambitious individuals who were often in competition with each other, rivalries invariably emerged between different cliques and even between individual officers within the same "ring."[78]

In the context of military operations, it might be expected that rivalries would become less intense as individuals subordinated their own ambitions to the task of defeating the enemy. As the BEF mobilized for war in August 1914, however, this system of patronage had a significant influence on the composition of its upper ranks. Not only was Wilson's coterie appointed to the Operations section at GHQ, but Lord Kitchener chose Sir Horace Smith-Dorrien to command II Corps against the wishes of Sir John French. The commander-in-chief's opposition likely stemmed in part from concern for the career of his own protégé, Haig. Thus, the association of ambitious officers in rival cliques around powerful patrons was a notable and important tendency in the upper ranks of the BEF in 1914.

Competition for command and staff posts, however, was not the only consequence of ambition among senior British officers. The preceding biographical sketches suggest that it also generated a desire for increased expertise in the military profession. In the decade prior to 1914, many senior officers were clearly concerned with expanding their own knowledge of modern warfare and improving the effectiveness of the army as a whole. This trend was part of the broader concern for "national efficiency" evident in Edwardian Britain. Smarting from military setbacks during the South African War, and confronted with what they perceived to be an increasingly aggressive German Empire, British elites embarked on a campaign to reestablish their nation's economic, political, and military competitiveness. The military misfortunes of "Black Week" in December 1899 had sparked concerns regarding British decline. Consequently, the army was subjected to considerable scrutiny in the aftermath of the South African War.[79] Given that senior British officers comprised part of the governing elite so preoccupied with national competitiveness, it is hardly surprising that many of them demonstrated an increased concern for military efficiency in this period.

This concern is evident in the heated debate over cavalry tactics between "reformers," led by Lord Roberts, and defenders of the *arme blanche*, such as Sir John French and Sir Douglas Haig.[80] In light of the harsh technological revelations of the First World War, it is tempting to belittle arguments in favor of traditional tactics advanced by French, Haig, and their allies. The length and intensity of the tactical debate suggests, however, that the cases of both sides represented the product of genuine reflection by capable officers. Defenses of traditional tactics probably contained an element of interest in the institutional survival of the mounted arm. Even if such were the case, however, the British cavalry was certainly not the last military organization to allow its preferred vision of warfare to influence its choice of tactics.

The improvement of military education is another indication of an increased concern for professional competency in the officer corps. In the decade before the First World War, under the guidance of commandants such as Henry Rawlinson and Henry Wilson, the Staff College at Camberley became more prestigious and practical, as students were directed away from pedantic classroom exercises toward preparations for modern war.[81] The opening of the Staff College at Quetta in 1907, with Tommy Capper as its commandant, is further evidence of the increased energy and resources devoted to the education of officers. The improvement of staff training apparently spurred some officers to continue their education independently. As Tom Bridges related in his memoirs: "[w]hile at Camberley I spent all my leaves abroad, either going to foreign manoeuvres and battlefield tours or to brush up on languages, visiting countries I had not seen, Norway, Sweden and Denmark. Fired by Henderson's 'Stonewall Jackson' I also went for a walking tour in the Shenandoah Valley in Virginia to make some sketches of the battlefields."[82]

Other officers were able to augment their staff training through assignments as military observers. For ambitious individuals, such appointments were subject to fierce and often bitter competition. In 1904, Aylmer Haldane was chosen over Henry Wilson to travel to Manchuria as an observer during the Russo-Japanese War. According to Haldane: "because I had been chosen to go to Japan I was to be the subject of his hostility from that time onwards."[83] Such animosities aside, it is evident that the state of military education in the British officer corps was improving in the years before the First World War. Through refinements to staff training, as well as increased travel and observation, British officers were becoming more knowledgable about their profession.

Linked to the growing importance of education was an increased recognition of the relevance of staff work, and the emergence of capable staff officers such as George Macdonogh. This tendency was manifested in the composition of the upper ranks of the BEF in 1914. Among the officers examined in the preceding section, only Sir John French did not attend the Staff College at Camberley. This high proportion of p.s.c.s is representative of the BEF as a whole. According to Brian Bond: "Taking into account the senior staff officers at GHQ, the Corps Commanders and their Brigadier-Generals General Staff, the Divisional commanders and their chief staff officers (GSOs 1) and the Commanding Officer of the Royal Flying Corps and his GSO 1, no less than 40 out of the 45 who held these appointments in the first three months of the war were p.s.c.s."[84] Thus, it is evident that in the decade preceding the First World War, ambitious soldiers in the upper ranks of the officer corps were progressing toward an increased level of professional competence.

This trend, however, was not unrestricted. Describing the limits of the broader national efficiency movement, Geoffrey Searle has commented: "The aim was to revive the competitiveness of Britain as a unit in rivalry with other Great Powers on the world stage, but to do this with minimal disturbance to the status quo."[85] Similarly, while officers were concerned with improving the efficiency of the army, the preceding sketches suggest that they sought to do so without abandoning habits and values which they had acquired as regimental officers. One such value was a strong penchant for physical recreation. Among the upper ranks of the BEF in 1914, there were numerous avid sportsmen, such as Henry Rawlinson, Henry Wilson, George Harper, Sir Horace Smith-Dorrien, and Hubert Gough, a renowned jockey in India in the 1890s.[86] Certainly, physical activity and especially riding had long been integral parts of soldiering, and it would have been remarkable if British soldiers had not displayed any interest in such pastimes, particularly given the emphasis on sport in the British public schools that produced many senior officers in 1914.[87]

This tendency was certainly not confined to the upper ranks of the officer corps. In the years prior to the First World War, officers and cadets participated in various forms of physical activity from their enrollment in the Royal Military Academy. At Sandhurst, such recreation occasionally reached violent extremes. As a cadet in 1907, Bernard Montgomery played rugby and participated in savage mélées with other companies. As he related in his memoirs: "Fierce battles were fought in the passages after dark; pokers and similar weapons were used and cadets often retired to hospital for repairs."[88] Physical recreation, in both peaceful and violent forms, also comprised an important component of regimental life. In a postwar interview, A.N. Acland, a subaltern in 1914, recalled that "almost every afternoon you got into dress after lunch and you went and played cricket or fished or something like that."[89] As a more dignified alternative to the intercompany frays at Sandhurst, officers donned gloves and sparred with their counterparts in other regiments. An account provided by Tom Bridges suggests that such events were not always easy to distinguish from the brawls at the Royal Military College. According to Bridges:

On one of those hot June week-ends of 1914 the German military Attaché came down and stayed with me in barracks. There was a lively Saturday guest-night when we entertained another regiment, and high spirits were released all around. My guest was horrified at the disorder. To see me having my nose rubbed on the floor by a subaltern was bad enough, but when a colonel put on the gloves with a Captain of his weight and got knocked into the fireplace, his nerve broke and he asked permission to retire. I would have liked to have seen the letter he wrote to Berlin for the Emperor's eye.[90]

In addition to a penchant for physical recreation, the preceding biographical sketches reveal among officers an aversion to narrow intellectualism, or pedantry. This attitude was particularly evident among older commanders such as Sir John French and Sir Horace Smith-Dorrien, neither of whom were known for the depth of their reading. Given the modernizing tendencies discussed earlier, it is clear that many senior officers in 1914 were not opposed to the study of warfare. Nevertheless, it is apparent that there remained a suspicion of individuals whose devotion to intellectual pursuits detracted from more sociable activities. The popularity of officers such as Sir Douglas Haig and George Macdonogh, for example, seems to have suffered because of this tendency. Conversely, as Brian Bond has observed, Henry Rawlinson's ability to increase the prestige of the Staff College throughout the officer corps stemmed in part from the fact that "no one could accuse him of being a theoretical bookworm."[91]

This opposition to narrow intellectualism was also evident among junior officers in the years immediately prior to 1914. In his memoirs, Hubert Gough commented on the study habits of officers in the mounted arm before the First World War. As he related:

Not one of them had read a book on tactics, Clery's or any other. To know your drill was sufficient. We led a cheerful, care-free life; what duties we had to do, and in which we were thoroughly proficient, were punctiliously attended to, but they did not call for much mental effort. Afternoons were usually free for most of the officers. We played polo and some cricket at the Aldershot Club in the summer.[92]

Nor was this attitude confined to the cavalry. J.F.C. Fuller noted critically of the officers he met upon joining the infantry: "of war they knew nothing, did not want to know anything, and considered themselves better soldiers for their ignorance."[93]

Among the officers examined in this chapter, many also favored approaches to command that involved the personal leadership of troops. One such approach was the cavalry spirit, which stressed the intuitive decision-making skills of the commander, rather than careful planning and staff work. The cavalry spirit had passionate adherents in Sir John French, Hubert Gough, and, to a lesser extent, Sir Douglas Haig. More prevalent, however, was a related approach emphasizing the maintenance of morale through close ties with the troops. Aylmer Hunter-Weston tended toward an organizer's role during preplanned battles. Nonetheless, he felt a close attachment to the troops of his 11th Infantry Brigade, and was capable of leading them personally in the midst of battle. Despite the fact that his position necessitated a managerial style of command, Sir John French understood the importance of morale and attempted to maintain close ties with the soldiers of the BEF. Even Tommy Capper, who clearly grasped the importance of staff officers in organizing operations, also favored the maintenance of morale through the personal leadership of these same officers. Capper consequently charged his own staff with the task of buoying the morale of the soldiers through self-sacrifice.

This preference for personal leadership was certainly not unique to the upper ranks of the BEF. In the prewar army, it figured prominently in the regimental officer's responsibilities. As G.D. Sheffield has argued, "officer-man relations" in the British Army during the First World War were characterized by the deferential conduct of other ranks in exchange for the paternalism of their officers. This paternalistic behavior included "setting an example of courage" on the battlefield, behaving in a "gentlemanly manner when out of action," and caring for the general well-being of their men.[94] Like recent examinations of the French and German armies during the First World War, Sheffield's study conceives of this "deferential/paternal relationship" in contractual terms, as a "bargain" between officers and other ranks. Implicit in this interpretation is the assumption that soldiers could opt out of this bargain and refuse to obey orders if the command structure above them failed to honor its perceived contractual responsibilities. As Leonard Smith has demonstrated, this occurred in the French 5th Infantry Division in 1917. According to Sheffield, however, the BEF generally remained "a loyal, hierarchically-minded and disciplined army with high morale" throughout the war.[95] He attributes this stability largely to the paternalistic behavior of British officers.

Paternalism was especially pronounced in the prewar officer corps. Indeed, officers of the Regular Army undoubtedly saw paternalism as a responsibility rather than a contractual obligation. Prior to the expansion of the army in late 1914, officers were relatively homogeneous in their social origins, coming from " 'traditional sources of supply': families with military connections; the gentry and peerage; and to some degree, the professions and clergy." Moreover, the vast majority had been educated at public schools. According to Sheffield, this social and educational background "ensured that by 1914 virtually all Regular officers were thoroughly paternalistic." This tendency was reinforced by the fact that the other ranks of the prewar army were drawn overwhelmingly from the working classes, and were therefore inclined to reciprocate the paternalism of their superiors with deference. The nature of service in the prewar army tended to calcify these attitudes. Regiments were composed of volunteers who spent seven years on active duty before serving for five additional years in the reserves. This relatively long term of active service enabled soldiers and officers to become reasonably familiar with one another in an environment where a shared sense of regimental loyalty further enhanced cohesion. Thus, paternalism and deference were well-established patterns of behavior among officers and other ranks of the Regular Army.[96]

The resulting bond between officers and other ranks has been described in glowing terms by historians of the British Army. According to R. Money Barnes: "there was a family feeling throughout the battalion. The officers were leaders in sports as in everything else; they were held in great respect by the men and generally speaking the whole system worked excellently."[97] It is certainly possible to exaggerate the degree of harmony within British regiments. Significantly, other ranks were subject to often harsh disciplinary measures. Moreover, as Sheffield has observed, relations between officers and their subordinates were generally rather distant. Nevertheless, it is evident that there existed an atmosphere of mutual respect between the two groups. In other words, the contract between officers and other ranks in the prewar army was established by precedent, clearly understood and agreeable to both sides.

Regimental officers were clearly amenable to the paternalistic role expected of them. In the words of A.N. Acland: "[o]f course, one loved one's men, and we hoped they loved us." [98] Nor was paternalism reserved for soldiers familiar to an officer. K.F.B. Tower, a subaltern in the 2/Royal Fusiliers, described his relationship with one reservist in his memoir of the 1914 campaign:

When at Noyelles trying to weed out the unfits, there was one most extraordinarily ugly little man in my company who couldn't march a bit and on each occasion had fallen out exhausted and sore footed. I told him he would have to leave the battalion and go back to the Base. He protested heavily and implored me to let him come along and fight with the Battalion and told me in tones of great pride that he had won first prize for waltzing on a table in Hackney for 13 hours! Eventually I gave way and let him come. That man tried his hardest. He fell out exhausted day after day. He fell out really badly on the day we reached Mons but struggled on and arrived in time to fight with the company during those two days and gave a v[ery] fine account of himself. On the second day of the Retreat he collapsed at the side of the road and died in my arms.[99]

As well as enhancing small-unit cohesion during active operations, paternalistic behavior undoubtedly provided officers with some degree of emotional satisfaction. Given these benefits, as well as the social and educational background of most British officers in 1914, it is not surprising that formation commanders, who had once been regimental officers themselves, continued to favor personal leadership of soldiers even as they occupied relatively senior posts in 1914.

CONCLUSION

Overall, a variety of trends and attributes influenced the way in which senior British officers approached their profession in the years preceding the First World War. Clearly, these individuals stood out from most members of the officer corps as unusually ambitious. This ambition led to the emergence of often contentious cliques and produced friction between officers competing for promotions. It also contributed, however, to a desire among senior officers to increase their own military expertise and the efficiency of the army as a whole. Officers addressed tactical dilemmas, worked to improve the standard of education in the officer corps, and increasingly recognized the importance of staff work. These modernizing trends existed alongside values and habits that stemmed from the experiences of formation commanders and staff officers as regimental officers. Senior officers thus demonstrated a fondness for personal leadership in battle as well as physical recreation. In addition, there remained a suspicion among many officers toward colleagues whose devotion to intellectual pursuits deterred from their participation in the more social aspects of soldiering.

This blend of traits was often present in individual officers. Henry Wilson and Henry Rawlinson, for example, made significant contributions to staff training at Camberley prior to the war, yet still retained reputations as avid sportsmen. Tommy Capper clearly recognized the value of staff work, while advocating the personal leadership and even the sacrifice of staff officers on the battlefield. Aylmer Hunter-Weston's conception of command encompassed both personal leadership and a managerial role well behind the front line. Certainly, not every officer in the British army exhibited this mixture of traits. George Macdonogh, for example, adhered to few, if any of the values and practices associated with regimental officers. Nevertheless, the majority of officers examined in this chapter demonstrate a mixture of modernizing tendencies and traits associated with leadership at the regimental level. In light of this blend of characteristics, these individuals may be termed "hybrid" officers.

The tendencies and traits displayed by "hybrid" officers had important implications for the exercise of command in the BEF at the beginning of the First World War. Some of these characteristics would prove quite beneficial in 1914. Despite the British Army's lack of experience in campaigns on the European continent, the increased education and staff training of senior officers left them much better prepared to conduct prolonged operations on a large scale than they had been even a decade earlier. Even traits generally associated with regimental leadership could prove useful when demonstrated by senior officers. An active lifestyle involving sport probably left senior commanders and staff officers better prepared physically for the strains of active campaigning than did an exclusive focus on intellectual pursuits. With some notable exceptions, such as Sir James Grierson, senior British officers appear to have been younger and in better physical condition than their French and German counterparts in 1914.[100] In addition, the preference of many commanders for personal leadership on the battlefield held the potential to enhance the cohesion and sustain the morale of British soldiers under the new and unfamiliar conditions of war in Europe.

Qualities characteristic of regimental officers, however, were not without their drawbacks, particularly when they were displayed by senior commanders and staff officers. While they could enhance the performance of "hybrid" officers on the battlefield, these traits could also interfere with their ability to adjust to the unprecedented nature of the 1914 campaign. An excessive focus on sport, for example, could divert the attention of officers from the serious study of warfare. Moreover, the bias against narrow intellectualism likely discouraged officers from developing clearly articulated ideas regarding the use of firepower on the battlefield. The tendency of many officers toward personal leadership on the battlefield also had its drawbacks. Under the unprecedented volume of fire that prevailed in 1914, such a practice placed experienced commanders in significant danger. Moreover, the desire for contact with the troops made it more difficult for officers to adjust to the unaccustomed task of commanding large formations in battle. While in previous conflicts, senior British commanders had often led their troops personally, the size of the BEF in 1914 required that they delegate considerable authority to staff and subordinate commanders. An emphasis on personal leadership on the battlefield discouraged officers from adapting to the new tasks before them. Thus, many of the traits displayed by "hybrid" officers in 1914 proved to be double-edged in nature. Along with the modernizing tendencies evident among senior officers, these qualities could be quite useful under the strain of active operations. Nevertheless, these traits also held the potential to undermine the operations of the BEF under the largely unprecedented conditions of 1914.

NOTES

1. J.M. Bourne, "Haig and the Historians," in Brian Bond and Nigel Cave, eds., *Haig: A Reappraisal 70 Years On* (London: Leo Cooper, 1999), 7.

2. Samuel Huntington, *The Soldier and the State* (Cambridge, MA: Harvard University Press, 1959), 8.

3. GHQ was divided into three principal sections: "G," under the chief of the general staff, which coordinated the planning and conduct of operations; "A," under the adjutant-general, which was concerned with discipline, military law, personnel and casualties; and "Q" under the Quartermaster-General, which supplied the army in the field. References to "GHQ" in this study refer to "G" section in particular, unless otherwise indicated.

4. The Marquess of Anglesey, *A History of the British Cavalry, 1816 to 1919, Vol. IV, 1899–1913* (London: Leo Cooper, 1986), 408; Richard Holmes, *The Little Field-Marshal: Sir John French* (London: Jonathan Cape, 1981), 82–93, 162–165.

5. Liddell Hart Diary, 28 March 1927, 11/1927/1, Liddell Hart Papers, Liddell Hart Centre for Military Archives, King's College, London (LHCMA).

6. Sir William Robertson, *Soldiers and Statesmen: 1914–1918* (Toronto: Cassell, 1926), 71.

7. Holmes, *The Little Field-Marshal*, 367.

8. L.A.E. Price-Davies to his wife, 10 November 1914, Price-Davies Papers, Imperial War Museum (IWM), London.

9. For a detailed account of the Curragh incident, see Holmes, *The Little Field-Marshal*, ch. 6, or Ian F.W. Beckett, *Johnnie Gough, V.C.* (London: Tom Donovan, 1989), ch. 8.

10. Gerard DeGroot, *Douglas Haig: 1861–1928* (London: Unwin Hyman, 1988), 145; Holmes, *The Little Field-Marshal*, 189.

11. Murray to Charles Deedes, 18 December 1930, Spears Papers, 2/3, LHCMA; Murray to Smith-Dorrien, 12 July 1919, "Murray Correspondence," WO 79/62, Public Record Office, Kew (PRO).

12. Edmonds Memoirs, III/8, Edmonds Papers, LHCMA. See also "Talk with Edmonds, 7/6/34," 11/1934/41, Liddell Hart Papers, LHCMA.

13. Holmes, *The Little Field-Marshal*, 221.

14. Edmonds Memoirs, III/8, LHCMA.

15. "Lieutenant-General Sir George M.W. Macdonogh, GBE, KCB, KCML," Walter Kirke Papers, Intelligence Corps Museum (ICM), Chicksands, Bedfordshire; Archibald Murray to Edward Spears, 22 December 1930, Edward Spears Papers, 2/3, LHCMA; Edmonds Memoirs, August 1914, Edmonds Papers, III/8, LHCMA. See also Victor Bonham-Carter, *The Strategy of Victory, 1914–1918: The Life and Times of the Master Strategist of World War I: Field-Marshal Sir William Robertson* (New York: Holt, Rinehart and Winston, 1963), 84.

16. "Lieutenant-General Sir George M.W. Macdonogh, GBE, KCB, KCML," Kirke Papers, ICM; Brian Bond, *The Victorian Army and the Staff College: 1854–1914* (London: Eyre Methuen, 1972), 244–270.

17. Count Edward Gleichen, *A Guardsman's Memories: A Book of Recollections* (London: Blackwood, 1932), 177.

18. Tom Bridges, *Alarms and Excursions: Reminiscences of a Soldier* (Toronto: Longman's, 1938), 252.

19. Holmes, *The Little Field-Marshal*, 145, 162; John Charteris, *At GHQ* (London: Cassell, 1931), 87.

20. Hubert Gough to Shaw-Sparrow, 25 December 1918, Shaw Sparrow Papers, Vol. I, 48203, British Library, London. Aylmer Haldane, *A Soldier's Saga* (London: Blackwood, 1948), 206.

21. "Lieutenant-General Sir George M.W. Macdonogh, GBE, KCB, KCML," Kirke Papers, ICM; Bernard Ash, *The Last Dictator* (London: Cassell, 1968), 130.

22. "Lieutenant-General Sir George Macdonogh, GBE, KCB, KCML," Kirke Papers, ICM; Tim Travers, *The Killing Ground: The British Army, the Western Front and the Emergence of Modern Warfare, 1900–1918* (London: Routledge, 1993), 287; Bond, *The Victorian Army and the Staff College*, 253.

23. Travers, *The Killing Ground*, 287.

24. Spears to Archie Murray, 8 May 1931, Spears Papers, 2/3, LHCMA.

25. "Lieutenant-General Sir George M.W. Macdonogh," Kirke Papers, ICM; Travers, *The Killing Ground*, 287, 289.

26. "Lieutenant-General Sir George M.W. Macdonogh, GBE, KCB, KCML," Kirke Papers, ICM; Bond, *The Victorian Army and the Staff College*, 159–160, 315; Holmes, *The Little Field-Marshal*, 213; John Ferris, "The British Army and Signals Intelligence in the Field during the First World War," *Intelligence and National Security*, 3:4 (October 1988), 23–48.

27. "Lieutenant-General Sir George M.W. Macdonogh, GBE, KCB, KCML," Kirke Papers, ICM.

28. "Lieutenant-General Sir George M.W. Macdonogh, GBE, KCB, KCML," Kirke Papers, ICM. See John Ferris and Uri Bar-Joseph, "Getting Marlowe to Hold His Tongue: The Conservative Party, the Intelligence Services and the Zinoviev Letter." *Intelligence and National Security*, 8:4 (October 1993), 113, for Macdonogh's belief in an "apolitical army."

29. Holmes, *The Little Field-Marshal*, 162.

30. Edmonds to Wavell, 17 June 1938, Allenby Papers, LHCMA.

31. George Barrow, *The Fire of Life* (London: Hutchinson, 1931), 118; Stephen Badsey, "Cavalry and the Development of Breakthrough Doctrine," in Paddy Griffith, ed., *British Fighting Methods in the Great War* (London: Frank Cass, 1996), 147.

32. Bond, *The Victorian Army and the Staff College*, 164.

33. Hubert Gough, *Soldiering On* (London: Arthur Barker, 1954), 95.

34. Gough, *Soldiering On*, 97; Bond, *The Victorian Army and the Staff College*, 164.

35. See, for example, Bourne, "Haig and the Historians," and John Hussey, "Portrait of a Commander-in-Chief," in Brian Bond and Nigel Cave, eds., *Haig: A Reappraisal 70 YearsOn* (London: Leo Cooper, 1999).

36. See, for example, DeGroot, *Douglas Haig*; Travers, *The Killing Ground*; Shelford Bidwell and Dominick Graham, *Fire-Power: British Army Weapons and Theories of War, 1904–1945* (London: Allen and Unwin, 1982); Robin Prior and Trevor Wilson, *Passchendaele; the Untold Story* (New Haven: Yale University Press, 1996).

37. Birch to Wavell, 15 December 1936, Allenby Papers, LHCMA. See also Barrow, *The Fire of Life*, 43–44.

38. "Historical Note," 11/1933/41, Liddell Hart Papers, LHCMA.

39. "Talk With Edmonds, 10/1/35," 11/1935/58; "Talk With Edmonds, 16/12/35," 11/1935/117; "Note on Duff Cooper's 'HAIG,' " 11/1935/132; Liddell Hart Papers, LHCMA.

40. Holmes, *The Little Field-Marshal*, 51; Travers, *The Killing Ground*, 10; DeGroot, *Douglas Haig*, ch. 4; DeGroot, "Ambition, Duty and Doctrine: Douglas Haig's Rise to High Command," in Bond and Cave, eds., *Haig: A Reappraisal*, 41.

41. "Talk with Edmonds: 5/2/37," 11/1937/4; "Talk With Edmonds, 16/12/35," 11/1935/117, Liddell Hart Papers, LHCMA.

42. Travers, *The Killing Ground*, 18–19.

43. "Letter to Sir A. Murray from Charles Deedes," Spears Papers, 2/3, LHCMA. See also Deedes to Murray, 16 December 1930, Spears Papers, 2/3, LHCMA; and "General Report on the Battle of Le Cateau, 26 August 1914," CAB 45/206, PRO.

44. Ash, *The Last Dictator*, 51.

45. On George V's influence over army appointments, see Ian F.W. Beckett, "George V and His Generals," in Matthew Hughes and Matthew Seligmann, eds., *Leadership in Conflict: 1914–1918* (London: Leo Cooper, 2000).

46. DeGroot, *Douglas Haig*, ch. 7; Haig Diary, 13 August 1914, National Library of Scotland (hereafter NLS), Edinburgh, and Haig Diary, WO 256/1, PRO.

47. Bond, *The Victorian Army and the Staff College*, 141.

48. A.J. Smithers, *The Man Who Disobeyed: Sir Horace Smith-Dorrien and His Enemies* (London: Leo Cooper, 1970), 130.

49. Smith-Dorrien Diary, 1–4 November 1914, CAB 45/206, PRO.

50. Holmes, *The Little Field-Marshal*, 131–133; Smithers, *The Man Who Disobeyed*, 90.

51. Charles Callwell, *Experiences of a Dug-Out: 1914–1918* (London: Constable, 1920), 57.

52. Smithers, *The Man Who Disobeyed*, 105, 160;   See French to Kitchener, 17 August 1914; Kitchener to French 18 August 1914; WO 33/713, PRO.

53. "Talk With Edmonds, 16/12/35," Liddell Hart Papers, 11/1935/117; "Talk With Edmonds, 5/2/37," Liddell Hart Papers, 11/1937/4; LHCMA.

54. Bond, *The Victorian Army and the Staff College*, 196–197; "Talk with Edmonds, 5/2/37," 11/1937/4, Liddell Hart Papers, LHCMA. See also Bidwell and Graham, *Fire-Power*, 81.

55. Holmes, *The Little Field-Marshal*, 127.

56. Rawlinson Diary, 7 September 1914, Henry Rawlinson Papers, Churchill College Archives, Cambridge (CCC).

57. "Talk With Lloyd George and Sir Hubert Gough (at the Atheneum)—28/11/35," 11/1935/107, Liddell Hart Papers, LHCMA.

58. Robin Prior and Trevor Wilson, *Command on the Western Front: The Military Career of Henry Rawlinson, 1914–1918* (Oxford: Oxford University Press, 1992), 394.

59. Bidwell and Graham, *Fire-Power*, 87; Peter Simkins, "Haig and His Army Commanders," in Bond and Cave, eds., *Haig: A Reappraisal*, 41.

60. Keith Simpson, "Capper and the Offensive Spirit," *Journal of the Royal United Services Institute*, 118:2 (June 1973), 51.

61. Gough, *Soldiering On*, 93.

62. Bond, *The Victorian Army and the Staff College*, 318, 208.

63. "Talk With Edmonds, 16/12/35," 11/1935/117, Liddell Hart Papers, LHCMA; Barrow, *The Fire of Life*, 123; Haldane, *A Soldier's Saga*, 269.

64. Montgomery to Edmonds, 4 February 1921, 7 Division War Diary, WO 95/1627, PRO.

65. Price-Davies to Mrs. Price-Davies, 13 November 1914, Price-Davies Papers, IWM; Simpson, "Capper and the Offensive Spirit," 54.

66. Travers, *The Killing Ground*, 287. Bond, *The Victorian Army and the Staff College*, 162.

67. Hunter-Weston to Mrs. Hunter-Weston, 11 November 1914, Hunter-Weston Papers, 48363, British Library, London.

68. Hunter-Weston to Elkington, 31 August 1916, Hunter-Weston Papers 48365, British Library.

69. Hunter-Weston to W.D.S. Brownrigg, 17 March 1934; Hunter-Weston to Mrs. Hunter-Weston, 30 August 1914; Hunter-Weston to Mrs. Hunter-Weston, 25 October 1914; Hunter-Weston Papers, 48363, British Library.

70. Hunter-Weston Diary, 26 August 1914, Hunter-Weston Papers, 48363, British Library.

71. "Account of the Action of the 11th Infantry Brigade on the night of 12th–13th September, 1914." 4 Division War Diary, WO 95/1439, PRO; E.K.G. Sixsmith, *British Generalship in the Twentieth Century* (London: Arms and Armour Press, 1970), 51.

72. Hunter-Weston to Mrs. Hunter-Weston, 9 November 1914, Hunter-Weston Papers, 48363, British Library.

73. Hunter-Weston Diary, 28 October 1914, Hunter-Weston Papers, 48363, British Library.

74. Price-Davies to Mrs. Price-Davies, 17 October 1914, Price-Davies Papers, IWM.

75. E.H. Beddington, "My Life," Edward Beddington Papers, LHCMA.

76. Edmonds Memoirs, III/9, Edmonds Papers, LHCMA; Travers, *The Killing Ground*, 11; Simkins, "Haig and the Army Commanders," in Bond and Cave, eds., *Haig: A Reappraisal*, 88.

77. J.M. Bourne, "British Generals in the First World War," in G.D. Sheffield, ed., *Leadership and Command: The Anglo-American Military Experience Since 1861* (London: Brassey's, 1997), 94–95.

78. On rivalries between rings, see Travers, *The Killing Ground*, ch. 1. On rivalries within the Wolseley ring in the 1880s, see Adrian Preston, ed., *In Relief of Gordon: Lord Wolseley's Campaign Journal of the Khartoum Relief Expedition* (London: Hutchinson, 1967), introduction; Ian F.W. Beckett, "Command in the Late Victorian Army," in Sheffield, ed., *Leadership and Command*, 37–56.

79. G.R. Searle, *The Quest for National Efficiency: A Study in British Politics and Political Thought, 1899–1914*, 2d ed. (London: Ashfield, 1990), xix.

80. Edward M. Spiers, "The British Cavalry, 1902–1914," *Journal of the Society for Army Historical Research*, 57:230, (Summer 1979), 71–79; The Marquess of Anglesey, *A History of the British Cavalry, 1816–1919, Vol. IV*; Gervase Phillips, "The Obsolescence of the Arme Blanche and Technological Determinism in British Military History," *War in History*, 9:1 (January 2002), 39–59.

81. Bond, *The Victorian Army and the Staff College*, ch. 6, 8.

82. Bridges, *Alarms and Excursions*, 55.

83. Haldane, *A Soldier's Saga*, 206.

84. Bond, *The Victorian Army and the Staff College*, 306.

85. Searle, *The Quest for National Efficiency*, xxiv.

86. Smithers, *The Man Who Disobeyed*, 26.

87. G.D. Sheffield, *Leadership in the Trenches: Officer-Man Relations, Morale and Discipline in the British Army in the Era of the First World War* (London: Macmillan, 2000), 44–47; Bourne, "British Generals in the First World War," 95; Geoffrey Best, "Militarism and the Victorian Public School," in B. Simon and I. Bradley, eds., *The Victorian Public School: Studies in the Development of an Educational Institution* (London: Gill and Macmillan, 1975) 129–146.

88. Bernard Montgomery, *The Memoirs of Field-Marshal the Viscount Montgomery of Alamein, K.G.* (London: Collins, 1958), 24. See also John Masters, *Bugles and a Tiger: A Volume of Autobiography* (New York: Viking, 1956), 42.

89. Peter Liddle interview with Lieutenant-General Floyer-Acland, August 1974, Tape 268, Liddle Collection, Brotherton Library, University of Leeds.

90. Bridges, *Alarms and Excursions*, 67.

91. Bond, *The Victorian Army and the Staff College*, 196.

92. Gough, *Soldiering On*, 34.

93. J.F.C. Fuller, *The Army in My Time* (London: Rich and Cowan, 1935), 53.

94. Sheffield, *Leadership in the Trenches*, 104–107.

95. Sheffield, *Leadership in the Trenches*, 72; Leonard V. Smith, *Between Mutiny and Obedience: The Case of the French Fifth Infantry Division during World War I* (Princeton: Princeton University Press, 1994). For a similar conception of this relationship in contractual terms, see Dennis Showalter, *Tannenberg: Clash of Empires* (Hamden CT: Archon, 1991), 254.

96. Sheffield, *Leadership in the Trenches*, 1–2.

97. R. Money Barnes, *The British Army of 1914* (London: Seeley, 1968), 38–39.

98. "Peter Liddle interview with Lieutenant-General Floyer-Acland," August 1974, Papers of A.N. Acland, Liddle Collection, Brotherton Library, University of Leeds. See also John Baynes, *Morale: A Study of Men and Courage* (New York: Praeger, 1967), ch. 7.

99. Tower Memoirs, K.F.B. Tower Papers, IWM.

100. On the German officer corps, see Showalter, *Tannenberg*. British commanders at the army and corps level were all younger than their counterparts in the German 8th Army in 1914. Moreover, as Showalter notes, "the German army never made quite as much of field sports and physical fitness as its British counterpart." See Douglas Porch, *The March to the Marne: The French Army, 1871–1914* (London: Cambridge University Press, 1981), 177; and Hew Strachan, *The First World War, Volume 1: To Arms* (Oxford: Oxford University Press, 2001), 226, for a brief discussion of the age and health of senior French officers.

2

Command in Crisis: Mons, Le Cateau, and the "Great Retreat"

The opening weeks of the First World War proved a difficult test for the BEF. After colliding with German forces around the Belgian town of Mons on 23 August, Sir John French's army embarked on hasty retirement into France. On the 25th, the two corps that constituted the BEF separated in an attempt to circumvent the seemingly impassable Forest of Mormal. Amid considerable confusion, however, they failed to reconnect later that day. As a result, Sir Horace Smith-Dorrien's II Corps was left alone to fight a significant action at Le Cateau on 26 August. In the aftermath of the battle, the two corps continued to retreat independently until 1 September, with Smith-Dorrien's force in disarray. It was only on 6 September, after retiring over 165 miles to the outskirts of Paris, that the exhausted BEF joined the French counteroffensive against the Germans.

Existing portrayals of the retreat from Mons have elevated the exploits of the "Old Contemptibles" to almost legendary status. Historians have emphasized the poise and professionalism of British soldiers on the battlefield as they checked superior German forces at Mons and Le Cateau and endured the privations of the retreat that followed.[1] Nonetheless, it is also apparent that the competence of British soldiers was undermined by the shortcomings of their leaders. Accounts of the retreat and biographies of senior officers suggest that the behavior of British commanders was often detrimental to the efficiency of the BEF as a whole. Scholars have noted GHQ's lack of control over operations, as well as the despondency of senior officers during the retreat. In the aftermath of the battle of Le Cateau, John Terraine has provided an unflattering portrait of GHQ, "in the agonies of a mental defeat that far surpassed anything suffered by the Army itself."[2]

Despite these revelations regarding the performance of British commanders, significant questions remain regarding the operations of the BEF in this period. Why did Sir Douglas Haig's I Corps and Sir Horace Smith-Dorrien's II Corps become separated on 25 August, leaving II Corps to face the enemy alone the following day? Why did the two formations continue to retire independently for nearly a week afterward? The inability of existing accounts to address these issues reflects a lack of attention to the dynamics of command in the BEF. While historians have highlighted the behavior of key commanders and staff officers in this period, they have not examined the complex array of alliances and animosities among senior British officers at the beginning of the First World War. Moreover, the communications system that linked formations during mobile operations remains poorly understood.

Through an analysis of these factors and their impact on the decisions of senior officers, it is possible to shed new light on the conduct of the retreat from Mons. With this intent, this chapter will examine the exercise of command in the BEF in August and early September 1914. Focusing in particular on GHQ and the two corps, it will argue that officers were handicapped by their inexperience in controlling large formations, particularly with unfamiliar technology and a command philosophy that encouraged ambiguity in crucial orders. Furthermore, rivalries among senior officers undermined the operations of the army throughout this period, contributing to the prolonged separation of the two corps that comprised the BEF, and hindering the recovery of the army from the losses sustained during this separation. The fact that the BEF survived the retreat intact was a significant accomplishment. Its commanders, however, did not always facilitate this process.

THE ASSEMBLY OF THE BEF

Following Britain's declaration of war on Germany on 4 August 1914, Henry Wilson's plan for the mobilization of the BEF was set in motion. By the 12th, British soldiers had begun crossing the English Channel in significant numbers (see Map 2.1). Eight days later, the BEF had completed its concentration in a "pear-shaped area between Maubeuge and Le Cateau, almost twenty-five miles long from north-east to south-west, and averaging ten miles wide."[3] The original contingent of the BEF numbered approximately 100,000 troops. It was composed of I and II Corps, commanded by Sir Douglas Haig and Sir Horace Smith-Dorrien, respectively. I Corps comprised 1 and 2 Divisions, while II Corps consisted of 3 and 5 Divisions. Each division contained three infantry brigades, four artillery brigades, and a heavy battery, as well as a squadron of cavalry. The infantry and artillery brigades were further divided into four battalions and three batteries, respectively. In addition to the divisional mounted troops, the BEF was accompanied by five brigades of cavalry, four of which comprised the Cavalry Division under Sir Edmund Allenby, and one which was attached to Haig's I Corps.[4]

While the battalions of the prewar army were composed of long-service volunteers, the necessity of replacing partially trained recruits in the ranks as well as soldiers detached on colonial garrison duty required the reenlistment of substantial numbers of reservists in August 1914. As Bidwell and Graham have

Map 2.1
British Area of Operations,
21 August–5 September 1914

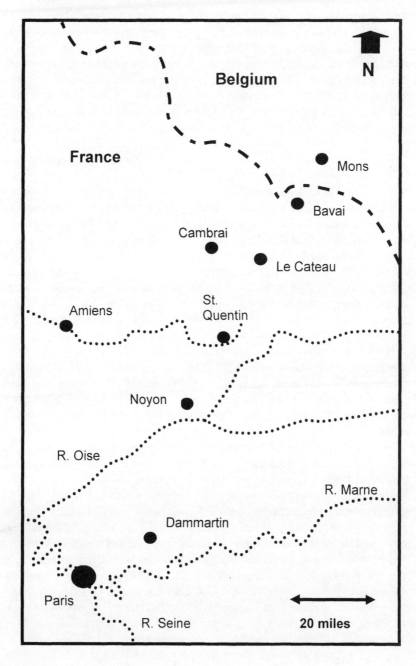

noted, reservists comprised up to 70 percent of the strength of British battalions in this period. Although these soldiers were often physically unprepared for the rigors of active operations, they had developed formidable tactical skills over years of service that they retained even after leaving the Regular Army. Indeed, the rapid fire and marksmanship of British infantry in 1914 have been well-documented.[5] In addition, reservists were recalled to their former regiments, often rejoining the same officers under whom they had served as regular soldiers. As a result, they were able to renew their relationships with their superiors with relatively little difficulty. Thus, the high proportion of reservists in British battalions in 1914 was offset by the experience and tactical proficiency of the officers and other ranks alike.

Staff Work

Although the battalions of the BEF proved reasonably well prepared for war in 1914, the army's command and control structure remained largely untested. An important element of this apparatus was the staff. Since the South African War the Staff Colleges at Camberley and Quetta had produced an unprecedented number of trained staff officers. These officers responded enthusiastically to the outbreak of war, often leaving their administrative posts in Britain to accompany the BEF to France. This widespread desire for active service ensured that the BEF had an ample supply of officers with formal staff training. Much of this enthusiasm, however, was based on the combined assumptions that the war would be short and decisive, and would require only a limited contribution from the British Army. This failure to appreciate the gravity of the impending conflict was reflected in the attitude of many officers. Sir James Marshall-Cornwall, a staff officer in I Corps in 1914, commented after the war: "I think most of us, in the junior ranks anyway, treated the First World War in rather light-hearted spirit, thinking like many senior officers did, that it would be all over by Christmas."[6]

This attitude did nothing to compensate for the inexperience of most staff officers. The command blunders of the South African War had underlined the importance of staff work and consequently sparked an improvement in the curriculum at Camberley. Nevertheless, aside from the war in South Africa, the army's practical experience consisted of small-scale colonial police actions. Thus, there existed a dearth of institutional knowledge regarding the handling of a force the size of the BEF in the field. Nor did staff officers have sufficient opportunity to develop such knowledge before the war. Even at GHQ, the impressive qualifications of senior staff officers were offset by their inexperience in the tasks required of them in 1914. Archie Murray, the CGS, had held a variety of senior staff posts during and after the South African War, while both Sir William Robertson, the quartermaster-general (QMG), and Henry Wilson, the "sub-chief" of the General Staff, had commanded the Staff College at Camberley. Prior to the war, however, GHQ had existed only during army maneuvers. Moreover, most of its members in 1914 had never participated in these exercises in the roles they would perform in the opening months of the conflict. Consequently, Murray, Robertson, Wilson, and the members of the Operations and Intelligence sections of GHQ found themselves executing largely unaccustomed tasks at the beginning of the First World War.[7] Charles Deedes, a member of the Operations Staff in this period, reflected on the resulting problems in his memoir of the 1914 campaign. According to Deedes: "Difficulties in mobilization, ignorance of each other's duties and functions, [and] a tendency to work in watertight compartments made the machine groan and creak considerably for the first few days."[8]

At the corps level, Sir Douglas Haig was the only formation commander in the British Army who possessed a permanent staff prior to mobilization in August 1914. Even the I Corps staff, however, required several inexperienced additions following the outbreak of the conflict. John Charteris, Haig's aide-de-camp and chief intelligence officer, described one of these new officers in a letter to his wife: "Colonel X, who has recently blossomed into a Staff officer, consulted me very confidentially. 'You know all about the army—tell me how many battalions are there in a division?' "[9] Haig's advisors nonetheless represented the most experienced and efficient staff in the British Army in 1914. In contrast, the staff of II Corps had to be improvised following mobilization. A similar situation prevailed in the divisions of the BEF, which had a peacetime establishment of only two staff officers per formation. Upon mobilization, each of the divisional staffs expanded to include six officers. If the motley crew that joined Thomas Snow's 4 Division is any indication, these individuals brought limited experience to their new posts. According to Sir James Edmonds, the division's chief staff officer in August 1914, the new additions were either incompetent or uninterested in staff duties. Even the most qualified, an instructor at Camberley, was a relative novice at staff work. As Edmonds related in his memoirs: "He...could not write a practical, only an academic, operation order; had never heard of a sliding time scale for marches, and knew nothing of the routine of preparing simultaneously sufficient copies of an order and of a march table. In fact, in the first days, he was a hindrance rather than a help."[10] In considering this description, it is wise to bear in mind the derisive tendencies of its source. The overall frailty of the 4 Division staff is further illustrated, however, by the fact that Edmonds himself was relieved after collapsing from exhaustion during the retreat from Mons.[11]

In the cavalry, trained and experienced staff officers proved even scarcer. Since the South African War, innovative officers within the mounted arm had introduced training in areas such as marksmanship and even the preparation of trenches. The cavalry nonetheless retained an institutional ethos that stressed independence and intuitive decision-making, qualities that did not encourage attention to staff duties.[12] Prior to August 1914, the British Cavalry Division had no permanent staff officers. Nor did the assortment of officers collected to fill its various positions have any significant background in staff work. Even the divisional chief of staff, John Vaughan, had no staff training or experience. Edmund Allenby, the commander of the division, was more fortunate in his selection of George Barrow as his chief intelligence officer.[13] During the retreat and afterward, Barrow repeatedly displayed his competence in staff work, despite a lack of practical experience. Nonetheless, the necessity of improvising an entire staff out of inexperienced officers increased the likelihood of problems for the cavalry division during the retreat from Mons. Overall, despite manifest improvements in staff training since the South African War, there existed at all levels of the BEF a paucity of practical experience in the command and control of large formations in August 1914. Even the senior staff at GHQ entered the war with little preparation for the duties that they would be required to perform. This dearth of experience foreshadowed difficulties for the control of the BEF under the strain of active operations.

Communications

Whatever the capabilities of British staff officers, proper coordination of the army also required efficient methods of communication. At the outset of the First World War, the British army was in the process of integrating real-time communications mechanisms, such as radio, telegraph and telephone, with older "human" methods of transferring information. The mixture of techniques that prevailed at the outset of the war reflected this period of transition. Divisional signal companies in 1914 comprised an assortment of systems that ranged from the modern to the archaic, including telephones, flags, and lanterns, and dispatch riders on motorcycles, bicycles, or horses. In addition, both GHQ and Allenby's Cavalry Division were equipped with radios. GHQ also employed liaison officers in cars to communicate with corps and divisions as well as neighboring French forces.[14]

Some of these communications systems proved to be impractical during the 1914 campaign. The few bulky radio sets available to the BEF were a nuisance to formations on the move. Ultimately, they proved more useful in communicating air reconnaissance and intercepting enemy radio transmissions than in conveying information between British headquarters.[15] The telephone and telegraph also had limited value during mobile operations. Unless formations remained stationary for more than a few hours, it was impractical to lay telephone cable between them. In the absence of such direct links between headquarters, staff officers were forced to rely on the existing Belgian and French telephone and telegraph systems that were usually located at railway stations. Given the rapid pace of the retreat, however, British formations rarely remained in the vicinity of a particular railway station for long enough to establish consistent communications with higher headquarters. The bulk of information was thus carried by dispatch riders and liaison officers.

In the midst of a hurried retreat, even such rudimentary methods of communication were fraught with complications. Not only did messengers have to navigate through largely unknown territory while attempting to locate the continually shifting headquarters of other formations, but they were usually forced to share roads with heavy civilian and military traffic. Motor vehicles facilitated the process, and the BEF had at its disposal a pool of skilled volunteer drivers. Cars and motorcycles of the early twentieth-century, however, were exceedingly slow and unreliable by modern standards. Edward Spears, a liaison officer between GHQ and the French 5th Army in 1914, was provided only with, "a small Sunbeam car with absurd showroom headlights that used to go out every few minutes during night journeys." Traveling close to German lines, Spears also risked attracting fire from friend and foe alike. As he related:

During the retreat I had many times to do with Germans, but they were not nearly so dangerous as the posts of Territorials or lunatic armed civilians that one met on the roads at frequent intervals....These posts had no idea of what they were expected to do, but very often, at night especially, they used to just fire and as they were often armed with shot guns, the chance of their doing damage was very great indeed.[16]

In addition to this range of handicaps, obstacles and hazards, vital information could be delayed by such mundane pitfalls as traffic accidents. Thus, despite the presence of devices such as the radio, telephone, and telegraph, the methods of conveying information available to British officers in August 1914 hardly represented a dramatic improvement in speed or reliability over previous conflicts. During mobile operations, real-time communications systems were available only infrequently. While automobiles held the possibility of expediting information, their effectiveness was limited by mechanical failure, traffic congestion, and human error. The instability of communications contributed to the difficulties of British officers as they grappled with the unaccustomed responsibilities of controlling the BEF during the initial stages of the war.

Exercise of Command

Unreliable communications systems and inexperienced staff officers were handicaps shared by all European armies in 1914. Certain characteristics of the British officer corps, however, held the potential to create additional problems from the beginning of the campaign. Martin Samuels has argued that the exercise of command in the British Army during the First World War was governed by a practice known as "umpiring." This policy limited the responsibility of senior commanders to the assignment of general objectives, leaving their subordinates to manage the details involved in directing them.[17] Umpiring undoubtedly eased the task of senior officers and allowed commanders in the field independence of action. Nevertheless, the imprecise orders entailed by such a policy could compound problems created by unreliable means of communication and the inexperience of British staff officers.

In addition, the contentious group of individuals at GHQ in 1914 distorted the chain of command in the upper ranks of the army from the beginning of active operations. Given the allegiance of "Uncle" Harper and the Operations section to Henry Wilson, Archie Murray's authority as chief of staff was threatened from the outset of operations. Sir John French's close relationship with the sub-chief further diminished Murray's influence. Moreover, Henry Wilson exacerbated the situation by privately influencing French, and surreptitiously undermining Murray's position with the help of Harper and his subordinates. As the CGS related after the war, the "War Office clique" that comprised the Operations section "entirely ignored me as far as possible, continually thwarted me, even altered my instructions."[18] Thus, even before the battle of Mons, Archie Murray had been effectively sidelined from the chain of command.

Similarly, George Macdonogh, another outsider to the ascendant faction at GHQ, was unable to exert any significant influence, despite his manifest capabilities. Macdonogh's cool relations with Wilson also resulted in the subordination of his Intelligence section to the Operations section at GHQ. After the war, the Intelligence chief made a series of allegations in correspondence with Sir James Edmonds. According to Macdonogh:

One of the worst features during the first 3 months of the war was the attitude of O[perations] to I[ntelligence]. Intelligence para.s of orders were often drafted by O without reference to I, information received from I was cooked or suppressed to suit O's preconceived notions, & the movements of the British & Allied troops were systematically concealed from me.[19]

With the marginalization of Murray and Macdonogh, the allegiance of the Operations section and the trust of the commander-in-chief made Henry Wilson the intellectual focal point of GHQ in the opening stages of the war. This situation had a detrimental impact on the decision-making process at General Headquarters. Wilson's predominance reduced the free exchange of ideas among senior staff officers. In addition, during active operations, the British communications system provided an erratic flow of information on which to base decisions. As a result of these two factors, GHQ proved vulnerable to what Robert Jervis has termed "premature cognitive closure." According to Jervis, this phenomenon is characterized by a tendency to assimilate incoming information into preexisting beliefs, so that all data but that which plainly contradicts those beliefs will be interpreted as consistent with them.[20] In specific terms, GHQ, in light of Wilson's predominance, tended to develop definite ideas regarding the operational situation of the BEF and adhere to them even when faced with mounting evidence to the contrary.

This inclination would have serious consequences for the army throughout the 1914 campaign. The tendency of senior officers to succumb to cognitive closure, however, was first manifested in August, as British units advanced into Belgium. At the beginning of the war, the operations of the BEF were framed by the broad directive which Sir John French received from Secretary of State for War Lord Kitchener. The order was problematic in that it contained two potentially discrepant instructions. On the one hand, Sir John French was to "support and cooperate with" the French Army. In light of the small size of the BEF and the limited availability of immediate reinforcements, however,

Kitchener emphasized that "the greatest consideration will devolve upon you as to participation in forward movements where large bodies of French troops are not engaged and where your force may be unduly exposed to attack."

As John Terraine has suggested, the ambiguous and even contradictory nature of these instructions was probably necessary due to the unknown situation faced by the allies.[21] Kitchener's orders nonetheless allowed French and his staff considerable leeway in directing the operations of the BEF. Because of the intellectual dominance of Henry Wilson at GHQ, it was almost inevitable that the British would advance in close cooperation with the French in the opening stages of the conflict. In addition to being a long-time admirer of the French Army, Wilson believed that the BEF could be the decisive factor in a war between France and Germany.[22] His careful planning for mobilization alongside the French in the years before 1914 was therefore paralleled by a conviction that the BEF ought to conform closely to the movements of its ally in the opening stages of the conflict. Given the path of the German advance in late August, the presence of the BEF on the French left flank proved auspicious for both Britain and France. In this respect, Wilson's ascendancy at GHQ was fortunate. Cooperation with the French Army, however, was not the only consequence of Wilson's dominance. Indeed, the sub-chief's admiration of the French Army also left him susceptible to the optimism of the French commander-in-chief, Joseph Joffre. In the week prior to the battle of Mons, Wilson consistently expressed confidence in the ability of the French and British armies to advance into Belgium.[23]

Wilson's intellectual dominance ensured that his optimism became the principal concept shaping the operations of the BEF leading into the battle of Mons. This confidence prevailed at GHQ despite increasing tensions with the leadership of the neighboring French 5th Army and the accumulation of evidence indicating the approach of considerable German forces. Its resiliency was demonstrated on 17 August, in the wake of a frosty encounter between Sir John French and General Lanrezac, commander of the neighboring French Fifth Army. The details of this meeting have been recounted elsewhere.[24] It is significant, however, that despite the fact that the two generals left with poor opinions of one another, the British commander-in-chief retained his confidence in the ability of both armies to conduct a joint offensive. Thus, following the concentration of the BEF on 20 August, GHQ ordered the force to advance the following morning.[25]

THE ADVANCE INTO BELGIUM AND THE BATTLE OF MONS, 21–23 AUGUST

The BEF encountered few difficulties as it moved north toward Belgium on 21 August. Unmolested by enemy forces, the army completed a relatively leisurely "peace march" of 10 miles, ostensibly alongside the French 5th Army. Unbeknownst to the British, Lanrezac's force in fact remained in defensive positions south of the River Sambre before being driven back by advancing

German forces.[26] During the day, however, British intelligence sources indicated threatening movements of enemy forces in front of the BEF as well. The Royal Flying Corps brought word of several German columns advancing directly into the path of the British Army. In addition, George Barrow, the recently installed intelligence chief of the Cavalry Division, took advantage of the railway telephone system, placing calls from Mons to stations further north in order to determine the direction of the German advance. By early afternoon, he had detected a steady flow of German troops to the west and southwest, with cavalry patrols probing southward toward Mons.

Neither air reconnaissance reports nor Barrow's discovery could disturb the self-assurance of GHQ. As Henry Wilson replied dismissively to Barrow's warning: "Information you have acquired and conveyed to C in C appears somewhat exaggerated."[27] The certainties of 21 August, however, would be tested further during the next twenty-four hours. Shortly after daylight on the 22nd, in front of the main body of the BEF, British troops clashed with the enemy for the first time, as the 4th Dragoon Guards of Henry de Lisle's 2nd Cavalry Brigade ambushed a German cavalry patrol north of Mons. By late morning it had become clear that the enemy was present in greater force, as the artillery of Hubert Gough's 3rd Cavalry Brigade was exchanging fire with German guns to the north.[28]

This altercation alerted British commanders to the necessity of making concrete preparations to meet the enemy. Consequently, the vague directives to advance that had hitherto emanated from GHQ were replaced by specific instructions for the disposition of the BEF in order to engage German forces. In light of the sparse coverage provided to the British left by French Territorial divisions, the Cavalry Division, previously employed as an advance guard, was ordered to move to the left flank.[29] I Corps had taken up positions around the fortress of Maubeuge, over ten miles south of Mons, during the morning of 22 August. At 1:30 pm, GHQ ordered Haig's corps to move northward to positions just southeast of Mons to connect with the right of II Corps, which held a line around the town and to the west of it along the Mons-Condé Canal.[30]

The last units of I Corps and the Cavalry Division did not reach their positions until early on the morning of 23 August. It was nonetheless fortunate that their movements were initiated by GHQ early in the afternoon of the 22nd, as subsequent news from the Fifth Army revealed that the BEF had become dangerously exposed. [31] The British advance had been carried out under the assumption that Lanrezac's force was moving forward in unison on its right. During the afternoon, however, Edward Spears arrived with the news that the Fifth Army was in fact retreating, and planned to continue the next day. Once British units reached their assigned positions for the 22nd, the BEF would sit nine miles in front of the French. The proposed French retirement on the 23rd threatened to expose the right flank of the BEF even further, given that GHQ was planning yet another advance.[32] The information related by Spears resulted in the postponement of these plans. At a late afternoon meeting at GHQ, Sir John French and Archie Murray informed the chief staff officers of both corps and the

Cavalry Division that the BEF would remain stationary the following morning. Nonetheless, even the French withdrawal did little to deflate the confidence prevalent at GHQ. Although the British commander-in-chief declined a subsequent request from Lanrezac that the BEF attack German forces on its right, Sir John French promised that his army would stand fast on its exposed position for the next twenty-four hours.[33]

British units began arriving near Mons on the evening of the 22nd. On the left of the army, the Cavalry Division took up positions south of the Mons-Condé Canal from the town of Thulin to Condé. The cavalry were replaced the following morning by the newly arrived 19th Infantry Brigade, temporarily under Allenby's orders. To the immediate right of the Cavalry Division was II Corps, which occupied the greatest length of the British line. Charles Fergusson's 5 Division held positions from the right of the cavalry along the canal to Mons. There it connected with 3 Division, commanded by Hubert Hamilton, which held the town and the salient that followed the canal northeast of it. To the right of II Corps was I Corps, which faced almost due east, and extended toward the French Fifth Army to the southeast.[34]

The Mons position was exceedingly difficult to defend. To the north of the Mons-Condé Canal, a broad swathe of forest extended along the entire length of the British front, concealing enemy movements to within two miles of the British lines. To make matters worse, the area west of Mons consisted of a series of small settlements interspersed with mines and slag heaps. This made it difficult for the British artillery to find firing positions south of the canal. The canal itself was not a particularly imposing barrier to the advancing Germans, with eighteen bridges spanning its width between Mons and Condé.[35] The salient to the northeast of Mons presented further difficulties, as it was exposed to advancing enemy forces on three sides.

The selection of this dubious defensive position stemmed from two factors. First, it is unlikely that senior members of GHQ actually visited the vicinity of Mons before 23 August. During this period, GHQ was located in the town of Le Cateau, approximately thirty miles to the south. While Sir John French visited units at the front on the 23rd, it seems that no senior officer from GHQ had traveled northward into Belgium beforehand. Nor did junior members of the staff venture far from their headquarters in this period. According to Charles Deedes: "The days spent at Le Cateau were for the most part uneventful and our time was spent in marking up the positions of our own and enemy troops on the map, with conferences and with interviews with all and sundry who looked upon O(a) as an enquiry office!"[36]

The choice of this position can also be explained by the fact that Sir John French and Henry Wilson had no intention of remaining on the defensive. GHQ issued no formal orders to advance on 23 August. Edward Spears's memoir of 1914, however, contains the transcript of a revealing telegram sent to Fifth Army headquarters at 1 am on the 23rd by Colonel V. Huguet, the French liaison officer at GHQ. The document indicates that Sir John French was prepared to comply with Lanrezac's earlier request and advance against German forces on the British right at midday, provided that air reconnaissance indicated no significant threat on his left. According to Spears, the explanation for this change of plans, "was really very simple: General Henry Wilson had become convinced that the right policy was to attack, and had brought the Commander-in-Chief round to his point of view."[37]

While they never came to fruition on the 23rd, French and Wilson's intentions evidently leaked out of GHQ the previous evening. In his diary entry for 22 August, Sir Horace Smith-Dorrien reflected on his position, commenting: "The Mons salient, which is held by the 9th Brigade, is an almost impossible one to defend, but I gather it is not expected that this is to be treated as a defensive position." Troops of 3 Division, stationed in the salient, were thus instructed to husband their efforts in constructing entrenchments along the Mons-Condé Canal. As "Kingy" Tower of the Royal Fusiliers, part of the 9th Brigade, related: "We worked away till about 9pm but we were told that we should be advancing the next morning so that we need not do too much."[38] Thus, on the eve of the battle of Mons, the physical and psychological distance of GHQ from realities at the front left British units largely unprepared for their first engagement of the war.

John Terraine has described the battle of Mons in considerable depth. For the purposes of this study, it is sufficient to note that enemy attacks early on 23 August came as a surprise to most British soldiers. German pressure on II Corps increased steadily throughout the morning. By 11 am, heavy attacks had developed against 3 Division in the Mons salient as von Kluck's First German Army stumbled unawares into the BEF. Although British rifle and machine-gun fire inflicted serious casualties on the Germans, the BEF was hindered by its poor positions. With no artillery positions from which to counter German guns, 3 Division eventually began to falter. Shortly after 1 pm, Hubert Hamilton reported to corps headquarters that the Germans had penetrated his defensive line.

Fortunately for II Corps, Smith-Dorrien had already ordered the preparation of a second position two to three miles south of the Mons-Condé Canal.[39] By 3 pm, the withdrawal of the corps was underway. Although a gap developed between 3 and 5 Division in the process, the Germans made no serious efforts to exploit it, apparently due to the damage inflicted on them by the British. By dusk, the German attack had subsided. Although II Corps had suffered approximately 1,600 casualties, the vast majority of them in 3 Division, it had retired successfully to the position prepared during the day. The relative calm that prevailed on the evening of 23 August, however, belied the extremely dangerous situation confronting the BEF. During the day, II Corps intelligence had identified elements of five German corps in the vicinity of Mons.[40] While the German First Army had been surprised by its collision with the BEF on the morning of 23 August, von Kluck was now well aware of its whereabouts. Any respite for the British was likely to be brief.

At Le Cateau, however, GHQ retained its unassailable confidence well into the evening of the 23rd. Much of this attitude can be attributed to the fact that Sir

John French and his staff had at best a fragmentary understanding of the day's events. While the commander-in-chief had met with Haig and Smith-Dorrien during the morning of the 23rd, he had subsequently left the vicinity to inspect the 19th Brigade at Valenciennes, leaving the management of the battle to GHQ.[41] French's staff had no discernible impact on events around Mons. The war diaries of both I and II Corps record little or no communication with GHQ during the day. II Corps sent a message to Le Cateau shortly after 3 pm, reporting the withdrawal of 3 Division and the subsequent development of the gap between its two divisions. It is not clear, however, whether GHQ replied to this message.[42]

Tenuous communications likely contributed to the isolation of the senior staff on 23 August. Given that roads between Belgium and France were clogged with military and civilian traffic in this period, it would have been quite difficult for liaison officers to complete the thirty-mile journey from Le Cateau to the vicinity of Mons. GHQ therefore remained comfortably insulated from the battle, and continued to entertain the cheerful scenarios generated by Henry Wilson. During the afternoon of the 23rd, the sub-chief of the General Staff determined that the BEF was opposed by no more than two corps. After convincing Sir John French and Archie Murray of the accuracy of his "careful calculation," Wilson drafted plans for an attack the next morning involving II Corps, the Cavalry Division, and the 19th Brigade. Fortunately for the BEF, before these orders could be issued, GHQ received a telegram from Joffre at 8 pm, stating that the British were opposed by 2 1/2 corps.[43] This figure, too, was a significant underestimate, but it nonetheless resulted in the jettisoning of Wilson's plan.

The optimism of GHQ was not yet fully quelled. At 8:05 pm, Sir John French, undoubtedly still influenced by Wilson's cheery assessment of the situation, ordered II Corps to "stand the attack" on its present positions the next morning. In addition, the Cavalry Division was ordered to advance at 5 am.[44] Once again it required a sobering visit from Edward Spears to extinguish the resilient confidence of GHQ. Between 11 pm and midnight, the liaison officer arrived with word that the French Fifth Army was retreating and leaving the right flank of the BEF uncovered.[45] This information, combined with the earlier news that the army faced superior German forces, finally dispelled the illusions of GHQ. Faced with disaster if the BEF attempted to stand on its own against overwhelming German forces, GHQ at last acknowledged the necessity of a retreat. Thus, the optimism of Sir John French and his staff had rendered the BEF unprepared for its first significant engagement with the Germans. Isolated from the battle of Mons by distance and unreliable communications, their continued misconceptions left the army equally unprepared for the traumatic retreat that would follow.

THE FOREST OF MORMAL, LANDRECIES, AND LE CATEAU, 24–26 AUGUST

In historical accounts of the 1914 campaign, the events of 24–25 August have largely been overshadowed by the battles of Mons and Le Cateau. The behavior of British commanders and staff officers on these two days, however, had critical consequences for the BEF during the rest of the retreat. Following the arrival of Edward Spears late on the 23rd with the news of the further withdrawal of Lanrezac's Fifth Army, GHQ summoned the chief staff officers of the two corps and the Cavalry Division to Le Cateau to receive orders. John Gough, the chief staff officer of I Corps, had arrived earlier in the evening.[48] It was not until 1 am on 24 August, however, that George Forestier-Walker of II Corps and John Vaughan of the Cavalry Division appeared at GHQ. The orders they received hardly justified the thirty-mile journey to Le Cateau (see Map 2.2). Archie Murray informed the staff officers that the BEF would retire to the vicinity of Bavai in the morning, but beyond the direction that I Corps would cover the retirement of II Corps while the cavalry made a "demonstration," he provided no further information. Thus, Haig and Smith-Dorrien were to arrange the details of the retreat among themselves.[49]

The circumstances surrounding this order have puzzled historians. Requiring the staff officers to make the considerable journey to Le Cateau inconvenienced them at a moment when time was clearly precious. It also contravened army protocol, which dictated that orders were conveyed "forward" from GHQ to the headquarters of lower formations. Moreover, the vague nature of the order scarcely warranted the assembly of the officers to receive it.[50] The indefinite character of the order stemmed from two factors. First, in directing Haig and Smith-Dorrien to arrange the details of the retirement themselves, Archie Murray was adhering to the philosophy of umpiring, which counseled respect for the operational realms of subordinate commanders. Second, even in the absence of such a consideration, it is unlikely that he could have provided more detailed instructions. Given the irrepressible optimism that had held sway at GHQ until the evening of the 23rd, the British staff had not planned for the possibility of a retreat, and thus had little idea of how to direct the two corps. As noted earlier, it is doubtful that most British staff officers had even been to the area between Bavai and Mons. The order to retire was thus limited to a vague instruction that Haig and Smith-Dorrien work out the details of the retreat themselves.

The summoning of staff officers to Le Cateau to receive this order appears to have been a product of discord at GHQ. Given the loyalty of "Uncle" Harper and the bulk of the operations section to Henry Wilson, Archie Murray encountered considerable difficulty in disseminating his own orders. As Lord Loch, the liaison officer between GHQ and II Corps, related in his diary on 24 August: "Harper has stuck his feet in the ground and refused to do anything for Murray— consequently someone had to write messages etc. so I did it."[51] The principal responsibility of liaison officers was the relaying of orders and information between GHQ and the corps and divisions. The fact that officers such as Loch

Map 2.2
Situation of the BEF, Night 25/26 August

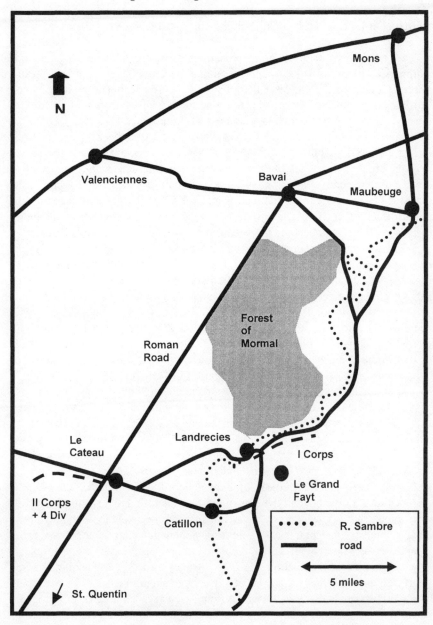

N

Mons

Valenciennes

Bavai

Maubeuge

Forest
of
Mormal

Roman
Road

Le
Cateau

Landrecies

I Corps

Le Grand
Fayt

II Corps
+ 4 Div

Catillon

•••••   R. Sambre

———   road

5 miles

St. Quentin

were diverted from this task undoubtedly impeded communications, and may explain the summoning of corps and divisional staff to Le Cateau. Thus, the ambiguity inherent in umpiring, the consequences of earlier optimism, and internal conflict combined to diminish the control of GHQ over the army in the initial stages of the retreat.

The ad hoc system of communications that prevailed in this period compounded these difficulties. Upon receiving the orders to retire at Le Cateau, Johnnie Gough was able to wire them back to I Corps headquarters near Mons shortly after 1 am. The I Corps staff thus had time to initiate preparations for the retirement before rousing Sir Douglas Haig at 2 am. Once Haig had learned of the planned withdrawal, he was consequently able to set his corps in motion fairly rapidly. Both Forestier-Walker and Vaughan, however, were forced to carry the orders by car back to their respective headquarters. As a result, Smith-Dorrien did not receive the directive from GHQ until between 2 and 3 am.[50] Not only was his inexperienced staff unprepared for the news, but they faced much more difficulty than Haig's subordinates in relaying the instructions to the units of II Corps, which had become disorganized during the previous day's battle.

While this method of conveying and distributing orders undoubtedly delayed the retirement of the BEF, it should not have had further consequences. Regardless of its ambiguity, the directive issued by GHQ clearly had instructed Haig to cover the retirement of Smith-Dorrien's corps. It also enjoined both commanders to make specific arrangements to this end. Nonetheless, upon receiving the order to retire, Haig determined that covering Smith-Dorrien's retreat "was an impossible role for I Corps," and commenced the withdrawal of his own force. Haig later visited Smith-Dorrien's headquarters at 6 am on the 24th, ostensibly to arrange for the cooperation of their respective formations.[51] By this hour, however, the I Corps commander had limited considerably the support he could offer by commencing his retreat without reference to II Corps. Both S.H. Lomax's 1 Division and Charles Monro's 2 Division were underway before 5 am on 24 August. For 3 Division, on the right of II Corps, the first news of any retirement came at 5:20 am when units of 2 Division on its right were observed falling back, thereby exposing its flank.[52]

In his diary, Haig provided no explanation for his withdrawal without reference to II Corps beyond the contention that the task assigned him by GHQ was "impossible." The exact rationale behind his decision to withdraw thus remains unclear. The practice of umpiring apparently allowed the two corps commanders considerable freedom in coordinating the retirement of their forces. Nonetheless, it did not permit Haig to disobey orders that instructed him specifically to cover the withdrawal of II Corps. It should be acknowledged that the I Corps commander was suffering from a stomach ailment in this period, which may have affected his judgment, causing him to initiate an excessively hasty withdrawal.[53] Such behavior by Haig, however, was not without precedent. As II Corps withdrew from its exposed positions around Mons the previous afternoon, Smith-Dorrien had requested a loan of troops from I Corps to fill the gap that developed between 3 and 5 Division. Citing increased artillery fire on his own force, Haig had declined. With the breach still open in the evening, George Forestier-Walker had traveled to Haig's headquarters to repeat the request in person. The I Corps commander had then grudgingly provided three battalions, noting afterward in his diary that the gap between 3 and 5 Divisions was "most easy to defend," and ultimately the battalions were not required. In the typed version of the diary, he added the remark: "The 2nd Corps HQ staff did not impress me!"[54]

Haig's inherent caution may have contributed to his reluctance to assist II Corps at Mons. Given that I Corps suffered only forty casualties on the 23rd, however, it is unlikely that enemy attacks were sufficient to cause its commander significant trepidation. Furthermore, the vindictive tone of Haig's diary suggests that cooperation between the two commanders was hindered by his rivalry with Smith-Dorrien. The precipitate withdrawal of I Corps on the morning of 24 August thus forms part of a broader pattern. While sickness and Haig's own prudence may have influenced his behavior during this period, professional jealousy toward Smith-Dorrien also contributed to Haig's failure to cooperate with II Corps as the retreat commenced. Thus, by the morning of the 24th, tensions between the corps commanders and discord at GHQ had exacerbated the difficulties of conducting a retirement under enemy pressure.

Haig's decision had adverse consequences for II Corps. On 24 August, von Kluck began to pressure the left of the BEF in hopes of driving it into the fortress of Maubeuge. Thus, while I Corps retired "smoothly and in good order," Smith-Dorrien's force once again bore the brunt of the German attack as the BEF made its way southward to the town of Bavai. In particular, Fergusson's 5 Division, retiring on the left flank of the BEF, fought continuous rearguard actions against German forces seeking to push the entire British army toward Maubeuge. The last troops of 5 Division did not reach their billets until after midnight. It was thus a battered II Corps that bivouacked in the vicinity of Bavai on the night of 24 August. There it connected with 2 Division of I Corps, which had experienced a quiet, albeit tiring, march from Mons. The BEF had suffered over 2,500 casualties on 24 August, the majority in 5 Division.[55] Nonetheless, the army remained intact despite continued German attacks.

As British soldiers retired during the 24th, Sir John French and Archie Murray struggled with the topographical challenges posed by their chosen path of retirement. The two spent most of the day at a hastily established "Advanced GHQ" in the town of Bavai, where they learned of the further withdrawal of Lanrezac's Fifth Army during the afternoon. Consequently, they had little choice but to continue the retreat the next morning, especially in light of the unremitting German pressure.[56] Directly in the path of the BEF, however, lay the Forest of Mormal, a thick wood approximately nine miles long and three to four miles wide. In planning to negotiate this obstacle, French and Murray were handicapped by a paucity of staff at their advanced headquarters, as the bulk of the Operations section remained at GHQ in the town of St. Quentin with Henry Wilson.[57] As a result, there were not sufficient staff officers at Bavai on 24 August to reconnoiter the Forest of Mormal. In the absence of reconnaissance reports, French and Murray were forced to rely on maps, which indicated that the only routes through the forest were dirt tracks unsuitable for vehicles.[58] There existed more substantial roads to the east and west of the forest. It appeared dangerous, however, to attempt to funnel the entire BEF to either side. To move both corps by the most direct line, the old Roman Road to the west of the forest, would create a substantial gap between the British Army and the French Fifth Army to its right, and expose it to the full weight of the German attack on its left flank. Bypassing the forest to the east involved two crossings of the River Sambre. It was deemed too difficult to send both corps by this path, especially given the proximity of French forces on the British right.[59]

During the afternoon of 24 August, French and Murray thus resolved to send the battered II Corps to the vicinity of Le Cateau via the Roman Road, while I Corps, still relatively unscathed, was instructed to find its way to the same town using roads to the east. This demarcation made the roads within the forest itself the responsibility of the I Corps commander, whether or not he chose to use them to move the bulk of his force. After the war Murray contended that GHQ Operation Order No. 7 of 24 August, which laid out the respective routes of both corps, should have made this fact plain to Haig. He also admitted that after issuing the order, he considered emphasizing the importance of maintaining touch with II Corps. Ultimately, however, Murray submitted to the protocol of umpiring, which stressed nonintervention in the operational responsibilities of subordinate commanders. As he maintained: "[w]e had been trained in the same school, and trained not to tell Commanders to do what was obvious as part of their duties."[60]

The desire to maintain cordial relations with field commanders clearly contributed to Archie Murray's decision to remain silent. In postwar correspondence regarding the order to circumvent the forest, he contended: "Army commanders do not issue special instructions on these commonplace points. Indeed...they would resent them." Whatever the reasons for his ambiguity, the chief of staff clouded the issued further by sending Haig a report on the 24th, which stated that all of the roads through the forest were in poor condition and thus unfit for heavy traffic.[61] Based on this information, Haig assumed that they were of little importance and directed I Corps to move entirely to the east of the forest. Whether or not this supposition was correct, Murray's silence created ambiguity in the orders issued by GHQ at a crucial point in the retreat.

The ambivalence of the CGS, combined with the practice of requiring staff officers to travel to GHQ to receive instructions, further obscured the army operation orders for 25 August by creating confusion over the start time of I Corps. French and Murray first articulated their plan for circumventing the forest to Haig when the latter visited Bavai on the afternoon of the 24th. At this meeting, Murray instructed the I Corps commander that the rearguard of his force was to have cleared the Maubeuge-Bavai-Eth Road by 8 am. In the evening, however, both Smith-Dorrien and Forestier-Walker of II Corps arrived at Bavai to receive orders, and emphasized that the continued pressure on their force necessitated an earlier start. As a result, when Murray issued Operation Order No. 7 at 8:25 pm, he changed the departure time for the entire BEF to 5:30 am the next morning. When Johnnie Gough arrived "rather late at night" to receive the same order, Murray again failed to underscore what seemed obvious, as he neglected to point out the changed start time.[62] Such an oversight would probably not have been significant under normal circumstances, but given that conflict at GHQ had complicated communications with the corps, the likelihood of errors had increased considerably. Requiring the undoubtedly exhausted Gough to travel to GHQ late at night, ostensibly to receive exactly the same information that had been given to Haig that afternoon, invited an oversight on his part. The fact that Murray neglected to draw attention to the single, but important alteration in the operation order further increased the possibility of I Corps misinterpreting its orders, with potentially dangerous results.

The next morning, the oversights of the 24th were laid bare as the army separated to bypass the Forest of Mormal. II Corps began retiring as early as 2 am, with most units clearing the Maubeuge-Bavai-Eth Road by 5:30 am and ultimately making their way to Le Cateau. I Corps, however, only began its march after a delay of up to five hours.[63] This late departure was the result of confusion regarding the intended start time of the corps as well as the late hour at which orders were received. On the evening of 24 August, Haig, who had been suffering from stomach trouble all day, had gone to bed before 9 pm. Control of the corps had thus gravitated into the hands of the already overworked Johnnie Gough. After traveling to GHQ to receive Operation Order No. 7, Gough may have overlooked the changed start time when issuing orders to 1 and 2 Divisions. According to the war diary of 1 Division, its units did not even begin their march on the morning of the 25th until 5 am. E.S. Bulfin's 2nd Brigade did not leave its billets until 8:30 am.[64] This would have prevented the rearguard of I Corps from clearing the Maubeuge-Bavai-Eth Road until well after 5:30 am. Even if Gough did instruct I Corps to commence its march according to Murray's instructions, it is unlikely that the order would have been received in time, due to the hour at which it was circulated. As the 2 Division war diary indicates, orders were not distributed to its units until 2:30 am on the 25th, and did not reach some until daylight.[65] While Johnnie Gough was late in issuing orders, it is difficult to fault him, as he was forced to perform tasks that were clearly the responsibility of GHQ. Rather, it was the failure of GHQ to issue instructions through liaison officers, combined with Murray's ambiguous approach to staff work, that created a significant delay in the retreat of I Corps on 25 August.

Although it was spared German attacks for most of the day, the difficulties of I Corps were compounded by the fact that it was forced to share the same road with retiring French forces.[66] The resulting congestion hindered its progress considerably at a time when its late start had increased the necessity for rapid movement, and it soon became clear that I Corps would be unable to realize its objective. By 4 pm, Haig, apparently in better health, had abandoned hope of reaching Le Cateau, and pulled the corps to a halt with its head at the town of Landrecies. Thus, rather than rejoining the rest of the BEF, I Corps went into billets directly south of the Forest of Mormal, still at least seven miles by road from its assigned destination.

Haig's decision to halt clearly exceeded the operational leeway permitted by umpiring, as it precluded his fulfillment of the objectives outlined in the previous evening's operation order.[67] In his diary, however, he went to great lengths to suggest that his actions met with the approval of GHQ. According to the I Corps commander, he was the principal architect of the British Army's plan of retreat for 25 August. By Haig's account, he visited French and Murray at Advanced GHQ at Bavai at about 4 pm on the 24th, where he convinced them of the necessity of continuing the retirement the following morning. At Murray's request, Haig then adjourned with his aide-de-camp, John Charteris, to a house in Bavai, where he determined a route by which his corps would march by roads east of the Forest of Mormal, "so that our head will reach Landrecies." Charteris then delivered a letter to Murray outlining this scheme, for which Haig claimed he received approval.[68]

In his diary, Haig took the trouble to include a copy of this letter in which he explained his plan to the chief of staff. Strangely, however, he neglected to include Murray's reply. This would seem to be a pivotal piece of evidence in Haig's case, given that Operation Order No. 7, devised by GHQ only a few hours after this alleged dialogue, gave no indication that it had ever taken place. Nor did Murray, in postwar correspondence regarding the separation of the BEF around the Forest of Mormal, refer to any such exchange of ideas.[69] Moreover, diaries of British commanders and staff officers express surprise at the failure of I Corps to reach Le Cateau. As Henry Wilson exclaimed: "Found to my disgust that I Corps were retiring E of Forest of Mormal & pulling up with head at Landrecies. This is mad. D.H. [Haig] says he cannot go any further but he ought to be made to go on to Le Cateau otherwise there will be an awkward gap and tomorrow the II Corps will be unsupported."[70]

Evidently, GHQ expected I Corps to arrive at Le Cateau, and its inability to do so caused considerable consternation. The inefficient system of distributing orders and Murray's failure to clarify the start time of I Corps no doubt contributed to the predicament of the BEF on the evening of 25 August. Nonetheless, Haig's elaborate attempt to deny that I Corps had failed to reach its assigned objective implies that he recognized his own liability in leaving a significant breach between the two corps, perhaps devising the alternative account out of concern for his reputation. Both Haig and Smith-Dorrien periodically sent excerpts of their diaries to the king during the initial stages of the war. Given Haig's ambitions, it was certainly in his interest to provide a favorable account of his own performance. It appears that these ambitions influenced his diary entry for 25 August, as he portrayed his halt at Landrecies as the result of careful planning, and neglected to mention its dangerous implications for II Corps.

In any case, the halt of I Corps at Landrecies proved short-lived. Despite instructions from GHQ to resume his march as soon as possible, Haig ordered I Corps to remain in billets until 2 am before continuing on to positions south of

Le Cateau.[71] In light of Archie Murray's earlier assurance that the roads within the Forest of Mormal were not capable of supporting heavy traffic, the I Corps commander apparently surmised that his force was safe from enemy predations. His decision to halt, however, was based on insufficient evidence. While Haig may have believed that the operations staff at GHQ had surveyed the wood thoroughly on 24 August, he did not direct his own staff to do the same on the 25th, when German forces had pushed further southward.[72] Haig thus halted his force directly in front of a forest that neither I Corps nor GHQ had reconnoitered.

Dangerous consequences were not long in materializing. Not only were roads within the forest capable of supporting considerable traffic, but unbeknownst to the British, German forces had penetrated the wood in motor vehicles during the afternoon of 25 August.[73] At about 7:30 pm, a detachment of the 3/Coldstream Guards, stationed at a crossroads just north of Landrecies, was surprised by a force of German soldiers disguised in French uniforms. While the Coldstreams recovered from their initial shock, they were forced to repel repeated German attacks, which continued for the rest of the night, only halting at 3 am the next morning.[74] The appearance of the Germans at Landrecies was accompanied by an almost simultaneous attack on the forces of I Corps at Maroilles, approximately three miles to the east. Sporadic fighting continued for the rest of the night in that vicinity as well. Despite the unexpectedness of the enemy incursion, it did not prove to be a concerted effort, as apparently the German forces in the area did not even comprise a full brigade. Only two of the six brigades of I Corps were involved in the actions of the night of the 26th, and even they were never threatened seriously.[75] The soldiers of I Corps had performed well in their first real engagement of the retreat, but in truth, they had not been faced with a substantial German attack.

Meanwhile, at I Corps headquarters in Landrecies, these altercations were perceived quite differently. According to John Charteris, when the attack opened on the evening of the 25th, the usually reserved Haig "was jolted out of his usual placidity. He said 'If we are caught, by God, we'll sell our lives dearly'."[76] Haig's alarm apparently manifested itself in an attempt to take charge of the impending engagement. By his own account, the I Corps commander single-handedly organized the town for defense, scolding the commander of the 4th Guards Brigade, Scott-Kerr, for the "sleepy" and "half-hearted" measures he had taken to that point.[77] While this description may contain some exaggeration, it is evident that Haig remained in Landrecies for several hours after the initial encounter with the Germans. Only after 11 pm did he move his headquarters to the village of Le Grand Fayt.[78]

By this point in the evening, the I Corps commander was apparently satisfied that the situation at Landrecies no longer required his personal intervention. Orders issued from Le Grand Fayt, however, suggest that he continued to believe that I Corps was in grave danger. At 12:30 am on 26 August, Haig instructed his troops to dump excess supplies and even cast off their packs in order to expedite the withdrawal of the entire corps southward.[79] Such an order, with its potentially troublesome repercussions should I Corps manage to survive the engagement, indicates the apprehension that prevailed at Haig's headquarters. Anxiety continued to abound at Le Grand Fayt throughout the early morning of 26 August, as Johnnie Gough reported to GHQ at 1:35 am that I Corps was under attack by four German divisions. In St. Quentin, over twenty miles southeast of Landrecies, GHQ already had a distorted impression of the plight of I Corps, as rumors had been circulating that its headquarters had been captured. When Gough's message arrived, the exhausted Archie Murray was fast asleep, but the commander-in-chief arranged for French forces to come up on the right of I Corps at daylight.[80] In the interim, however, these measures did little to soothe the commander of I Corps. In a message dispatched to GHQ at 3:50 am, after the German attack had ceased, Haig requested further assistance from Smith-Dorrien's corps, suggesting that "troops near LE CATEAU should cooperate by advancing straight on LANDRECIES."[81]

By the early morning of the 26th, however, II Corps was preparing to meet a much more threatening situation in the vicinity of Le Cateau. Although its departure was not delayed to the same extent as I Corps, difficulties had plagued Smith-Dorrien's force throughout 25 August. As they retired along the Roman Road, the units of II Corps were forced to contend with continued German pressure as well as the presence of French troops and refugees.[82] During the day, the corps was bolstered by the arrival of Thomas Snow's 4 Division, which shielded 3 and 5 Divisions as well as Allenby's cavalry and the 19th Brigade as they marched southward. While 4 Division served as an effective covering force, its presence further complicated the retirement. During the afternoon and evening of the 25th, three infantry divisions and an independent brigade, four cavalry brigades, as well as all of their associated transport converged on the town of Le Cateau. As dusk fell, delays abounded and units became separated. As late as 12:35 am on the 26th, 3 Division reported to II Corps headquarters that three battalions of its 7th Brigade remained at large. Even at this hour, most of 4 Division was still en route to Le Cateau.[83] The retirement of Smith-Dorrien's force thus continued into the early morning of 26 August.

It was in this context that Edmund Allenby arrived at II Corps headquarters near Le Cateau around 2 am. There, he informed Smith-Dorrien that the Cavalry Division had become dispersed. Given the independent spirit of the four cavalry brigadiers, Allenby's inexperienced staff proved unable to control them in the confusion that prevailed during the 25th. With only one brigade left under his control, the commander of the Cavalry Division advised Smith-Dorrien that he was presently unable to cover the retirement of II Corps. Allenby also suggested that Smith-Dorrien's force would be attacked if it could not get underway by 5 am.[84] At this point, II Corps was in no condition to continue the retreat. The last units of 3 Division did not arrive at Le Cateau until 4 am, and most units of 4 Division did not reach their positions until daylight. While Allenby and Smith-Dorrien were discussing the situation, Hubert Hamilton arrived and confirmed the disarray of 3 Division, stating that his troops would be unable to continue the retirement until 9 am. Faced with the prospect of his "retirement turning into a rout," Smith-Dorrien resolved to disregard orders from GHQ to resume the retreat, and remain on his current positions around Le Cateau. He secured the cooperation of Snow's 4 Division and the cavalry remaining under Allenby's control, and informed GHQ of his decision.[85]

Sir John French and his staff had already spent 25 August in a state of trepidation. Throughout the evening, alarming messages had been arriving from I Corps. While these were generally exaggerated, they cannot have been reassuring to GHQ, especially in light of the long-standing and close relationship between Sir John French and Sir Douglas Haig. Consequently, any subsequent information that arrived at GHQ was interpreted through a filter of anxiety. Arriving under these circumstances, the news that Smith-Dorrien intended to face the enemy at Le Cateau had a devastating impact on the collective psyche of GHQ. Upon receiving Smith-Dorrien's telegram shortly before 5 am, Sir John French and his staff rapidly concluded that II Corps was doomed. The low opinion of the II Corps commander that prevailed at GHQ encouraged this conclusion. The fact that it was Smith-Dorrien, rather than the well-respected Haig, who had resolved to defy orders and fight made the decision seem all the more catastrophic. After trying to convince French to force II Corps to retire, Henry Wilson apparently fell into a depression. As he remarked blackly in his diary: "This will lead to disaster, or ought to." Archie Murray was asleep when Smith-Dorrien's message arrived, but upon reading it shortly after he awoke, he promptly fainted.[86] While Sir John French did not succumb to distress to the same extent as his subordinates, he too concluded that Smith-Dorrien's decision meant the almost certain destruction of II Corps. Thus, instead of bringing the two corps back together, the commander-in-chief resolved to salvage I Corps by directing Haig either to retreat southwest on St. Quentin, or southeast, to gain shelter with the French on his right.[87]

Back at Le Grand Fayt, Haig and his staff remained apprehensive, and in fact continued to expect reinforcement from II Corps. When Hugh Dawnay, the liaison officer between GHQ and I Corps, arrived at 6 am with the commander-in-chief's new instructions, it became evident that such assistance would not be forthcoming. Haig thus chose to ignore the orders, as well as a message sent four hours later directing I Corps to rejoin II Corps at Busigny, to the southwest.[88] While the policy of umpiring afforded the I Corps commander a degree of freedom in carrying out orders, it did not allow him to disregard them deliberately. Haig's behavior can best be explained by his continued impression that his own force was in serious danger, as well as his professional opinion of Sir John French. Although Haig's career had benefited from his long connection with the commander-in-chief, he did not necessarily trust French's judgment. As a result, Haig, who remained unaware of the plight of II Corps, interpreted French's failure to send reinforcements to his aid early on the morning of the 26th as evidence that the commander-in-chief had abandoned I Corps erroneously. As he remarked in his diary: "GHQ had evidently given my corps up as lost from their control!"[89]

In the absence of what he perceived to be adequate support from his commander, Haig continued his retreat directly southward on 26 August. Although panic may have influenced his actions at Landrecies on the evening of the 25th, it is apparent that neither Haig's anxiety nor his illness endured throughout the next day as I Corps retired under minimal pressure. In a postwar letter to Sir Basil Liddell Hart, A.H. Burne, an officer in I Corps, reported encountering a rather poised corps commander at 7 am on 26 August. According to Burne, Haig was "smiling, spick & span & most confident looking. His appearance reassured us all."[90] In spite of his apparent recovery, however, Haig continued to demonstrate little concern for the fate of II Corps. After the war, Edmonds alleged that the I Corps commander "had definite word" of the movement of German forces across his front on the 26th to attack Smith-Dorrien's right flank. While this is impossible to confirm, Haig was undoubtedly aware that II Corps was in some difficulty. The I Corps and 1 Division war diaries note that during the day artillery could be heard from the direction of Le Cateau. In addition, E.S. Bulfin, commander of the 2nd Brigade of 1 Division, commented in his diary: "gather there was a bit of a mix up at Le Cateau." Haig proved more concerned for the safety of his own force than for the rest of the army, however, leaving II Corps to face the Germans alone.[91]

The exploits of British soldiers at Le Cateau have been recounted elsewhere. It is nonetheless useful to examine briefly the impact of the aforementioned command decisions on the course of the battle. Sir John French's decision to "save" I Corps, and Haig's subsequent departure, deprived II Corps of much-needed support at Le Cateau. To make matters worse, French failed to inform Smith-Dorrien of the location of I Corps. East of the town, 5 Division had taken up positions on the assumption that it would connect with units of Haig's force when they arrived. With I Corps retiring southward on the 26th, however, the right flank of II Corps remained exposed throughout the battle of Le Cateau.[92]

Ultimately, it was German exploitation of this open flank that necessitated the withdrawal of II Corps. In an effort to destroy what he believed to be the entire British Army, von Kluck directed his First Army to engage the BEF while enveloping both of its flanks. This envelopment was slow in transpiring. Throughout the morning, units of 4 and 3 Divisions, occupying the left and center of the British position, respectively, withstood increasing artillery and infantry attacks. On the right, however, the situation of 5 Division became progressively more precarious. By noon, infantry of the German III Corps had begun to turn the right flank of the division.[93] The independent initiatives of the British cavalry were of little help to Fergusson's force. During the morning, Hubert Gough's 3rd Cavalry Brigade stumbled accidentally into the battle on the right of II Corps. From hastily selected positions, two guns of the brigade's battery shelled the attacking Germans until early afternoon, aiding the embattled infantry on its left. Apparently, however, Gough made no effort to contact nearby commanders. As a result, he had little idea of the broader course of the battle, and inadvertently withdrew his force at a critical moment. As Gough admitted in his memoirs: "the position which I held was…important to the right admitted in his memoirs: "the position which I held was...important to the right flank of the II Corps, but unfortunately, owing to my entire ignorance of the situation, I did not hold it as long as I might have done."[94]

Shortly afterward, German pressure against the right flank of 5 Division necessitated its retirement. Beginning around 2:30 pm, British units began the difficult and dangerous process of extricating themselves from close contact with the enemy.[95] Although Smith-Dorrien's force suffered heavily during this withdrawal, the bulk of II Corps had escaped by evening. In total, British units suffered 7,812 casualties and lost 38 guns on 26 August. Though they were fighting outnumbered, II Corps and 4 Division had inflicted at least as many casualties on the enemy. The fact that they had been left to fight unsupported, however, stemmed from the inability of senior British officers to conduct the retirement under enemy pressure. As the BEF withdrew from Mons, inexperience, the ambiguities of umpiring, and discord at GHQ led to the failure of I and II Corps to reconnect after bypassing the Forest of Mormal. In the confusion that ensued, the peculiar relationships between Sir John French, Sir Douglas Haig, and Sir Horace Smith-Dorrien contributed to the abandonment of Smith-Dorrien's force. While the units of II Corps performed well at Le Cateau, they were left in disarray as they retired southward on the night of 26 August.

THE "GREAT RETREAT": 27 AUGUST–5 SEPTEMBER

The events of 25–26 August left the BEF separated and disoriented. Although German pressure subsided on subsequent days, however, anxiety continued to abound among senior British officers. As a result, the army was slow to reestablish its composure as the retreat drew to an end. The collective disposition of GHQ had begun to deteriorate as ominous news arrived from both Haig and Smith-Dorrien on the night of 25/26 August. As British units fought at Le Cateau on the 26th, depression among senior officers at St. Quentin intensified. Following Smith-Dorrien's telegram indicating his decision to face the enemy, the next communication between GHQ and II Corps took place around 7 am, when Smith-Dorrien contacted St. Quentin using the French railway telephone system. Henry Wilson took the call, and the II Corps commander summarized the situation facing his force. As Smith-Dorrien related in his diary: "I explained the state of affairs, and that we should put up a real grand fight, but that as our men were too weary to march there was a real possibility, with both our flanks *en l'air* and a vastly superior number of the enemy against us, of our being surrounded."[96]

While historians have described this exchange, they have not speculated regarding its effects on the parties involved. For Smith-Dorrien, the phone call provided an opportunity to justify his decision personally without the risk of betraying his apprehension in a face-to-face encounter. His task was made easier by the fact that Henry Wilson was an officer of lesser rank with no authority to overrule him. Thus, the exchange with the sub-chief of staff seems to have bolstered his resolve. According to Charles Deedes, who transcribed the conversation in St. Quentin, the II Corps commander "spoke very cheerfully and one could not help admiring the strength of character that he displayed."[97]

The phone call affected Henry Wilson quite differently. At 7 am on 26 August, the sub-chief had already spent a sleepless night wracked by anxiety over the situation of both corps. He also had no conception of the predicament of II Corps beyond the information conveyed in Smith-Dorrien's early morning telegram. Moreover, he received the call in a noisy train station, "amid the clatter of instruments and the excited conversation of French officials." Under these circumstances, he likely gleaned no more than a fragmentary understanding of the situation at Le Cateau. Given Wilson's apprehension on the morning of the 26th, the limited information he received in the phone call would hardly have been sufficient to alleviate his concerns. Indeed, he reportedly warned Smith-Dorrien: "[i]f you stay and fight there will be another Sedan."[98]

Thus, the early morning phone conversation apparently intensified Henry Wilson's anxieties regarding II Corps. In light of the sub-chief's intellectual leverage at GHQ, his despondency spread rapidly among senior staff officers. According to Deedes: "Things seemed so black that when it was decided to move GHQ back to Noyon I was not sorry to be sent on ahead and to get away from the depressing atmosphere at St. Quentin."[99] The decision to relocate GHQ provides further evidence of the gloom that prevailed in the upper ranks of the BEF. Not only was Noyon at least fifty miles by road from Le Cateau, but GHQ moved in the midst of the battle without even informing Smith-Dorrien.[100]

Such behavior on the part of GHQ indicates that senior officers held little hope for II Corps following the telephone conversation between its commander and Wilson. Nevertheless, it would be erroneous to accept James Edmonds's postwar allegation to Liddell Hart that Sir John French and his staff "gave up II Corps as lost" in the aftermath of Le Cateau. Significantly, despair at GHQ diminished when the II Corps commander materialized at Noyon at 2 am on the 27th. After learning that Smith-Dorrien's force had escaped annihilation, Sir John French and his staff quickly initiated efforts to restore its cohesion. By 2:30 am, several officers from GHQ had been dispatched to St. Quentin, with instructions to reorganize the scattered units retiring southward from Le Cateau.[101]

On the morning of 27 August, the troops of II Corps and 4 Division were badly in need of direction. After leaving the battlefield in considerable disarray the previous afternoon, they had become even more disorganized and exhausted as they marched southward in the darkness. Nor did daylight offer the prospect of relief. After the punishment they had suffered the previous day, many British troops fully expected the enemy to exploit their disarray on the 27th. A.H. Habgood, a medical officer, related in his diary: "As we thought this day would see the end of the Expeditionary Force, we shared our private stock of rum with the men."[102] In light of the confusion that prevailed on the morning of 27 August, the task of reorganizing II Corps and 4 Division entirely was well beyond the immediate capabilities of the inexperienced British staff. As Smith-Dorrien related in his diary: "[g]reat efforts were made by the Staff to get units together as much as possible, but as some of them had lost almost all their officers it was not for the next two or three days that we were able to get certain of them together."[109]

Nevertheless, staff officers managed to reduce the confusion by progressively sorting through the masses of soldiers passing through St. Quentin. In addition, they made arrangements to ensure that the troops were fed. Soldiers were directed along particular roads based on the divisions, brigades, and battalions to which they belonged. Sir William Robertson aided in the process by leaving food along the roadside in piles from which troops could draw rations. In addition to their organizational duties, staff officers attempted to restore the morale of the soldiers as they marched through St. Quentin. On the morning of the 27th, Frederic Coleman, a chauffeur drafted to perform staff work in St. Quentin, received the following instructions from an unidentified senior staff officer:

"Cheer them up as you keep them on the move," he said. "They are very downhearted. Tell them anything, but cheer them up. They've got their tails down a bit, but they are really all right. No wonder they are tired! Worn out to begin with, then fighting all day, only to come back all night—no rest, no food, no sleep—poor devils! Yes, they are very downhearted. Tell em where to go, and cheer 'em up—cheer 'em up."[110]

No British officer had a greater impact on morale in this period than Sir John French. In the days after Le Cateau, the commander-in-chief visited British troops, delivering impromptu speeches in an attempt to lift their spirits. These efforts apparently had a significant impact on the soldiers of II Corps in the aftermath of the battle. In his memoirs, C.D. Baker-Carr, also a chauffeur in 1914, offered the following tribute to the commander-in-chief during the retreat: "Sir John French may not have been a great soldier in the modern sense of the word, but he was a great leader of men. His unfailing cheerfulness and courage at that time were of inestimable benefit in keeping up the morale of the soldiers, and if he ever realised the desperate plight of the Army under his command, he never showed the slightest sign of it."[111]

Efforts by GHQ to salvage the army were not limited to the organization and encouragement of retreating soldiers. More broadly, the decision to continue the retirement southward in the aftermath of Le Cateau apparently reflected the desire of Henry Wilson to continue operating alongside the French. Given that GHQ had exercised only tenuous control over the BEF since 23 August, an alteration in the line of retreat would undoubtedly have been difficult. Nevertheless, it is evident that in the aftermath of Le Cateau, senior staff officers explored the possibility of retiring westward to the English Channel. In a 1937 conversation with Liddell Hart, a staff officer under Sir William Robertson recalled that during the retreat, the quartermaster-general had instructed him to find a suitable port for evacuating the BEF on the west coast of France.[112] The fact that GHQ did not attempt to retire to the southwest to place the army in closer proximity to an evacuation point suggests a determination by Wilson, the dominant personality at GHQ, to remain in contact with the French.

This decision proved auspicious in the days following Le Cateau. Under the impression that he had defeated the entire BEF in the battle, von Kluck allowed the German First Army to rest on the night of 26 August. In addition, he assumed that the British were retiring to the southwest toward Calais and Boulogne, and thus sent a pursuing force of cavalry in that direction. In reality, the BEF was withdrawing southward. Smith-Dorrien's force retired unmolested to St. Quentin, where it halted briefly before continuing its march during the afternoon. By evening, units of 5 Division and 19th Brigade had reached as far south as Olezy, forty miles from Le Cateau. Thus, Wilson's resolution to continue the retirement southward in the aftermath of Le Cateau allowed Smith-Dorrien's force to elude its pursuers. It is perhaps because of this decision that the staff officer W.H. Bartholemew claimed in 1927 that the sub-chief "saved the British Army" during the retreat from Mons.[107]

Notwithstanding these efforts to preserve the army, GHQ had concluded by the evening of 27 August that the BEF was no longer an effective military force. This belief stemmed from the observations of senior officers with no experience of warfare on the scale of 1914. For soldiers accustomed to the limited casualty levels of colonial campaigns, the losses suffered by II Corps at Le Cateau likely seemed catastrophic. Ernest Swinton, the official press officer attached to the BEF in 1914, recalled Henry Wilson's troubled reaction upon seeing casualties at the Aisne. According to Swinton: "though showing his sensibility, he exhibited a certain blindness to realities and a lack of sense of proportion."[108]

The sub-chief of staff was clearly affected by the condition of II Corps after Le Cateau. As he remarked in his diary on the 27th, "the 3rd & 5th Divisions don't exist." Wilson's despondency spread rapidly at GHQ. That evening, Colonel Huguet, the French liaison at GHQ, embellished on the sub-chief's appraisal in a message to GQG, stating: "Conditions are such that for the moment the British army no longer exists."[109] In light of the exhaustion and disarray of Smith-Dorrien's force on 27 August, such judgments were not entirely erroneous. Nor were they necessarily harmful, provided they remained open to adjustment as the situation changed. In subsequent days, however, the BEF encountered no serious pressure from the enemy, and the condition of II Corps slowly improved. Despite this recovery, French and his staff were unable to abandon the notion that Smith-Dorrien's force had been shattered at Le Cateau, and that the army thus remained in grave danger. For the second time since the beginning of the campaign, GHQ succumbed to cognitive closure.

The grim conclusions of senior officers in the wake of Le Cateau were manifested in their skittish behavior in the ensuing week. According to Frederic Coleman: "GHQ took 'some watching' in those days. If one turned around it was likely to disappear to the southward."[110] The departures of the staff from Le Cateau on the 25th and St. Quentin on the 26th were only the first two in a series of hurried relocations. During the evening of 1 September, the sound of gunfire, combined with reports of approaching German cavalry, sparked a rapid exodus from the town of Dammartin. According to C.D. Baker-Carr, "[t]he departure from Dammartin was a panic-stricken flight. Rumours of thousands of Uhlans in the woods near by arrived every moment. Typewriters and office equipment were flung into the waiting lorries." In the commotion surrounding the withdrawal, the members of the Operations Section forgot to inform Neville Macready, the adjutant-general of the BEF. Macready only learned of the relocation after nearly being hit by an automobile containing George Macdonogh, who "shouted out that he was off to Paris, and disappeared along a deserted street."[111]

The repeated disappearances of GHQ undoubtedly hindered its control over the army during the retreat. The misperceptions of senior officers also influenced their command decisions in this period. These decisions had a direct, and often detrimental impact on the recovery of the BEF. Late in the evening of 27 August, Henry Wilson issued an order directing that all ammunition and baggage not required by the army was to be abandoned, thus allowing tired troops to be carried on transport wagons.[112] The "sauve qui peut" order, as it was later termed, was clearly excessive given the relative calm that had prevailed since Le Cateau, and it betrayed the desperation that endured at GHQ. It also damaged the fragile morale of the retreating soldiers. According to Frederic Coleman: "The 4th Division carried out the order before it was countermanded, and eleven wagonloads of kit were burned in huge piles by the roadside—by no means a reassuring sight." Lord Loch concurred, remarking in his diary: "It has just put a cap on the demoralisation."[113]

The misconceptions of GHQ notwithstanding, the army continued to retreat unassailed on the 28th. The retirement of I Corps was sufficiently smooth that Sir Douglas Haig pledged to support an attack by Lanrezac's Fifth Army on his right. Haig, who had been consistently unhelpful to Smith-Dorrien thus far in the campaign, offered the assistance of his artillery to the French, and stated that his infantry "could join in pursuit" if necessary.[114] Any such arrangements, however, were swiftly vetoed by GHQ. In view of the slackening pursuit on 28 August, Sir John French and his staff had planned an extended halt for the fatigued soldiers of Haig's force as well as the ostensibly shattered II Corps. As the commander-in-chief related in a telegram to the War Office on the 28th, "I am nearly sure of securing two or three days' rest." French's distrust of Lanrezac may have left him reluctant to place his own troops at risk for his ally.[115] His refusal to assist stemmed primarily, however, from the belief that his army remained scattered and disorganized. Consequently, while Lanrezac attacked the German Second Army at Guise on 29 August, the BEF stood by.[116]

While the commander-in-chief's refusal to support the Fifth Army did nothing for relations between the British and French armies, it proved propitious for the BEF. Indeed, the halt on the 29th benefited exhausted soldiers as well as staff officers, who were showing signs of intense stress by this point in the retreat. Smith-Dorrien noted in his diary on 28 August that "some of the Staffs of Brigades and Divisions are quite worn out and almost unequal to working out orders." That day, the chief staff officer of 3 Division, F.R.F. Boileau, "went quite off his head," shooting himself in the arm, and subsequently dying from the wound. In addition, on the night of 29 August, Edmonds, the chief of staff of 4 Division, collapsed and had to be replaced. As early as 26 August, John Vaughan, the chief of staff of the Cavalry Division, had also collapsed.[117] While one day of rest was not sufficient to allay the fatigue incurred by the army since the battle of Mons, it was undoubtedly appreciated by British soldiers and officers alike.

Although the misperceptions of senior officers allowed the BEF a much needed rest on 29 August, they had the opposite effect the next day. During the afternoon of the 29th, initial reports arrived indicating that the French had been defeated at Guise. Consequently, GHQ hastily ordered a retreat for the following day. It gradually became evident, however, that the Fifth Army had in fact pushed back the Germans. This elicited a sheepish addendum from GHQ. Admitting that "The C-in-C would not have ordered this further retirement if he had known what he does now," the new order enjoined corps commanders to limit their retirement to the daylight hours.[118] Thus, while the excessive concern of GHQ had resulted in a brief respite for the army on the 29th, it also dashed any hopes for a longer rest.

The events of 29 August apparently brought GHQ to the realization that an extended halt was not feasible in such close proximity to the enemy. Consequently, on the 30th, Sir John French first articulated his infamous plan to withdraw the BEF behind the Seine "for at least ten days" to refit. Historians have documented French's scheme, as well as Lord Kitchener's subsequent intervention to suppress it.[119] While the two Field-Marshals exchanged telegrams, however, the retirement of the BEF continued with few interruptions. Contact was limited to cavalry skirmishes on 31 August, as British rearguards brushed against elements of von Kluck's First Army, which had turned southeast in order to strike the flank of the French Fifth Army. As the retreat continued, the spirits of the soldiers began to recover. As Lord Loch summed up on the 31st: "Morale improving, but GHQ still have nerves."[120]

In addition to restoring morale, the uninterrupted retirement enabled the BEF to regain its cohesion. On 1 September, the gap between I and II Corps, which had existed since 25 August, was finally closed. Given the traumatic circumstances of their separation, the cool relations between the two corps commanders, and Haig's repeated indifference to the plight of II Corps, it is not entirely surprising that the two formations remained separated for an entire week. Nevertheless, it is significant that throughout this period, GHQ made few efforts to draw them together. Sir John French and his staff attempted to direct Haig's force to the southeast to rejoin II Corps on the morning of 26 August. Afterward, however, the perceived necessity of saving the remnants of Smith-Dorrien's force took precedence over reorganizing the BEF for nearly a week as GHQ did not enjoin the two corps to reunite.[121]

The distraction of GHQ also contributed to an unplanned reorganization of the British cavalry in this period. In the days following the dispersal of the Cavalry Division on 25 August, three of its four brigades gradually reconnected under their commander. Hubert Gough's 3rd Brigade, however, ignored Allenby's orders and veered eastward on the 26th, subsequently attaching itself to I Corps.[122] This unusual development stemmed from several factors. Since the beginning of the campaign, Allenby's inexperienced staff had been unable to control four brigades during mobile operations. These difficulties were compounded by the independent mindset of the brigadiers. Hubert Gough, in particular, harbored ambitions that led him to abandon Allenby as well as II Corps at a critical point in the retreat. After the war, the commander of the 3rd Brigade contended that he had left the Cavalry Division in hopes of obtaining more effective leadership under Haig. Other cavalry officers, however, alleged that Gough "was determined to go off on his own and make a name for himself."[123]

Sir Douglas Haig clearly assisted in Gough's secession from the Cavalry Division. Indeed, the I Corps commander began issuing orders to the 3rd Cavalry Brigade on 27 August, without consulting Allenby, a rival of his at Camberley. Gough's transfer also received the blessing of GHQ. This likely resulted in part from his close relationship with Haig and the commander-in-chief. As George Barrow contended after the war: "had he [Gough] not been *persona grata* with French & Haig he would have been sent straight back to England."[124] It is significant that GHQ did not notify Allenby of the transfer prior to issuing Operation Order No. 13 on 31 August.[125] While a variety of factors contributed to Hubert Gough's unauthorized abandonment of the Cavalry Division, the failure of GHQ to inform Allenby until well after the fact suggests that senior officers remained indifferent to the situation of the cavalry in the week after Le Cateau. Thus, the preoccupation of GHQ with salvaging the ostensibly shattered II Corps again led it to neglect the task of reorganizing the army.

The retirement of the BEF continued into early September with little disruption. On the 4th, however, French commanders discerned an opportunity to strike back against the flagging German armies, and developed concrete plans for an offensive against their pursuers. Historians have examined the events that led to the participation of the BEF in this offensive.[126] For the purposes of this study, it is sufficient to note that misconceptions at GHQ continued to influence the decisions of senior officers even at this stage of the retreat. During the day on 4 September, British officers were apprised of two different French offensive plans that dictated an advance on the 6th and 7th, respectively. The counteroffensive beginning on the latter date required the further withdrawal of the BEF to make room for the French Sixth Army on its left. Under the impression that this plan had been approved by Joffre himself, Archie Murray issued orders during the evening of the 4th for a continuation of the retirement the following morning.[127]

Later that evening, however, Joffre in fact ordered the offensive to commence on the 6th, a scenario that did not require the withdrawal of the BEF on 5 September. Joffre's orders did not reach GHQ until 4 am on the 5th. By that time the main body of II Corps had been underway for several hours, and I

Corps and the newly formed III Corps, under E.P. Pulteney, were just beginning their retreat. While it was too late to cancel the retirement, it was certainly possible to halt the movement of British units before they reached their assigned billets.[128] Nevertheless, GHQ did not alter the order, apparently due to a lack of enthusiasm for Joffre's offensive plan. Even at this stage of the retreat, GHQ still believed that the army, particularly II Corps, remained in a shattered state. Sir Douglas Haig related in his diary on 4 September that Sir John French continued to entertain the notion of withdrawing the BEF behind the Seine in order to refit.[129] The army therefore continued its retirement on the 5th, subjecting the soldiers to a full day's march on the day before the planned counteroffensive. Moreover, the BEF began the advance well behind the intended positions from which it was supposed to attack on the 6th. Thus, even in early September, the battle of Le Cateau cast a long shadow over the decision-making process at GHQ. Despite the gradual recovery of II Corps and the reorganization of the army, Sir John French and his staff continued to believe that the BEF had been rendered ineffective as a fighting force. Decisions based on this conviction did nothing to aid its recovery. Consequently, at the beginning of the advance, the BEF remained an exhausted army.

CONCLUSION

The retreat from Mons placed severe stress on the BEF. From the outset of the retirement, soldiers were forced to contend with physical and mental fatigue in addition to enemy pressure. The battalions of the BEF performed well in this period, repelling heavy German heavy attacks and regaining their cohesion after Le Cateau despite the manifest difficulties involved in withdrawing from contact with the enemy. Senior British officers, however, were often less successful in controlling the army. Suffering from the same fatigue as their subordinates, commanders and staff officers were repeatedly confronted with decisions for which they had no precedent. Unfamiliar technology, such as the telephone, compounded the problems caused by exhaustion. Facing many of the same challenges, French and German officers encountered serious difficulties in controlling their forces in August 1914.[130]

Significantly, however, many of the problems faced by the British Army in this period stemmed from characteristics that were likely peculiar to the upper ranks of the BEF. The inexperience of senior officers in controlling large formations meant that responsibilities of staff officers and methods for the dissemination of orders were not clearly defined. In the absence of established procedures, officers allowed professional rivalries as well as loyalties between patrons and protégés to influence the way they exercised command. This tendency had a detrimental effect on the operations of the BEF throughout the retreat. The ascendancy of Henry Wilson left GHQ prone to cognitive closure at the outset of active operations. As a result, the BEF was unprepared for both the German attack at Mons and the retirement that followed. Once the retreat began, the increased marginalization of Archie Murray by Wilson and his allies at GHQ hampered the direction of operations and placed further responsibility on corps staff officers. With these officers executing additional and unaccustomed tasks, the possibility of errors increased just as the BEF began the dangerous process of withdrawing while under enemy pressure.

As the army approached the Forest of Mormal, the practice of umpiring did little to clarify matters, as Murray's ambiguous orders compounded confusion already prevalent due to internal conflict at GHQ. As a result, the two corps of the BEF failed to reconnect after dividing to bypass the forest. Once the consequences of the continued separation of the BEF became manifest in the early hours of 26 August, the possibility of I and II Corps reuniting became progressively more remote. In an atmosphere of heightened anxiety, the complex relationship between GHQ and the two corps commanders further undermined the effective exercise of command, leading GHQ to abandon II Corps on the morning of the 26th. Sir Douglas Haig also contributed to the Sir Horace Smith-Dorrien's difficulties at Le Cateau. Throughout the retreat, Haig consistently failed to support his rival in command of II Corps. While the wayward behavior of Allenby's cavalry brigades did nothing to help Smith-Dorrien on 26 August, Haig's indifference to the plight of II Corps was particularly detrimental, as it left Smith-Dorrien's force to fight with its flank unsupported.

Although GHQ recovered from its collective distress enough to aid in the reorganization of II Corps in the aftermath of Le Cateau, Sir John French and his staff never fully regained their composure following the traumatic night of 25/26 August. By the evening of the 27th, GHQ had once again succumbed to cognitive closure, concluding that II Corps had been rendered ineffective as a military force. Even as the retirement continued largely unmolested on subsequent days, GHQ persisted in issuing pessimistic directives that impeded the recovery of the army. Thus, while the "Old Contemptibles" performed well throughout the retreat from Mons, their commanders often proved unequal to the strains of the 1914 campaign.

NOTES

1. See, for example, James Edmonds, *Military Operations: France and Belgium, 1914* (London: Macmillan, 1933); Robert Asprey, *The First Battle of the Marne* (New York: Lippincott, 1962); Lyn Macdonald, *1914* (London: Michael Joseph, 1987); John Terraine, *Mons: The Retreat to Victory*, 2d ed. (London: Leo Cooper, 1991).

2. Terraine, *Mons*, 164.

3. Edmonds, *Military Operations: France and Belgium, 1914*, 49. See also Terraine, *Mons*, 21–32, 40–44.

4. Shelford Bidwell and Dominick Graham, *Fire-Power: British Army Weapons and Theories of War, 1904–1945* (London: Allen and Unwin, 1982), 13, 29.

5. Terraine, *Mons*, 94; Frederick Maurice, *Forty Days in 1914* (London: Constable, 1921), 81–82; Bidwell and Graham, *Fire-Power*, 41–42.

6. "Peter Liddle interview with Sir James Marshall-Cornwall," May 1974, Papers of Sir James Marshall-Cornwall, Liddle Collection, Brotherton Library, University of

Leeds; Brian Bond, *The Victorian Army and the Staff College: 1854–1914* (London:Eyre Methuen, 1972), 299.

7. Victor Bonham-Carter, *The Strategy of Victory, 1914–1918: The Life and Times of the Master Strategist of World War I: Field-Marshal Sir William Robertson* (New York: Holt, Rinehart and Winston, 1963), 84; Charles Callwell, *Experiences of a Dug-Out, 1914–1918* (London: Constable, 1920), 12; Richard Holmes, *The Little Field-Marshal: Sir John French* (London: Jonathan Cape, 1981), 152.

8. Peter Scott, ed., "The View from GHQ: The Second Part of the War Diary of General Sir Charles Deedes, KCB, CMG, DSO," *Stand To!*, 11 (Summer 1984), 9.

9. John Charteris, *At GHQ* (London: Cassell, 1931), 9.

10. Edmonds Memoirs, III/8, Edmonds Papers, Liddell Hart Centre for Military Archives, King's College, London (LHCMA).

11. Bond, *The Victorian Army and the Staff College*, 299.

12. This argument is developed in Nikolas Gardner, "Command and Control in the 'Great Retreat' of 1914: The Disintegration of the British Cavalry Division," *The Journal of Military History*, 63:1 (January 1999), 29–54.

13. Sir Archibald Wavell, *Allenby: A Study in Greatness* (London: 1940), 128–130. Cited in Bond, *The Victorian Army and the Staff College*, 309; John Shea to Wavell, 8 December 1938, Allenby VI/I, Allenby Papers, LHCMA. George Barrow to Wavell, undated, Allenby VI/I, Allenby Papers, LHCMA

14. Edmonds Memoirs, III/8, Edmonds Papers, LHCMA. A.J. Smithers, *The Man Who Disobeyed: Sir Horace Smith-Dorrien and His Enemies* (London: Leo Cooper, 1970), 165. Edward Spears, *Liaison—1914*, 2d ed. (London: Eyre and Spottiswood, 1968); Frederick Coleman, *From Mons to Ypres with French: A Personal Narrative* (Toronto: William Briggs, 1916); C.D. Baker-Carr, *From Chauffeur to Brigadier-General* (London: Benn, 1930); A. Rawlinson, *Adventures on the Western Front: August 1914–June 1915* (London: Andrew Melrose, 1925).

15. See John Ferris, "The British Army and Signals Intelligence in the Field during the First World War," *Intelligence and National Security*, 3:4 (October 1988), 23–48.

16. Spears to Sir John French, 16 May 1919, Spears Papers 2/3, LHCMA.

17. Martin Samuels, *Command or Control? Command, Training and Tactics in the British and German Armies, 1888–1918* (London: Frank Cass, 1995), 51.

18. Archie Murray to Charles Deedes, 18 December 1930, Spears Papers 2/3. LHCMA.

19. Macdonogh to Edmonds, 22 November 1923, CAB 45/141, Public Record Office, Kew, (PRO).

20. Robert Jervis, *Perception and Misperception in International Politics* (Princeton: Princeton University Press, 1976), 187–194. See also Richard Ned Lebow, *Between Peace and War: The Nature of International Crises* (Baltimore: Johns Hopkins University Press, 1981), 105.

21. Terraine, *Mons*, 37.

22. Bond, *The Victorian Army and the Staff College*, 258–261.

23. Spears, *Liaison 1914*, 163–64; Holmes, *The Little Field-Marshal*, 197–198.

24. Terraine, *Mons*, 53–56. Holmes, *The Little Field-Marshal*, 208–209.

25. GHQ Operation Order No. 5, 20 August 1914, GHQ War Diary, WO 95/1, PRO.

26. Terraine, *Mons*, 73–74; GHQ War Diary, 21 August 1914, WO 95/1, PRO.

27. Henry Wilson to Cavalry Division, 21 August 1914, 12:45 pm, Cavalry Division War Diary, WO 95/1096, PRO; George Barrow to Wavell, undated, Allenby 6/VI,

Allenby Papers, LHCMA.

28. Terraine, *Mons*, 77; Henry de Lisle, "My Narrative of the Great German War," De Lisle Papers, LHCMA; Cavalry Division War Diary, 22 August 1914, WO 95/1096, PRO; Edmonds, *Military Operations: France and Belgium, 1914*, 62.

29. Cavalry Division War Diary, 22 August 1914, WO 95/1096. De Lisle, "My Narrative," De Lisle Papers, LHCMA.

30. Haig Diary, 22 August 1914, National Library of Scotland (NLS); WO 256/1, PRO.

31. 1 Division War Diary, 23 August 1914, WO 95/1227; Cavalry Division War Diary, 23 August 1914, WO 95/1096, PRO.

32. Terraine, *Mons*, 83–84.

33. Terraine, *Mons*, 85; Spears to Sir John French, 16 May 1919, Spears 2/3, Spears Papers, LHCMA. II Corps War Diary, 22 August 1914, WO 95/630, PRO.

34. Terraine, *Mons*, 87-88; Cavalry Division War Diary, 23 August 1914, WO 95/1096, PRO. 19th Brigade War Diary, 23 August 1914, WO 95/1364, PRO.

35. Maurice, *Forty Days in 1914*, 82–83; Loch Diary, 22 August 1914, Loch Papers, IWM; Smith-Dorrien Diary, 23 August 1914, CAB 45/206, PRO; Edmonds, *Military Operations: France and Belgium, 1914*, 65.

36. Scott, "The View From GHQ: The Second Part of the War Diary of General Sir Charles Deedes," 9.

37. Spears, *Liaison 1914*, 163.

38. Tower Memoirs, K.F.B. Tower Papers, IWM; Smith-Dorrien Diary, 22 August 1914, CAB 45/206, PRO.

39. 3 Division to II Corps, 1:23 pm, 23 August 1914, Smith-Dorrien Papers, IWM. II Corps to 3 Division, 7 am, 23 August 1914, 3 Division War Diary, WO 95/1375; 3 Division War Diary, 23 August 1914, WO 95/1375; 5 Division War Diary, 23 August 1914, PRO.

40. II Corps Intelligence War Diary, 23 August 1914, WO 95/629, PRO; Terraine, *Mons*, 104–105.

41. Terraine, *Mons*, 89.

42. II Corps War Diary, 23 August 1914, WO 95/630, PRO.

43. Henry Wilson Diary, 23 August 1914, Henry Wilson Papers, IWM. See also Terraine, *Mons*, 106.

44. Cavalry Division War Diary, 23 August 1914, WO 95/1096, PRO; II Corps War Diary, 23 August 1914, WO 95/630.

45. Holmes, *The Little Field-Marshal*, 217. Henry Wilson Diary, 23 August 1914, Wilson Papers, IWM.

46. Haig Diary, 23 August 1914, NLS; WO 256/1, PRO.

47. Edmonds, *Military Operations: France and Belgium, 1914*, 97. Johnnie Gough to I Corps, 1:30 am, 24 August 1914, Smith-Dorrien Papers, IWM. II Corps War Diary, 24 August 1914, WO 95/630, PRO.

48. Terraine, *Mons*, 107. Edmonds Memoirs, III/9, Edmonds Papers, LHCMA.

49. Loch Diary, 24 August 1914, Lord Loch Papers, IWM.

50. Johnnie Gough to I Corps, 1:05 am, 1:30 am, 24 August 1914, Smith-Dorrien Papers, IWM. Haig Diary, 24 August 1914, NLS; WO 256/1, PRO. Smith-Dorrien to Becke, 9 July 1919, Smith-Dorrien Papers, IWM.

51. Smith-Dorrien to Maurice, 27 July 1919, Smith-Dorrien Papers, IWM; Haig Diary, 24 August 1914, NLS; WO 256/1, PRO.

52. 1 Division War Diary, 24 August 1914, WO 95/1227, PRO. 2 Division War Diary, 24 August 1914, WO 95/1283, PRO. 3 Division War Diary, 24 August 1914, WO 95/1375. II Corps War Diary, 24 August 1914, WO 95/630, PRO.

53. Haig Diary, 24 August 1914, NLS; WO 256/1, PRO; Charteris, *At GHQ*, 17.

54. Haig Diary, 23 August 1914, NLS; WO 256/1, PRO.

55. Edmonds, *Military Operations: France and Belgium, 1914*, 112.

56. Terraine, *Mons*, 110–112.

57. Scott, "The View From GHQ: The Second Part of the War Diary of General Sir Charles Deedes," 9.

58. Terraine, *Mons*, 91–93. Edmonds, *Military Operations: France and Belgium, 1914*, 119. Edmonds notes that the divisional cavalry of I Corps had in fact traveled through the Forest of Mormal during its advance to Mons.

59. Maurice, *Forty Days in 1914*, 101.

60. Murray to Edmonds, 5 January 1927, CAB 45/129, PRO; Murray to Deedes, 18 December 1930, 2/3, Spears Papers, LHCMA; GHQ Operation Order No. 7, 24 August 1914, 8:25 pm., GHQ War Diary, WO 95/1, PRO.

61. Murray to Edmonds, 5 January 1927, CAB 45/129, PRO. Edmonds to Murray, 7 January 1927, CAB 45/129, PRO. Haig Diary, 24 August 1914, NLS; WO 256/1, PRO.

62. Murray to Deedes, 18 December 1930, 2/3 Spears Papers, LHCMA.

63. Smith-Dorrien Diary, 25 August 1914, CAB 45/206, PRO. "Commander-in-Chief's Diary", 25 August 1914, GHQ War Diary, WO 95/1, PRO. Loch Diary, 25 August 1914, Loch Papers, IWM.

64. Bulfin Diary, 25 August 1914, CAB 45/140; 1 Division War Diary, 25 August 1914, WO 95/1227, PRO; Haig Diary, 24 August 1914, NLS; WO 256/1, PRO. Murray to Deedes, 18 December 1930, 2/3 Spears Papers, LHCMA.

65. 2 Division War Diary, 25 August 1914, WO 95/1283, PRO.

66. I Corps War Diary, 25 August 1914, WO 95/588; GHQ War Diary, 25 August 1914, WO 95/1, PRO; Spears, *Liaison 1914*, 216–217.

67. Montgomery-Massingberd to Edmonds, 9 May 1933, CAB 45/206, PRO; Smith-Dorrien to Becke, 29 December 1914, Smith-Dorrien Papers, IWM.

68. Haig Diary, 25 August 1914, NLS; WO 256/1, PRO. I Corps War Diary, 25 August 1914, WO 95/588, PRO.

69. See for example, Murray to Deedes, 18 December 1930, Murray to Spears, 22 December 1930, 2/3 Spears Papers, LHCMA, Murray to Edmonds, 5 January 1927, "Copy of Correspondence. Lord Haig & Sir H. Smith-Dorrien. Mons & Le Cateau," CAB 45/129, PRO.

70. Wilson Diary, 25 August 1914, Henry Wilson Papers, IWM. See also Smith-Dorrien Diary, 25 August 1914, CAB 45/206, PRO; Loch Diary, 25 August 1914, Lord Loch Papers, IWM.

71. Wilson Diary, 25 August 1914, Henry Wilson Papers, IWM. French Diary, 25 August 1914, John French Papers, IWM; Haig Diary, 25 August 1914, NLS; WO 256/1. Edmonds, *Military Operations, France and Belgium: 1914*, 123.

72. Liddell Hart to A.H. Burne, 19 December 1933, 1/131/35, Liddell Hart Papers, LHCMA.

73. Edmonds to Spencer Wilkinson, 15 March 1916, 2/1, Edmonds Papers, LHCMA; A. Rawlinson, *Adventures on the Western Front*, 46.

74. "Action at Landrecies, August 25th–26th, 1914." I Corps War Diary, WO 95/588, PRO. Haig Diary, 25 August 1914, NLS; WO 256/1, PRO.

75. "6th Infantry Brigade. Action at MAROILLES—August 25th/26th, 1914." I Corps War Diary, WO 95/588, PRO. "Note on Duff Cooper's 'HAIG'." Liddell Hart Papers, 11/1935/132, LHCMA. Haig Diary, 25 August 1914, NLS; WO 256/1, PRO.

76. Charteris, *At GHQ*, 18; "Talk with Edmonds. 7/12/33." 11/1933/26, Liddell Hart Papers, LHCMA.

77. Haig Diary, 25 August 1914, NLS; WO 256/1, PRO. I Corps War Diary, 25 August 1914, WO 95/588, PRO.

78. Haig Diary, 25 August 1914, NLS; WO 256/1, PRO.

79. Haig Diary, 26 August 1914, NLS; WO 256/1, PRO. J. Gough to GHQ, 26 August 1914, 1:35 am, Edmonds Papers 6/1, LHCMA. Bulfin Diary, 25 August 1914, CAB 45/140, PRO.

80. J. Gough to GHQ, 1:35 am, 26 August 1914, Edmonds Papers, 6/1; Clive Diary, 25 August 1914, Sir Sidney Clive Papers, LHCMA; French Diary, 26 August 1914, John French Papers, IWM; "Peccavi—Contra Veritatum. How Opinions Must Yield to Facts." 11/1935/160, Liddell Hart Papers, LHCMA; Wilson Diary, 26 August 1914, Henry Wilson Papers, IWM; Spears, *Liaison 1914*, 222.

81. Haig to GHQ, 3:50 am, 26 August 1914, Edmonds Papers, 6/1, LHCMA.

82. Terraine, *Mons*, 126, 129.

83. T. D'O Snow, "Account of the Retreat of 1914," CAB 45/129; II Corps War Diary, 26 August 1914, WO 95/630, PRO.

84. II Corps War Diary, 26 August 1914, WO 95/630; John Shea to Edmonds, 19 October 1919; Allenby to Smith-Dorrien, 4 June 1919, CAB 45/129, PRO; John Vaughan to Smith-Dorrien, 24 June 1919; Smith-Dorrien to Archie Murray, 21 July 1919, WO 79/62; Cavalry Division War Diary, 25 August 1914, WO 95/1096, PRO.

85.Smith-Dorrien Diary, 26 August 1914, CAB 45/206; Smith-Dorrien to Archie Murray, 2 July 1919, WO 79/62; John Shea to Edmonds, 19 October 1919, CAB 45/129, PRO.

86. Wilson Diary, 26 August 1914, Henry Wilson Papers, IWM; "Talk with Edmonds, 7/12/33," 11/1933/26, Liddell Hart Papers, LHCMA.

87. "Talk with Edmonds, 7/12/33," 11/1933/26, Liddell Hart Papers, LHCMA. Montgomery-Massingberd to Edmonds, 9 May 1933, CAB 45/206, PRO.

88. GHQ to I Corps, 10 am, 26 August 1914, Edmonds Papers, 6/1, LHCMA.

89. Haig Diary, 26 August 1914, NLS. This entry does not appear in the typed version of the diary.

90. Lieutenant-Colonel A.H. Burne to Liddell Hart, 8/12/33, 1/131/32, Liddell Hart Papers, LHCMA.

91. I Corps War Diary, 26 August 1914, WO 95/588; 1 Division War Diary, WO 95/1229; Bulfin Diary, 26 August 1914, CAB 45/140, PRO; "Talk with Edmonds, 5/2/37," 11/1937/4, Liddell Hart Papers, LHCMA. For a detailed account of the separation of I and II Corps, see Nikolas Gardner, "Command in Crisis: The British Expeditionary Force and the Forest of Mormal, August 1914," *War & Society*, 16:2 (October 1998), 13–32.

92. Edmonds, *Military Operations: France and Belgium, 1914*, 152–155; 5 Division War Diary, 26 August 1914, WO 95/1510; "General Report on the Battle of Le Cateau, 26 August 1914," CAB 45/206, PRO.

93. "General Report of the Battle of Le Cateau," CAB 45/206, PRO.

94. Gough, *The Fifth Army* (London: Hodder and Stoughton, 1931), 28; Beddington Memoir, cited in Bonham-Carter, *The Strategy of Victory*, 92.

95. Edmonds, *Military Operations: France and Belgium, 1914*, 175; II Corps War Diary, 26 August 1914, WO 95/630, PRO.

96. Smith-Dorrien Diary, 26 August 1914, CAB 45/206, PRO. See also Scott, "The Second Part of the War Diary of General Sir Charles Deedes," 10.

97. Scott, "The Second Part of the War Diary of General Sir Charles Deedes", 10. On the use of the telephone in the German army in 1914, see Dennis Showalter, "Even Generals Wet Their Pants: The First Three Weeks on the Eastern Front, August 1914," *War & Society*, 2:2 (September 1984), 61–86.

98. Edmonds Memoirs, III/9; Edmonds, "A Telephone Conversation at Le Cateau," VI/1, Edmonds Papers; "Talk with Edmonds, 7/12/33," 11/1933/26, Liddell Hart Papers, LHCMA; Scott, "The Second Part of the War Diary of General Sir Charles Deedes," 10.

99. Scott, "The Second Part of the War Diary of General Sir Charles Deedes," 10.

100. "True Extract From *On the Road From Mons, with an Army Service Officer. By Its Commander* (London: Hurst and Blackett, 1916)" in II Corps War Diary, WO 95/630, PRO. See also Smith-Dorrien Diary, 26 August 1914, CAB 45/206, PRO; Coleman, *From Mons to Ypres with French*, 25–26.

101. John French Diary, 27 August 1914, John French Papers, IWM; Smith-Dorrien Diary, 26 August 1914, CAB 45/206, PRO; Loch Diary, 26 August 1914, Lord Loch Papers, IWM; Scott, "The Second Part of the War Diary of General Sir Charles Deedes," 11; "Talk with Edmonds, 7/12/33," 11/1933/26, Liddell Hart Papers, LHCMA.

102. Habgood Diary, 27 August 1914, A.H. Habgood Papers, IWM. Edmonds Diary, 6/4, Edmonds Papers, LHCMA; See also Herbert Stewart, *From Mons to Loos: Being the Diary of a Supply Officer* (London: Blackwood, 1916), 51; Tower Memoir, K.F.B. Tower Papers, IWM.

103. Smith-Dorrien Diary, 27 August 1914, CAB 45/206, PRO.

104. Coleman, *From Mons to Ypres with French*, 28–29.

105. Baker-Carr, *From Chauffeur to Brigadier*, 27. See also Liddell Hart Diary, 28 March 1927, 11/1927/1, Liddell Hart Papers, LHCMA; William Robertson, *Soldiers and Statesmen*, 71; "Casualty," *"Contemptible"* (Philadelphia: Lippincott, 1916), 53.

106. "Talk with General Ironside, 6/5/37," 11/1937/33, Liddell Hart Papers, LHCMA.

107. Liddell Hart Diary, 28 March 1927, 11/1927/1, Liddell Hart Papers, LHCMA; 5 Division War Diary, 27 August 1914, WO 95/1510; 19th Brigade War Diary, 27 August 1914, WO 95/1364, PRO; Edmonds, *Military Operations: France and Belgium, 1914*, 184–185.

108. Ernest Swinton, *Eyewitness: Being Personal Reminiscences of Certain Phases of the Great War, Including the Genesis of the Tank*, 2d ed. (New York: Arno, 1972), 30.

109. Terraine, *Mons*, 163; Wilson Diary, 27 August 1914, Wilson Papers, IWM.

110. Coleman, *From Mons to Ypres with French*, 63.

111. Neville Macready, *Annals of an Active Life, vol. 1* (London: Hutchinson, 1924), 207; Baker-Carr, *From Chauffeur to Brigadier*, 29.

112. GHQ War Diary, 27 August 1914, O 95/1, PRO. See also, "Account of the Retreat of 1914," CAB 45/129, PRO; Smith-Dorrien Diary, 27 August 1914, CAB 45/206, PRO. Edmonds Memoirs, III/9, Edmonds Papers, LHCMA.

113. Loch Diary, 28 August 1914, Loch Papers, IWM; Coleman, *From Mons to Ypres with French*, 47.

114. I Corps to GHQ, 28 August 1914, 7 pm, Haig Diary, NLS; WO 256/1; II Corps War Diary, 28 August 1914, WO 95/630, PRO. Bulfin Diary, 28 August 1914, CAB

45/140, PRO. I Corps War Diary, 28 August 1914, WO 95/588, PRO.

115. Holmes, *The Little Field-Marshal*, 228; French to War Office, 28 August 1914, WO 33/713, PRO.

116. Smith-Dorrien Diary, 29 August 1914, CAB 45/206, PRO. II Corps War Diary, 29 August 1914, WO 95/630, PRO.

117. John Shea to Wavell, undated, Allenby Papers, LHCMA; "Account of the Retreat of 1914," CAB 45/129, PRO. 4 Division War Diary, 29 August 1914, WO 95/1439; Smith-Dorrien Diary, 28 August 1914, CAB 45/206, PRO; Frederick Maurice Diary, 31 August 1914, F.B. Maurice Papers, LHCMA; Loch Diary, 28 August 1914, Loch Papers, IWM.

118. GHQ Operation Order No. 11, 29 August 1914, 9 pm; Murray to I and II Corps, 29 August 1914, GHQ War Diary, WO 95/1, PRO.

119. Terraine, *Mons*, 180–190; Holmes, *The Little Field-Marshal*, 232–235.

120. Loch Diary, 31 August 1914, Lord Loch Diary, IWM; Cavalry Division War Diary, 31 August 1914, WO 95/1096, PRO; Terraine, *Mons*, 179. Holger Herwig, *The First World War: Germany and Austria-Hungary, 1914–1918* (New York: Arnold, 1997), 99–100.

121. GHQ to I Corps, 10 am, 26 August 1914, 6/1, Edmonds Papers, LHCMA. GHQ Operation Orders 9–13, 27–31 August 1914, WO 95/1, PRO; Terraine, *Mons*, 193.

122.Phillip Chetwode to Archibald Wavell, 20 June 1938; John Shea to Wavell, 8 December 1938; George Barrow to Wavell, n.d., VI/I, Allenby Papers, LHCMA; Gough, *The Fifth Army*, 33–34; 3rd Cavalry Brigade War Diary, August 1914, WO 95/1130; Cavalry Division War Diary, 29 August 1914, WO 95/1096, PRO.

123. Roseberry to Wavell, 15 August 1938, VI/I, Allenby Papers, LHCMA. See also Chetwode to Wavell, 20 January 1938; Shea to Wavell, 8 December 1938; VI/I, Allenby Papers, LHCMA; Hubert Gough, *Soldiering On* (London: Arthur Barker, 1954), 117.

124. Barrow to Wavell, n.d., VI/I, Allenby Papers; "Note on Duff Cooper's 'HAIG'," 11/1935/132, Liddell Hart Papers, LHCMA.

125. GHQ Operation Order No. 13, 31 August 1914, WO 95/1, PRO; Cavalry Division Operation Order No. 4, 30 August 1914, WO 95/1096, PRO.

126. See Terraine, *Mons*, 198–213, or Asprey, *The First Battle of the Marne*, ch. 8.

127. GHQ Operation Order No. 16, 6:35 pm, 4 September 1914, WO 95/1, PRO.

128. Edmonds, "General Sir John French on September 4th," Edmonds Papers, LHCMA.

129. Haig Diary, 4 September 1914, NLS; WO 256/1, PRO.

130. On command in the French Army, see Leonard V. Smith, *Between Mutiny and Obedience: The Case of the French Fifth Infantry Division during World War I* (Princeton: Princeton University Press, 1994), ch. 3. On the German army, see Herwig, *The First World War*, ch. 3, and Dennis Showalter, *Tannenberg: Clash of Empires* (Hamden CT: Archon, 1990).

3

The Advance to the Aisne and the Advent of Trench Warfare, 6–30 September

On 6 September, the BEF joined the French Army on the offensive, advancing against the overextended German forces that had pursued them during the preceding two weeks. Over the next three days the British Army pushed through successive enemy rearguards on the Petit Morin and Marne rivers. When the Germans initiated a general withdrawal on the 9th, the BEF pursued them northward, before stalling against formidable enemy positions north of the River Aisne on 13 September. After three days of largely fruitless attempts to break through German lines on the Aisne, the army strengthened its own positions and settled into the deadly monotony of trench warfare until its transfer to Flanders at the beginning of October.

Historians have offered varying assessments of the performance of the BEF in this period. Sympathetic interpretations characterize the British advance as a qualified success. While John Terraine suggests that, "nowhere, and at no time, did it present the traditional aspect of victory," he nonetheless contends that the British and French advance into the gap between the German First and Second Armies "made the battle of the Marne the decisive battle of the war."[1] Other scholars have been more critical. In *The First Battle of the Marne*, Robert Asprey contends: "If the BEF, instead of advancing less than twelve miles on September 9 had pushed fifteen or twenty miles forward, they would have netted a tactical victory that possibly could have become decisive."[2]

Despite the differing intensity of their criticisms, existing accounts agree that the BEF did not defeat the Germans decisively during the advance to the Aisne. Beyond noting the fatigue of British soldiers in the wake of the retreat, however, historians have done little to determine why this was the case. In an attempt to explain what Georges Blond called the "excessive *lenteur* of the British," this chapter will examine the operations of the BEF during the period 6–15 September.[3] It will also consider the stalemate that ensued along the Aisne during the last two weeks of the month, a period overlooked by historians of the British Army. Focusing on the exercise of command at GHQ and the corps level, this chapter will illuminate the way in which senior officers conducted the first offensive operations of the war, as well as their initial reaction to the advent of trench warfare. It will argue that the caution and inexperience of British officers prevented the BEF from disrupting the German retirement to the River Aisne. Subsequently, despite the revival of optimism in the upper ranks of the army, the army suffered heavy casualties in unsuccessful attempts to dislodge the enemy from formidable defensive positions. While the ensuing stalemate allowed British officers to respond to the unprecedented nature of the 1914 campaign, this response was influenced by the double-edged traits characteristic of "hybrid" officers as well as the continued prevalence of rivalries in the upper ranks of the army.

THE ADVANCE TO THE AISNE, 6–12 SEPTEMBER

The Initial Stages, 6–7 September

As the BEF moved forward on the morning of 6 September, it did not face an easy task. In itself, the terrain over which the army was to advance presented considerable challenges. The path of the BEF crossed the river valleys of the Grand Morin, the Petit Morin, the Marne, the Ourcq, and the Aisne (see Map 3.1). None of these rivers, with the exception of portions of the Petit Morin, could be traversed without the use of bridges, most of which had been destroyed by the British and French during the retreat. Moreover, the heights on the north side of each river valley afforded excellent defensive positions to the retiring Germans. In addition to the obstacles in its path, the continued retreat of the BEF on 5 September had left its formations between 10 and 20 miles from German positions. Thus, the army was not within easy striking distance of the enemy as it took the offensive.[4]

Nor was the condition of the BEF conducive to a rapid advance. The army had sustained considerable punishment over the preceding two weeks, and the ranks of many units remained depleted by casualties. In a wire to Lord Kitchener on the 6th, Sir John French reported that he had received only 13,000 reinforcements to offset losses of 488 officers and 19,532 men since the battle of Mons.[5] For those soldiers who had survived the retreat, its cumulative effects were not easily shaken off. In a postwar interview, Sir James Marshall-Cornwall, a member of the 3 Division staff, described the soldiers of his formation: "They had marched 200 miles with their backs to the enemy and they were really physically worn out when they had to advance again."[6]

Nevertheless, the end of the retreat did much to restore the morale of the BEF. Numerous accounts of this period note the renewed enthusiasm of exhausted British soldiers for the prospect of striking back at their pursuers. In Charles Fergusson's 5 Division, which had suffered heavily during the retreat, the divisional war diary recorded on 6 September: "[s]pirits have been rising all

Map 3.1
BEF Area of Operations, 6–9 September 1914

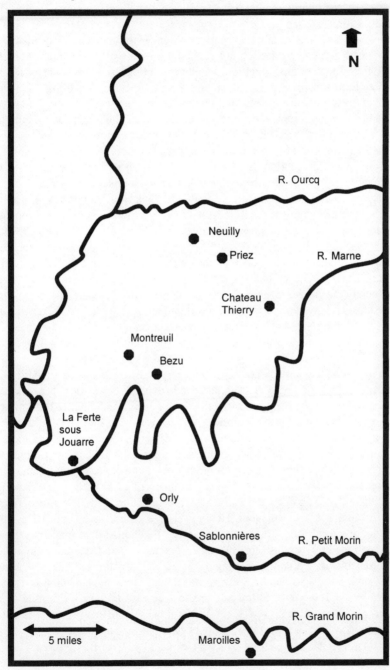

day."[7] Such was not the case, however, at GHQ. While pressure from Joffre and Lord Kitchener had compelled a reluctant Sir John French to join the French counteroffensive, many senior British officers were initially quite averse to committing the battered army to an advance alongside their allies. At GHQ, Henry Wilson was a notable exception. After learning of French plans to advance on 4 September, the sub-chief of the General Staff recovered relatively quickly from the pessimism that had shaped his outlook since Le Cateau. In the days that followed, he advocated an aggressive advance, hectoring Sir John French on the importance of "pushing like the devil in pursuit."[8]

Despite pressure from Wilson, the commander-in-chief remained cautious. French's wariness stemmed in part from his continued concern for the condition of the BEF in light of its sufferings over the previous two weeks. Archie Murray shared this bleak perception of the state of the army, and discouraged French from committing to the offensive.[9] The commander-in-chief's rocky relationship with his French counterparts also contributed to his lack of enthusiasm. Sir John French's animosity toward his allies likely subsided following Franchet D'Esperey's replacement of Charles Lanrezac as commander of the French Fifth Army. It was rekindled, however, on 5 September as the allied armies prepared to advance. Amid the confusion regarding the participation of the BEF, Joffre contacted Lord Kitchener and requested British cooperation in the offensive. Subsequently, Joffre met with Sir John French on the afternoon of the 5th and obtained his support. Unaware of this development, Kitchener wired French that evening, informing him that "General Joffre considers it essential that you should fully realize that it is most important that you should cooperate most vigorously with him."[10]

Given that he had already assured Joffre personally of British participation in the attack, Sir John French was annoyed by the news that the French commander-in-chief had appealed to a higher authority. As he replied sharply to Kitchener on the 6th: "If my desire to act vigorously is doubted by General Joffre, I can only state that he is doing a great disservice to my force and me."[11] While Joffre's attempts to secure the assistance of the BEF were ultimately successful, they had the effect of straining relations between himself and Sir John French. This likely reinforced the reluctance of both French and Murray to commit the army to an aggressive advance in conjunction with their allies. Thus, for the first time in the campaign, Henry Wilson's optimism was stifled by his more cautious superiors. Consequently, army operation orders made no great demands on the army to push forward on 6 September. The first operation order of the offensive, issued on the evening of the 5th, simply directed that "the army will advance eastward, with a view to attacking." This movement was to be preceded by the rotation of all three corps to face east during the morning of 6 September.[12] Due to the time spent performing this maneuver, it was late morning before most of the army actually began to advance. The three corps then moved forward carefully behind a screen of cavalry, with E.P. Pulteney's III Corps on the left, Smith-Dorrien's II Corps in the middle, and Haig's I Corps on the right.

Despite this delay in commencing the advance, the BEF soon encountered German forces in strength. On the right of the army, the advanced guard of 1 Division, Ivor Maxse's 1st (Guards) Brigade, reported artillery fire followed by advancing German infantry shortly after 10 am.[13] Upon receiving this information, senior officers showed little enthusiasm for a significant engagement with the enemy. Maxse's report, combined with rumors of additional enemy forces in the vicinity of I Corps, induced Sir Douglas Haig to halt until II Corps arrived on his left. Sir John French confirmed the I Corps commander's decision and ordered Smith-Dorrien to move forward in support.[14] Haig's corps never achieved any significant momentum on the 6th. Despite the arrival of II Corps on his left, and orders from GHQ to resume the advance to Maroilles, just south of the Grand Morin, Haig proved reluctant to press on in light of air reconnaissance indicating the continued proximity of two German brigades. Thus, he halted at 6:30 pm, well short of his assigned destination. Smith-Dorrien's corps continued its march into the evening without encountering enemy forces. By the night of the 6th, it stood on the south bank of the Grand Morin, ahead of both III Corps on its left and I Corps on its right.[15] While the army advanced approximately eleven miles on 6 September, it had no contact with the enemy aside from the brief and inconclusive engagements of the morning.

GHQ continued to plot the offensive cautiously on the evening of the 6th, taking pains to ensure contact with French forces on the right of the BEF. When Sir John French and Archie Murray learned late that night that Conneau's adjacent cavalry corps had not pushed forward as far as expected, they cancelled operation orders calling for an advance at 5 am and deferred any movement until further reports arrived of French progress.[16] This postponement may have been prudent, but it resulted in significant delays on the morning of 7 September as GHQ did not issue instructions to advance until 8 am, after Allenby's cavalry had gained touch with the French. These orders did not filter down to the divisional level until at least 10 am, and most units did not actually begin moving forward until 11 am.[17]

To complicate matters further, GHQ had ordered only a three-hour march to ensure that the BEF did not outrun the French cavalry. Consequently, the entire army was forced to halt in the early afternoon until new orders were distributed. These delays resulted in an average advance for the BEF of "under eight" miles, bringing the total distance covered since the beginning of the advance to approximately nineteen miles.[18] Given the travails endured by the army over the preceding weeks, this was not an insignificant accomplishment. Nevertheless, the pace of the advance on 6–7 September did not allow the BEF to disrupt the operations of the Germans to any significant extent. In addition, on the evening of the 7th, the only British units across the Grand Morin, the first of the series of rivers the army had to negotiate, were the 3rd and 5th Cavalry Brigades. While Sir John French stated confidently in a wire to Kitchener that "all three corps will make the Marne to-morrow," the tentative movements of the army during the first two days of the advance did not suggest that German forces were in great jeopardy.[19]

Fatigue may have diminished the pace and intensity of the advance in its initial stages. Anecdotal evidence indicates, however, that British soldiers were hardly pushed to the limits of their endurance during 6–7 September. According to an anonymous narrative of the experiences of the East Lancashire Regiment, part of Snow's 4 Division: "We seemed to be sitting about in the sun during a considerable part of each day, and the marches were generally short, but this was no doubt due to tactical or other reasons which were not obvious to us."[20] Thus, rather than stemming solely from the fatigue of British soldiers, the halting advance of the BEF on 6–7 September reflected the continued caution of senior officers such as Sir John French, Archie Murray and Sir Douglas Haig. As a result, the BEF had little impact on the German army during the first two days of the advance.

The wariness of GHQ in this period is also evident in the tight leash it kept on the British cavalry. Beginning on 6 September, the cavalry began operating in two separate formations. Briggs's 1st Brigade, De Lisle's 2nd Brigade, and Bingham's 4th Brigade remained under Allenby in the Cavalry Division. Hubert Gough's 3rd Brigade and Phillip Chetwode's 5th Brigade now formed an independent force under Gough's command, which was designated 2 Cavalry Division in mid-September.[21] Throughout the advance, these two formations covered the rest of the BEF, moving in front of the army and on its right. While British infantry had little contact with the enemy on 6–7 September, the cavalry encountered German mounted troops from the outset of the advance. At approximately 7:30 am on the 6th, Henry De Lisle's 2nd Brigade engaged enemy cavalry screening a larger force of infantry moving southeast. De Lisle related in his memoirs that the skirmish ended with "the 4th Dragoon Guards and the 9th Lancers again distinguishing themselves."[22]

Despite this success, the 2nd Cavalry Brigade did not disrupt the movement of the German infantry. Instead, Allenby ordered it to hold its positions until the arrival of I Corps, which was to advance later in the morning. Shortly after allowing the enemy column to pass, De Lisle observed the curious spectacle of the same German troops returning in the direction from which they had come. This was apparently part of the withdrawal of two corps of von Kluck's First Army to the northwest to meet Manoury's 6th French Army, which was advancing from Paris. As De Lisle noted in his memoirs, his force "could have hampered this movement," but his superiors were taking no chances.[23] The cavalry thus regarded the German march passively. Allenby's unwillingness to allow the 2nd Cavalry Brigade to disrupt the German retirement likely stemmed in part from a desire to maintain control of his division after the wayward behavior of his brigades during the retreat. Orders restraining the cavalry during the initial stages of the advance, however, were not entirely the product of Allenby's trepidation. In postwar correspondence with George Barrow, Sir Archibald Wavell defended Allenby, arguing: "as regards opportunities missed by the Cavalry in the Advance...I think it would have been a very difficult decision, even for a bold man like Allenby, to push ahead in the circumstances. For the Commander-in-Chief, as you know, did not trust the French, and was very averse from pushing on ahead of them."[30]

On the morning of 7 September, caution at GHQ prevented the cavalry from exploiting two tactical successes. Just after 6 am, De Lisle's 2nd Brigade encountered German cavalry patrols on the right flank of the BEF and its advanced guard charged an enemy squadron. According to De Lisle, who observed the clash, "the 9th Lancers went through the 9th Garde Dragonen as if they were tissue paper." Shortly afterward, he witnessed another skirmish in which the 18th Hussars thwarted a German cavalry charge with dismounted rifle fire. De Lisle had no opportunity to capitalize on these victories, however, as orders soon arrived from GHQ instructing him to hold his position. As a result, the 2nd Cavalry Brigade remained stationary for the next three hours, watching German ambulances remove wounded troopers from the battlefield.[31]

The Pursuit, 8–12 September

While senior British officers remained cautious during the first two days of the advance, the movements of von Kluck's First Army were creating significant opportunities in the path of the BEF. Early on 6 September, von Kluck had directed II and IV Corps of his army to withdraw from in front of the British in order to meet Manoury's French Sixth Army on his right. During the day, the threat from Manoury intensified. In the evening, von Kluck thus ordered his III and IX Corps, which were also situated in front of the BEF on the right flank of the German Second Army, to retire to the line of the Petit Morin to join II and IV Corps. This withdrawal created a considerable gap between the German First and Second Armies directly north of the British. If the BEF could penetrate this breach, held by only two German cavalry corps, it would be able to operate against the flanks of the two German armies while they were engaged by French forces. On the 7th, French commanders drew this gap to the attention of GHQ and urged the British to exploit it.[32] This request, combined with continued agitation by Henry Wilson, elicited more assertive orders from Sir John French and Archie Murray. GHQ Operation Order No. 18, issued at 7:25 pm on the 7th, directed all three corps to continue the advance the next morning, "attacking the enemy wherever met." Rather than the intermittent marches of the previous two days, the order directed British infantry units to be underway by 6 am, and to continue advancing until they reached the Marne.[33]

A more aggressive offensive required detailed planning in order to minimize the mutual interference of adjacent units. Beyond the aforementioned order, however, GHQ did not provide any such guidance. As a result, British forces encountered significant difficulties on 8 September as they encountered German rearguards along the Petit Morin and the Marne. Given that the two rivers met in front of III Corps, Pulteney's force faced fewer obstacles than the rest of the army, as it had only the Marne to cross. Thus, while the other two corps and the cavalry struggled to negotiate the Petit Morin, III Corps, on the left, reached the south bank of the Marne near the town of La Ferte sous Jouarre by late morning. There, however, its units found nearby bridges either destroyed or occupied by the Germans, with the enemy holding strong positions on the other side of the river. Unable to dislodge the enemy from these positions by evening, Pulteney's corps remained south of the Marne on the night of the 8th.[28]

To the right, both II Corps and I Corps achieved more success in evicting German rearguards from the north bank of the Petit Morin. Nonetheless, once they crossed the river, the advance of both formations was hindered by a lack of coordination between units. In II Corps, units of 5 Division managed to cross the river during the afternoon. Apparently, however, neither 5 Division nor II Corps informed 4 Division, to the left, or 3 Division, to the right, of their whereabouts. As a result, British artillery on the south side of the Petit Morin shelled units of 5 Division during the afternoon. Similarly, in I Corps, British guns shelled units of 2 Division, disrupting their advance considerably.[29] The first day of determined advance by the BEF thus produced mixed results. While both I and II Corps had dislodged strong rearguards on the Petit Morin, further progress was hindered by friendly fire. Overall, British formations had advanced an average of about ten miles. Aside from III Corps, however, they had yet to reach the Marne.

With the intent of pressuring the flanks of the German First and Second Armies, GHQ pressed the advance on 9 September. Operation Order No. 19, issued on the evening of the 8th, directed the BEF to "continue the advance north to-morrow at 5 am, attacking rear-guards of the enemy wherever met."[30] German rearguards, however, proved no easier to overcome on the 9th than they had the previous day. At La Ferre sous Jouarre, III Corps faced at least four enemy battalions in easily defensible positions north of the Marne, supported by artillery. It was not until this rearguard began to retire after 4 pm that infantry of the 11th Brigade, part of 4 Division, could begin crossing the river. Further progress north of the river was hindered by poor coordination between infantry and artillery units in 4 Division. This problem stemmed from the rudimentary methods of artillery spotting that prevailed in this period. C.L. Brereton, commander of an artillery battery in 4 Division, described his attempts to support the crossing of the infantry. According to Brereton: "About 6.30 pm an East Lancs officer pointed out to me what looked like a section of guns on the north side of the river, at about 1800 yards range. It was getting dark, and I could not see very well, but did what looked like very good shooting."

The next day, Brereton discovered that the "guns" on which he had directed his fire were in fact two bushes. In addition, his shells had wounded two British soldiers and killed a German prisoner, without assisting the advance of 4 Division.[31] Thus, at the end of 9 September, the bulk of Pulteney's force remained south of the Marne. To compound the difficulties of III Corps, 4 Division lost its commander, Thomas Snow, who was injured in a fall from his horse and returned to England for the rest of 1914. Snow was succeeded by Brigadier-General H.F.M. "Fatty" Wilson, the commander of the 12th Brigade.

The rest of the army faced considerably less opposition. The advance of I and II Corps faltered, however, due to continued caution among senior officers.

After finding bridges across the Marne unguarded and intact, advanced guards of II Corps were across the river by 9 am. By late morning, however, air reconnaissance reports indicating the presence of up to three enemy divisions in the vicinity compelled GHQ to halt the entire army, with Smith-Dorrien's advanced guards near the towns of Montreuil and Bezu, just north of the Marne.[32] By mid-afternoon, further reconnaissance revealed the earlier warnings to be false. This allowed II Corps to resume its advance, but Smith-Dorrien's formation did not move beyond Montreuil and Bezu on the 9th. While this lack of progress was partly a result of the wariness of GHQ, it also reflected the hesitancy of formation commanders within II Corps when its units encountered rather weak enemy rearguards near Bezu during the afternoon. According to K.F.B. Tower, whose battalion was part of the advanced guard of 3 Division: "The whole of the II Corps was held up for a whole 24 hours by one company and a battery of guns."[33] This delay stemmed less from the strength of enemy positions or the fatigue of British soldiers than from a simple lack of determination on the part of British commanders at the brigade level and above. According to another regimental officer in 3 Division: "A few encouraging words from behind would have driven us, I know, 6 miles further."[34] Apparently, however, commanders from the brigade level upward did little to press the advance of II Corps on the afternoon of 9 September.

Haig's I Corps had also pushed advanced guards over the Marne by mid-morning when orders arrived from GHQ to halt. As was the case with Smith-Dorrien's force, however, it proved difficult to resuscitate the advance of I Corps following its extended pause during the afternoon. This was due at least in part to the hesitancy of subordinate commanders. After ordering his force to continue its advance at 3 pm, Haig discovered that Monro's 2 Division was in fact retiring to the south bank of the Marne. The 2 Division war diary maintained that the exposed position in which it was forced to halt necessitated a retirement. Haig was less charitable, commenting in his diary that Monro's withdrawal demonstrated "what might happen with nervous commanders who are ready to make use of any excuse to avoid coming to conclusions with the enemy!"[35]

The afternoon halt of I Corps and its subsequent difficulties in moving forward delayed its progress on the 9th significantly. In addition, when the corps finally got underway again, its advance was soon cut short by GHQ. According to the *Official History*, Sir John French ordered Haig to halt late in the afternoon, as "no French troops had come up on the right."[36] This is a curious explanation, given that the intent of the British advance was to relieve the pressure on the embattled French armies on either flank. In order to do so, it was necessary for the BEF to penetrate the gap between the German armies opposing the French and operate against their flanks. This entailed that the British operate well in front of the French. It would seem that the reluctance to continue the advance stemmed from continued trepidation on the part of Sir John French and his staff. While GHQ had begun to press the advance more aggressively as early as 8 September, the psychological effects of the retreat from Mons did not immediately disappear.

The advance of the BEF was not without effect. The progress of British units across the Marne on the morning of the 9th helped induce the retirement of the German First and Second Armies later that day.[37] Significantly, the news of this withdrawal was sufficient to eliminate the caution that remained at GHQ. Before instructions even arrived from Joffre that evening, Sir John French directed the army to pursue the Germans northward in hopes of overtaking von Kluck's First Army, which was moving east across the British front. The GHQ Operation Order called for the army to continue its advance at 5 am the next morning, again "attacking the enemy wherever met."[38] This order produced mixed results. While III Corps managed to cross the Marne and move up into line with II Corps on its right, Pulteney's force did not encounter any German resistance in the process. For Smith-Dorrien's formation, however, 10 September proved to be the most successful day of the advance. Preceded by the 3rd and 5th Cavalry Brigades, II Corps engaged the retiring Germans throughout the day, with Hamilton's 3 Division collecting over 600 prisoners and 6 field guns. Gough's cavalry captured an additional 450 prisoners. The accomplishments of II Corps clearly satisfied its commander. As Smith-Dorrien remarked optimistically in his diary: "today is the first which has made me come to the conclusion that there is real evidence of our enemy being shaken, for the roads are littered and the retreat is hurried."[39]

Haig's I Corps achieved only limited success on 10 September. At 8:30 am, the advanced guard of 2 Division attacked a column of the German First Army on its flank, taking 400 prisoners. Shortly afterward, the artillery of Bulfin's 2nd Brigade, again the advanced guard of 1 Division, opened on enemy detachments and "veritably plastered them in column of fours."[40] The advance of I Corps suffered again, however, due to poor communications between British units. At approximately 10 am, artillery units of 1 Division erroneously fired on the Royal Sussex and Loyal North Lancashire Regiments of Bulfin's Brigade as they advanced near the town of Priez. According to the 1 Division war diary, this error was the result of an absence of "any mutual system of intercommunication arranged between the infantry and the [artillery] Brigade originally detailed to support the attack."[41]

This lack of contact between the infantry and artillery brigades of 1 Division stemmed from the haphazard deployment of artillery detachments by divisional commanders. As Shelford Bidwell and Dominick Graham have noted, British divisional commanders in 1914 had no set procedures for the distribution of artillery units under their command. Many chose to maintain the four artillery brigades allotted to each infantry division under their own control, rather than assigning them to individual infantry brigades. As a result, infantry and artillery brigades within the same division often operated independently of one another, in this case with unfortunate consequences. On the morning of 10 September, the problem was compounded by the further lack of communication between divisions. Observing the guns of 1 Division firing on Bulfin's infantry, the artillery of 2 Division and 1st Cavalry Brigade opened on it as well.[42]

Monro's 2 Division suffered similar problems during the morning when the Royal Berkshire Regiment of the 6th Brigade was shelled by guns of 3 Division to the left.[49] The advanced guards of both divisions were sufficiently shaken by the experience of being bombarded by British artillery that Haig ordered a halt just before 1 pm to allow them to regroup near the town of Neuilly. The corps made little progress during the rest of the day. Its troubles continued later in the afternoon, however, as the 4th (Guards) Brigade, on the left of 2 Division, discovered that forces of 3 Division had already occupied its chosen billeting positions. Thus, the poor coordination of units within I Corps, as well as a lack of communication between I Corps, II Corps, and the Cavalry Division, prevented greater success for Haig's force on 10 September. For the entire army, the day was somewhat discouraging. According to the *Official History*, while the BEF as a whole captured nearly 1,800 prisoners on the 10th, "it was a disappointment that the enemy had not been more severely punished."[50]

The possibility of the BEF overtaking the retiring Germans diminished on the evening of 10 September. Before the distribution of GHQ's operation order for the following day, instructions arrived from Joffre directing the French Fifth and Sixth Armies and the BEF to turn to the northeast in pursuit of the enemy. Sir John French thus ordered a continuation of the advance in that direction. Despite the optimism of GHQ, this directive presaged significant problems for the BEF, especially given the lack of orchestration which had characterized the advance of the army on the 10th. Whether or not a pivot to the northeast would bring the British and French any closer to the Germans, it narrowed the British area of operations to such an extent that it was impossible to allot separate roads to each division. As a result, the advance on 11 September faltered as British staff officers struggled with the administrative challenges of funneling the army into a reduced front (see Map 3.2).[51]

On the left of the army, the advance of III Corps was plagued by problems from the beginning of the day. "Fatty" Wilson's 4 Division was forced to halt before 7 am, as it discovered that the road assigned to it by III Corps did not exist. While the advanced guard, formed by Haldane's 10th Brigade, pushed forward across the countryside, the divisional staff requested further instructions from corps headquarters regarding the route to be taken by the divisional and brigade ammunition columns. At 7:30 am, they received the unhelpful response that these units should simply follow the infantry. The 4 Division staff replied that an ammunition column "was mechanical transport and could not follow fighting troops" off main roads. Eventually the columns were redirected and ordered to rejoin the rest of the division at the end of the day.[52]

For the advancing infantry, delays continued. Shortly after 8 am, the advanced guard reported to 4 Division headquarters that it had reached another road, but had run into the rear of French transport moving northeast. While the French agreed to share their route, the advanced guard was blocked again within an hour by units of Fergusson's 5 Division, which were also using the road. To make matters worse, the advance of 5 Division itself was obstructed by Chetwode's 5th Cavalry Brigade. III Corps spent most of 11 September at the

Map 3.2
Advance of the BEF, 11–14 September 1914

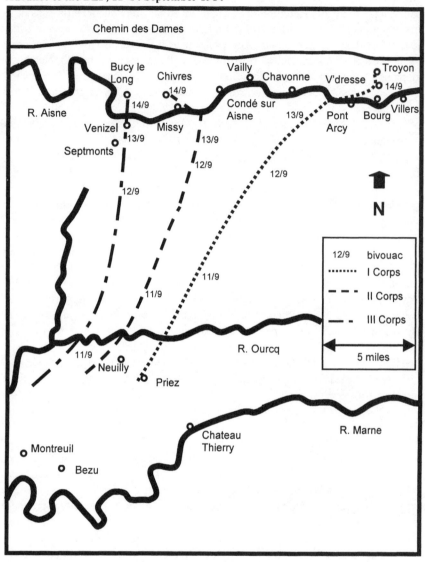

rear of this long column. Although the force finally began to move forward by mid-afternoon, its progress was hampered further by heavy rain, which rendered the roads almost impassable. For C.L. Brereton's artillery battery, the miscues of the staff continued to have repercussions into the evening, as the unit was directed to the wrong billeting area for the second night in a row.[47] Thus, while units of III Corps had reached the south bank of the Ourcq by the evening of 11 September, their sluggish advance had no impact on the retreating enemy.

I Corps encountered similar difficulties due to the narrowing of the British front. Monro's 2 Division was forced to share roads with both 3 Division on its left and 1 Division on its right. On the right of 1 Division, the French XVIII Corps impeded the advance of Bulfin's 2nd Brigade. The resulting delays, combined with the deterioration of the roads due to rain during the afternoon, hindered the progress of I Corps. According to the 2 Division war diary, Monro's force managed "a rate of ten miles in twelve hours without encountering any opposition from the enemy."[48] Only II Corps, which began the day in front of both I and III Corps, managed to advance on the 11th without obstruction from units on its flanks. Nonetheless, Smith-Dorrien's formation was forced to march behind the 3rd and 5th Cavalry Brigades on roads that turned to mud once it began raining.[49] Thus, while the weather was hardly conducive to a rapid advance, the BEF was also delayed for the second consecutive day by the uncoordinated movements of its separate components. As the British pursuit continued in a disorderly fashion, the German Army retired almost unmolested to the River Aisne.

Despite the marked lack of success of the British pursuit on 10–11 September, GHQ remained ambitious on the evening of the 11th, directing the army to seize crossings over the Aisne and occupy the high ground on the north bank of the river the next day.[50] On the 12th, however, the poor weather, combined with the cramped front on which the BEF was forced to operate, continued to cause congestion on roads leading toward the Aisne. Moreover, when advanced guards arrived at the river, they found all of the bridges in the front of the army either heavily damaged, destroyed, or guarded by enemy detachments. Consequently, the only British units even to reach the south bank of the Aisne were the leading units of III Corps and the cavalry formations covering the center and right of the army. The bulk of the BEF bivouacked well behind these advanced guards and had no contact with the enemy. The 5 Division war diary characterized 12 September as, "a pouring wet day and men under arms from 5.30am to 5.30pm with no results."[51]

As the German army consolidated its positions north of the Aisne on the night of the 12th, the pursuit effectively came to a close. While the BEF had captured over 2,000 prisoners since 8 September, its performance in this period was a disappointment to many senior officers.[52] The hesitant nature of the British advance in its initial stages, however, stemmed in part from the circumspection of these same individuals. In addition, as optimism gradually replaced trepidation in the upper ranks of the BEF and the German armies began to retire, the inexperience of British officers resulted in a lack of control and coordination between units that disrupted the advance considerably. As a result, the BEF was unable to inflict significant losses on the Germans before they reached formidable positions north of the Aisne.

THE BATTLE OF THE AISNE: 13–30 SEPTEMBER

The End of the Advance, 13–15 September

On the evening of 12 September, Sir John French and his staff remained optimistic, persisting in their plans to push across the Aisne. Since the beginning of the German retirement on the 9th, senior officers at GHQ had regained their confidence. According to C.D. Baker-Carr: "Nobody doubted but that the beginning of the end had come. The enemy had shot his bolt and we had him on the run. Even Henry Wilson, the ablest thinker in the British Army, was prophesying a German *debacle* and talking of chasing them back to the Rhine."[53] Wilson was sufficiently confident that he apparently overlooked the possibility that the enemy might make a stand on the formidable defensive positions north of the Aisne. As the sub-chief of Staff commented in his diary on 12 September: "[w]e drove the enemy over the Aisne without any trouble." Since the beginning of the German retirement, the commander-in-chief had come to share Wilson's opinion. As Sir John French stated in an optimistic wire to Lord Kitchener on the night of the 12th: "Very heavy rain falling to-night, making roads most difficult. Should much hamper enemy's retreat. Pursuit continues at daybreak."[54]

The tone of French's telegram likely stemmed in part from his desire to reassure Kitchener that he had recovered from his despondency of late August. Nevertheless, it is evident that neither the commander-in-chief nor his senior staff members anticipated serious difficulties in crossing the Aisne. The GHQ Operation Order issued on the evening of 12 September directed the army to continue the "pursuit," advancing over the Aisne and well beyond the heights above.[55] Such an order was not necessarily indicative of renewed cognitive closure at GHQ. On two occasions in August, Sir John French and his staff had adhered to conclusions regarding the situation of the army despite abundant evidence to the contrary. On 12 September, however, they had received little information suggesting a German stand on the Aisne. Nor is it likely that the confidence of the French encouraged British officers to question their assumptions. Therefore, the increasing optimism of GHQ following the German retirement on 9 September was not entirely without basis.

Nevertheless, the topography of the Aisne river valley could present serious difficulties for the BEF if the Germans mounted a defense north of the river. The Aisne itself was entirely unfordable, and all of the bridges in the British front were guarded by the enemy, heavily damaged, or destroyed. The river valley was one to two miles in width, with little cover to conceal the movement of troops. On either side, steep slopes rose up to 300 feet to heights above. In order to cross the Aisne, British units had to traverse the river valley, in which they were vulnerable to German fire. The British artillery, located on the heights south of the valley, was unable to neutralize German guns due to the difficulty of locating the enemy positions on the heights to the north.[56] Consequently, the infantry had to cross the river in the face of enemy infantry and artillery fire without significant support from British guns.

On the morning of 13 September, the BEF made its first attempts to continue the pursuit over the Aisne. On the left of the army, III Corps made significant progress, as Hunter-Weston's 11th Brigade moved forward under cover of darkness to take the bridge spanning the Aisne at the town of Venizel. While this enterprise secured a passage over the river, subsequent attempts to push beyond it proved unsuccessful, as units of the 11th Brigade found the enemy entrenched several hundred yards behind the crest of the ridge north of the Aisne.[57] By mid-morning, it was clear that further progress would be impossible without considerable artillery support. The efforts of British guns from positions on the heights south of the Aisne, however, caused more harm than help. On three separate occasions, between 11 am and 3 pm, the 11th Brigade complained to 4 Division headquarters that the guns of 5 Division were shelling its troops.[58] Thus, while III Corps had established positions across the Aisne by the end of the day, it was unable to progress beyond the ridge north of the river and its units remained vulnerable to enemy fire.

Smith-Dorrien's formation had even less success than III Corps. With the three bridges in its front, at Missy, Conde sur Aisne, and Vailly, all heavily damaged and guarded by German infantry, it was impossible to cross the river until late afternoon, when the 14th Brigade of 5 Division constructed a temporary pontoon bridge west of Missy. At the same time, units of 3 Division managed to reach the north bank via a plank extended over a gap in a damaged bridge at Vailly. By the end of 13 September, both divisions of II Corps held what the 3 Division war diary termed "a rather precarious position across the Aisne with two brigades."[59] Like II Corps, I Corps found the bridges in its front in German hands. Eventually, however, troopers of De Lisle's 2nd Cavalry Brigade discovered an aqueduct that enabled infantry, cavalry, and even artillery to cross the river. The rest of the Cavalry Division, the infantry and some of the guns of 1 Division crossed the Aisne and reached Vendresse on the heights north of the river during the afternoon, but they were unable to make further headway against German entrenchments.[60] Thus, all three corps held rather exposed positions north of the Aisne at the end of the day.

The situation of the BEF on the night of 13 September was difficult. Not only had the British been unable to break through enemy positions north of the Aisne, but those positions only grew stronger as reinforcements arrived during the day.[61] This intensified the tactical dilemma facing the army. It was impossible to dislodge the Germans without adequate artillery support. The topography of the Aisne river valley, however, rendered such support exceedingly hard to provide. Under such conditions, careful planning of the offensive and the coordination of artillery and infantry of separate brigades, divisions and even corps was necessary. Unfortunately for British soldiers on 14 September, the continued confidence of GHQ resulted in the disregard of such exigencies. On the night of the 13th, Sir John French and his staff were still under the impression that the German army was retiring. Thus, orders issued by GHQ for 14 September remained confident, directing that, "the Army will continue the pursuit tomorrow at six am. and act vigorously against the retreating enemy."[62]

Contrary to the notions prevalent at GHQ, the enemy was not retreating. By the morning of 14 September, the Germans were strongly entrenched in their positions, and throughout the day they made a concerted effort to force the BEF back over the Aisne. While units of II and III Corps maintained their positions north of the river, they suffered heavily from enemy artillery fire. Attempts by British guns to respond to this fire proved ineffectual. From the heights south of the Aisne, or in exposed positions in the river valley itself, the artillery was unable to locate the German guns on the heights to the north. Consequently, the infantry of both corps remained pinned down by German fire throughout the day.[63] On the right of the British line, I Corps made limited headway. By placing guns forward with the infantry, Samuel Lomax, the commander of 1 Division, was able to increase the potency of his artillery. As a result, 1 Division advanced later in the morning, passing over the Chemin des Dames, a road running parallel to the river on top of the heights. During the afternoon, strong German counterattacks pushed the British back, inflicting heavy losses in the process. When these attacks subsided, Haig ordered the entire corps to push forward at 6:30 pm. By this time, however, the force had suffered over 3,300 casualties, including 160 officers, and had no remaining reserves. The attack thus made little progress, and the troops returned to the positions they had held during the afternoon, just below the crest of the heights.[64]

The heavy British casualties on 14 September were finally sufficient to shake the optimism of Sir John French and his staff. Rather than ordering the army to advance aggressively, as it had since the crossing of the Marne, GHQ directed the corps commanders to act the next morning according to instructions conveyed personally by the commander-in-chief. Although he was in the process of realizing that the enemy was no longer in retreat, Sir John French had not abandoned entirely the hope of advancing further. As he related in his diary: "I think it very likely that the enemy is making a determined stand, but to-morrow will show."[65] Thus, while French instructed Pulteney and Haig to consolidate their positions on the 15th, he directed Smith-Dorrien to continue the attack. Against German positions that had been strengthened overnight by both wire and additional troops, the efforts of II Corps stood little chance of success. Attempting to take the heights above the Aisne with the same ineffective artillery support that had prevailed on previous days, Fergusson's 5 Division made little headway on the morning of 15 September. By early afternoon, its efforts were terminated.[66]

The utter lack of progress of 5 Division throughout 15 September, combined with the intensity of German shelling of the entire army, was enough to convince Sir John French that the German retirement was in fact over. As he wired Kitchener that evening: "we have been opposed not merely by rearguards but by considerable forces of the enemy which are making a determined stand in a position splendidly adapted to defence." The commander-in-chief's subsequent orders reflected this realization, as he impressed upon all units "the absolute importance of effective entrenchments." At 8:30 pm, Operation Order No. 26 finally brought the advance to a close, stating: "The Commander-in-Chief wishes the line now held by the Army to be strongly entrenched, and it is his intention to assume the general offensive at the first opportunity."[67]

As Edmonds observed in the *Official History*, this directive "proved to be the official notification of the commencement of trench warfare."[68] With no further orders emanating from GHQ following the distribution of nearly identical instructions the next evening, British units spent the balance of September holding the same tenuous positions along the Aisne. As an account prepared by 2 Division for I Corps headquarters related of the period following 15 September: "The following days were all much alike. Periods of heavy shell fire directed now on one part of our line and now on another, and often against nothing in particular; hostile infantry attacks, usually very local in character, heavy rifle fire during the night, have been the normal occurrences."[69] This account is representative of the experiences of all three corps in this period. For the rest of September, the BEF endured daily artillery bombardments, as well as sporadic infantry attacks. Only in the last three days of the month did the pressure subside.[70] As the stalemate continued into late September, British commanders resolved to transfer the BEF to the left of the allied line. On the afternoon of 1 October, GHQ directed the army to move north to Flanders, ordering the three corps to withdraw in succession, with II Corps beginning the next morning.[71]

The Mounting Costs of the Campaign

German initiatives in the second half of September were wholly unsuccessful in driving British units back over the Aisne. Nevertheless, enemy attacks in this period exacted a significant material and human toll on an army that had already suffered heavily during the first month of active operations. Even by mid-September, the BEF faced shortages of a variety of essential provisions and equipment, including food, clothing, field kitchens, and entrenching tools.[72] While the stalemate at the Aisne enabled the supply services to begin replenishing these items, operations in the second half of September depleted British ammunition supplies to critical levels. On the 17th, Sir John French informed the War Office that the BEF had supplies of only 270 rounds for each of its howitzers, and 180 for each field gun. Nor were plentiful supplies awaiting shipment in England. On 20 September the War Office replied tersely: "On 22nd September, 100 rounds per 60pr [field] gun will be sent you, 100 rounds per gun on 29th September, 100 rounds per gun on 6th October. There will be difficulty in maintaining supplies at this rate after this."[73]

This disbursement of ammunition was woefully insufficient, especially given the profligate expenditure of German artillery. Even when the severity of German bombardments relented in early October, E.S. Bulfin estimated that each gun firing on his 2nd Brigade shot an average of twenty shells per day. In order to mount a reply to the German fire, British batteries were forced to exceed their daily quota of shells, which led to the further reduction of that quota on subsequent days. As a result, by the beginning of October, Bulfin's guns were restricted to a meager daily allowance of two and a half rounds.[74]

Operations on the Aisne also inflicted heavy casualties on the BEF. I Corps, which bore the brunt of the fighting in the final stages of the offensive, suffered losses of nearly 350 officers and more than 6,500 other ranks between 13 September and the end of the month. Bulfin's 2nd Brigade reported 1,581 casualties in September, over 25 percent of its fighting strength.[75] Although neither II Corps nor III Corps endured the same level of punishment, they too were subjected to incessant German artillery fire. During the period 12–26 September, II Corps reported casualties of 136 officers and 3,075 other ranks. Combined with losses sustained earlier in the campaign, operations on the Aisne left the BEF significantly depleted. Between the beginning of the war and the end of September, Smith-Dorrien's corps had suffered casualties in the range of 520 officers and 12,900 other ranks.[76] In the same period, Haig's I Corps had lost approximately 470 officers and 9,500 other ranks.[77] Casualty totals for III Corps and the cavalry divisions are more difficult to determine. A conservative estimate suggests, however, that Pulteney's force had lost over 240 officers and 5,100 other ranks, while the casualties to the British cavalry amounted to at least 50 officers and 500 other ranks.[78] Thus, by the end of September, the BEF had sustained losses amounting to at least 1,280 officers and 26,500 other ranks, over 25 percent of its initial strength.

This damage was not entirely irreparable. Broadly defined, casualties encompass a wide range of afflictions including minor injuries and ailments. It is therefore likely that a significant proportion of these figures represent soldiers who were able to return to active service within a fairly short period of time. Moreover, at this stage of the war there remained a supply of trained reservists available to replace those troops killed or seriously wounded. Since the end of the retreat, the ranks of II Corps had in fact been replenished by successive drafts of reinforcements. These drafts had been arriving, however, at an unsustainable rate. According to the *Official History*, within a month of the battle of Mons: "the supply of Regular reservists for many regiments had been exhausted, and...men of the Special Reserve—the militia of old days—were beginning to take their place."[79] Even these reserves were insufficient to counteract the steadily mounting losses on the Aisne. The cumulative effect of casualties on the army is evident in the decision made in mid-September to disperse the newly arrived 6 Division, under Major-General J.L. Kier, to relieve depleted British formations. While officers at GHQ initially debated where to place Kier's division in the British line, the condition of the original units of the BEF dictated its use as reinforcements.[80]

Of even greater concern than the overall rate of casualties was the dwindling supply of experienced officers. The leadership of officers at the regimental level had played a vital role in maintaining the cohesion of the BEF during the first month of the war. Given that junior officers often led by example on the battlefield, it is hardly surprising that they suffered heavy losses during this period. These casualties, however, were not easily replaced. Not only was there a shortage of trained officers in England to serve as replacements, but those reinforcements that began to arrive following the retreat were not of the same caliber as their predecessors. The superior effectiveness of the original contingent of officers in the BEF stemmed from two factors. First, their leadership skills had been acquired through years of service, both at home and abroad. Such experience could not be simulated during a brief training period in England. In November 1914, the chief staff officer of 3 Division, Frederick Maurice, compared these seasoned officers to their replacements, commenting: "A few of them are worth dozens of the Sandhurst boys who have to be shoved straight into the firing line, before they can get their legs."[81]

Second, over the course of their careers, the original officers of the BEF had become familiar to the other ranks in their battalions. This undoubtedly strengthened the contractual relationship between officers and their subordinates at the beginning of the First World War. Replacement officers likely joined the BEF in the fall of 1914 with a clear conception of their paternalistic responsibilities to these subordinates. As unfamiliar faces in their battalions, however, they could not immediately recreate the bond that had existed between their predecessors and the other ranks. It therefore proved difficult to reestablish the effectiveness of British units with replacement officers, particularly those with little combat experience and no familiarity with the troops they were assigned to lead. On 13 September, Sir John French outlined the problem in a wire to Lord Kitchener requesting further reinforcements. As he explained:

Unless experienced officers are sent in sufficient numbers at once, the whole course of the campaign may be affected and services of officers retained in England never be required. The essential requirement is in point of quality rather than quantity if we are to press our present advantages. The best and most experienced officers must be sent at once. Some of the officers sent out to me are really useless. Nothing but the best will do.[82]

Thus, notwithstanding the optimism of senior British officers, the BEF was unable to dislodge the German Army from its formidable positions above the Aisne. As a result, British units were subjected to repeated attacks throughout the second half of September. By the end of the month, the BEF faced serious shortages of ammunition and officers.

CONFRONTING TRENCH WARFARE: OFFICERS' RESPONSE TO STALEMATE ON THE AISNE

Tactical Solutions and Stopgaps

Despite continuing casualties, the stalemate on the Aisne allowed British soldiers to adjust to the unprecedented scale and intensity of the 1914 campaign.

With their planning responsibilities reduced by the lull in mobile operations, commanders and staff officers had an opportunity to consider their experiences of the previous month and devise more efficient methods of conducting the war. While the diaries and correspondence of senior officers in this period contain independent reflection regarding the nature of the conflict, analysis was also encouraged by GHQ. On 24 September, Henry Wilson requested "instructions" from the staffs of all three corps for the benefit of newly arriving formations, based on experience gained in the initial stages of the war.[83] In response, each corps submitted a detailed report in late September or early October.

The overriding theme in the reports of all three corps, as well as in other recorded observations of British officers, was the dominance of artillery during the 1914 campaign. In light of this recognition, the reports emphasized the necessity of defensive measures to counter the effects of enemy artillery. Foremost among these were well-prepared entrenchments for infantry, sited behind the crest of hills or ridges to protect them from direct fire from enemy guns. Entrenchments in 1914 certainly did not rival the sophistication of the British trench system that developed in subsequent years. Neither, however, were they simply shallow depressions designed only to provide temporary cover before the next advance. The reports directed the preparation of front-line trenches with regular traverses, obstacles such as wire in front, rudimentary drainage systems, and communication trenches linking them to rear areas. They also recognized the importance of protecting British guns, suggesting the concealment of artillery positions from enemy aircraft.[84]

British officers also recommended and implemented measures to increase the effectiveness of their own artillery. During the advance, a lack of coordination between infantry and artillery had hindered the operations of the BEF. This problem was exacerbated by the impossibility of direct fire, as the dominance of German artillery on the Aisne had forced British guns to operate out of sight of the infantry. Cooperation thus required an efficient communications system between front-line infantry units and the artillery positions behind them. Yet at the beginning of the war, messages were conveyed from infantry positions to the artillery via a complicated route through the headquarters of infantry brigades and even divisions. As a result, the information that reached the gunners was often neither timely nor accurate.[85] In the absence of a direct link to the front, the only alternative to this system was direct observation by the gunners themselves. Even when visual contact was possible, however, it proved difficult for them to differentiate friend from foe.

British officers recognized this problem, and advocated techniques that enhanced coordination of the two arms, as well as improving the indirect fire of the artillery. Both of these ends were furthered by the use of forward observation posts in the front lines. Connected to their batteries by telephone, artillery officers in these positions could direct the fire of their batteries onto enemy trenches and guns, and prevent the inadvertent shelling of British troops. In practice, this means of controlling fire was far from perfect. As Paddy Griffith has remarked, observation posts, "were often entirely non-existent, or manned intermittently by relatively junior officers, who could see little of what was going on and who enjoyed only very flimsy communications with their parent battery."[86]

Despite these limitations, British staff officers deemed observation posts equipped with telephones to be an effective method of directing fire in conjunction with the tactical needs of the infantry. The posts also served to make a particular section of the front the responsibility of each battery. This practice, combined with the policy of designating "zones" of enemy territory to the guns of each division, imposed some order on the fire of the artillery where none had prevailed during the advance. The allocation of artillery zones apparently began following the end of the British offensive. On 13 September, when guns of 5 Division repeatedly shelled infantry units of the adjacent 4 Division north of the Aisne, neither divisional nor corps war diaries contain any reference to the existence of separate artillery zones. On the 22nd, however, 5 Division requested permission to shell an enemy position in the zone of 4 Division.[87] By limiting the fire of the guns of each division to a particular zone, and by tying each battery within the divisional artillery to a specific frontage within that zone through a communications link, many of the mishaps of the advance were prevented.

The most revolutionary method of increasing the effectiveness of British artillery fire in 1914 was by aerial observation, a practice used by the Germans since the battle of Mons. The British Army had experimented with the technique prior to the war, but failed to develop it in the absence of any manifest necessity for its use.[88] It was only when the terrain of the Aisne river valley rendered the British unable to locate German gun positions that senior officers began to explore seriously the potential of aerial observation. The BEF apparently first attempted it during active operations on 15 September, when Pulteney's III Corps assigned aircraft to the divisional heavy and howitzer batteries. The technique caught on relatively quickly. On 26 September, 3 Division reported to II Corps headquarters that a pilot equipped with wireless had facilitated hits on several previously hidden German positions. By early October, the following procedure, described by the staff of I Corps, prevailed throughout the BEF: "The hostile batteries are first located as accurately as possible by aeroplane; these results are then communicated to divisions and an hour at which fire is to be opened is fixed. At that hour the aeroplane again goes up, observes the fire, and signals any necessary corrections by wireless."[89] While the superiority of German positions and ammunition supplies remained, aerial observation allowed the BEF to improve the effectiveness of its artillery.

Clearly, British officers quickly embraced new tactics and technology in September 1914. They did not deem these innovations to be a sufficient response, however, to the unprecedented scale and intensity of the conflict. Measures such as well-sited trenches and concealed artillery positions certainly allowed a margin of physical safety for British soldiers. In addition, improved methods of artillery spotting provided a more effective means of countering enemy guns. Nonetheless, officers also recognized that these measures did not remove the risk to soldiers on the Aisne, particularly in light of the destructive power of enemy weapons. Thus, commanders and staff officers also placed heavy emphasis on traditional martial virtues such as morale, discipline, and personal bravery. Certainly, the preservation of morale and discipline is essential to any army, and it would be surprising if British officers had not encouraged it. The way in which they did, however, held the potential to diminish the value of the tactical innovations they introduced in September 1914. Senior officers maintained, for example, that significant losses could actually enhance British morale while eroding that of the enemy. The 1 Division War Diary contains considerable praise for the South Wales Borderers and the Welsh Regiment of the 3rd Brigade, who suffered heavily while holding trenches above the Aisne between 14 and 21 September. As the diary states:

The moral effect of maintaining them so long was good for our men and must have impressed the enemy with the temerity and hardihood of our troops. Heavily shelled every day, in spite of their entrenchments suffering losses continually, the Welsh and SWB maintained their positions with utmost confidence and were always ready for night enterprise as a welcome change from the day's inactivity.[90]

This feat may indeed have impressed the enemy. It is debatable, however, whether enduring eight consecutive days of enemy fire for no tangible purpose bolstered the morale of the two battalions in question. Nevertheless, the 1 Division staff deemed the moral importance of the feat to outweigh any losses suffered in the process. In contrast to the Welsh and South Wales Borderers, troops who were unable to maintain their positions under fire were treated with disdain. During an inquiry into the temporary evacuation of trenches by the West Yorkshire Regiment on 20 September, Sir Douglas Haig commented scornfully: "I find it difficult to write in temperate language regarding the very unsoldierlike behaviour of the W. Yorks on the 20th....It rests with them to regain the good name and reputation which our infantry holds, and which they have by their conduct on the 20th forfeited."[91]

Such failures of courage were perceived to stem from a loss of morale, a result of prolonged periods on the defensive. As the II Corps staff observed: "It has been found that during a retirement, or during the occupation of a defensive position, the morale of officers and men is apt to deteriorate to an alarming degree unless drastic steps are taken to counteract this tendency." Given that soldiers were much safer in defensive positions than while attacking, it is not abundantly clear why their morale should have diminished when they were not on the offensive. Nonetheless, British officers clearly believed that the failure to attack had negative psychological effects on the other ranks. The immediate antidote to this problem was strict discipline. Even more effective were measures designed to maintain the "offensive spirit" of the troops. As the II Corps report continued: "The best preventative is probably to insist on small local attacks and enterprises, even with the knowledge that they must entail loss of men on missions of minor importance."[92] Trench raids, a practice that prevailed throughout the war, seem to have emerged on the Aisne with this intent. On 4

October, Sir Douglas Haig gave the following description of one such undertaking by the 1/Coldstream Guards of 1 Division:

A single sentry was found in the first trench, where he was bayonetted before he could give warning. A second trench was found to be lightly held and all its occupants dealt with. A little further on was a third trench, and here a sharp fight occurred in which the Coldstream Guards had a few casualties. Having effected their object, they made their way back to their own lines, after having shot or bayonetted at least 20 of the enemy; our casualties were one officer and seven men wounded, two men missing or killed. This shewed a fine soldierly spirit.[93]

Absent from Haig's detailed account is any definition of the purpose of the foray, beyond causing limited casualties to the enemy in an effort to sustain an aggressive "soldierly spirit." Throughout the war, trench raids proved useful in determining the strength and identity of enemy forces opposite the British. In the autumn of 1914, however, they were apparently employed simply as a means of preserving morale during prolonged periods on the defensive. George Barrow, Sir Edmund Allenby's chief of staff in 1914, suggested in his memoirs that such initiatives were not successful in achieving their intended purpose. As he related:

In the matter or raids...the Higher Command showed too little understanding of the nature of the British soldier. Raids for specific purposes: "to destroy a mine-head or mortar or other weapon which is causing trouble, or to obtain information or identification which cannot be secured otherwise" (to quote from our Field Service Regulations) were often necessary, but the Higher Command were not content with this range and urged raids to be undertaken for the purpose of maintaining the offensive spirit of our men.[94]

It is difficult to determine with any precision the actual impact of trench raids on the morale of British soldiers in this period. Nonetheless, it is sufficient to note that even at the risk of considerable casualties, officers encouraged such initiatives as a means of maintaining morale and discipline among the soldiers in the face of superior German fire-power. Thus, while British officers introduced tactical innovations that undoubtedly enhanced the effectiveness of the BEF, they continued to emphasize values and concepts that did not always prove beneficial to British soldiers holding positions on the Aisne.

Promotions and Removals

The attachment of British officers to such values also influenced the promotion and removal of commanders in September 1914. Despite the dispersal of the British Cavalry Division during the retreat, as well as the impact of modern firepower on the Aisne, senior officers continued to hold the independence of action associated with the cavalry spirit in high regard. No officer benefited from this fondness for the cavalry spirit more than Hubert Gough. Even after his desertion of Allenby during the retreat, Sir John French awarded Gough command of 2 Cavalry Division in mid-September.[95] This promotion was likely a reflection of Hubert Gough's connections with French and Sir Douglas Haig. Nevertheless, he was not the only cavalry officer to be rewarded for his independent initiatives. Henry De Lisle had also operated without reference to his commander for an extended period during the retreat. Moreover, he subsequently incurred his commander's wrath on 13 September when he crossed the Aisne without consulting Allenby. Not only did De Lisle keep his command of the 2nd Cavalry Brigade, however, but he succeeded Allenby at the head of 1 Cavalry Division when the latter took command of the newly formed Cavalry Corps in October 1914.[96]

Among infantry commanders, senior British officers showed a clear preference for individuals who displayed personal bravery under fire and a stoic acceptance of losses suffered by their formations. No British infantry commander in 1914 exhibited these qualities to a greater extent than Edward Bulfin, commander of the 2nd Brigade in S.H. Lomax's 1 Division. On the Aisne, Bulfin's brigade had spearheaded the advance of I Corps in the final stages of the offensive. It then bore the brunt of German attacks during the ensuing stalemate until it was relieved by Walter Congreve's 18th Brigade on 19 September. Throughout this period, Bulfin displayed a grim determination in the face of heavy losses. According to John Charteris, a member of Haig's I Corps staff: "Bulfin was really almost peevish when he was told that his brigade was to be pulled out for a short rest and replied 'We never asked to be taken out—we can hang on here quite well.' "[97]

Bulfin's steadfastness on the Aisne impressed his superiors. Sir Douglas Haig's diary, generally a source of criticisms of other officers, contains a description of Bulfin as "a tower of strength," and "one of my stoutest hearted brigadiers." In late October, Sir John French recommended Bulfin, along with Aylmer Haldane and Aylmer Hunter-Weston, for promotion to Major-General for distinguished conduct in the field. As French informed Lord Kitchener: "these officers have never once failed in the most trying circumstances, and have done great service for their country."[98] In II Corps, Smith-Dorrien praised courageous behavior among his own brigadiers. As he described Count Gleichen, commanding the 15th Brigade: "He is quite undisturbed by the heaviest shell fire and most alarming situations, and is a most efficient Brigadier."[99]

Officers perceived to be deficient in courage, tenacity, and stoicism did not fare so well in 1914, regardless of their other attributes. This is evident in an examination of the career of Ivor Maxse, commander of the 1st (Guards) Brigade at the beginning of the war. Maxse later attained prominence commanding 18 Division at the Somme, and XVIII Corps during 1917 and 1918. Paddy Griffith has characterized him as one of the "undoubted elite" of British commanders during the war.[100] Despite his subsequent repute, however, Maxse's performance in 1914 was distinctly mediocre in the eyes of other officers. After losing his rearguard battalion on 27 August, Maxse proved cautious during the rest of the retreat and tentative during the advance to the Aisne. This trepidation incurred the scorn of his superiors. On 6 September, Haig commented in his diary that Maxse "seemed to have lost his fighting spirit which used to be so noticeable at Aldershot in peace time!" Maxse's command of the 1st (Guards) Brigade ended under rather unusual circumstances in mid-September. Upon his promotion to major-general, Sir John French promptly sent him back to England to command the newly formed 18 Division, recommending him to Lord Kitchener as "an excellent trainer of troops."[101]

At first glance, Maxse's reassignment appears entirely legitimate and even astute. As a major-general, he was entitled to command a division. Sir John French was also correct in his estimation of Maxse's training skills, and his decision ultimately paid dividends for the BEF. Within the context of the 1914 campaign, however, French's justification for sending Maxse back to England seems rather dubious. At this stage of the war, it would have appeared highly unlikely to the commander-in-chief that Maxse would return before the end of hostilities. In mid-September, the notion that the conflict would continue even beyond the spring of 1915 was by no means widely accepted. French himself remained optimistic that the Germans would soon be defeated.[102] The task of organizing and training 18 Division, however, took more than a year, and it only reached the front in 1916. By sending the commander of the 1st Guards Brigade home for such a purpose, Sir John French effectively indicated that he was content to do without Maxse's services for the duration of the war.

A willingness to part with an experienced commander was certainly not typical of the commander-in-chief. Given the losses suffered by the BEF throughout 1914, Sir John French proved exceedingly reluctant to sacrifice officers to command formations of the "Kitchener armies" being raised in England. Even formation commanders were in increasingly short supply by mid-September 1914. Around the time of Maxse's reassignment to 18 Division, there existed vacancies at the head of the 4th Guards Brigade and the 6th Brigade. In October, the commands of 1, 3, and 5 Divisions would also become vacant. The reasons behind this proliferation of vacancies will be discussed in subsequent chapters. For the present, it is sufficient to note that despite the dearth of experienced senior commanders in 1914, Ivor Maxse was deemed unsuitable for a command in the field.[103]

The commander of the 6th Brigade, R.H. "New Zealand" Davies, was removed under similar circumstances in September 1914. The retreat from Mons apparently took a heavy toll on Davies, a member of the New Zealand Staff Corps. As Haig related to his wife on 4 September: "little New Zealand Davies has disappointed me: the want of sleep and food has quite changed him." The I Corps commander's dissatisfaction stemmed from his subordinate's lack of resolve. In his diary, Haig characterized Davies as "very jumpy and nervous." On the recommendation of Charles Monro, commander of 2 Division, the 6th Brigade commander was removed on the 22nd. Haig nonetheless recommended Davies for a divisional command, noting in his diary: "he has many good qualities and trains and leads men well."[104]

Given that both Davies and Maxse had served under Haig prior to the war, the I Corps commander may have attempted to soften the circumstances of their removal. Neither promotions nor new appointments, however, disguised the fact that these officers had failed by the standards of their contemporaries in the autumn of 1914. Thus, traditional values and concepts continued to influence promotions and removals as well as the day-to-day operations of the BEF in this period. Qualities such as courage and tenacity under fire were beneficial to the cohesion of the army under the unprecedented weight of enemy fire that prevailed on the Aisne. By themselves, however, they did little to facilitate the adjustment of the BEF to the conditions of the 1914 campaign.

Tensions and Rivalries in the Upper Ranks of the Army

Just as traditional leadership qualities of British officers remained largely unchallenged in late September 1914, patterns of behavior that had prevailed in the upper ranks of the BEF since the beginning of the campaign persisted as well. Despite the lull in mobile operations, tensions continued to abound at GHQ as well as between the commanders of I and II Corps. Following the end of the British offensive on 15 September, GHQ enjoyed a period of relative respite after the strain of the opening weeks of the war. Temporarily relieved of most of their organizational duties, staff officers found themselves with few responsibilities for the first time in the conflict. In his account of the 1914 campaign, Charles Deedes described the daily routine at GHQ in this period as "rather monotonous." This characterization, however, was followed by a comment suggesting the continued prevalence of intrigue among senior staff officers in this period. According to Deedes:

I always think that one knows too much at a large headquarters or at the War Office, especially if one is occupying a subordinate position and unable to have very much influence over affairs. One sees too the ambitions of individuals more plainly disclosed than when one is in close contact with the enemy and one is more concerned with beating him than with making one's own career![105]

This rather cryptic remark was likely a reference to the continuing struggle between Archie Murray and Henry Wilson. During the advance to the Aisne, Wilson had struggled to assert himself over Murray and alleviate the caution of the commander-in-chief. By mid-September, he had managed to reestablish much of his influence at GHQ. At the end of the month, he was apparently able to convince the Sir John French to move the BEF to Flanders.[106] The sub-chief's renewed ascendancy at GHQ was not a wholly negative development. Wilson was responsible for useful initiatives such as the compilation of tactical notes by the corps staffs during late September. Nevertheless, his distortion of the chain of command at GHQ once again left senior officers prone to cognitive closure as the BEF resumed the offensive. As the army attempted to advance into Flanders, the dominance of the optimistic Wilson would have adverse effects on the operations of the army.

Outside of GHQ, friction prevailed between the commanders of I and II Corps. Tensions between Haig and Smith-Dorrien flared in mid-September, as the BEF encountered strong German positions north of the Aisne. On the 15th, the I Corps commander complained to Sir John French of the failure of the 3 Division artillery to support 2 Division the previous day. According to Haig, the artillery brigade in question arrived around midday north of the river near Pont Arcy, where I Corps had erected a pontoon bridge. After a member of Haig's staff requested that it support the hard-pressed 2 Division, the brigade had simply crossed the bridge and "retired from the scene of the action." As Haig continued: "In the interest of the Army, the reason why this body of Artillery failed to co-operate at a critical moment should be ascertained."[107]

A subsequent investigation initiated by Smith-Dorrien revealed Haig's claims to be groundless. While the artillery brigade had indeed retired, it had done so in order to find suitable positions south of the river from which it could support 2 Division. This entailed some delay. According to the II Corps commander, the brigade was impeded further by the fact that it was shelled heavily as it crossed the bridge at Pont Arcy. Smith-Dorrien's account is corroborated by the diary of J.L. Mowbray, who witnessed a discussion in which the commander of the 3 Division artillery brigade, "promised help" to officers of 2 Division. Mowbray was also present when the brigade suffered a direct hit as it attempted to cross the bridge.[108] Thus, despite Haig's accusations, the artillery of II Corps did in fact attempt to assist 2 Division and suffered considerably in doing so.

Rather than a deliberate distortion of the events of the 14th, Haig's account may have simply reflected his own incomplete understanding of the situation. The fact that he brought the situation to the attention of GHQ, however, suggests a desire on his part to undermine Smith-Dorrien's standing with Sir John French. Evidently, this was not standard procedure for addressing misunderstandings between commanders, and it did little to improve Haig's relations with the II Corps commander. As Smith-Dorrien informed GHQ rather bitterly: "I am sorry the GOC 1st Corps is adopting the policy of reporting what he considers my failures to support him through the Field Marshal, but I shall not alter my own policy, which is to inform him direct of any action of his troops which appear to me should be known by the Corps Commander."[109]

Haig also used his personal diary to undermine his rival. Given that he sent a copy to the king, the I Corps commander could effectively portray himself to George V as the most competent senior commander in the BEF by documenting Smith-Dorrien's apparent shortcomings. Haig attempted to do this in early October when he took over Smith-Dorrien's front following the departure of II Corps to Flanders. Upon learning that a bridge over the Aisne in this area remained in enemy hands, he remarked indignantly in his diary: "the action of the 2nd Corps and particularly of the 3rd Division (H. Hamilton) on 13th September, will want a lot of explaining!" Haig expressed further disapproval after discovering several bodies of British soldiers left unrecovered after being shot by Germans guarding the bridge. Careful to identify the culprits as troops of II Corps, he commented: "I cannot think how our troops (3rd Divn) could have allowed these men to remain so many weeks so close to our front, unburied."[110]

Like Haig's earlier charge, these criticisms appear to be unfounded. On 16 September, GHQ had ordered Smith-Dorrien specifically not to attack the bridge at Condé, owing to the strength with which it was held.[111] With regard to the bodies that Hamilton's division apparently treated with such indifference, the same Germans who had shot them from the bridge would likely have prevented them from being recovered. Despite their lack of credibility, such comments and accusations received an uninterrupted audience with the king in 1914. While Smith-Dorrien also sent a copy of his diary to George V, his account of the campaign is largely free of criticisms of other officers. Nor was Smith-Dorrien aware of the condemnations which Haig included in his own diary. Consequently, from the king's perspective, the I Corps commander's criticisms went unchallenged. It is therefore likely that George V accepted at least some of them as valid. In this way, Haig's diary served as a tool to advance his career at the expense of Sir Horace Smith-Dorrien.

In addition, by drawing the failings of II Corps to the attention of Sir John French, Haig took advantage of the commander-in-chief's dislike of Smith-Dorrien. Despite their inaccuracy, Haig's accusations may have fuelled Sir John French's desire to replace the II Corps commander. In light of French's existing antipathy toward Smith-Dorrien, and the II Corps commander's disregard of orders at Le Cateau, the commander-in-chief had probably entertained the idea of removing him before the Battle of the Aisne. Haig's allegations provided Sir John French with additional evidence to support such an initiative. Concern for his own tenuous relationship with Smith-Dorrien's patron, Lord Kitchener, probably discouraged French from attempting to oust the II Corps commander in this period. Nevertheless, Haig's criticisms of his rival during the Battle of the Aisne likely enhanced Sir John French's desire to remove Smith-Dorrien from the BEF.

While the I Corps commander used his handwritten diary as a means of enhancing his own career prospects, an examination of the typescript copy of his diary suggests that Haig also retained a more general concern for his reputation long after 1914. To this version of the diary, Haig added comments that attempted to link a retirement by 3 Division on 14 September to Smith-Dorrien's decision to fight at Le Cateau. Commenting on the withdrawal, Haig remarked: "It was impossible to rely now on some of the regiments of the 3rd Divn which had been so severely handled at Mons and Le Cateau." In parentheses, he added: "We had every reason to regret now the ill-considered decision of the 2nd Corps commander to give battle at Le Cateau."[112]

This assessment is hardly convincing. Even if 3 Division had lost heavily during the retreat, Smith-Dorrien's decision to fight at Le Cateau had proven to be correct, and was recognized as such by most British officers in 1914.[113] It is impossible to determine when this addition was made to the original text of the diary. The extent of Haig's alterations, however, suggests that they were not carried out until after the war. Thus, it can be assumed that this criticism of Smith-Dorrien's stand at Le Cateau was not part of the I Corps commander's attempt to further his career in 1914. Rather, the comment appears to reflect a more general concern for his reputation as a commander. Given the renown attained by Smith-Dorrien for his stand at Le Cateau, and the conspicuous absence of I Corps at this crucial engagement, Haig was undoubtedly uncomfortable regarding his role during this episode of the 1914 campaign. Consequently, he attempted to disparage Smith-Dorrien's decision to fight at Le Cateau in the final version of his diary in order to detract from his own failings in this period.

Haig's alterations to the typescript copy of his diary obviously had no impact on relations between himself and Smith-Dorrien in September 1914. Nonetheless, by unraveling Haig's motives in preparing both versions of his diary, it is possible to gain further insights into the mindset of the I Corps commander and his relationships with other officers in 1914. While modifications to the typescript version appear to indicate a general concern for his reputation, the contents of the original version suggest that Haig used his diary in 1914 as a means of depicting himself as a superior commander to Smith-Dorrien. Moreover, Haig's complaints to GHQ regarding the behavior of units of II Corps provide further evidence of his desire to undermine Smith-Dorrien's already shaky relationship with Sir John French. It is difficult to determine the impact of these efforts in 1914. Significantly, however, tensions between French and Smith-Dorrien would have adverse effects on the operations of II Corps during the First Battle of Ypres.

CONCLUSION

The end of the retreat from Mons boosted the morale of British soldiers. In the upper ranks of the BEF, however, senior officers proved slow to recover from the crises of late August. Consequently, officers at GHQ as well as formation commanders directed the British counteroffensive hesitantly in its initial stages. While caution in the upper ranks of the army began to dissipate by 8 September, the inexperience of British staff officers hindered the progress of the BEF, even after the German Army began retreating. Not only did GHQ do little to direct the operations of infantry and cavalry units, but corps and divisional staffs often failed to coordinate units within their respective formations. As a result, the advance was impeded by interference between units as well as friendly fire, and the BEF was unable to disrupt the orderly retirement of German forces before they crossed the Aisne.

By 12 September, senior officers had regained their collective confidence, ordering the continuation of the pursuit on subsequent days. Given the strength of German positions north of the Aisne, however, the buoyant mood at GHQ proved costly. The British artillery depleted its ammunition supplies in attempting to match the considerable expenditure of German guns. Moreover, British units lost heavily in the aggressive attacks ordered from 13 to 15

September and continued to suffer casualties as they held vulnerable positions along the river in the second half of September. By the end of the month, the army faced a growing shortage of experienced junior officers.

The lull in offensive operations after 15 September allowed British officers an opportunity to respond to the unprecedented nature of the 1914 campaign and address these growing human and materiel shortages. While they introduced a variety of tactical innovations that improved the effectiveness of the army, officers also emphasized concepts which held the potential to diminish the value of these innovations. Certainly, qualities such as courage and tenacity under fire proved valuable to the BEF as it endured enemy fire along the Aisne. They were not necessarily conducive, however, to the reduction of casualties. Just as the doubled-edged traits discussed in Chapter 1 persisted in this period, so too did rivalries in the upper ranks of the BEF, particularly at GHQ and between Sir Douglas Haig and Sir Horace Smith-Dorrien.

These tendencies augured poorly for the weakened BEF as it prepared to move to the left of the allied line. The courage and tenacity of British commanders under fire would prove pivotal during October 1914. Without moderation, however, such qualities could also result in excessive casualties to soldiers and their commanders. Continued rivalries in the upper ranks of the army also had dangerous implications. At GHQ, Henry Wilson's dominance left Sir John French and his staff prone to cognitive closure. In addition, tensions between senior commanders threatened to undermine cooperation between formations. Thus, despite the relative respite provided by the advance and subsequent stalemate on the Aisne, the "hybrid" officers of the BEF continued to encounter difficulties adjusting to the necessities of the 1914 campaign.

NOTES

1. John Terraine, *Mons: The Retreat to Victory*, 2d ed. (London: Leo Cooper, 1991), 215.

2. Robert Asprey, *The First Battle of the Marne* (New York: Lippincott, 1962), 151.

3. Georges Blond, *The Marne*, trans. H. Eaton Hart (London: Macdonald, 1965), 229.

4. James Edmonds, *Military Operations: France and Belgium, 1914, vol. 2* (London: Macmillan, 1925), 296–297, 312; "Talk With A.H. Burne re the Marne, 1914," 11/1934/38, Liddell Hart Papers, Liddell Hart Centre for Military Archives, King's College, London (LHCMA).

5. French to Kitchener, 6 September 1914, WO 33/713, Public Record Office, Kew (PRO).

6. "Peter Liddle interview with Sir James Marshall-Cornwall," May 1974, Papers of Sir James Marshall-Cornwall, Liddle Collection, Brotherton Library, University of Leeds.

7. 5 Division War Diary, 6 September 1914, WO 95/1510, PRO; See also J.M. Craster, ed., *'Fifteen Rounds a Minute': The Grenadiers at War, August to December 1914* (London: Macmillan, 1976), 69; E.S. Bulfin Diary, 6 September 1914, CAB

45/140, PRO; Mowbray Diary, 6 September 1914, Major J.L. Mowbray Papers, Imperial War Museum, London (IWM).

8. Henry Wilson Diary, 4–7 September 1914, Henry Wilson Papers, IWM.

9. Richard Holmes, *The Little Field-Marshal: Sir John French* (London: Jonathan Cape, 1981), 239.

10. Kitchener to French, 5 September 1914, WO 33/713, PRO.

11. French to Kitchener, 6 September 1914, WO 33/713, PRO.

12. GHQ Operation Order No. 17, 5 September 1914, GHQ War Diary, WO 95/1, PRO.

13. 5 Division War Diary, 6 September 1914, WO 95/1510, PRO; See also J.M. Craster, ed., *'Fifteen Rounds a Minute': The Grenadiers at War, August to December 1914* (London: Macmillan, 1976), 69; E.S. Bulfin Diary, 6 September 1914, CAB 45/140, PRO; Mowbray Diary, 6 September 1914, Major J.L. Mowbray Papers, Imperial War Museum, London (IWM).

14. Henry Wilson Diary, 4–7 September 1914, Henry Wilson Papers, IWM.

15. Richard Holmes, *The Little Field-Marshal: Sir John French* (London: Jonathan Cape, 1981), 239.

16. Kitchener to French, 5 September 1914, WO 33/713, PRO.

17. French to Kitchener, 6 September 1914, WO 33/713, PRO.

18. GHQ Operation Order No. 17, 5 September 1914, GHQ War Diary, WO 95/1, PRO.

19. 1 Division War Diary, 6 September 1914, WO 95/1227, PRO; Haig Diary, 6 September 1914, Haig Papers, NLS; WO 256/1, PRO.

20. Haig Diary, 6 September 1914, NLS, WO 256/1, PRO; 1 Division War Diary, 6 September 1914, WO 95/1227; Bulfin Diary, 6 September 1914, CAB 45/140, PRO.

21. Smith-Dorrien Diary, 6 September 1914, CAB 45/206, PRO; Haig Diary, 6 September 1914, NLS; WO 256/1, PRO.

22. 1 Division War Diary, 7 September 1914, WO 95/1227; I Corps War Diary, 7 September 1914, WO 95/588; Smith-Dorrien Diary, 6 September 1914, CAB 45/206; 2 Division War Diary, 6 September 1914, WO 95/1283, PRO.

23. Haig Diary, 7 September 1914, NLS; WO 256/1, PRO; 1 Division War Diary, 7 September 1914, WO 95/1227; 2 Division War Diary, 7 September 1914, WO 95/1283; 4 Division War Diary, WO 95/1439; 5 Division War Diary, WO 95/1510, PRO.

24. Edmonds, Military Operations: France and Belgium, 1914, 343.

25. French to Kitchener, 7 September 1914, WO 33/713; GHQ War Diary, 7 September 1914, WO 95/1, PRO.

26. "Anonymous Account of the 1st Battalion East Lancashire Regiment, August–September 1914," Miscellaneous 154, Item 2388, IWM. See also Craster, ed., *'Fifteen Rounds a Minute,'* 69.

27. GHQ Operation Order No. 17, 5 September 1914, GHQ War Diary, WO 95/1; 2 Cavalry Division War Diary, 15 September 1914, WO 95/1117, PRO.

28. De Lisle, "My Narrative of the Great German War," De Lisle Papers, LHCMA; Cavalry Division War Diary, 6 September 1914, WO 95/1096, PRO.

29. De Lisle, "My Narrative," De Lisle Papers, LHCMA; Frederick Maurice, *Forty Days in 1914* (London: Constable, 1921),177.

30. Archibald Wavell to George Barrow, 9 July 1938, VI/I, Edmund Allenby Papers, LHCMA.

31. Frederic Coleman, *From Mons to Ypres With French: A Personal Narrative*

(Toronto: William Briggs, 1916), 95–98; De Lisle, "My Narrative," De Lisle Papers, LHCMA; Cavalry Division War Diary, 7 September 1914, WO 95/1096, PRO.

32. "The Battle of the Marne, 1914." Edmonds V/4/4/2, Edmonds Papers, LHCMA.

33. GHQ Operation Order No. 18, 7 September 1914, GHQ War Diary, WO 95/1, PRO.

34. III Corps War Diary, 8 September 1914, WO 95/672; 4 Division War Diary, 8 September 1914, WO 95/1439; 19th Infantry Brigade War Diary, 8 September 1914, WO 95/1364, PRO.

35. George Jeffreys Diary, 8 September 1914, cited in Craster, ed., 'Fifteen Rounds a Minute,' 70; 1 Division War Diary, 8 September 1914, WO 95/1227; 5 Division War Diary, 8 September 1914, WO 95/1510, PRO; Count Edward Gleichen, The Doings of the Fifteenth Infantry Brigade, August 1914 to March 1915 (London: Blackwood, 1917), 95.

36. GHQ Operation Order No. 19, 8 September 1914, GHQ War Diary, WO 95/1; French to Kitchener, 9 September 1914, 8.50am, WO 33/713, PRO.

37. Brereton Diary, 9 September 1914, C.L. Brereton Papers, IWM; 4 Division War Diary, 9 September 1914, WO 95/1439, PRO.

38. Smith-Dorrien Diary, 9 September 1914, CAB 45/206; II Corps War Diary, 9 September 1914, WO 95/629, PRO.

39. Tower to Wavell, 20 February 1931, "Action of 3rd Division, Crossing the Marne, 9th September 1914." 3 Division War Diary, WO 95/1375; II Corps War Diary, 9 September 1914, WO 95/629, PRO.

40. James Harter to Wavell, January 1931, "Action of 3rd Division, Crossing the Marne 9th September 1914." 3 Division War Diary, WO 95/1375, PRO.

41. Haig Diary, 9 September 1914, NLS; WO 256/1, PRO; 2 Division War Diary, 9 September 1914, WO 95/1283, PRO.

42. Edmonds, Military Operations: France and Belgium, 1914, 334.

43. Holger Herwig, The First World War: Germany and Austria-Hungary, 1914–1918 (New York: Arnold, 1997), 104.

44. GHQ Operation Order No. 20, 9 September 1914, 8:15 pm, GHQ War Diary, WO 95/1, PRO.

45. Smith-Dorrien Diary, 10 September 1914, CAB 45/206; II Corps War Diary, 10 September 1914, WO 95/629; 3 Division War Diary, 10 September 1914, WO 95/1375, PRO.

46. Bulfin Diary, 10 September 1914, CAB 45/140; I Corps War Diary, 10 September 1914, WO 95/588, PRO; Haig Diary, 10 September 1914, NLS; WO 256/1, PRO.

47. 1 Division War Diary, 10 September 1914, WO 95/1227, PRO; Brodie Diary, 10 September 1914, E. Craig-Brown Papers, IWM; F.A. Bolwell, With a Reservist in France (London: Routledge, 1916), 38.

48. 1 Division War Diary, 10 September 1914, WO 95/1227, PRO; Brodie Diary, 10 September 1914, Craig-Brown Papers, IWM; Bulfin Diary, 10 September 1914, CAB 45/140, PRO; J.G.W. Hyndson, From Mons to the First Battle of Ypres (London: Wyman, 1933), 41; Shelford Bidwell and Dominick Graham, Fire-Power: British Army Weapons and Theories of War, 1904–1945 (London: Allen and Unwin, 1982), 20.

49. Haig Diary, 10 September 1914, NLS; WO 256/1, PRO.

50. Edmonds, Military Operations: France and Belgium, 1914, 362; 2 Division War Diary, 10 September 1914, WO 95/1283; I Corps War Diary, 10 September 1914, WO

95/588; 1 Division War Diary, 10 September 1914, WO 95/1227, PRO.

51. Edmonds, *Military Operations: France and Belgium, 1914*, 365; GHQ Operation Order No. 21, 10 September 1914, WO 95/1, PRO.

52. 4 Division War Diary, 11 September 1914, WO 95/1227, PRO.

53. Brereton Diary, 11 September 1914, C.L. Brereton Papers, IWM; 4 Division War Diary, 11 September 1914, WO 95/1227, PRO.

54. 2 Division War Diary, 11 September 1914, WO 95/1283; Bulfin Diary, 11 September 1914, CAB 45/140; 1 Division War Diary, 11 September 1914, WO 95/1227, PRO.

55. Smith-Dorrien Diary, 11 September 1914, CAB 45/206; II Corps War Diary, 11 September 1914, WO 95/629, PRO.

56. GHQ Operation Order No. 22, 11 September 1914, GHQ War Diary, WO 95/1, PRO.

57. 5 Division War Diary, 12 September 1914, WO 95/1283; II Corps War Diary, 12 September 1914, WO 95/629; III Corps War Diary, 12 September 1914, WO 95/668, PRO.

58. See, for example, Haig Diary, 10–11 September 1914, NLS; WO 256/1, PRO; Wilson Diary, 10 September 1914, Henry Wilson Papers, IWM; Loch Diary, 10–12 September 1914, Loch Papers, IWM.

59. Brereton Diary, 11 September 1914, C.L. Brereton Papers, IWM; 4 Division War Diary, 11 September 1914, WO 95/1227, PRO.

60. 2 Division War Diary, 11 September 1914, WO 95/1283; Bulfin Diary, 11 September 1914, CAB 45/140; 1 Division War Diary, 11 September 1914, WO 95/1227, PRO.

61. Smith-Dorrien Diary, 11 September 1914, CAB 45/206; II Corps War Diary, 11 September 1914, WO 95/629, PRO.

62. GHQ Operation Order No. 22, 11 September 1914, GHQ War Diary, WO 95/1, PRO.

63. 5 Division War Diary, 12 September 1914, WO 95/1283; II Corps War Diary, 12 September 1914, WO 95/629; III Corps War Diary, 12 September 1914, WO 95/668, PRO.

64. See, for example, Haig Diary, 10–11 September 1914, NLS; WO 256/1, PRO; Wilson Diary, 10 September 1914, Henry Wilson Papers, IWM; Loch Diary, 10–12 September 1914, Loch Papers, IWM.

65. C.D. Baker-Carr, *From Chauffeur to Brigadier-General* (London: Ernest Benn, 1930), 40.

66. French to Kitchener, 12 September 1914, WO 33/713, PRO; Wilson Diary, 12 September 1914, Henry Wilson Papers, IWM.

67. GHQ Operation Order No. 23, 12 September 1914, GHQ War Diary, WO 95/1, PRO.

68. Edmonds, *Military Operations: France and Belgium, 1914*, 371; Haig Diary, 13 September 1914, NLS; WO 256/1, PRO; Loch Diary, 12–14 September 1914, Loch Papers, IWM.

69. 4 Division War Diary, 13 September 1914, WO 95/1439; Aylmer Hunter-Weston, "Account of the Action of the 11th Brigade on the night of 12th–13th September, 1914," 4 Division War Diary, WO 95/1439, PRO.

70. Brereton Diary, 13 September 1914, C.L. Brereton Papers, IWM; 4 Division War Diary, 13 September 1914, WO 95/1439, PRO.

71. 3 Division War Diary, 13 September 1914, WO 95/1375; 5 Division War Diary, 13 September 1914, WO 95/1510; II Corps War Diary, 13 September 1914, WO 95/629, PRO.

72. Haig Diary, 13 September 1914, NLS; WO 256/1; 1 Division War Diary, 13 September 1914, WO 95/1227; I Corps War Diary, 13 September 1914, WO 95/588, PRO; De Lisle, "My Narrative," De Lisle Papers, LHCMA.

73. Edmonds, *Military Operations: France and Belgium, 1914*, 465.

74. GHQ Operation Order No. 24, 13 September 1914, GHQ War Diary, WO 95/1; Kitchener to French, 13 September 1914, WO 33/713, PRO; Wilson Diary, 13 September 1914, Henry Wilson Papers, IWM.

75. II Corps War Diary, 14 September 1914, WO 95/629; 5 Division War Diary, 14 September 1914, WO 95/1510; 4 Division War Diary, 14 September 1914, WO 95/1439; III Corps War Diary, 14 September 1914, WO 95/668, PRO.

76. Bulfin Diary, 14 September 1914, CAB 45/140; "Operations of the 1st Corps on the River Aisne, 13th to 30th September 1914," I Corps War Diary, WO 95/588; 1 Division War Diary, 14 September 1914, WO 95/1227; 2 Division, "Passage of the River Aisne," I Corps War Diary, WO 95/588, PRO; Haig Diary, 14 September 1914, NLS; WO 256/1, PRO.

77. French Diary, 14 September 1914, Lord French Papers, IWM; GHQ Operation Order No. 25, 14 September 1914, GHQ War Diary, WO 95/1, PRO.

78. 5 Division War Diary, 15 September 1914, WO 95/1510, PRO.

79. GHQ Operation Order No. 26, 15 September 1914, GHQ War Diary, WO 95/1; II Corps War Diary, 15 September 1914, WO 96/629; Kitchener to French, 15 September 1914, WO 33/713, PRO.

80. Edmonds, *Military Operations: France and Belgium, 1914*, 430.

81. 2 Division, "Passage of the River AISNE," I Corps War Diary, WO 95/588, PRO.

82. GHQ War Diary, 16–30 September 1914, WO 95/1; I Corps War Diary, 16–30 September 1914, WO 95/588; II Corps War Diary, 16–30 September 1914, WO 95/629; III Corps War Diary, 16–30 September 1914, WO 95/672, PRO.

83. GHQ Operation Order No. 28, 1 October 1914, WO 95/1, PRO; French to Kitchener, 2 October 1914, WO 33/713, PRO.

84. III Corps War Diary, 21 September 1914, WO 95/668; Smith-Dorrien Diary, 19 September 1914, CAB 45/206; II Corps War Diary, 17, 19 September 1914, WO 95/588, PRO.

85. French to War Office, 17 September 1914, WO 33/713; War Office to French, 20 September 1914, WO 33/713, PRO.

86. Bulfin Diary, 2 October 1914, CAB 45/140, PRO. See also Wilfrid Abel Smith Diary, 19 September 1914, in J.M. Craster, ed., *'Fifteen Rounds a Minute,'* 96.

87. Bulfin Diary, 30 September 1914, CAB 45/140; "Operations of the 1st Corps on the River AISNE, 13th to 30th September, 1914." I Corps War Diary, WO 95/588, PRO.

88. Smith-Dorrien Diary, 4 September 1914, 26 September 1914, CAB 45/206, PRO; Edmonds, *Military Operations: France and Belgium, 1914*, 363n.

89. Haig Diary, 5 September 1914, NLS; WO 256/1, PRO; Edmonds, *Military Operations: France and Belgium, 1914*, 363n; "Operations of I Corps on the River Aisne, 13–30 September 1914," I Corps War Diary, WO 95/588, PRO.

90. "Summary of Operations of the IIIrd Corps," III Corps War Diary, WO 95/668, PRO; Edmonds, *Military Operations: France and Belgium, 1914*, 224, 363n.

91. Edmonds, *Military Operations: France and Belgium, 1914*, 440.

92. Wilson Diary, 18–19 September 1914, Henry Wilson Papers, IWM.

93. Maurice to Mrs. Maurice, 5 November 1914, F.B. Maurice Papers, LHCMA. See also Loch Diary 23 September 1914, Lord Loch Papers, IWM; Charles Calwell, *The Life of Sir Stanley Maude, Lieutenant-General, KCB, CMG, DSO* (London: Constable, 1920), 138.

94. French to Kitchener, 13 September 1914, WO 33/713, PRO.

95. "MEMORANDUM" from Sub-Chief of Staff, Henry Wilson, 24 September 1914, II Corps War Diary, WO 95/588, PRO.

96. "Memorandum," I Corps War Diary, WO 95/588; "Notes, Based on the Experience Gained by the Second Corps, During the Campaign," October 1914, II Corps War Diary, WO 95/629; "Report of III Corps," III Corps War Diary, WO 95/668, PRO.

97. Bidwell and Graham, *Fire-Power*, 68; Mowbray Diary, 2 October 1914, J.L. Mowbray Papers, IWM.

98. Paddy Griffith, *Battle Tactics of the Western Front: The British Army's Art of Attack, 1916–1918* (New Haven: Yale University Press, 1994), 41.

99. 4 Division War Diary, 13 September 1914, WO 95/1439; 5 Division War Diary, 13 September 1914, WO 95/1510; III Corps War Diary, 13 September 1914, WO 95/668; II Corps War Diary, 13 September 1914, WO 95/629, PRO.

100. Bidwell and Graham, *Fire-Power*, 101–102.

101. "Memorandum," I Corps War Diary, WO 95/588; II Corps War Diary, 26 September 1914, WO 95/629; III Corps War Diary, 15 September 1914, WO 95/668, PRO; Haig Diary, 16 September 1914, NLS; WO 256/1, PRO.

102. 1 Division War Diary, 14 September 1914, WO 95/1227, PRO.

103. Haig's handwritten comment on Lomax to I Corps, 23 September 1914, I Corps War Diary, WO 95/588, PRO.

104. "Notes," II Corps War Diary, WO 95/630, PRO

105. Haig Diary, 4 October 1914, NLS; WO 256/1, PRO.

106. George Barrow, *The Fire of Life* (London: Hutchinson, 1931), 158.

107. 2 Cavalry Division War Diary, 15 September 1914, WO 95/1142; French to Kitchener, 10 September 1914, WO 33/713, PRO.

108. GHQ War Diary, 9 October 1914, WO 95/1, PRO; De Lisle, "My Narrative," De Lisle Papers, LHCMA; Nikolas Gardner, "Command and Control in the 'Great Retreat' of 1914: The Disintegration of the British Cavalry Division," *The Journal of Military History*, 63:1 (January 1999), 29–54.

109. John Charteris, *At GHQ* (London: Cassell, 1931), 39. See also Haig Diary, 20 September 1914, NLS; WO 256/1, PRO.

110. French to Kitchener, 24 October 1914, WO 33/713, PRO; Haig Diary, 20, 27 September 1914, NLS; WO 256/1, PRO.

111. Smith-Dorrien Diary, 22 September 1914, CAB 45/206, PRO.

112. Griffith, *Battle Tactics of the Western Front*, 83. See also Bidwell and Graham, Fire-Power, 126, and Martin Samuels, *Command or Control? Command, Training and Tactics in the British and German Armies, 1888–1918* (London: Frank Cass, 1995), 121–123.

113. French to Kitchener, 17 September 1914, WO 33/713, PRO; Haig Diary, 6 September 1914, NLS; WO 256/1; Bulfin Diary, 2 September 1914, CAB 45/140, PRO.

114. Rawlinson Diary, 1 October 1914, Rawlinson Papers, 1/1, CCC.

115. John Baynes, *Far From a Donkey: The Life of General Sir Ivor Maxse* (London: Brassey's, 1995), 119. Correspondence between Maxse and his wife, Mary, lends weight

to this interpretation. In a letter to her husband, Mary informed him that she had learned from another officer that Maxse was returning to England because he "wanted a rest."

116. Haig Diary, 22 September, 18 September 1914, NLS, WO 256/1, PRO; Haig to Mrs. Haig, 4 September 1914, Haig Papers, NLS.

117. Scott, ed., "The View from GHQ: the Second Part of the Diary of General Sir Charles Deedes, KCB, CMG, DSO," *Stand To!*. 11 (Summer 1984), 16.

118. Wilson Diary, 17, 22, 23, 28 September, 3, 4 October 1914, Henry Wilson Papers, IWM. The circumstances surrounding the transfer of the BEF will be discussed in the following chapter.

119. Haig to CGS, 15 September 1914, II Corps War Diary, WO 95/630, PRO.

120. Mowbray Diary, 14 September 1914, J.L. Mowbray Papers, IWM; Smith-Dorrien to GHQ, 16 September 1914, II Corps War Diary, WO 95/630, PRO.

121. Smith-Dorrien to GHQ, 16 September 1914, II Corps War Diary, WO 95/630, PRO.

122. Haig Diary, 8,9 October 1914, NLS; WO 256/1, PRO.

123. II Corps War Diary, 16 September 1914, WO 95/629, PRO.

124. Haig Diary, 14 September 1914, WO 256/1, PRO.

125. Ian F.W. Beckett, *The Judgment of History: Sir Horace Smith-Dorrien, Lord French and 1914* (London: Tom Donovan, 1993); Holmes, *The Little Field-Marshal*, 222–224.

4

The Costs of Confidence: Command and the Demise of II Corps, 1–30 October

For the BEF, the 1914 campaign culminated in a series of engagements known collectively as the First Battle of Ypres. The battle commenced in early October as British units advanced alongside the French Army with the intention of turning the German flank in northern France. When the allied forces collided with enemy units attempting a similar flanking movement, GHQ extended the British front northward into Belgium in search of open territory over which to advance. The arrival of British units in the vicinity of Ypres, however, coincided with a German offensive launched with the intention of winning the war before winter. Thus, rather than advancing, the BEF was forced to defend its precarious positions until the abatement of German counterattacks in mid-November. The army fought desperate engagements throughout this period. As Sir James Edmonds noted in the *Official History*, while British soldiers faced only seven days of "critical" combat in August and September, they endured twenty such days in October and November.[1] The BEF ultimately succeeded in repelling the enemy counteroffensive, inflicting significant damage on the German Army in the process. While precise casualty figures are impossible to determine, Edmonds estimated German losses in northern France and Belgium at 134,000 killed, wounded, and missing. The British stand at Ypres played a key role in foiling German efforts to win the war in 1914. Holger Herwig has characterized the German offensive in Flanders as a "debacle."[2] Nevertheless, the success of the British Army came at a high price. Despite its expansion to include six corps, "First Ypres" left the BEF depleted to the point of collapse.

The unprecedented scope of the First Battle of Ypres compelled the official historian to treat it as six separate engagements. While one can understand the dynamics of command in the British Army during the battle without resorting to this level of detail, it is not possible to comprehend the behavior of the British command system in this period within the confines of one chapter. An effective means of examining command, as well as the more general experiences of the BEF during this period, is to view the First Battle of Ypres from the perspective of the principal British corps that participated. Different corps shouldered the burden of combat during each phase of the battle. These particular formations consequently provide the clearest illustration of the challenges British commanders faced in this period. An examination of the experiences of separate British corps, in rough chronological succession, will illuminate the behavior of the British command system as the battle progressed and intensified during October and November 1914.

Accordingly, the following four chapters will discuss the operations of different corps of the BEF during the First Battle of Ypres. This chapter will examine Sir Horace Smith-Dorrien's II Corps in October. The first three weeks of this month saw the gradual transfer of the BEF to the left of the Allied line. On 11 October, II Corps, the first British formation to arrive, spearheaded an offensive aimed at turning the German flank. The advance continued until the 20th, when the enemy replied with a counteroffensive, the thrust of which fell against Smith-Dorrien's force until GHQ withdrew the entire corps from the British line eight days later. While II Corps was not the only element of the BEF involved in active operations in October, none of the other British corps participated in the advance for its full duration. An assessment of the dynamics of command within II Corps, as well as the relationship between Sir Horace Smith-Dorrien and GHQ, will therefore offer particularly useful insights into the problems of command during the advance in northern France and Flanders.

While historians have chronicled the First Battle of Ypres, the exercise of command in the BEF in this period remains poorly understood. Focusing primarily on the regimental level, the *Official History* provides few insights into the conduct of operations by senior officers. Glimpses of the behavior of British commanders are offered by Holmes's *The Little Field-Marshal*, and *Death of an Army*, Anthony Farrar-Hockley's account of First Ypres. Both studies note the mercurial temperament of Sir John French throughout October, suggesting that the commander-in-chief's mood swings often tended toward excessive optimism. In addition, they are critical of Sir Horace Smith-Dorrien, emphasizing his pessimism regarding the condition of II Corps in late October.[3]

Beyond these observations regarding individual officers, however, there has been no sustained analysis of relationships among senior commanders. Nor have scholars considered the influence of fundamental notions about warfare held by British officers on their conduct in this period. Through an examination of the experiences of II Corps, this chapter will assess the impact of command relationships as well as basic ideas and values of officers on the operations of the BEF in October 1914. It will argue that dysfunctional relationships in the upper ranks of the army compounded the difficulties of II Corps during the advance and the subsequent German counteroffensive. As a result of his strained relations with Lord Kitchener and the distorted internal dynamics of GHQ, Sir John French pressed the advance of II Corps despite evidence of increasing enemy opposition. Tensions between the commander-in-chief and Sir Horace Smith-Dorrien further complicated the exercise of command as Smith-Dorrien attempted to conceal the depleted condition of his force and deflect criticism for its performance. Friction between senior commanders compounded the difficulties facing junior officers in II Corps. The heroic efforts of these officers prevented the disintegration of Smith-Dorrien's force in the face of intensifying enemy attacks. They only did so, however, at the cost of soldiers whose training and experience proved irreplaceable.

THE TRANSFER OF THE BEF AND THE DYNAMICS OF GHQ, OCTOBER 1914

Historians have identified a variety of factors that led to the transfer of the BEF to the left of the Allied line. They have done little, however, to determine their relative weight. A comprehension of the fundamental reasons behind this move is essential in order to understand the fortunes of the army in October 1914. A cursory examination of the situation of the BEF in late September suggests several reasons for the transfer. On the Aisne, the position of the BEF between two French armies necessitated that the British line of communications cross that of the French forces on its left. A shift to the north would both shorten the British line and reduce its interference with French logistics. Moreover, the need to streamline British communications promised to become more pressing with the expected arrival of five divisions of British and Indian reinforcements during the month of October.[4] In addition to simplifying Allied logistical arrangements, redeployment in Flanders would place the British Army in a better position to defend French and Belgian ports on the English Channel (see Map 4.1). Concerned with maintaining the safety of the ports, Winston Churchill, then first lord of the admiralty, proposed the move during his visit to GHQ on 17 September. The progressive German advance toward the Belgian city of Antwerp in late September lent credence to Churchill's argument. The loss of Antwerp would place Allied control of the ports in jeopardy, a fact that had serious implications for the safety of British supply lines.

In themselves, these were compelling reasons for the relocation of the army. There is little evidence, however, to suggest that these considerations had a significant impact on GHQ in late September. Rather, senior British commanders and staff officers favored the transfer to Flanders primarily on the assumption that it would allow them to escape the stalemate on the Aisne and resume offensive operations. Henry Wilson was apparently the first senior member of GHQ to advocate the move. After conferring with the first lord of the admiralty on the 17th, the sub-chief of the General Staff commandeered Churchill's idea and set about convincing his malleable commander-in-chief of its merits. Fearing a return to Belgium after the traumatic experience of the retreat from Mons, Sir John French apparently expressed trepidation. Nonetheless, Wilson's reasoning

Map 4.1
BEF Area of Operations, October–November 1914

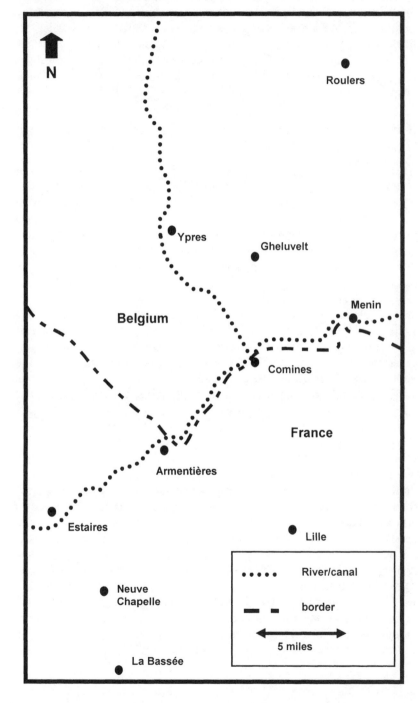

proved irresistible, and on 27 September, French approached Joffre regarding the possibility of the transfer of the BEF to the left of the French line.[5]

The commencement of the German bombardment of Antwerp the following day underlined the urgency of reinforcing the Allied left flank. French and Wilson, however, were less concerned with the plight of the city and the implications of its capture than with securing an opportunity to advance. In his diary, Henry Wilson showed little interest in the progress of the German siege. Informed of the impending fall of Antwerp on 3 October, he commented nonchalantly that the loss of the city, "tho[ugh] not serious, will be a bother." In correspondence with Lord Kitchener, Sir John French expressed more concern for the fate of Antwerp. French's apparent anxiety regarding the safety of the city, however, stemmed largely from a desire to placate the secretary of state for war, with whom his relationship remained rather tenuous. Kitchener's opinion of the commander-in-chief may have recovered from its nadir during the retreat from Mons. French nevertheless remained reluctant to challenge openly the wishes of his superior, who was clearly concerned with the fate of Antwerp. Thus, in response to Kitchener's inquiries during the first week of October regarding the possibility of the BEF participating in the relief of the city, French repeatedly stressed that Antwerp was his "first objective."[6]

French's declarations, however, were not unequivocal. In fact, the commander-in-chief's telegrams to Kitchener indicate that he had little intention of making a serious effort to save the Belgian city. His professions of concern for Antwerp notwithstanding, French refused to abandon or even postpone the planned advance of the BEF in an attempt to alleviate German pressure on the city. On 7 October, he declared: "I would be glad to embark on any enterprise which promises the successful relief of Antwerp, but I am sure that the most effective and quickest way of doing this, if it is at all possible, is to continue our present plans."[7] This explanation demonstrates clearly that French attached only secondary importance to Antwerp. On the 7th, the commander-in-chief's "present plans" included the assembly of British troops around the French town of St. Omer, approximately 100 miles southeast of the besieged Belgian city. This would allow the BEF to advance into Flanders alongside the French forces on its right. As Kitchener himself had pointed out four days earlier, however, a concentration point this far west would render the BEF unable to reach Antwerp in time to alleviate increasing German pressure.[8] Thus, despite his claims of concern for the fate of Antwerp, Sir John French shared Henry Wilson's desire to move to Flanders in order to resume offensive operations.

The eagerness of the two officers was based on a profound confidence regarding the possibility of attaining decisive results against the German flank. Optimistic despite the fall of Antwerp on 9 October, Henry Wilson predicted enthusiastically in his diary: "I think we are going to hit the extreme right of the Germans & hit it hard."[9] The commander-in-chief expressed similar sentiments. While French may have reacted warily to the sub-chief's initial suggestion that the BEF move to the left, he had been suffused with Wilson's optimism by the beginning of October. As Henry Rawlinson noted in his diary on the 1st: "He [French] seems to think the war will finish in the spring."[10]

From the perspective of the entrenched British positions on the Aisne, the left flank certainly appeared to offer significant offensive opportunities. It is thus not surprising that senior British officers initially expressed optimism about the move. Such an outlook, however, would prove dangerously tenacious in the ensuing weeks. This attachment to the advance stemmed from several factors. First, Sir John French remained uncomfortably aware that he had deliberately disregarded Kitchener's suggestions that he divert the BEF to relieve Antwerp. Given the subsequent fall of the Belgian city and his delicate relationship with the secretary of state for war, French undoubtedly felt concerned for the permanency of his command should the offensive fail to produce concrete results. The commander-in-chief's perceived investment in the success of the advance thus left him reluctant to abandon offensive efforts.

Even if French's commitment wavered, the internal dynamics of GHQ undermined any serious reassessment of prospects for a British advance. As noted in the preceding chapter, Henry Wilson had reestablished his dominance at GHQ by early October. Significantly, Wilson proved extremely optimistic in this period. The sub-chief maintained close relationships with senior French officers, particularly Ferdinand Foch, commanding the French armies in the northern section of the Allied line. Bolstered by the cheerful predictions of Foch and other French commanders, Wilson remained confident regarding the prospects of an offensive in northern France and Flanders. Even when the advance showed signs of faltering, the charismatic Wilson was able to persuade subordinates and superiors alike of the necessity of continuing to press forward.[11] Thus, Sir John French's desire to advance was bolstered by the optimism of his influential sub-chief of Staff.

Debate at GHQ over the wisdom of the advance was circumscribed further by the enduring rift between the Operations and Intelligence subsections. On a personal level, friction remained between the head of Intelligence, George Macdonogh, and both Henry Wilson and "Uncle" Harper. During the advance to the Aisne, Macdonogh had broken his collarbone in an automobile accident. Perceiving an opportunity to remove a source of dissenting opinion at GHQ, Wilson attempted to replace the Intelligence chief with an officer of his own choosing. In light of vociferous protests from the Intelligence staff, as well as the fact that Macdonogh's injury did not interfere with the performance of his duties, Wilson ultimately relented.[12] Nevertheless, it is highly unlikely that this episode improved relations between the taciturn head of Intelligence and his colleagues.

Thus, several mutually reinforcing tendencies combined to sustain the confidence of senior British officers as the army began its advance in October. Henry Wilson's resilient optimism augmented the commander-in-chief's desire to produce concrete results from the offensive. In addition, the continued marginalization of George Macdonogh and Intelligence at GHQ diminished the impact of information that might have undermined the plans of Sir John French and the sub-chief of Staff. Consequently, as the BEF embarked on the "race for the flank," senior officers were unlikely to reassess their expectations of a successful offensive against the German Army.

THE TRANSFER TO FLANDERS AND THE ADVANCE OF II CORPS

The advance of II Corps began within the context of profound optimism at GHQ. On 30 September, three days after Sir John French's initial request, Joffre agreed to the transfer of the BEF to positions on the Allied left. Eager to commence operations against the German right flank, GHQ wasted little time in initiating the removal of British forces from the Aisne. Sir John French issued orders to his corps commanders at a conference the next morning, directing II Corps to begin vacating its positions in the middle of the British line on the night of 1 October. The withdrawal progressed smoothly, and Smith-Dorrien's troops began boarding trains for northern France by noon on the 5th (see Map 4.2).[18]

Despite the efficient departure of II Corps from the Aisne, the optimistic plans of GHQ began to unravel before Smith-Dorrien's force could even begin its advance. To prevent the obstruction of their own communications, the French refused to allow II Corps to detrain at the town of St. Omer, its intended concentration point near the Belgian border. Instead, the British were forced to disembark at Abbeville, over fifty miles to the southwest. The French hastily provided buses to expedite the transport of II Corps from Abbeville to the vicinity of St. Omer. In the absence of any prior planning by French or British staff, however, the transfer was plagued by delays.[19] Consequently, II Corps was not ready to advance until 11 October. Nonetheless, in spite of this rather clumsy transfer, the optimism of GHQ remained unshaken. As Smith-Dorrien's force assembled near Bethune, approximately twenty miles southeast of St. Omer, both Archie Murray and Henry Wilson expressed satisfaction in their diaries regarding its progress.[20]

In light of the condition of II Corps, this confidence was not warranted. As noted in the preceding chapter, II Corps had sustained losses amounting to approximately 520 officers and 12,900 other ranks by early October. As a proportion of the original strength of II Corps, these totals represent approximately 30 percent of its other ranks and 50 percent of its officers.[21] Some of these casualties had undoubtedly returned to their units by the beginning of the advance. Nevertheless, it seems unlikely that Smith-Dorrien's force retained more than three-quarters of its original contingent of soldiers and more than two-thirds of the cadre of officers who had fought at Mons. The high rate of casualties among the officers of II Corps proved particularly significant for two reasons. First, according to the *Official History*, only 485 officers had joined the BEF as reinforcements by the beginning of October.[22] Given that these individuals were likely divided between the three British corps and the cavalry, this number was clearly insufficient to erase the considerable deficit of officers that prevailed in II Corps. Moreover, as discussed in the preceding chapter, it

Map 4.2
II Corps Area of Operations, 11–30 October 1914

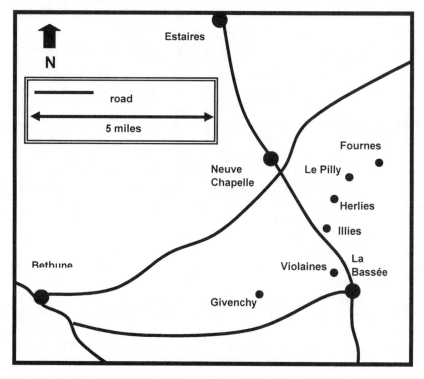

proved difficult to find experienced replacements for the original officers of the BEF. Thus, the high rate of officer casualties in the first six weeks of the campaign resulted in a paucity of effective leadership at the regimental level of II Corps as it began its advance in early October.

Given the nature of the terrain in northern France and Flanders, this deficiency was particularly detrimental to the effectiveness of Smith-Dorrien's force. The flat countryside of the region was intersected by numerous canals, hedgerows, and dikes, and strewn with farms, small villages, coal pits, and slag heaps.[18] Such a cluttered landscape created considerable difficulties for the advancing British Army. As the level terrain precluded effective artillery observation, guns were forced to deploy among the infantry in order to support its forward movement. Impediments such as canals, dikes, and pits, however, checked the rapid progress of the artillery, consequently inhibiting the advance of the rest of the army.[19] Even more significantly, the numerous obstacles enabled small bodies of enemy troops to establish isolated yet obstinate defensive positions that further hindered the British advance. This situation held the potential to create a spiral of increasing casualties in II Corps. Subduing enemy positions entailed the dispatch of small detachments, led by regimental officers who suffered significant casualties in the process.[20] Casualty levels would intensify as the dwindling number of veteran officers fell and were replaced by relative novices who were compelled to perform the same difficult task.

The growing German presence on the Allied left flank increased the likelihood of such losses. Even before II Corps began its advance on the 11th, there was evidence of the arrival of enemy forces in the vicinity. In postwar correspondence with Edmonds, George Macdonogh alleged that intelligence reports indicating the approach of German units were consistently ignored by the Operations Section at GHQ, even after he "made a devil of a row" around 10 October. The Intelligence Section was not the only source of such information. As Smith-Dorrien noted in his diary on the 10th, German attacks on the French forces to the right of II Corps necessitated that he begin his advance as quickly as possible. The following day, an intercepted wireless transmission divulged that the Germans were planning a concerted attack on the French on the 12th.[21] Thus, despite the optimism prevalent at GHQ in early October, II Corps faced serious difficulties as it began advancing. Weakened by heavy losses sustained earlier in the campaign, Smith-Dorrien's formation was forced to negotiate difficult terrain in the face of stiffening enemy opposition.

The substantial area of operations assigned to II Corps compounded these difficulties. Orders issued by GHQ at the beginning of the offensive directed the force to advance on a front approximately eight miles long.[22] The size of this front equalled or exceeded that occupied by any other British corps in 1914. Given the terrain in its vicinity and the proximity of enemy forces, the task of covering so much territory strained the depleted resources of II Corps. In a report submitted in late 1914, Smith-Dorrien contended that he was forced to employ his corps reserve in the front line as early as the second day of the offensive. The extent of the front allotted to II Corps may have reflected the optimism of GHQ. It may also have stemmed from a lack of experience on the part of senior staff in the conduct of large-scale operations. In any case, it complicated the already onerous task facing II Corps as it began its advance.

Predictably, the offensive faltered from the outset. From positions southeast of the French village of Bethune, II Corps moved forward on the morning of 11 October, flanked on either side by French forces. Smith-Dorrien's intention was to use 5 Division, on the right of II Corps, to occupy the German forces molesting the French immediately to the south, while wheeling around 3 Division, on the left, to attack the Germans in flank. This effort was impeded, however, by a lack of coordination with allied forces. As Smith-Dorrien's force attempted to advance on the 11th, it found the roads in its front blocked by French cavalry and ammunition columns moving northward to take up positions on its left.[23] While the departure of these units left II Corps with a clear path the next morning, enemy resistance increased throughout the 12th. In front of II Corps during the initial stages of the advance were elements of two cavalry corps, supported by artillery. These units took advantage of the local terrain to impede the movement of British forces. According to Smith-Dorrien, German cavalry and jaegers took up positions afforded by the terrain, and "cleverly disputed every village, stream and hedgerow," inflicting approximately 300 casualties on his force.[24]

On 13 October, the tentative advance of II Corps ground to a virtual halt. To the north, Pulteney's III Corps and Allenby's newly formed Cavalry Corps began to move forward without serious opposition.[25] Smith-Dorrien's force, however, faced multiple counterattacks as elements of the German Sixth Army arrived in the vicinity. These forays did not comprise a concerted effort on the part of the enemy. Nevertheless, the momentum of II Corps was not sufficient to suppress them. Consequently, Smith-Dorrien's formation made almost no headway. While the arrival of additional enemy forces undoubtedly hindered the progress of II Corps, it is evident that Smith-Dorrien's tentative advance in this period was not due solely to the strength of German opposition. Charles Deedes recalled: "We learnt from intercepted wireless messages sent out by the German commander (General von der Marwitz) that our advance was 'slow' and 'hesitating' and evidently did not cause him any anxiety."[26]

This lack of progress stemmed in part from poor coordination with French forces on either flank of Smith-Dorrien's formation. On 12–13 October, both divisions of II Corps reported delays caused by the absence or obstruction of French units on their flanks.[27] Rather than reflecting the ineptitude of either the British or the French, these failures were likely inevitable, as the two armies attempted to coordinate their advance with only rudimentary communications and different languages of operation. In any case, the slow advance of II Corps from 11 to 13 October cannot be ascribed solely to a lack of coordination with the French. The principal factor inhibiting Smith-Dorrien's force was its growing scarcity of experienced officers. This shortage became manifestly clear early on 13 October, as German cavalry and jaegers, hitherto content to oppose II Corps from the relative safety of defensive positions, began initiating counterattacks. While the enemy attacks were apparently uncoordinated, they proved sufficient to disrupt completely the advance of a British force suffering from increasing deficiencies at the lower levels of its command structure.

These deficiencies become evident in an examination of the experiences of Sir Charles Fergusson's 5 Division on 13 October. Advancing on the right of II Corps, the division incurred the vast majority of casualties suffered by Smith-Dorrien's force during the day. German attacks fell most heavily on the 15th Brigade, in the middle of the 5 Division line. While they did not comprise an organized attempt to overwhelm the British advance, the enemy initiatives took a heavy toll on a brigade already depleted during the 1914 campaign. Its commander, Count A.E.W. Gleichen, later described the 13th as "a terrible day," with three of the brigade's four battalions suffering heavy losses.[28]

Misfortune fell first upon the Cheshire Regiment, on the left of the brigade. This battalion had been decimated during the retreat from Mons, with its commanding officer falling alongside most of his troops on 24 August.

Successive drafts had replenished the ranks of the Cheshires during September. Due to the scarcity of replacement officers, however, the unit was led by a captain until the arrival of a permanent commander, Major Vandeleur, on 7 October. In his memoir of 1914, Gleichen described the new commander of the Cheshires as "a first-rate sensible fellow."[29] On 13 October, however, Vandeleur's inexperience had adverse consequences for his battalion. Leading half a company on a scouting party during the morning, Vandeleur and his second-in-command, Major Young, were attacked by superior German forces near the village of Rue d'Ouvert. The party found shelter in a farmhouse and managed to resist enemy attacks for the rest of the day, but by evening its position had become untenable. Wounded, and cut off from reinforcements, Vandeleur surrendered.[30]

The commander of the Cheshires can hardly be held responsible for the presence of hostile forces in the vicinity of the 15th Brigade. Nevertheless, his judgment in accompanying the scouting party along with his second-in-command was more questionable. The absence of its two senior officers throughout 13 October handicapped the battalion headquarters precisely when the plight of the scouting party necessitated rapid action. Had either Vandeleur or Young remained behind on the morning of the 13th, it seems likely that a more concerted effort would have been made to determine the whereabouts of the ill-fated reconnaissance force. With both officers forward, however, the battalion was effectively decapitated. The junior officers of the unit did not make an effort to locate the missing detachment and, consequently, remained under the mistaken impression that the entire scouting party had been killed or captured early in the morning.[31] Evidently, Vandeleur's inexperience contributed to the demise of a half company of the Cheshire battalion, including its two senior officers. These losses would further inhibit the effectiveness of the unit as fighting intensified in subsequent days.

The Cheshire Regiment was not the only battalion to suffer from the inexperience of its officers on 13 October. To its immediate right, the Bedfordshire Regiment incurred heavy casualties in an unsuccessful attempt to hold the village of Givenchy. The Bedfords mounted an obstinate defense, holding their positions under an intense German artillery bombardment until casualties compelled their withdrawal late in the afternoon. The battalion evidently retired in considerable disarray. Lord Loch, the liaison between GHQ and II Corps, commented in his diary on 13 October that the Bedfords "are said to have broke." Their failure to recover one of the battalion's two machine guns supports this description.[32] An even more significant indicator of the Bedfords' haste was the fact that they neglected to notify the adjacent Dorsetshire Regiment of their retirement. This had disastrous consequences for the latter unit. Expecting their left flank to be covered by the Bedfords, the Dorsets were surprised by simultaneous attacks on their front and left. Quickly overwhelmed by enemy fire, the battalion initiated an abrupt withdrawal, abandoning a machine gun and two artillery pieces. By the time they finally regrouped approximately half a mile to the west, the Dorsets had suffered 490 casualties, 13 of them officers. According to the 5 Division war diary, only 5 officers remained with the battalion on the night of the 13th.[33]

Clearly, the Germans exerted significant pressure on the Bedford and Dorset positions on 13 October. The disorderly retirement of both battalions, however, indicates the inability of regimental officers to maintain the discipline of their troops under fire. This stemmed from both quantitative and qualitative deficiencies among the officers of both units. Even before the engagement on the 13th, the Dorsetshire battalion retained only 18 officers, well short of its full establishment of 30. In addition, these officers evidently included a large number of replacements, less experienced, and less familiar to the other ranks than their predecessors. The following day, Sir John French implored Lord Kitchener to provide him with capable reinforcements, declaring: "we need well-trained officers very much." Similarly, Lord Loch referred in his diary to "half-trained" officers as a primary factor behind the difficulties of II Corps.[34] In the case of the 15th Brigade on 13 October, this profound lack of experienced regimental officers resulted in heavy losses to three of its battalions. Moreover, casualties suffered on the 13th further weakened the brigade just as German resistance began to increase.

Command deficiencies in 5 Division were not limited to its regimental officers. The German attacks on 13 October revealed similar weaknesses at the brigade level, particularly in the 13th Brigade, advancing on the immediate right of Count Gleichen's force. Like many units in Smith-Dorrien's corps in October, the 13th Brigade was led by a relatively inexperienced commander. Its original brigadier, G.J. Cuthbert, had been diagnosed as "seedy" and relieved of his command at the beginning of the month.[35] Consequently, his replacement, Brigadier-General Hickie, was still adjusting to the new responsibilities of his position when the British offensive began. On 13 October, the task of advancing under enemy pressure exceeded Hickie's undeveloped capabilities as a brigade commander. During the morning, the French force to the right of 5 Division requested that the 13th Brigade support its advance. According to the divisional war diary, however, "Hickie considered [the] open ground so unfavourable between his right and enemy's position that he declined to cooperate without orders from superior authority." This decision had adverse consequences for units on both flanks of the 13th Brigade. Not only was the French attack thwarted, but German forces in Hickie's front also fired on the Dorsets of the 15th Brigade on his left.[36] Thus, the hesitancy of the inexperienced commander of the 13th Brigade produced casualties in adjacent units on the morning of 13 October.

If the terrain in front of the 13th Brigade imperiled its advance, Hickie's superiors did not consider it sufficient to justify his inaction. The inexperienced brigadier was replaced the same day by Colonel Martyn, a battalion commander in the 13th Brigade. In his diary, Smith-Dorrien explained euphemistically that Hickie "had to go sick."[37] The immediacy of his dismissal following the failure of the 13th Brigade to support adjacent units, however, suggests a close connection between the two events. Apparently, Hickie's superiors removed him as soon as his unwillingness to advance became apparent. Nonetheless, the fact that his replacement was equally untested indicates that the profound shortage of experienced regimental officers in 5 Division also prevailed at the brigade level, with similarly negative effects on the performance of the division.

The multiple crises of 13 October left 5 Division a depleted force. The advance of S.P. Rolt's 14th Brigade, on the left of Fergusson's force, was postponed due to the lack of progress of units on its flanks, and consequently the brigade remained largely intact that night.[38] While German attacks on the rest of the division had abated by evening, the other two brigades were considerably shaken. Gleichen's 15th Brigade had suffered particularly heavily during the day, and as darkness set in, its battered units clung to makeshift positions without brigade reserves to repel further enemy attacks. Fergusson's divisional reserve consisted of only two companies until 10 pm, when Smith-Dorrien transferred a battalion from 3 Division to bolster the beleaguered force. The II Corps commander acknowledged the weariness of Fergusson's force in his operation order issued on the night of 13 October. While he directed 3 Division to continue its advance the next morning, Smith-Dorrien acknowledged that 5 Division "may not be in a position to participate in the next day's operations."[39]

Despite the combination of factors contributing to the plight of II Corps on the night of 13 October, accountability for its lack of progress fell squarely on the shoulders of Charles Fergusson. When Sir John French met with Smith-Dorrien during the day on the 13th, the II Corps commander apparently informed him that Fergusson lacked resolve and should be relieved at once. The commander-in-chief concurred and wired Kitchener that night, requesting a new commander for 5 Division. As French informed the Secretary of State for War: "[a] fighting commander is all-important in these times."[40] Five days later, Fergusson was replaced by Major-General F.L.N. Morland. The 1914 campaign had undoubtedly taken its toll on the commander of 5 Division. Nevertheless, given the dearth of effective leadership in many British units, the difficulties presented by the terrain in which they were operating, and the presence of German opposition, it hardly seems plausible to attribute the sluggish advance of II Corps solely to the poor leadership of Charles Fergusson. In his diary, Lord Loch commented perceptively on the circumstances of the Fergusson's removal, reflecting:

Fergusson is blamed and said to show want of decision. I think he is not to blame. His Division is scattered over a front of 5 1/2 miles of very enclosed country—no supports or reserves only a firing line—a man might be excused if he hesitated to attack in these circumstances even with the best troops, but with shaken half-trained men and half-trained officers, it is very natural to hesitate.[41]

Moreover, as the events of 14 October demonstrated, 5 Division was not alone in its inability to advance. While Fergusson's force remained stationary on the 14th, Hubert Hamilton's 3 Division attempted to move forward on its left. Suffering from a shortage of capable officers similar to that of 5 Division, however, Hamilton's force managed to mount only a feeble attack in the morning before it was thrown on the defensive by several German counterattacks. As Sir John French related to Kitchener in a telegram that evening, three of these attacks nearly succeeded in breaking the units of 3 Division, "because ignorant and untrained company officers made no attempt to rally their men."[42] The commander-in-chief recognized that the primary reason for the floundering advance of 3 Division was its deficiency of capable leadership at the regimental level. During a meeting with French on the 14th, Smith-Dorrien apparently admitted that a shortage of proficient regimental officers hindered both of his divisions. As French related in his diary: "He [Smith-Dorrien] says they have never got over the shock of Le Cateau—that the officers he has been sent to replace his tremendous losses are untrained & ignorant, and there is no great fighting spirit throughout the corps."[43]

It is difficult to attribute either the scarcity of capable officers or the apparent malaise afflicting II Corps to Charles Fergusson. Nor is it clear how these difficulties could have been alleviated by the removal of the commander of 5 Division. It thus appears that the primary motivation behind his replacement lay elsewhere. Indeed, rather than stemming from his ineffectiveness as a commander, Fergusson's dismissal was largely a product of the fractious system of relationships in the upper ranks of the army. The faltering advance of II Corps from 11 to 13 October did nothing to alleviate Sir John French's concerns regarding the permanency of his post. The commander-in-chief's worries about his own position inclined him to redirect as much responsibility as possible for the slow advance. His chilly relationship with the commander of II Corps provided French with a convenient target. Consequently, as II Corps struggled forward in October, Sir Horace Smith-Dorrien undoubtedly felt considerable pressure from his commander-in-chief. In a similar state of anxiety regarding the safety of his post, Smith-Dorrien reacted in the same way as Sir John French, shifting the onus for the slow advance onto Charles Fergusson, whose division had encountered the greatest opposition. While the difficulties of II Corps had little to do with Fergusson's leadership of 5 Division, his dismissal apparently served to relieve pressure on his superiors.

The trajectory of Charles Fergusson's career following his replacement lends weight to this argument. Similar to the case of Ivor Maxse of the 1st (Guards) Brigade, the pretext for the removal of the commander of 5 Division was his promotion to Lieutenant-General. Unlike Maxse, however, Fergusson was not assigned a training position that precluded his prompt return to active operations. He thus rejoined the BEF less than three months after his dismissal, replacing Smith-Dorrien as commander of II Corps upon the promotion of the latter to head the Second Army in late 1914.[44] Fergusson's return to command a larger formation, under the same officer who had recently sacked him, suggests that his superiors retained considerable confidence in his capabilities. In light of Fergusson's swift return to command, as well as his lack of culpability for the sluggish advance of II Corps in October, it appears that his dismissal was a product of tensions among Lord Kitchener, Sir John French, and Sir Horace Smith-Dorrien. While Fergusson's removal may have alleviated these tensions, it also deprived II Corps of an experienced leader at a crucial juncture of the 1914 campaign.

The relief of Charles Fergusson did little to ease the problems of II Corps. Nor did the continued determination to advance that prevailed at GHQ. Throughout this period, when bad news followed good in rapid succession, Sir John French's mercurial disposition regularly fluctuated between optimism and despair. Nonetheless, French's bouts of depression never persisted. The commander-in-chief's concern for his post, combined with the influence of the optimistic Henry Wilson, ensured that French would continue the advance if at all possible.[45] Thus, while senior officers recognized that II Corps faced serious problems on 13 October, orders emanating from GHQ suggest that they had again succumbed to the cognitive closure that had influenced their behavior during the retreat from Mons. On the evening of the 13th, French and his staff remained intent on advancing. In light of the losses suffered by 5 Division on the 13th, Smith-Dorrien requested the temporary use of one of the nearby divisions of Pulteney's III Corps that evening. GHQ, however, refused to authorize this loan, specifically directing Pulteney not to assist II Corps, but to continue eastward toward the German flank. On the night of 14 October, despite incurring further losses during the day, II Corps was enjoined to continue its advance the following morning.[46] These continued orders to attack took a heavy toll on Smith-Dorrien's force. While the confidence of GHQ remained intact, neither the difficulties of the terrain nor the presence of the enemy diminished after 13 October. As a result, both 3 and 5 Divisions continued to sustain casualties on subsequent days, including a relatively large proportion of regimental officers. Such losses compounded the already serious shortage of officers in the corps, further reducing its effectiveness.

Although the vast majority of officer casualties in Smith-Dorrien's force occurred at the regimental level, the corps suffered an additional setback on 14 October, when Hubert Hamilton, commander of 3 Division, was killed by a shell while observing the progress of his troops from an exposed position.[47] Hamilton's death appears peculiar in light of the rather notorious seclusion of senior British commanders from the violent realities of combat in the years after 1915. As Martin van Creveld has noted, this isolation resulted from the difficulties of controlling large forces as well as a recognition of the dangers of enemy artillery.[48] In October 1914, however, the emphasis on personal leadership prevalent throughout the officer corps had yet to be tempered by either the managerial responsibilities of a mass army or a healthy respect for modern firepower. Thus, in comparison to later years, brigadiers and even divisional commanders proved quite reckless in exposing themselves to enemy fire. While this exposure usually took place under the pretense of observing the battlefield, the extent to which it occurred was out of all proportion to the benefits it conferred to formation commanders, particularly given the availability of staff officers to perform such tasks. Thus, its underlying purpose was apparently to serve as an example to subordinate troops. One commander prone to this behavior was Walter Congreve, commanding the 18th Brigade of 6 Division. According to his biographers, Pamela Fraser and L.H. Thornton:

Each day, with the exception only of Sundays, Congreve inspected his front line morning and evening. Sometimes, when he had a visitor, he would go round his line a third time for his visitor's benefit. On such occasions his companion would have no cause to pronounce his walk lacking in interest, for his host much disliked getting wet and far preferred walking dry shod—completely indifferent to the target which he was presenting to the enemy—along the top.[49]

Similar conduct led to Hubert Hamilton's demise on 14 October. Billy Congreve, his aide-de-camp, provided the following description of the general's death in his diary: "He and Thorpe [staff officer] were out to the north of Vielle Chapelle; he had gone to see personally why our left was hung up. They were dismounted and standing on the road, when a salvo of shrapnel burst right over them. One bullet hit him in the forehead, and he died almost immediately."[50] While the leadership of the 3 Division commander may have bolstered the morale of his subordinates, his demise compounded the difficulties of II Corps. With the loss of Hubert Hamilton and the impending departure of Charles Fergusson, Smith-Dorrien's force was deprived of two experienced senior commanders at a point when heavy casualties at the lower levels of its command structure had already rendered its task exceedingly difficult.

Casualties continued to accumulate on 15 October, as GHQ sustained the listless advance of II Corps against enemy opposition. With the arrival of its new commander, Colin Mackenzie, 3 Division made some progress alongside French forces on its left. Nevertheless, its gains fell considerably short of the hopes of the II Corps commander. As Smith-Dorrien commented ruefully in his diary: "It has taken four days for the left flank of my wheel to get forward three miles." Moreover, this success came at a heavy cost. According to the divisional war diary, its units only made headway after "severe fighting" that further depleted their numbers. By the end of the 15th, the 2/Royal Scots Battalion of the 8th Brigade had lost 15 officers and 500 other ranks in four days, and was commanded by a 2nd Lieutenant.[51]

While 3 Division made only modest progress on 15 October, heavy casualties since the beginning of the advance had reduced 5 Division to a state of paralysis. Facing entrenched enemy positions, the commanders of the 13th and 14th Brigades did not even attempt an advance, reporting their men, "too exhausted for vigorous offensive action." In light of its devastating losses two days earlier, Gleichen's 15th Brigade was in no condition to advance unsupported. Thus, 5 Division remained stationary on 15 October. While this respite undoubtedly spared Fergusson's force additional casualties, the advance had already taken a heavy toll on both divisions. Lord Loch recorded in his diary that II Corps had lost 93 officers and 1,745 other ranks between 12 and 15 October.[52] Although such figures appear small in comparison to the losses suffered by the corps at Le Cateau, they nonetheless had a profound impact on a force already depleted by the travails of the 1914 campaign. By the end of the 15th, even Henry Wilson acknowledged the plight of Smith-Dorrien's force, remarking in his diary: "the 3rd & 5th Divs are not fighting units at this moment."[53]

Despite this recognition, GHQ did not amend its offensive plans. Operation Order No. 36, issued at 11:40 pm on the 15th, enjoined the BEF to advance eastward, "attacking the enemy wherever met." Even the battered II Corps was directed to advance with the intent of drawing closer to Pulteney's III Corps to the north. Against the opposition that had prevailed on 15 October, this task was likely beyond the diminished capabilities of Smith-Dorrien's force. On the morning of the 16th, however, the weary units of 3 and 5 Division discovered that the enemy had evacuated its positions of the previous day. The absence of any opposition enabled both divisions to move forward cautiously. Mackenzie's 3 Division captured the town of Neuve Chapelle and pushed eastward, while 5 Division, still under the discredited Charles Fergusson, regained Givenchy, which it had lost on the 13th.[54]

Rather than signalling the long-awaited return to mobile operations, however, this advance likely resulted from Falkenhayn's desire to draw the BEF forward before launching his own counteroffensive. As the units of both divisions discovered on the morning of the 17th, the Germans had not gone far, occupying villages to the east and fortified isolated outposts afforded by the terrain. These new positions posed a formidable obstacle to the depleted units of II Corps. As Lord Loch noted: "every village has to be almost blown down with guns."[55] Smith-Dorrien's force was thus unable to replicate its gains of the 16th on subsequent days. On 17 October, 3 Division advanced to the southeast, overwhelming German positions around the village of Herlies with bayonet charges. Over the next two days, however, Mackenzie's troops repeatedly failed to capture the neighboring community of Illies, approximately one mile to the southwest.[56]

To the right, 5 Division encountered similar difficulties in its attempts to capture the town of La Bassée from 17 to 19 October. Despite admonitions from II Corps, and the replacement of Charles Fergusson by the ostensibly more aggressive T.L.N. Morland on the 18th, the division proved consistently unable to take the town.[57] The minimal progress of II Corps after the 16th caused considerable exasperation in the upper ranks of the army. According to Sir Douglas Haig, Sir John French commented to him on the 17th that Smith-Dorrien's corps "had not done well." The following day, Henry Wilson remarked sourly in his diary that 5 Division "made no real attempt to take La Bassée."[58]

The irritation of GHQ notwithstanding, it is hardly surprising that the advance of II Corps foundered after 17 October. In light of the casualties it had sustained since the 11th, the new German positions likely presented insurmountable obstacles to the weary and depleted force. In addition, the bitter experiences of the previous week had left many of the remaining officers of its units reluctant to incur further losses in attacks that promised only a remote chance of success. As Lord Loch recorded in his diary on the 18th: "It is all very well to order an attack but if Regimental officers do not obey and Brigadiers do not enforce the order it is hard to get on."[59] While Loch provided no explanation for the apparent dissipation of initiative among brigade and regimental commanders, Count Gleichen's memoir yields some insight into their difficulties after 17 October. As the commander of the 15th Brigade recalled:

We were continually being urged to advance and attack, but how could we? There was nothing to attack in front of us except La Bassée, a couple of miles off, and we could not advance a yard in that direction without exposing our flank to a deadly enfilade fire from across the Canal, for the Germans were still strongly holding that infernal railway triangle, and nothing availed to get them out of it.[60]

The strength of German positions, the heavy losses already sustained by the units of II Corps, and the growing hesitancy of their officers combined to extinguish the advance of II Corps by 19 October. Aside from a successful local initiative by the Royal Irish Regiment of 3 Division to occupy positions near the village of Le Pilly, the rest of the corps remained stationary that day. As Lord Loch observed: "attacks are practically abandoned as far as we are concerned."[61] While senior officers at GHQ continued to express annoyance, offensive efforts had subsided not a moment too soon, as the arrival of considerable enemy forces in front of II Corps foreshadowed an enemy counteroffensive. On the 18th, Smith-Dorrien recorded "distinct signs of an increase in the strength of the Germans." The following day, Henry Wilson fumed over the impending attacks in his diary. As the sub-chief of Staff remarked: "it is perfectly maddening. Owing to nothing but absolute incompetence, and want of regimental officers we have lost the finest opportunity of the war & are now going to be thrown on the defensive."[62]

Wilson's comment indicates the acknowledgement by GHQ of the termination of the advance of II Corps. It is also significant, however, in that it demonstrates the unrealistic optimism that the sub-chief had retained since the outset of the advance. This attitude strengthened Sir John French's resolve, burdening II Corps with unrealistic orders to attack strong enemy positions. The inability of Smith-Dorrien's force to meet the expectations of GHQ resulted indirectly in the removal of Charles Fergusson. In addition, these repeated efforts to advance simply compounded the "want of regimental officers" that Wilson decried on the 19th, producing a spiral of increasing ineffectiveness in the units of Smith-Dorrien's force. As a German counteroffensive loomed on 19 October, the lackluster advance of II Corps had left it an exhausted force.

THE GERMAN COUNTEROFFENSIVE AND THE DEMISE OF II CORPS

The German counteroffensive did not come as a surprise. In light of the increasing numbers of enemy troops in the vicinity, II Corps orders issued on the evening of the 19th enjoined both 3 and 5 Divisions to "hold resolutely to the ground won today." The instructions retained a glimmer of optimism, suggesting that divisional commanders were "at liberty" to press forward when appropriate. The enemy quickly scuttled any remaining hopes of an advance, however, launching attacks against II Corps, III Corps, and the Cavalry Corps on the morning of 20 October. The attacks fell particularly heavily on II Corps, which continued to hold a front of approximately eight miles. In the 5 Division line, the Manchesters of the 14th Brigade were driven from their advanced trenches during the afternoon. While the fighting subsided by 4 pm, the battalion nonetheless suffered 200 casualties before retiring to new positions.[63]

Although the eviction of the Manchesters constituted the only breach of the 5 Division line on the 20th, Colin Mackenzie's 3 Division incurred more serious damage. On its left, the Royal Irish Regiment of the 8th Brigade had advanced and occupied the village of Le Pilly on the evening of 19 October. Owing to the failure of adjacent French forces to take the nearby village of Fournes, however, the battalion remained in an exposed position that night. The commanding officer of the Royal Irish, Major Daniell, recognized the danger of his unit's position, and attempted to secure support from adjacent British forces. Unfortunately for Daniell, the Middlesex Regiment on his right proved too weak to advance. Consequently, the Royal Irish remained dangerously exposed when the German counteroffensive commenced on the morning of 20 October.[64]

The precarious position of Daniell's force did not escape the attention of the II Corps commander. Smith-Dorrien met with the commander of 3 Division during the 20th and arranged for the withdrawal of the Royal Irish Regiment after dark.[65] By then, however, it was too late. As the adjutant of the battalion, M.C.C. Harrison, related three years later, German attacks became serious early on 20 October and continued throughout the day. Enemy pressure gradually took its toll on the Royal Irish Regiment, as most of the unit's officers were killed or wounded as the day progressed. Harrison himself was wounded twice while leading troops to threatened points in the battalion's position. By late afternoon, the force was no longer able to mount an effective resistance. Despite efforts by the nearby Royal Fusiliers to relieve the German pressure on Daniell's force, the remains of the Royal Irish were surrounded and cut off.[66] Of the 20 officers and 800 other ranks who attacked on the 19th, only 2 officers and less than 100 other ranks escaped the next day. The Royal Irish Regiment was subsequently replaced by an entirely new battalion.[67]

A variety of factors contributed to the demise of the Royal Irish on 20 October. The inability of the French to take Fournes on the left of the battalion, combined with the frailty of British units on the right, left Daniell's force exposed on the eve of the enemy counteroffensive. That the Royal Irish remained in such a perilous position overnight, however, appears to have resulted partly from the inexperience of the new commander of 3 Division. Colin Mackenzie possessed the authority to withdraw the Royal Irish Regiment on the night of 19 October. Nevertheless, evidence of its precarious position did not compel him to do so. Shortly after 4 pm on 19 October, the British received word that French possession of Fournes was "unlikely" that night.[68] This would have indicated that the Royal Irish Regiment would be unsupported until at least the next day. In spite of this knowledge, as well as evidence of impending enemy attacks, Mackenzie did not take the opportunity to withdraw the battalion under the cover of darkness. Daniell's force thus remained in its positions at Le Pilly on the 20th when Smith-Dorrien visited 3 Division headquarters and requested its withdrawal. Whether Mackenzie's failure to act stemmed from inexperience or indecision, it proved costly for 3 Division on 20 October. Thus, even at the divisional level, the profound shortage of officers had adverse consequences for Smith-Dorrien's force.

The annihilation of the Royal Irish Regiment on 20 October stemmed in large part from Mackenzie's inaction. It is nonetheless significant that the battalion's commander, Major Daniell, did not request the withdrawal of his unit, even after recognizing its exposed position. Daniell's unwillingness to concede ground may have been an expression of the regimental pride that animated British battalions of the Regular Army. In 1914, officers and other ranks alike exhibited a strong sense of loyalty to the regiments in which they served. As John Baynes has observed: "the cornerstone of the relationship between officers and other ranks was their common devotion to the regiment."[69] This attitude seems to have influenced the behavior of British units during the First Battle of Ypres. In particular, the ability of a battalion to hold its position until relieved became a point of regimental pride. F.A. Bolwell, a member of the 1st Loyal North Lancashires, offered evidence of this phenomenon in his account of the 1914 campaign. According to Bolwell: "it is a rule with the Regular Army that, on being relieved, trenches have to be handed over precisely as they were taken over, any that may be lost having to be retaken."[70]

On 19–20 October, a sense of regimental pride may have deterred the commander of the Royal Irish Regiment from abandoning his positions. This sentiment was also evident in 5 Division on the 21st. Despite the intensification of enemy attacks on the 21st, Morland's division remained largely intact, repelling enemy assaults with concentrated infantry fire. Particularly successful was the Cheshire Regiment of Gleichen's 15th Brigade. Bearing the weight of German pressure against 5 Division for the second consecutive day, the battalion held firm around the village of Violaines. [71] Given the devastating losses already suffered by the Cheshires in 1914, their performance on 20–21 October is surprising. The unit was practically destroyed during the retreat from Mons, and again lost heavily on 13 October. Even after the replacement of most of its original members, however, it is evident that the unit retained a strong measure of regimental pride that facilitated cohesion and proved a useful weapon against German attacks. This sentiment came to the fore on the evening of 21 October, as II Corps attempted to regain its equilibrium after two days of enemy pressure. In light of the heavy losses incurred resisting German attacks, T.L.N. Morland evidently considered withdrawing the Cheshires from Violaines to a more easily defensible position as part of a general readjustment of the 5 Division line. Aside from the obvious and exceptional case of the retreat from Mons, this was the first instance in 1914 in which a British formation had planned a voluntary withdrawal. However prudent such a relocation may have been, it did not meet with the approval of the commander of the Cheshires. Upon learning of Morland's plan, he objected strongly. After the war, John Headlam related to Edmonds his memory of the officer "pleading" with Morland to be allowed to hold Violaines on the night of the 21st. The new commander of 5 Division proved unable to resist such pressure. As Headlam recalled, Morland eventually agreed, "against, I imagine, his own better judgement," and allowed the Cheshires to retain their positions. [72]

As had been the case in 3 Division the previous day, the decision of an inexperienced commander had serious consequences. With Morland's permission, the Cheshire Regiment passed a quiet night in Violaines. At 6 am on the 22nd, however, German troops advanced under cover of fog, taking the Cheshires by surprise. A battalion at full strength might have been able to recover from such a shock. Casualties incurred during the advance, however, had left the Cheshire Regiment without sufficient officers to rally the troops. As a result, the unit fell back in considerable disorder, pulling with it elements of the neighboring Dorsetshire Regiment. Before they managed to regroup, the Cheshires had lost one-third of their remaining strength of 600. The senior surviving officer in the battalion was a 2nd Lieutenant. [73] Thus, the experiences of 3 Division on 20 October were repeated in Morland's force two days later. A lack of effective leadership at the divisional level allowed the stubbornness of a regimental commander to go unchecked, with devastating results. Certainly, regimental pride was important to the cohesion of the BEF in 1914. In the absence of a commander capable of controlling it, however, such spirit could be costly.

The disintegration of the Cheshire Regiment on 22 October was a clear indication of the physical fragility of 5 Division. Its weakness was further underlined by the inability of Morland's force to dislodge the Germans from their newly won positions in Violaines, which intruded between the 14th Brigade and Gleichen's 15th Brigade. [74] The failure of Morland's counterattacks on the 22nd resulted directly from exhaustion and a profound shortage of officers. The diary of A.N. Acland, a subaltern in the 1st Duke of Cornwall's Light Infantry (DCLI) of the 14th Brigade, provides a useful window of insight into these problems in 5 Division. By 22 October, Acland's unit had been in action for eleven consecutive days. After enduring concerted enemy attacks since the 20th, the DCLI were relieved at approximately 5:30 am on the 22nd. By the time they reached their reserve positions, however, the soldiers could hear the clamor of the German attack on Violaines. As the sole divisional reserve, the exhausted battalion was ordered immediately to counterattack German positions in the nearby village of Rue de Marais. As Acland recorded, the remaining strength of the DCLI consisted of "eight officers and about three hundred men, and very, very weary we all were."[75] The house-to-house fighting required to drive the enemy from the village was beyond the capabilities of this beleaguered force. The unit made little headway into Rue de Marais, and eventually fell back. Counterattacks by neighboring battalions proved similarly fruitless. On the night of the 22nd, the positions lost by the Cheshires that morning remained in enemy hands.[76]

The shaky performance of 5 Division finally convinced Smith-Dorrien of the danger of exposing it to further enemy attacks. After visiting Morland during 22 October, he discovered that the division was in a "worse state of affairs" than he had imagined. This revelation apparently compelled the commander of II Corps to send a lengthy message to GHQ that night, detailing the condition of 5 Division and proposing to withdraw the line of his entire corps immediately. As Smith-Dorrien explained in the letter, ten days of fighting and digging had rendered the troops of 5 Division so exhausted that battalion commanders feared that they would be unable to awaken the troops in the event of a night attack. Moreover, the shortage of officers, novice and experienced alike, further diminished the fighting capabilities of the division. As a result, Smith-Dorrien contended that the units of 5 Division had not mounted a determined resistance to German attacks on the 22nd. Nor, in his view, was the morale of the division sufficient to withstand further enemy pressure.[77]

Given the continued optimism of GHQ and Smith-Dorrien's concerns regarding his position as II Corps commander, this frank description is surprising. Significantly, however, Smith-Dorrien did not impart this information to Sir John French on his own volition. Rather, he hesitated to inform GHQ of the weakness of Morland's division until he was forced to do so by his subordinates. The principal catalyst in this process was Lord Loch, who related in his diary that after observing the condition of Smith-Dorrien's force on the 22nd, "I made up my mind that the 5th Division would not stand if attacked and that 3rd Division, though better, was in a bad state." The chief staff officer of II Corps, George Forestier-Walker, agreed with Loch's assessment. Smith-Dorrien, however, remained reluctant to bring such discouraging news to the attention of GHQ. Taking advantage of his position as liaison officer, Loch thus informed Sir John French directly. As Loch continued in his diary:

Smith-Dorrien would not tell the C-in-C, so I gathered, so I made up my mind to report it myself. I luckily did not find Smith-Dorrien at the HQ so I left a message with Forestier-Walker as to what I was going to say—F. Walker agreed with me and said he would do his best to get Smith-Dorrien to own up. I reported to the C-in-C and did not hide anything.[78]

In light of the fact that Loch had already disclosed the condition of II Corps with Forestier-Walker's support, Smith-Dorrien had little choice but to own up himself on the evening of the 22nd. He thus detailed the infirmities of his force in the letter mentioned above. Friction with Sir John French, however, had left the II Corps commander sufficiently concerned regarding his command that he hesitated to reveal the plight of his formation, even at the risk of further losses.

Whatever the circumstances behind Smith-Dorrien's decision to readjust his line, it provided his weakened force with a badly needed rest. After retiring between one and three miles to the west during the night of 22–23 October, II Corps enjoyed a day of relative peace on the 23rd. Beyond intermittent shelling, the Germans made no effort to disrupt the consolidation of the new British positions. While this lull in the enemy counteroffensive provided a brief opportunity to reorganize, the predicament of II Corps could not be mitigated in only one day. Smith-Dorrien's force had suffered over 5,000 casualties since the beginning of the advance, and those troops that remained unscathed were exhausted. Furthermore, the positions to which II Corps had hastily retired offered poor protection against a concerted enemy attack. In addition to the fact that it extended nearly eight miles, the new line remained exposed to German fire. Nor did the high water table throughout the region facilitate the construction of functional trenches. Given the absence of sandbags and wire due to the original intent of the advance, the difficulties presented by the soggy ground were not easy to alleviate.[79] Thus, the new defensive positions left the dissipated units of II Corps exceedingly vulnerable in the event of renewed German pressure.

Such pressure was not long in materializing. By the night of 23 October, German infantry had begun testing the new British line. While these incursions did not prove particularly threatening, shelling resumed the next morning and intensified throughout the 24th. Late in the afternoon, German infantry attacked Maude's 14th Brigade on the left of 5 Division, near its junction with 3 Division. The brigade held its ground, apparently inflicting heavy losses on its attackers. In light of the considerable casualties already suffered by 5 Division, however, senior commanders and staff officers expressed particular concern for the cohesion of Morland's force. As Lord Loch reflected in his diary the previous day: "3rd Division [is] in [a] strong position, but I am still very nervous about 5th Division."[80] Despite this apprehension, the weight of the German offensive against II Corps would fall on 3 Division for the remainder of the month. Shortly after the pressure on the 14th Brigade subsided on the evening of the 24th, the Germans launched concerted attacks against the 8th and 7th Brigades, in the middle and on the right of 3 Division, respectively. McCracken's 7th Brigade managed to repel the enemy onslaught. To the left, however, the German infantry was more successful, chasing the Gordon Highlanders from their trenches and occupying a portion of the 8th Brigade line until a counterattack by the adjacent 4/Middlesex Regiment dislodged them.[81]

As German attacks continued on the morning of 25 October, the battered units of 3 Division began to waver. After repulsing enemy attacks during the night, the Royal Irish Rifles of the 7th Brigade abandoned their trenches shortly before noon. As was the case the previous night, the 3 Division line was restored with the assistance of neighboring units. Enemy attacks continued throughout the 25th, however, with no sign of abating. Nor could the tired troops of II Corps anticipate imminent support. Although Indian infantry had begun replacing French cavalry to the left of the BEF, the bulk of the Indian Corps had not yet arrived in the theater of operations. Thus, on the evening of 25 October, the exhausted and depleted units of II Corps clung to their positions with little prospect of relief.[82] In this context, Sir Horace Smith-Dorrien concluded that his line was in grave danger of disintegrating. In his diary, the II Corps commander commented on the flight of the Gordon Highlanders the previous evening, suggesting that other units in II Corps had been reduced to a similar state. As he explained:

It is difficult to blame the battalion in question too much—one of the most renowned [sic] battalions in the Army—for it lost eighty percent of its numbers and all its officers except two or three in August, and has been kept going by drafts, mostly of Special Reserve, and quite young inexperienced officers with one or two exceptions. The battalion has never had a chance of shaking down, for it has been fighting incessantly ever since and for the last fourteen days has been engaged in most nerve-trying warfare, day and night, and they are physically worn out. This I regret to say is the condition of many other battalions also.[83]

Smith-Dorrien's recognition of the acute fragility of his corps impelled him to travel personally to GHQ on the evening of 25 October. There he informed Sir John French and his staff that his line was in serious danger of crumbling during the night.[84] Historians have criticized the II Corps commander for accepting the judgments of his subordinates without sufficient skepticism. Anthony Farrar-Hockley has suggested that Smith-Dorrien's "sensitive and affectionate nature" rendered him vulnerable to pessimistic reports regarding the weakened condition of his troops. Richard Holmes concurs, suggesting that: "it is not unreasonable to conclude, in this instance, that Sir Horace was unduly influenced by the gloomy representations of his divisional commanders."[85]

Given that II Corps did not collapse on the night of 25 October, it is tempting to accept such judgments of its commander. These assessments, however, will not bear serious scrutiny for two reasons. First, contrary to the assertions of Anthony Farrar-Hockley, it is evident that Smith-Dorrien's attachment to his troops was balanced by his concern for his own career. In light of his tenuous relationship with Sir John French, it is highly doubtful that Smith-Dorrien would express his trepidation to the commander-in-chief unless he felt it absolutely imperative. Indeed, on the night of the 22nd, Smith-Dorrien had proved reluctant to inform GHQ of the necessity of withdrawing his force until Loch and Forestier-Walker effectively obliged him to do so. The fact that he had been forced to confess his anxieties to French three days earlier probably left the commander of II Corps even less inclined to reveal the frailty of his force on the 25th. It is thus quite unlikely that Smith-Dorrien would again divulge his alarm to the commander-in-chief unless it was supported by substantial evidence.

There remains the possibility, as Richard Holmes has suggested, that such evidence derived from the inexperienced and ostensibly pessimistic divisional commanders of II Corps. By 25 October, however, it is difficult to imagine that the worsening situation of both divisions required a pessimistic slant in order to persuade Smith-Dorrien of its gravity. The increasing frequency of units abandoning their trenches in II Corps would have been cause for concern among all but the most unobservant or indifferent commanders. As his diary indicates, Smith-Dorrien was well aware of this unsettling trend. Nor was the II Corps commander alone in his anxiety on the night of 25 October. His arrival at GHQ around midnight was in fact preceded by that of Lord Loch, who warned Sir John French that 3 Division was "very shaky."[86] Thus, Smith-Dorrien's warning to GHQ reflected neither his own sentimental disposition nor the distorted perceptions of his divisional commanders. Rather, it was an accurate representation of the deteriorating condition of II Corps as it struggled under continuing German pressure.

Smith-Dorrien's news did little to increase his standing at GHQ. According to Henry Wilson, Sir John French was "rather short" with the II Corps commander upon receiving his news. Fortunately for II Corps, however, the German counteroffensive had sapped GHQ of some of the optimism that it had retained during the advance. Wilson and French may still have held high hopes for the progress of I and IV Corps on the left of the BEF. By the night of 25 October, however, they needed no further convincing of the plight of Smith-Dorrien's force.[87] As a result, GHQ reacted quickly upon learning of the condition of II Corps. The following day, the corps began to receive significant reinforcements, comprising two British and three French artillery batteries, four French infantry battalions, three infantry battalions of the Indian Army, sundry French cavalry units, and the entire 2nd British Cavalry Brigade.[88]

The arrival of substantial support on the 26th enabled 5 Division to weather continued German attacks. French forces shortened Morland's line and allowed British commanders to relieve their troops for the first time since II Corps had departed the Aisne.[89] Once again, however, German attacks fell most heavily against Mackenzie's 3 Division. Despite the arrival of Indian reinforcements, the 7th Brigade lost the village of Neuve Chapelle during the afternoon, as the long-suffering Royal Irish Rifles fled their trenches after being "crushed" by heavy artillery fire. The 7th Brigade launched a counterattack that evening that proved partially successful in clearing Neuve Chapelle of the enemy. The Germans nonetheless retained positions east of the village, which rendered it untenable by 3 Division.[90]

Smith-Dorrien's warnings to GHQ on the 22nd and 25th indicate clearly that he recognized the declining effectiveness of his force. Nevertheless, the ever-present concern of the II Corps commander for his position undoubtedly intensified following his hostile reception by Sir John French on the night of 25 October. Thus, despite the manifest deterioration of II Corps, the recovery of Neuve Chapelle took on an inordinate significance in his mind following the loss of the village on the 26th. The next morning, Smith-Dorrien renewed his efforts to recapture the position, initiating a joint counterattack by French, Indian, and British forces. Such a diverse array of troops created significant organizational challenges. As the II Corps commander later explained: "Owing to the mixing up of different units and nationalities, amongst others the 47th Sikhs, French Chausseurs, 9th Bhopal Infantry, South Lancashire Regiment, Royal Fusiliers, etc., it was difficult to coordinate an attack." The attempt to retake Neuve Chappelle was also impeded by what the II Corps war diary termed the "great weariness" of the 7th Brigade.[91] By late afternoon, the force had made only limited progress in clearing the village.

Just before dusk, a renewed German bombardment overwhelmed the feeble British advance. Under heavy shell fire, the Royal Irish Rifles again evacuated their trenches, accompanied by the adjacent Wiltshire Regiment. According to Smith-Dorrien: "night fell with our line broken, NEUVE CHAPELLE in the hands of the enemy, and our troops in a semi-circle round the North, West and South of the village."[92] The troops of 3 Division were in no state to mount further efforts to regain the position. As Billy Congreve, a staff officer in 3 Division, related in his diary on the 27th:

The Battalions of the 7th Brigade, who are holding these trenches, are nearly done for, for this incessant shelling with the big shells is very terrible. They have hardly any officers left, and the men are few and rather nerve-broken. It's getting on for three weeks' hard and continuous fighting now, always under fire by day and driving off desperately hard pushed attacks by night.[93]

In light of the condition of the troops, neither Mackenzie nor Morland appears to have favored the prospect of mounting further counterattacks on the night of the 27th. Nevertheless, Smith-Dorrien proved unwilling to concede German control of the village. Bypassing the commander of 5 Division, he instructed Stanley Maude to retake Neuve Chapelle that evening with his ostensibly stronger 14th Brigade as well as the remaining Cheshires and Dorsets of the 15th Brigade. By disregarding the two divisional commanders, such a directive contravened the command philosophy of umpiring. Smith-Dorrien's indifference toward this policy on the evening of 27 October indicates the strength of his desire to retake Neuve Chapelle. It soon became evident, however, that the troops he had assigned to the counterattack were not up to the task. According to Stanley Maude's Brigade-Major, Dyck-Cunyngham, when the Cheshires and Dorsets arrived, "one could see at once that they were not in a fit state to make the attack." Rather than assault an unfamiliar position in pitch darkness with exhausted troops, Maude demurred.[94]

Despite the condition of his force and the complete failure of counterattacks on the 27th, the II Corps commander obstinately renewed his attempts to recapture Neuve Chapelle the following day. Predictably, these efforts proved futile. In addition to suffering from the same poor coordination that had prevailed on 27 October, the counterattack planned by Smith-Dorrien for the morning of the 28th was delayed by fog until 11 am.[95] Even in the absence of these factors, however, three weeks of accruing fatigue and losses had sapped British units of their cohesion. Billy Congreve's diary provides a glimpse of the chaos that ensued as the advance of 3 Division floundered in the face of German opposition late in the afternoon. As Congreve, a lieutenant, related:

It was getting dark now, and when I got to Pont Logy I found to my horror that the ____'s and ____'s were retiring, goodness only knows why. I felt inclined to sit down and cry, but hadn't time. The men said they had had orders to retire; there were very few officers about. The Officer Commanding, a Captain I think he was, saluted me and called me "sir," which shows he was pretty far gone. So I ordered him about just as I wanted.[96]

The dubious justification for Smith-Dorrien's repeated attempts to retake Neuve Chapelle was further underlined in the aftermath of the failed 28 October attack, when the II Corps commander "came to the conclusion that the village was of no use to the enemy, as they could not stay in it with all our guns turned onto it, and therefore I decided to make no further attempts to re-take it."[97] The enemy came to a similar realization, evacuating Neuve Chapelle on the night of the 28th. This sudden abdication of the village by both armies reflects rather poorly on Smith-Dorrien's judgment. Had he determined that Neuve Chapelle was untenable on the 26th, his corps might have been spared two days of intense fighting. The desire of the II Corps commander to appear resolute in the eyes of GHQ, however, led him to unnecessary lengths to recapture the village. Rather than using his artillery to drive the enemy from Neuve Chapelle immediately following its loss, he resorted to repeated and ill-advised attempts to recapture it. The abortive counterattacks proved costly. On the 28th alone, the British lost 65 officers and 1,466 other ranks in an effort to take a position that the enemy abandoned voluntarily after dark.[98]

Combined with Smith-Dorrien's warnings on the 22nd and 25th, the unsuccessful efforts of II Corps to regain Neuve Chapelle in subsequent days finally convinced Sir John French and his staff that the formation was no longer reliable. Late on the night of the 27th, the commander-in-chief thus resolved to relieve the entire corps with Sir James Willcocks's newly arrived Indian Corps.

As Smith-Dorrien did not learn of the impending withdrawal of his force until he met with French the next day, the news came too late to halt his counterattack on the 28th. While he recognized the exhaustion of II Corps, the commander-in-chief nonetheless surmised that its difficulties originated elsewhere. As he explained cryptically in a wire to Lord Kitchener on the night of 27 October: "Both Divisions need rest badly and are tired out. I am not well satisfied as to their condition, although they have had a hard time. When they are clear of the trenches I will find out what is wrong."[99] Although he did not indicate as much to Kitchener, French evidently suspected that the failures of II Corps stemmed from its commander. Consequently, upon withdrawing the force, French placed it in reserve under his direct control, effectively removing Smith-Dorrien from the chain of command. The units of II Corps continued to play an important role as reserves as the First Battle of Ypres reached its climax in subsequent days. Their commander, however, was left without significant responsibilities. Following the relief of his force on 30 October, Smith-Dorrien and his staff spent the next three weeks on hiatus, shooting game in the French countryside and even enjoying a short visit to England.[100] Thus, despite Smith-Dorrien's costly attempts to demonstrate his resolve by retaking Neuve Chapelle, he was ultimately marginalized at the critical point in the 1914 campaign.

Largely oblivious to the friction among senior commanders, the units of II Corps commenced their withdrawal on the night of 28 October. For three successive nights, troops of the Indian Corps gradually replaced Smith-Dorrien's force. On the morning of 31 October, the II Corps commander formally relinquished command of the line to Sir James Willcocks. Smith-Dorrien's force had suffered heavily during October, especially given its depleted condition at the beginning of the month. On the 29th, the II Corps commander reported the casualties to his force since the beginning of the advance as 358 officers and 8,204 other ranks.[101] The battered troops of II Corps welcomed their relief after three weeks of continuous fighting. As Count Gleichen reflected: "It was with a feeling of extreme thankfulness that we left the horrible mud-plain of Festubert and Givenchy, with its cold, wet climate and its swampy surroundings and its dismal memories, for both Dorsets and Cheshires had suffered terribly in the fighting here. And the pleasantest feeling was to hear the noise of the bursting shells grow less and ever less as we worked north-westwards."[102]

Most units would enjoy only a brief rest, as intensifying German pressure soon necessitated their redeployment elsewhere along the British line. Stanley Maude's 14th Brigade and much of the II Corps artillery were assigned to bolster the Indian Corps and never actually left their positions.[103] Nevertheless, the relief of II Corps on 31 October marked the end of its participation as a coherent entity in the First Battle of Ypres. When Sir Horace Smith-Dorrien led his force back into the British line on 18 November, the crisis had passed.

CONCLUSION

Smith-Dorrien's II Corps played a pivotal role in the preservation of the British line in late October 1914 as it withstood repeated German attacks from the 20th until its relief up to ten days later. Significant casualties were inevitable in the face of continuous enemy pressure. Nevertheless, the condition of II Corps upon its withdrawal did not result solely from German attacks. Rather, the progressive deterioration of Smith-Dorrien's force throughout October derived in part from the behavior of senior British officers. In the upper ranks of the BEF, key decisions were influenced significantly by personal alliances and animosities. In light of his tenuous relationship with Lord Kitchener, particularly after the fall of Antwerp, Sir John French felt considerable pressure to produce concrete results from the offensive. His determination to press the advance of II Corps was encouraged by Henry Wilson, who retained his informal authority at GHQ in early October. With the consequent marginalization of Archie Murray and George Macdonogh's Intelligence Section, GHQ initiated the advance of II Corps on a broad front with little consideration for the condition of Smith-Dorrien's force, the terrain in its vicinity, or the arrival of enemy forces.

The tense relationship between Sir Horace Smith-Dorrien and Sir John French paralleled that between the commander-in-chief and Lord Kitchener. Consequently, Smith-Dorrien complied with orders from GHQ and pushed his tired force forward despite a clear awareness of its depleted condition. He also deflected responsibility for the faltering advance of II Corps by sacking experienced commanders such as Charles Fergusson. Even after the beginning of the German counteroffensive, Smith-Dorrien's concern for his position led him to conceal the rapidly deteriorating condition of his corps and even to launch futile counterattacks in an effort to demonstrate his resolve.

Dysfunction in the upper ranks of the army forced the battalions of II Corps to rely on regimental pride and the personal leadership of junior officers. These qualities undoubtedly accounted for much of the limited success of Smith-Dorrien's advance. More importantly, they prevented the collapse of the II Corps line in late October. Nevertheless, a dependence on these traits proved costly. Leading attacks against strong enemy positions exacted a heavy toll among the regimental officers of Smith-Dorrien's force. Such behavior had unfortunate consequences further up in the ranks as well, as Hubert Hamilton's deliberate contempt for enemy fire led to his death on 14 October. In the absence of effective leadership at the divisional level, the fierce pride of British regiments could also have dangerous consequences, as was demonstrated by the demise of the Royal Irish Regiment on 20 October. Ultimately, an excessive reliance on regimental pride and personal leadership proved unsustainable against unrelenting German attacks. By late October, II Corps had been rendered ineffective by heavy losses. While its units were dispersed throughout the British line during the latter stages of the First Battle of Ypres, it was only after the arrival of substantial reinforcements in late November and December that II

Corps regained any semblance of fighting efficiency. The force that emerged, however, was fundamentally different from that which had embarked for France in August. The original incarnation of II Corps had met its end in late October, as tensions and rivalries among senior officers distracted them from the exigencies of active operations.

NOTES

1. James Edmonds, *Military Operations: France and Belgium, 1914*, vol. 2 (London: Macmillan, 1925), v.

2. Holger Herwig, *The First World War: Germany and Austria-Hungary, 1914–1918* (New York: Arnold, 1997), 116; Edmonds, *Military Operations: France and Belgium, 1914*, 467–469. This figure includes casualties incurred fighting the French Army as well as the BEF.

3. Anthony Farrar-Hockley, *Death of an Army* (New York: Morrow, 1968), 38–130; Richard Holmes, *The Little Field Marshal: Sir John French* (London: Jonathan Cape, 1981), 243–248.

4. Peter Scott, ed., "The View from GHQ: The Third Part of the Diary of General Sir Charles Deedes, KCB, CMG, DSO," *Stand To!* 12 (Winter 1984), 28. Edmonds, *Military Operations: France and Belgium, 1914*, 29; Farrar-Hockley, *Death of an Army*, 40.

5. Holmes, *The Little Field-Marshal*, 242; Wilson Diary, 24–26 September 1914, Henry Wilson Papers, Imperial War Museum, London (IWM). On the intention of advancing into Flanders, see Edmonds, *Military Operations: France and Belgium, 1914*, 29; Kitchener to French, 3 October 1914, WO 33/713, Public Record Office London (PRO).

6. French to Kitchener, 4 October 1914. See also French to Kitchener, 6 October, 7 October 1914; Kitchener to French, 3 October, 7 October 1914, WO 33/713, PRO.

7. French to Kitchener, 7 Oct 1914. See also French to Kitchener 6 October 1914, WO 33/713, PRO.

8. Kitchener to French, 3 October 1914, WO 33/713, PRO.

9. Wilson Diary, 9 October 1914, Henry Wilson Papers, IWM. See also Wilson to Henry Rawlinson, undated, October 1914, Henry Rawlinson Papers, 1/1, Churchill College, Cambridge (CCC); Scott, "The View from GHQ: The Third Part of the War Diary of General Sir Charles Deedes," 28.

10. Rawlinson Diary, 1 October, 15 October 1914, Rawlinson Papers, 1/1, CCC. See also Victor Bonham-Carter, *The Strategy of Victory, 1914–1918: The Life and Times of the Master Strategist of World War I: Field-Marshal Sir William Robertson* (New York: Holt, Rinehart and Winston, 1963), 101.

11. Wilson Diary, 25 September, 8 October, 14–16 October 1914, Henry Wilson Papers, IWM.

12. Walter Kirke, "Lieut-General Sir George M.W. Macdonough, GBE, KCB, KCML," Walter Kirke Papers, Intelligence Corps Museum (ICM), Chicksands, Bedfordshire.

13. GHQ War Diary, 1 October 1914, GHQ Operation Order No. 28, 3pm, 1 October 1914, WO 95/1; II Corps War Diary, 1 October 1914, WO 95/629; II Corps Operation

Order No. 27, 12:45 pm, WO 95/630; II Corps War Diary, 5 October 1914, WO 95/629, PRO; Wilson Diary, 30 September 1914, Henry Wilson Papers, IWM.

14. 3 Division War Diary, 10 October 1914, WO 95/1375; Smith-Dorrien Diary, 6, 9 October 1914, CAB 45/206, PRO. Loch Diary, 10 October 1914, Lord Loch Papers, IWM; Charles Callwell, *The Life of Sir Stanley Maude* (London: Constable, 1920), 126.

15. Murray Diary, 9 October 1914, Archibald Murray Papers, IWM; Wilson Diary 11 October 1914, Henry Wilson Papers, IWM.

16. R. Money Barnes, *The British Army of 1914* (London: Seely, 1968); Count Edward Gleichen, *The Doings of the Fifteenth Infantry Brigade, August 1914 to March 1915* (London: Blackwood, 1917), 2.

17. Edmonds, *Military Operations: France and Belgium, 1914*, 467.

18. Smith-Dorrien Diary, 12 October 1914, CAB 45/206, PRO; II Corps War Diary, 13 October 1914, WO 95/629, PRO; John Headlam to Edmonds, 2 April 1923, CAB 45/182, PRO; Arthur Conan-Doyle, *The British Campaign in France and Flanders, 1914* (London: Hodder and Stoughton, 1916), 206; A. Corbett-Smith, *The Marne—And After*, (Toronto: Cassell, 1917), 198; Farrar-Hockley, *Death of an Army*, 46–47.

19. II Corps War Diary, 13 October 1914, WO 95/629, PRO; Aylmer Haldane to 4 Division Headquarters, 28 October 1914, 4 Division War Diary, WO 95/1440, PRO; Corbett-Smith, *The Marne—And After*, 198; Conan-Doyle, *The British Campaign in France and Flanders*, 206.

20. Smith-Dorrien Diary, 15 October 1914, CAB 45/206, PRO; French to Kitchener, 14 October 1914, WO 33/713, PRO; Conan-Doyle, *The British Campaign in France and Flanders*, 209.

21. Smith-Dorrien Diary, 10–11 October 1914, CAB 45/206, PRO; "General Smith-Dorrien's Report on Operations of II Corps, 11th October to 18th November 1914," II Corps War Diary, WO 95/630; Macdonogh to Edmonds, 22 November 1923, CAB 45/141, PRO. See also Loch Diary, 9 October 1914, Lord Loch Papers, IWM.

22. "General Smith-Dorrien's Report on the Operations of II Corps, 11th October to 18th November 1914," II Corps War Diary, WO 95/630; GHQ Operation Orders No. 33 and No. 34, 10, 11 October 1914, WO 95/1, PRO.

23. II Corps War Diary, 11 October 1914, WO 95/629; Smith-Dorrien Diary, 11–12 October 1914, CAB 45/206, PRO.

24. Smith-Dorrien Diary, 12 October 1914, CAB 45/206; GHQ War Diary, 12 October 1914, WO 95/1; II Corps War Diary, 12 October 1914, WO 95/629; 5 Division War Diary, WO 95/1510, PRO.

25. GHQ War Diary, 13 October 1914, WO 95/1; III Corps War Diary, 13 October 1914, WO 95/668; Cavalry Corps War Diary, 13 October 1914, WO 95/572, PRO.

26. Scott, "The View from GHQ: The Third Part of the War Diary of General Sir Charles Deedes," 28; Smith-Dorrien Diary, 13 October 1914, CAB 45/206, PRO. See also II Corps War Diary, 13 October 1914, WO 95/629; 3 Division War Diary, 13 October 1914, WO 95/1375; 5 Division War Diary, WO 95/1510, PRO.

27. II Corps War Diary, 12 October 1914, WO 95/629; "Report on operations of the 3rd Division from 11th to 30th October 1914," 3 Division War Diary, WO 95/1375, PRO.

28. Gleichen, *The Doings of the Fifteenth Infantry Brigade*, 163; Smith-Dorrien Diary, 13 October 1914, CAB 45/206, PRO; Conan-Doyle, *The British Campaign in France and Flanders*, 207–208.

29. Gleichen, *The Doings of the Fifteenth Infantry Brigade*, 147; John Terraine, *Mons: The Retreat to Victory*, 2d ed. (London: Leo Cooper, 1991), 119.

30. 5 Division War Diary, 13 October 1914, WO 95/1510, PRO; Gleichen, *The Doings of the Fifteenth Infantry Brigade,* 160–162.

31. Gleichen, *The Doings of the Fifteenth Infantry Brigade*, 162.

32. Loch Diary, 13 October 1914, Lord Loch Papers, IWM; Gleichen *The Doings of the Fifteenth Infantry Brigade*, 163–165.

33. 5 Division War Diary, 13 October 1914, WO 95/1510; GHQ War Diary, 13 October 1914, WO 95/1; Smith-Dorrien Diary, 13 October 1914, CAB 45/206; PRO; Gleichen, *The Doings of the Fifteenth Infantry Brigade*, 164–165; Loch Diary, 13 October 1914, Lord Loch Papers, IWM.

34. French to Kitchener, 14 October 1914, WO 33/713, PRO; Loch Diary, 15 October 1914, Lord Loch Papers, IWM.

35. Gleichen, *The Doings of the Fifteenth Infantry Brigade*, 141.

36. 5 Division War Diary, 13 October 1914, WO 95/1510; II Corps War Diary, 13 October 1914, WO 95/629, PRO; Gleichen, *The Doings of the Fifteenth Infantry Brigade*, 164–165.

37. Smith-Dorrien Diary, 13 October 1914, CAB 45/206, PRO.

38. II Corps War Diary, 13 October 1914, WO 95/629, PRO.

39. II Corps War Diary, 13 October 1914, WO 95/629; 5 Division War Diary, 13 October 1914, WO 95/1510, PRO.

40. French Diary, 13 October 1914, John French Papers, IWM; French to Kitchener, 14 October 1914, 12:05 am, WO 33/713, PRO.

41. Loch Diary, 15 October 1914, Lord Loch Papers, IWM.

42. French to Kitchener, 14 October 1914, 6:33 pm, WO 33/713; 5 Division War Diary, 14 October 1914, WO 95/1510; 3 Division War Diary, WO 95/1375, PRO.

43. French Diary, 14 October 1914, John French Papers, IWM.

44. Callwell, *The Life of Sir Stanley Maude*, 144; Smith-Dorrien Diary, 18 October 1918, CAB 45/206, PRO. Despite his promotion, Fergusson would continue to suffer from machinations in the upper ranks of the army. For an account of his removal in June 1916 to enable the promotion of Hubert Gough to command the Second Army, see Tim Travers, *The Killing Ground: the British Army, the Western Front and the Emergence of Modern Warfare, 1900–1918* (London: Routledge, 1993), 11.

45. Wilson Diary, 14–15 October 1914, Henry Wilson Papers; French Diary, 13 October 1914, John French Papers, IWM. See also Holmes, *The Little Field-Marshal*, 243–249, for an account of French's fluctuating spirits during October 1914.

46. III Corps War Diary, 13 October 1914, WO 95/668; II Corps War Diary, 14 October 1914, WO 95/629, PRO.

47. Smith-Dorrien Diary, 14 October 1914, CAB 45/206; 3 Division War Diary, 14 October 1914, WO 95/1375; French to Kitchener, 14 October 1914, 6:33 pm, WO 33/713, PRO.

48. Martin van Creveld, *Command in War* (Cambridge MA: Harvard University Press, 1985), 156–157. On this tendency in the British Army in particular, see, for example, Martin Samuels, *Command or Control? Command, Training and Tactics in the British and German Armies, 1888–1918* (London: Frank Cass, 1995), 59, 130; Travers, *The Killing Ground*, 108–109; Paul Fussell, *The Great War and Modern Memory* (New York: Oxford University Press, 1975), 82–85.

49. Pamela Fraser and J.H. Thornton, *The Congreves: Father and Son, General Sir Walter Norris Congreve, V.C., Bt-Major William LaTouche Congreve, V.C.* (London: John Murray, 1930), 128–129.

50. Congreve diary in Fraser and Thornton, *The Congreves*, 232. See also Ernest Hamilton, *The First Seven Divisions: Being a Detailed Account of the Fighting from Mons to Ypres* (New York: Dutton, 1916), 154.

51. 3 Division War Diary, WO 95/1375; PRO; Smith-Dorrien Diary, 15 October 1914, CAB 45/206, PRO. Hamilton, *The First Seven Divisions*, 154; Fraser and Thornton, *The Congreves*, 233.

52. Loch Diary, 17 October 1914, Lord Loch Papers, IWM; 5 Division War Diary, 15 October 1914, WO 95/1510, PRO.

53. Wilson Diary, 15 October 1914, Henry Wilson Papers, IWM.

54. II Corps War Diary, 16 October 1914, WO 95/629; 3 Division War Diary, 16 October 1914, WO 95/1375; 5 Division War Diary, 16 October 1914, WO 95/1510; Smith-Dorrien Diary, 16 October 1914, CAB 45/206; GHQ Operation Order No.36, 15 October 1914, GHQ War Diary, WO 95/1, PRO.

55. Loch Diary, 17 October 1914, Lord Loch Papers, IWM. See also Smith-Dorrien Diary, 16, 18 October 1914, CAB 45/206, PRO.

56. 3 Division War Diary, 19 October 1914, WO 95/1375; II Corps War Diary, WO 95/629, PRO.

57. 5 Division War Diary 17–19 October 1914, WO 95/1510; II Corps War Diary, 17–19 October 1914, WO 95/629, PRO.

58. Haig Diary, 17 October 1914, NLS; WO 256/2, PRO; Wilson Diary, 18 October 1914, Wilson Papers, IWM.

59. Loch Diary, 18 October 1914, Lord Loch Papers, IWM.

60. Gleichen, *The Doings of the Fifteenth Infantry Brigade*, 177. See also 5 Division War Diary, 19 October 1914, WO 95/1510, PRO; Aylmer Haldane, *A Brigade of the Old Army* (London: Arnold, 1920), 145.

61. Loch Diary, 19 October 1914, Loch Papers, IWM; 3 Division War Diary, 19 October 1914, WO 95/1375; 5 Division War Diary, 19 October 1914, WO 95/1510; II Corps War Diary, 19 October 1914, WO 95/629, PRO.

62. Wilson Diary, 19 October 1914, Henry Wilson Papers, IWM.

63. 5 Division War Diary, 20 October 1914, WO 95/1510; II Corps War Diary, 20 October 1914, WO 95/629; GHQ War Diary, 20 October 1914, WO 95/1; III Corps War Diary, 20 October 1914, WO 95/668; Cavalry Corps War Diary, 20 October 1914, WO 95/572, PRO; Archibald Home, *A Diary of a World War I Cavalry Officer* (Tunbridge Wells: Costello, 1985), 31; II Corps to 3 and 5 Divisions, 19 October 1914, 7 pm, II Corps War Diary, WO 95/630, PRO.

64. M.C.C. Harrison, "Operations of the 2nd Battalion, The Royal Irish Regiment, on 18th 19th and 20th October," 8th Brigade War Diary, WO 95/1416, PRO.

65. "General Smith-Dorrien's Report on Operations of II Corps, 11th October to 18th November 1914," II Corps War Diary, WO 95/630; Smith-Dorrien Diary, 20 October 1914, CAB 45/206, PRO.

66. Harrison, "Operations of 2nd Battalion, The Royal Irish Regiment," 8th Brigade War Diary, WO 95/1416; "General Smith-Dorrien's Report on Operations of II Corps," II Corps War Diary, WO 95/630, PRO. Hamilton, *The First Seven Divisions*, 168; Conan-Doyle, *The British Campaign in France and Flanders*, 212.

67. GHQ to War Office, 22 October 1914, 9 am, WO 33/713, PRO; Loch Diary, 21 October 1914, IWM.

68. II Corps War Diary, 19 October 1914, WO 95/629, PRO.

69. John Baynes, *Morale: A Study of Men and Courage: The Second Scottish Rifles at the Battle of Neuve Chapelle, 1915* (New York: Praeger, 1967), 169. See also John Masters, *Bugles and a Tiger: A Volume of Autobiography* (New York: Viking, 1956), 122–123.

70. F.A. Bolwell, *With a Reservist in France: A Personal Account of all the Engagements in Which the 1st Division 1st Corps Took Part, Viz: Mons (Including the Retirement), the Marne, the Aisne, First Battle of Ypres, Neuve Chappelle, Festubert, and Loos* (London: Routledge, 1916), 102. See also Hamilton, *The First Seven Divisions*, 6.

71. II Corps War Diary, 21 October 1914, WO 95/629; "General Smith-Dorrien's Report on Operations of II Corps," II Corps War Diary, WO 95/630; 3 Division War Diary, 21 October 1914, WO 95/1375; Smith-Dorrien Diary, 20 October 1914, CAB 45/206; II Corps War Diary, WO 95/629, PRO; Gleichen, *The Doings of the Fifteenth Infantry Brigade*, 178.

72. Headlam to Edmonds, 2 April 1923, CAB 45/182; 5 Division War Diary, 21 October 1914, WO 95/1510, PRO.

73. Smith-Dorrien to GHQ, 22 October 1914, II Corps War Diary, WO 95/629; "General Smith-Dorrien's Report on Operations of II Corps, 11th October to 18th November 1914," II Corps War Diary, WO 95/630; Smith-Dorrien Diary, 22 October 1914, CAB 45/206, PRO; Loch Diary, 22 October 1914, Loch Papers, IWM; Gleichen, *The Doings of the Fifteenth Infantry Brigade,* 179–180.

74. GHQ War Diary, 22 October 1914, WO 95/1; 5 Division War Diary, 22 October 1914, WO 95/1510; Smith-Dorrien to GHQ, 22 October 1914, II Corps War Diary, WO 95/629, PRO.

75. Acland Diary, 22 October 1914, A.N. Acland Papers, Liddle Collection, Brotherton Library, University of Leeds.

76. Loch Diary, 22 October 1914, Loch Papers, IWM; 5 Division War Diary, 22 October 1914, WO 95/1510, PRO.

77. Smith-Dorrien to GHQ, 22 October 1914, II Corps War Diary, WO 95/629; Smith-Dorrien Diary, 22 October 1914, CAB 45/206, PRO; Wilson Diary, 22 October 1914, Henry Wilson Papers, IWM.

78. Loch Diary, 22 October 1914, Loch Papers, IWM.

79. Edmonds, *Military Operations, France and Belgium*, vol. 2, 206; Gleichen, *The Doings of the Fifteenth Infantry Brigade*, 181–182; Smith-Dorrien Diary, 22 October 1914, CAB 45/206; Loch Diary, 23 October 1914, Loch Papers, IWM.

80. Loch Diary, 23 October 1914, Loch Papers, IWM; GHQ War Diary, 23 October 1914, WO 95/1, PRO.

81. 3 Division War Diary, 24 October 1914, WO 95/1375; II Corps War Diary, 25 October 1914, WO 95/629; "General Smith-Dorrien's Report on Operations of II Corps, 11th October to 18 November," II Corps War Diary, WO 95/630; Smith-Dorrien Diary, 25 October 1914, CAB 45/206, PRO.

82. 3 Division War Diary, 25 October 1914, WO 95/1375; II Corps War Diary, 25 October 1914, WO 95/629; Smith-Dorrien Diary, 25 October 1914, CAB 45/206, PRO.

83. Smith-Dorrien Diary, 25 October 1914, CAB 45/206, PRO.

84. Smith-Dorrien Diary, 25 October 1914, CAB 45/206, PRO; Wilson Diary, 25 October 1914, Henry Wilson Papers; Loch Diary, 25 October 1914, Lord Loch Papers; Murray Diary, 25 October 1914, Archibald Murray Papers, IWM.

85. Holmes, *The Little Field-Marshal*, 247; Farrar-Hockley, *Death of an Army*, 120.

86. Loch Diary, 25 October 1914, Loch Papers, IWM.

87. Wilson Diary, 25 October 1914, Henry Wilson Papers, IWM; GHQ War Diary, 23 October 1914, WO 95/1; II Corps to 5 Division, 23 October 1914, 9:26 pm, 5 Division War Diary, WO 95/1510; French to Kitchener, 26 October 1914, 9:05 am, WO 33/713, PRO.

88. Wilson Diary, 25 October 1914, Henry Wilson Papers, IWM; Smith-Dorrien Diary, 26 October 1914, CAB 45/206, PRO; Gleichen, *The Doings of the Fifteenth Infantry Brigade,* 187–188.

89. Gleichen, *The Doings of the Fifteenth Infantry Brigade,* 188; 5 Division War Diary, 26 October 1914, WO 95/1510; II Corps War Diary, 26 October 1914, WO 95/629, PRO.

90. "General Smith-Dorrien's Report on Operations of II Corps, 11th October to 18th November," II Corps War Diary, WO 95/630; Smith-Dorrien Diary, 26 October 1914, CAB 45/206; II Corps War Diary, 26 October 1914, WO 95/629; 3 Division War Diary, WO 95/1375, PRO.

91. "General Smith-Dorrien's Report on Operations of II Corps, 11th October to 18th November," II Corps War Diary, WO 95/630; II Corps War Diary, 27 October 1914, WO 95/629, PRO. See also 3 Division War Diary, 27 October 1914, WO 95/1375, PRO.

92. "General Smith-Dorrien's Report on Operations of II Corps, 11th October to 18th November," II Corps War Diary, WO 95/630, PRO.

93. Fraser and Thornton, *The Congreves*, 238.

94. Callwell, *The Life of Sir Stanley Maude*, 135–136. See also Wing to II Corps, 31 October 1914, II Corps War Diary, WO 95/629, PRO.

95. "General Smith-Dorrien's Report on Operations of II Corps, 11th October to 18th November," II Corps War Diary, WO 95/630; 3 Division War Diary, 28 October 1914, WO 95/1375; 5 Division War Diary, 28 October 1914, WO 95/1510; Smith-Dorrien Diary, 28 October 1914, CAB 45/206, PRO.

96. Fraser and Thornton, *The Congreves*, 245–246.

97. "General Smith-Dorrien's Report on Operations of II Corps, 11th October to 18th November," II Corps War Diary, WO 95/630, PRO.

98. Hamilton, *The First Seven Divisions*, 208–209.

99. French to Kitchener, 27 October 1914, 11:30 pm, WO 33/713; GHQ War Diary, 27 October 1914, WO 95/1; Smith-Dorrien Diary, 28 October 1914, CAB 45/206, PRO.

100. Smith-Dorrien Diary, 30 October–18 November 1914, CAB 45/206, PRO.

101. Smith-Dorrien Diary, 29 October 1914, CAB 45/206, PRO; Conan-Doyle, *The British Campaign in France and Flanders*, 225; GHQ War Diary, 28–31 October 1914, WO 95/1; Indian Corps War Diary, 28–31 October 1914, WO 95/1088, PRO.

102. Gleichen, *The Doings of the Fifteenth Infantry Brigade*, 199.

103. Smith-Dorrien Diary, 31 October 1914, CAB 45/206, PRO.

5

Losing the Race for the Flank: The First Incarnation of IV Corps, 9–25 October

Sir Henry Rawlinson's IV Corps was the last contingent of the Regular Army to join the BEF in 1914. Comprised of 7 Division and 3 Cavalry Division, the corps was conceived by Lord Kitchener in early October as an independent expeditionary force assigned to prevent the German capture of Antwerp. When it was unable to reach the Belgian city before its capitulation, the secretary of state for war placed the force under the orders of GHQ. After formally designating the contingent as IV Corps, Sir John French directed Rawlinson to join the offensive on the left of the BEF. Before he could make any significant gains, however, the German Army initiated its counteroffensive on October 20, launching heavy attacks against Rawlinson's corps. As both divisions incurred increasing losses over the next week, GHQ disbanded the force, attaching 3 Cavalry Division to Allenby's Cavalry Corps and placing 7 Division temporarily under Sir Douglas Haig in I Corps. Without a formation to command, Rawlinson returned to England. Until the arrival of 8 Division in Flanders in mid-November, IV Corps ceased to exist.

While the operational debut of IV Corps has received little scholarly scrutiny, existing accounts of this period allude to friction between senior officers, especially Sir Henry Rawlinson and Sir John French.[1] The impact of this particular relationship on the operations of IV Corps, however, has not been considered. Nor has there been any analysis of command within the corps itself. The experiences of Rawlinson's force during this period thus remain poorly understood. Even its unusual dismantling has yet to be explained. Accordingly, this chapter will assess the impact of command on the operations of IV Corps from its attachment to the BEF on 9 October until its dispersal between 25 and 27 October. It will argue that the optimism of senior officers, combined with their ambiguous orders, undermined relations between Sir Henry Rawlinson and GHQ during the short-lived advance of IV Corps. Under the pressure of the

German counteroffensive, this strained relationship, as well as discord among officers within 7 Division exacerbated problems created by the inexperience of Rawlinson and his subordinates, leaving the battalions of IV Corps exceedingly vulnerable to enemy attacks. While the leadership and personal bravery of junior officers prevented the line from disintegrating, 7 Division was left exhausted and depleted after only a week of German attacks. Frustrated with Rawlinson, Sir John French dispatched him to England, placing his divisions in the care of more trustworthy commanders.

GHQ AND IV CORPS AT THE OUTSET OF THE ADVANCE

Sir Henry Rawlinson's IV Corps had its genesis in Lord Kitchener's ill-fated attempt to prevent the fall of Antwerp in early October 1914. As German pressure on the city increased, Kitchener commandeered Thompson Capper's 7 Division and Julian Byng's 3 Cavalry Division, both of which were preparing for their assignment to the BEF. Placing the two divisions under Rawlinson's command, the secretary of state for war despatched them to Belgium on 4 October. Even before the force finished disembarking, however, it became clear that its task would be impossible. By the night of the 8th, heavy shelling had forced the Belgian Army and a small detachment of British Royal Marines to abandon Antwerp. Consequently, Kitchener placed Rawlinson's contingent under the orders of GHQ on 9 October.[2]

Eager to secure significant results from his proposed offensive in northern France and Flanders, Sir John French wasted little time in incorporating Rawlinson's force into his plans. After officially identifying the new formation as IV Corps, French instructed its commander to hold positions around the Belgian town of Courtrai until the arrival of II Corps and Allenby's newly formed Cavalry Corps, on the "13th or 14th October at the latest." Joined by the rest of the BEF, IV Corps would form the left wing of the British advance (see Map 5.1).[3] Subsequent developments necessitated the modification of French's plan. The approach of German forces from Antwerp on the 11th and the slow progress of the other British formations forced the withdrawal of IV Corps on the night of 13 October, "to help the II and III Army Corps get out of their present position."[4] Despite this delay, Sir John French remained hopeful that IV Corps would quickly relieve the pressure on the rest of his force and enable a general advance. After a meeting with the commander-in-chief on the 15th, Rawlinson noted in his diary: "He [French] is, I think somewhat optimistic, but that is better than the other extreme."[5]

The attitude of the commander-in-chief derived in part from the reputed quality of IV Corps, particularly 7 Division. Even in comparison to the other divisions of the BEF in 1914, accounts of contemporary observers suggest a widespread perception of Capper's division as a superior formation. This venerable reputation stemmed primarily from the fact that 7 Division was composed of battalions summoned from foreign garrison duty at the beginning of the war. These units contained a minimal proportion of reservists compared to

Map 5.1
I and IV Corps Area of Operations, October–November 1914

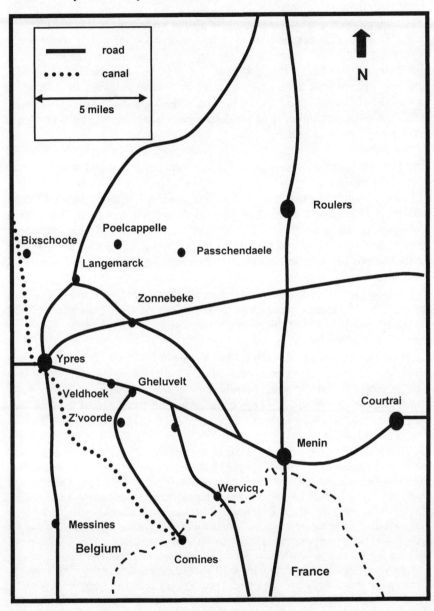

those mobilized in England in August 1914.[6] Particularly formidable among the battalions of Capper's division were the 1/Grenadier Guards and 2/Scots Guards of the 20th Brigade, commanded by H.G. Ruggles-Brice. Long perceived as elite infantry units within the British Army, the strong traditions and dignified bearing of the Guards were conspicuous even in a military organization where fierce regimental pride was commonplace. According to J.M. Craster, the historian of the 2/Grenadier Guards: "The Brigade of Guards, the modern Household Division, did not have a monopoly of discipline, smartness and professionalism in the BEF, but as an elite they did believe in the highest standards in all three, believe in them, demand them and maintain them, whatever the cost. They might be matched, but never beaten."[7]

Sir John French's confidence in the capabilities of IV Corps was enhanced further by the fact that its two divisional commanders demonstrated the qualities of courage and self-sacrifice favored by British officers in 1914. At the head of 7 Division, Tommy Capper exemplified the "hybrid" nature of many senior officers in this period. At Camberley and during his command of the Staff College at Quetta from 1906 to 1911, Capper had demonstrated a sincere interest in his profession, earning the praise of many of his contemporaries. Capper's conception of his role as an officer, however, placed considerable value on traditional notions such as personal bravery and self-sacrifice. The 7 Division commander lived up to these ideals on the battlefield, providing a visible example to his troops. According to C.D. Baker-Carr: "Day after day he [Capper] exposed himself in the most reckless fashion. He wasn't brave; he simply did not know what fear meant."[8]

Julian Byng did not enjoy the same prominence as Capper in the prewar army. Nevertheless, the commander of 3 Cavalry Division demonstrated a similar emphasis on personal bravery during the campaign of 1914. Toby Rawlinson, brother of the IV Corps commander and a member of the IV Corps staff, observed Byng under fire on 21 October. According to Rawlinson:

On my return to the main road I found that General Byng had gone on in the direction of Neuve Eglise, and I came up with him at a little roadside cafe on the slope commanding the valley between the hill of Kemmel and the village of Neuve Eglise. There was no doubt that the enemy was holding the crest of the opposite hill, and our own line had not yet descended into the valley. The General therefore ordered some coffee in the little cafe, and, to my astonishment, refused to partake of it in the house, but insisted that the table should be brought out into the road. He then sat down to his coffee in full view of both the enemy's line on the opposite hill and of our own men, who were then descending into the valley. This was done with the most complete unconcern in order that he might be able to observe the advance of our line. There was not the least suggestion of bravado, though it was obvious to everyone that he was offering himself as a most exceptionally favourable target to the enemy.[9]

Despite the obvious hazards of such behavior, senior British officers placed a premium on personal bravery in 1914. Indeed, the courage and resolve of

Edward Bulfin during the battle of the Aisne had resulted in his promotion to Major-General. The fact that both Capper and Byng were prone to similar conduct was thus likely an encouragement to Sir John French as IV Corps joined the BEF. Combined with the perceived proficiency of 7 Division, the presence of two courageous divisional commanders heightened the optimism of the commander-in-chief as Sir Henry Rawlinson's force prepared to advance into Flanders.

In light of the spirited leadership and relatively robust condition of IV Corps in early October, particularly in comparison to Smith-Dorrien's depleted II Corps, Sir John French's confidence is not unfathomable. Nonetheless, his desire to strike the German flank led the commander-in-chief to ignore several factors limiting the effectiveness of Rawlinson's formation. First, IV Corps could muster neither the manpower nor the firepower of a complete corps. While the other three British infantry corps consisted of two full infantry divisions, Rawlinson's force contained a single infantry division and a comparatively weak cavalry division. Indeed, 3 Cavalry Division was even smaller than the other two British mounted formations in 1914. While 1 and 2 Cavalry Divisions were composed of two and three brigades, respectively, Byng's force comprised less than two brigades, due to the absence of three squadrons from Kavanagh's 7th Cavalry Brigade. Thus, 3 Cavalry Division mustered a total of only 4,000 troops in addition to the 18,000 of Capper's 7 Division.[10]

The low tooth-to-tail ratio of cavalry units further diminished their strength in 1914. This was particularly the case during dismounted engagements, when one of every four troopers was required to remain in rear of the action as a "horse-holder," along with farriers and other support personnel. In such situations, a full cavalry brigade could raise only 600 rifles. Consequently, for almost all of October 1914, the effective strength of Byng's division consisted of less than 1,200 troops, slightly more than a single infantry battalion. In addition, rather than the 54 field guns, 18 howitzers, and four 60-pound heavy guns assigned to most British infantry divisions, 3 Cavalry Division possessed only twelve field guns. Capper's 7 Division was also short of firepower. Prior to embarking for Belgium in early October, the division received only 48 field guns and eight 4.7-inch naval guns used during the South African War.[11] Thus, the perceived quality of IV Corps was offset by its limited human and material resources.

A second impediment to the effectiveness of Rawlinson's force was its rapid mobilization. Recently summoned from overseas garrisons, many of its battalions had arrived in England with little time to spare before being sent to relieve Antwerp. According to Hugo Montgomery, Capper's chief of staff in 1914, the last units of 7 Division only joined the formation "about a week or ten days before we started for Belgium."[12] Byng's cavalry assembled in even greater haste. Two regiments of Makings's 6th Cavalry Brigade arrived from South Africa only four days before setting sail for the continent, and saw many of their horses for the first time at the Belgian port of Zeebrugge. Thus, at the beginning of October, both the infantry and cavalry components of IV Corps arrived in Belgium with little or no experience operating in large formations.[13] Nor did the hasty mobilization of Rawlinson's force give its troops sufficient opportunity to prepare for the physical rigors of active service. Colonial garrison duty did little to simulate the marching required during active operations in Europe. Thus, well into October, the IV Corps commander complained of the poor conditioning of his troops, commenting on the 17th: "[t]he VII Div is composed of fine material and very well commanded but the men are not yet fit having come from the colonies. The result being that they are not good marchers....Byng's Cav[alry] Div are a fine body of men and horses but they have also got to learn to march."[14]

A third factor hindering IV Corps in October 1914 was the inexperience of its senior officers. While Sir Henry Rawlinson had commanded 4 Division briefly during September, neither of his divisional commanders had seen action in 1914.[15] In addition, the growing shortage of trained personnel in England left IV Corps and its two divisions with makeshift staffs comprised of largely inexperienced officers. On 18 October, Sir Douglas Haig provided the following description of the IV Corps staff in his diary:

I was amused with Rawlinson's staff. His General Staff consists of two Regulars. R.A.K. Montgomery R.A. and Dallas (who had a bad sun stroke in India) from War Office....Amery, the writer of the "Times History of the South African War" was in charge of his Intelligence Section, while Toby Rawlinson (his brother) acted as Mess President. The latter is now graded as Colonel, though he left the 17th Lancers as a subaltern! Joe Laycock and the Duke of Westminster were ADCs....There were two or three other officers about, who in peace time were connected with motors or polo ponies![16]

While not particularly gracious, this was a reasonably accurate depiction of the inexperience of the IV Corps staff. Toby Rawlinson, for example, had left the army and become a race-car driver prior to the war. In August 1914, he joined the BEF as a civilian chauffeur before being assigned to the IV Corps staff two months later. Rawlinson had neither formal staff training nor even an official rank until Sir John French summarily appointed him a colonel upon his attachment to his brother's staff. During the First Battle of Ypres, his duties apparently consisted of conveying information in a car armed with a machine-gun and decorated with a Union Jack as well as two German helmets.[17] While Toby Rawlinson was an exceptional case, his meager qualifications as a staff officer, along with Haig's description of his colleagues, indicates the limitations of the IV Corps staff. The ill-preparedness of its members, even in comparison to the staff officers of other formations in 1914, foreshadowed difficulties for Rawlinson's force during active operations.

An additional threat to the effective exercise of command in IV Corps was the prevalence of discord in its upper ranks. At the divisional level, the primary source of such problems was the highly-regarded Tommy Capper. As discussed in Chapter 1, Capper's capabilities were marred by limited interpersonal skills. Friction also distorted Sir Henry Rawlinson's relations with other senior British commanders. Prominent among them was Sir Douglas Haig, whose I Corps operated adjacent to IV Corps during October. It is difficult to trace hostility between the two officers to any particular incident. It is likely, however, that the ambitious Haig viewed the younger, more articulate Rawlinson with a strong measure of professional jealousy.[18] Haig's dislike of Rawlinson is evident in records of their interactions in 1914. John Charteris observed the first meeting between the two commanders in 1914 in the Belgian town of Poperinghe. According to Charteris: "We met General Rawlinson there, just back from Antwerp way. There is a good deal of the melodramatic about Rawlinson. He was flying an enormous Union Jack on his car, and D.H.'s [Haig's] first remark was rather caustic—'I thought only the King and the C-in-C are permitted to fly the Union Jack.' Rawlinson's reply was that it helped encourage the inhabitants."[19]

Haig's diary contains numerous derisive comments regarding Rawlinson and his force. Aware that his personal reflections on the campaign were read by the king, the I Corps commander displayed little restraint in criticizing his younger rival. In addition to his unkind description of Rawlinson's staff, Haig made a variety of disparaging comments regarding the poor performance of IV Corps and the excessive caution of its divisional commanders. As he remarked on 21 October: "Byng had only some 50 casualties in his whole division yesterday. A small number considering the nature of this war and all that is at stake!"[20] Haig's references to IV Corps and its commander are similar to his negative comments regarding Sir Horace Smith-Dorrien and II Corps. It thus seems evident that the I Corps commander perceived Rawlinson as a rival much like Smith-Dorrien. Although Haig's attempts to undermine Rawlinson in 1914 appear to have been confined to his diary, his attitude did nothing to enhance cooperation between I Corps and IV Corps during the First Battle of Ypres.

Hostilities ran even deeper between the IV Corps commander and Sir John French. Animosity between the two likely stemmed in part from Rawlinson's rivalry with French's protégé, Haig. As Richard Holmes has noted, however, tensions between the commander-in-chief and Rawlinson originated as early as 1904, when they clashed over the appointment of another of French's protégés to a staff position. Afterward, French remained suspicious of Rawlinson, a member of the Roberts ring.[21] Discord between the two lingered in August 1914. In his diary, Rawlinson asserted that his omission from the original contingent of the BEF resulted from French's displeasure over his conduct on maneuvers the previous year. Whether or not this allegation was true, tensions between the two officers flared soon after the arrival of the IV Corps commander in Belgium. The fact that Rawlinson originally reported directly to Lord Kitchener undoubtedly vexed the commander-in-chief.[22] Difficulties in establishing his authority over IV Corps following its transfer to the BEF aggravated French's annoyance. Because of Rawlinson's initial independence, the commander-in-chief had no means of communicating directly with IV Corps headquarters upon its subordination to GHQ. Until a direct link was established on 12 October, messages traveled through the War Office, where they were apparently delayed due to Lord Kitchener's insistence on monitoring all telegraphic exchanges.[23]

As a result of this practice, telegrams between IV Corps and GHQ did not always reflect current conditions, or command relationships, by the time they reached their final destination. Sir John French apparently received an outdated message from Henry Rawlinson on the 11th, indicating that IV Corps remained independent of GHQ. The receipt of this telegram was sufficient to inflame the suspicions of the commander-in-chief. As he replied irritably: "I do not understand whether you consider yourself under my orders or not."[24] Explanatory telegrams from Rawlinson and Kitchener assuaged Sir John French's concerns. Nevertheless, the professional relationship between the commander-in-chief and Sir Henry Rawlinson was clearly frayed by suspicion from the outset of the advance of IV Corps in October 1914. This relationship, combined with Douglas Haig's animosity toward the IV Corps commander and friction between Tommy Capper and his colleagues, held the potential to undermine the operations of IV Corps in October 1914. The formation faced even more serious difficulties due to its limited size and the ill-preparedness of its troops, as well as the inexperience of its senior commanders and staff officers. Thus, regardless of the reputed quality of the units of IV Corps, Sir John French proved excessively optimistic as he ordered the advance of Rawlinson's force upon its attachment to the BEF.

THE ADVANCE OF IV CORPS, 14–19 OCTOBER

The units of IV Corps arrived in the vicinity of Ypres on 14 October. Given the unseasoned condition of the troops, the 60-kilometer march from the vicinity of Ghent left both divisions extremely tired.[25] Fortunately for the soldiers, however, they were not required to move forward with any urgency during the next three days, as the slow progress of II Corps and III Corps to the south rendered an advance by Rawlinson's force unnecessary. Thus, GHQ did not order a concerted advance by IV Corps from 15 to 17 October. While both divisions moved forward cautiously on the 16th to a line east of Ypres, IV Corps remained largely stationary up to 18 October.[26] Following the brief advance on the 16th, 3 Cavalry Division occupied a line running from the village of Poelcappelle southward to the village of Zonnebeke. From there, 7 Division held positions extending further south across the Ypres-Menin Road to the village of Zandvoorde. The total front occupied by IV Corps measured eight miles, a manageable distance against the negligible opposition that prevailed before 18 October. Once IV Corps began to encounter significant German forces, however, the attenuation of Rawlinson's relatively weak force would prove dangerous.

From 15 to 17 October, the units of IV Corps observed increasing German activity to the east. On the 16th and 17th, 7 Division noted that German troops were constructing trenches around the towns of Wervicq and Menin, to the east of the British position. In addition, on 16 October, Pulteney's adjacent III Corps had detected a planned enemy counteroffensive through Menin and Courtrai, directly in front of IV Corps.[27] These ominous indications did not deflate the optimism of senior British commanders and staff officers. Sir John French remained determined throughout October to attain significant results from an offensive against the German flank. If the commander-in-chief retained any doubts about the prospects for a British advance on the 17th, they were erased by a meeting with Ferdinand Foch as well as the continued buoyancy of Henry Wilson. That evening, GHQ Operation Order No. 38 directed a "vigorous attack" on the morning of the 18th in conjunction with the French. With the exception of I Corps, which had not yet completed its transfer from the Aisne, the entire BEF was ordered to advance.[28]

From Sir Henry Rawlinson's perspective, the increasing enemy presence in front of his force, as well as its forward position relative to the rest of the army, cast considerable doubt on the wisdom of a determined forward movement on 18 October.[29] Moreover, the language of Operation Order No.38 appeared to counsel prudence for two reasons. First, while the document called for a "vigorous attack" by the entire army, such an order did not necessarily require that every corps attack with equal intensity. This was particularly the case when one formation held positions in advance of the others, as IV Corps did throughout this period. The operation order for 16 October, for example, had enjoined the army to advance, "attacking the enemy wherever met." Rawlinson's force, however, was directed to push forward, but "not move much in advance of the left of the III Corps."[30] Given this precedent set by GHQ orders two days earlier, it was conceivable that Operation Order No. 38 did not necessarily require an aggressive advance by IV Corps.

Second, the vocabulary employed in the operation order to characterize the movement of Rawlinson's force was considerably less enthusiastic than that used to describe the advance of the other British corps. GHQ directed II Corps to "attack and capture La Bassée," while III Corps was ordered to move down the banks of the River Lys, "attacking the enemy wherever met." By contrast, IV Corps was instructed only to "move on" Menin, a phrase that apparently had no specific meaning in army parlance.[31] Thus, given the wording of the order, the forward position of IV Corps and the mounting evidence of a strong enemy presence in its front, it seems quite possible for Rawlinson to have interpreted Operation Order No. 38 as something less than a wholehearted invocation to attack.

In accordance with such an interpretation, the IV Corps commander ordered only a cautious advance on the morning of the 18th. Covered by Byng's cavalry, 7 Division moved approximately 4,000 yards in the direction of Menin before taking up positions late in the morning. It soon became clear, however, that GHQ had envisioned a much more aggressive effort. Around noon, the liaison officer between GHQ and IV Corps, L.A.E. Price-Davies, arrived at Rawlinson's headquarters, where he learned to his surprise that IV Corps had ceased its advance for the day. A further visit to 7 Division headquarters confirmed this information, which Price-Davies relayed back to his superiors.[32] The revelation that IV Corps had not even attempted to capture Menin caused considerable consternation at GHQ. During the afternoon two unidentified staff officers visited Capper's headquarters, apparently to confirm that he had stopped short of the town. Shortly afterward, orders arrived from Archie Murray, directing IV Corps to take Menin without further delay. By the time the order was distributed, however, and the necessary arrangements were made to ensure cooperation between the two divisions of Rawlinson's force, it was too late to execute the attack on the 18th. Thus, Rawlinson postponed the assault on the town until the next day.[33]

Senior officers at GHQ clearly expected a more assertive advance by IV Corps on the 18th. Henry Wilson expressed irritation with Rawlinson in his diary, remarking that the IV Corps commander: *"never moved.* What on earth he was at I don't know. He says he was not ordered to attack Menin, but he *was* ordered to take a 'vigorous offensive' & 'move on Menin.' How that could be construed into doing nothing I can't imagine." Even the usually laconic Archie Murray commented in his diary that "IV Corps failed to move."[34] Observing the annoyance of his superiors, L.A.E. Price-Davies blamed himself for the failure of Rawlinson's force to capture Menin. In a letter to his wife, the liaison officer explained that upon arriving at IV Corps headquarters on the 18th, he ought to have either informed Rawlinson that his abbreviated advance did not meet the expectations of GHQ, or else immediately reported his discovery to his superiors. By continuing in his daily routine to visit 7 Division headquarters, he delayed the transmission of crucial information to GHQ until it was too late for IV Corps to attack Menin that day. "I don't know what bewitches me to do these things," Price-Davies lamented to his wife, "[i]t is the first time I have had the chance of showing whether I am worthy of my post or not & I have failed."[35]

This explanation sheds some light on the failure of IV Corps to attack on the afternoon of 18 October. Price-Davies can hardly be held responsible, however, for the confusion that prevailed over the meaning of Operation Order No. 38. This misunderstanding stemmed from the ambiguous language of the document as it pertained to IV Corps. By instructing Rawlinson's force to "move on" Menin, while directing II Corps to "attack and capture" La Bassée, the order left the intentions of GHQ for IV Corps open to considerable interpretation, particularly by a staff with little experience. The composition of GHQ operation orders was ultimately the responsibility of Archie Murray. Despite his lack of influence in this period, the fact that Murray commented in his diary on Rawlinson's failure to follow the order suggests that it was issued with his prior knowledge. It thus seems apparent that even relatively experienced British staff officers such as Murray had yet to master the finer points of staff work in October 1914.

In addition to suggesting a lack of proficiency on the part of senior staff at GHQ, this misunderstanding illustrates the conviction of Sir John French and his advisors that Rawlinson's force did not face opposition sufficient to threaten its advance on Menin. This conviction prevailed throughout the 18th despite considerable evidence to the contrary. In addition to the indications on previous days of significant German forces in front of IV Corps, Tommy Capper received further reports on the afternoon of 18 October suggesting the presence of considerable numbers of the enemy at Courtrai, approximately five miles east of Menin. Officers from GHQ discounted this report, however, informing Capper that there was "nothing much" in Courtrai.[36] Subsequent events would demonstrate that this information was incorrect. Nor did it represent the views of the Intelligence Section at GHQ. After the war, George Macdonogh asserted to Edmonds that he had gathered "quite a lot of information" indicating the arrival of new German units in front of the BEF on 18 October.[37] Nonetheless, reports provided by both Macdonogh and field commanders such as Capper did little to deter senior commanders and staff officers from their offensive plans on 18 October. Not only did the officers who visited Capper's headquarters dismiss reports of German forces gathering at Courtrai, but orders from GHQ that evening implored IV Corps to attack Menin the next morning.[38] Thus, the determination of Sir John French and his staff to press the advance of IV Corps prevailed despite evidence of considerable German forces arriving in the vicinity.

Suitably admonished by GHQ, the commander of IV Corps made a genuine effort to orchestrate an attack on Menin on 19 October. In addition to sending members of his staff to liaise with the two divisional commanders, Sir Henry Rawlinson himself traveled to 7 Division to monitor Capper's advance on Menin.[39] During the morning, the forward movement progressed relatively smoothly. Covered on the left by Byng's cavalry, units of 7 Division reached a point about three miles north of Menin by 10:30 am. Here, however, the advance came to an abrupt halt, as a strong enemy detachment attacked Rawlinson's force in flank from the north. At approximately 11:30 am, the IV Corps commander received air reconnaissance reports revealing the approach of an enemy division from Courtrai, which the GHQ staff had reported empty the previous day. Subsequent information indicated two more divisions arriving from north of the same town. It later became evident that these formations were the lead divisions of three German corps. In total, 5 1/2 German infantry corps and a cavalry corps were advancing toward the BEF and allied forces to the north on 19 October.[40] In light of this information, Sir Henry Rawlinson terminated his attack just before noon. Enemy pressure increased throughout the afternoon, however, forcing 3 Cavalry Division to fall back around 4 pm to positions between the villages of Zonnebeke and Langemarck. This in turn necessitated the withdrawal of Capper's division to the line that it had occupied in the morning through Zonnebeke, Gheluvelt, Kruiseke, and Zandvoorde.[41] Later in the evening, GHQ issued a more feasible directive for IV Corps on 20 October, enjoining Rawlinson to maintain and entrench his positions.

The setbacks encountered by IV Corps on the 19th apparently led the commander-in-chief to reduce his expectations of Rawlinson's force. Significantly, however, the orders did not shorten the extended front occupied by IV Corps. Moreover, they instructed Haig's newly arrived I Corps to advance on Rawlinson's left. Clearly, the growing evidence of large enemy forces east of Ypres on 18 and 19 October did little to diminish the determination of GHQ to press the British offensive. IV Corps had made no progress after two days of attempted advances, and numerous sources suggested the arrival of enemy troops in substantial numbers. Rather than disabusing Sir John French and Henry Wilson of their plans, however, the failure of the IV Corps advance simply lowered their opinion of Sir Henry Rawlinson. The commander-in-chief was particularly annoyed. On the 19th, French remarked in his diary that the IV Corps commander had "disappointed" him.[42] Thus, by 19 October, the gap between the unrealistic expectations of GHQ and the performance of IV Corps had resulted in the erosion of the already shaky relationship between Sir John French and Sir Henry Rawlinson. In addition, the optimistic plans of French and his staff had left IV Corps on an extended front on the eve of the German counteroffensive.

THE DEPLETION OF 7 DIVISION AND THE DISPERSAL OF IV CORPS, 20–27 OCTOBER

Despite the mounting evidence of approaching German forces on 18 and 19 October, GHQ did nothing to encourage caution on the part of corps commanders. Consequently, the positions established by IV Corps following the abortive attack on Menin were not chosen for their defensive merits. The front occupied by Rawlinson's diminutive corps still extended eight miles, from Langemarck south to Zandvoorde. The length of the IV Corps line was roughly equivalent to that held by II Corps during this period. In terms of the dismounted troops it was able to muster, however, IV Corps was likely even weaker than Smith-Dorrien's force, despite the depleted condition of both 3 and 5 Divisions. As Toby Rawlinson noted in his memoir of the war, the units of IV Corps were dispersed over the front at a rate of only one man every seven yards. Such a sparsely defended position would prove fragile under heavy German attacks, particularly since it formed a conspicuous salient in the allied line.[43] Thus, as the battalions of Rawlinson's force took up positions on their extended front, they were unknowingly exposing themselves to the full thrust of impending enemy attacks.

The German counter-offensive began early on 20 October. Attacks fell first on French forces to the right of IV Corps, compelling their withdrawal by 10am. The French retirement exposed the left of Byng's cavalry, which then fell back around noon. This in turn uncovered 7 Division just as frontal attacks developed against both divisions of IV Corps. Lawford's 22nd Brigade, on the left of Capper's force, endured pressure from the front and left throughout the day. In spite of its tenuous positions, 7 Division held fast on the 20th, losing 5 officers and 136 other ranks during the day, the bulk of these in the 22nd Brigade.[44] Neither Capper's division nor the forces adjacent to it, however, would be so fortunate on the 21st, when severe German attacks fell all along the front of I Corps, IV Corps, and the Cavalry Corps to the south. The arrival of German forces in the vicinity was hardly a surprise to GHQ. Nevertheless, it is evident that Sir John French's investment in the offensive continued to override the wiser counsel of George Macdonogh's Intelligence Section. Thus, GHQ operation orders for 21 October directed I Corps to advance, closely supported on its right by 3 Cavalry Division, while 7 Division held its positions.[45]

On the morning of the 21st, these instructions had particularly negative consequences for I Corps, the supposed spearhead of the British advance. Assured of a negligible German presence in front of it, Haig's force collided with advancing enemy units. Combined with the unexpected withdrawal of French forces on the left, German attacks halted the advance of I Corps. While units of IV Corps did not attempt to move forward, they were nonetheless subjected to considerable pressure. Late in the morning, enemy infantry temporarily broke through Watts's 21st Brigade, in the center of the 7 Division line.[46] Difficulties also arose on the right of Capper's front, as attacks on Hubert Gough's adjacent 2 Cavalry Division created a breach between it and 7 Division. Fortunately for Sir Henry Rawlinson, the suspension of Haig's advance had left Byng's cavalry unoccupied, and the IV Corps commander was thus able to transfer it to the right of 7 Division, thereby filling the gap.[47]

The greatest pressure, however, fell on the already beleaguered 22nd Brigade on the left of Capper's line. Holding the corner of 7 Division's salient, Lawford's force suffered under heavy and accurate artillery fire throughout the day. As early as 8 am, Tommy Capper reported to IV Corps headquarters that the condition of the 22nd Brigade was "critical." Although the advance of I Corps on the left eased the situation temporarily around 2 pm, enemy artillery fire forced the retirement of Lawford's brigade two hours later, "by which time their trenches had been wholly annihilated."[48] The IV Corps war diary diplomatically described the withdrawal of the 22nd Brigade as a "slight rectification" of the 7 Division line.[49] In reality, heavy German shelling caused Lawford's force to retire in considerable disarray. Given the casualties incurred by the battalions of the 22nd Brigade since the 19th, this is hardly surprising. By the night of 21 October, the 1st Royal Welch Fusiliers had lost 23 officers and 750 other ranks, over 75 percent of its strength.[50]

Despite the intensity of German attacks, particularly on the 21st, responsibility for the rapid depletion and consequent retirement of the 22nd Brigade fell on its commander. Commenting on the withdrawal of the brigade in his diary, Sir Douglas Haig suggested that it had stemmed from the inexperience of Lawford and his force, rather than the intensity of the German bombardment or the brigade's unfavorable positions. As he remarked on 22 October: "Lawford is new to the game and so are his troops. Except for a few shells, all was quiet when I arrived."[51] In considering the opinions expressed in Haig's diary, it is important to keep in mind his professional jealousy of Sir Henry Rawlinson. It is significant, however, that Haig attributed the retirement of the brigade to Lawford, rather than attempting to pin responsibility on the IV Corps commander. Rawlinson himself offered a more specific indictment of Lawford. In a letter written to Tommy Capper on 22 October, he maintained that the losses of the 22nd Brigade resulted from the failure of its commander to locate positions on rearward slopes, safe from direct observation by enemy gunners. As

Rawlinson declared: "It is clear that the Brigade which he [Lawford] commands was not handled skillfully during yesterday's action & that the heavy losses were largely due to the bad siting of trenches. The Brigadier alone must be held responsible for this."[52]

Undeniably, Lawford had little experience leading a brigade in the combat conditions of 1914. Nevertheless, to blame him for the retirement of the 22nd Brigade, or even the vulnerability of its trenches, does not appear to be justified. Given the losses suffered by the brigade by the afternoon of 21 October, Haig's suggestion that Lawford withdrew without just cause is rather dubious. Further doubt is cast on this accusation by the fact that the commander of the 22nd Brigade does not appear to have been in any way deficient in personal bravery. Frederic Coleman's memoir of 1914 provides a vivid example of Lawford's behavior under fire, related to the author by a junior officer in the 22nd Brigade. On 7 November, the brigade was directed to execute a counterattack after German forces broke the British line around Ypres. With only three officers remaining in the entire brigade, Lawford took charge. Coleman related the subaltern's account as follows:

"The General," said the young officer, "plugged on ahead of all of us, waving a big white stick over his head and shouting like a banshee. There was no stopping him. He fairly walked into the Germans, and we after him on the run. We took the German trench in front of us and held it, but they mowed us down getting up there. How Lawford escaped being hit is more than anyone can tell. I can see him now, his big stick waving in the air, and he shouting and yelling away like mad, though you couldn't hear a word of what he said above the sinful noise."[53]

One example of Lawford's boldness in early November is not sufficient to disprove allegations of his timidity on 21 October. It nonetheless raises further doubts about Haig's explanation for the withdrawal of the 22nd Brigade.

Sir Henry Rawlinson's account was more accurate than that provided by Haig in that it identified the poor location of trenches as an important factor prompting the withdrawal of the 22nd Brigade. As Arthur Conan-Doyle suggested in his account of 1914: "It may be that the Seventh Division, having had no previous experience in the campaign, had sited their trenches with less cunning than would have been shown by troops who had already faced the problem of how best to avoid high explosives."[54] Rawlinson was also correct in pointing out to Capper that the location of trenches was the responsibility of the brigadier. Under the prevailing command philosophy of umpiring, the duties of the corps and divisional commanders would not have extended beyond the selection of a general line of defense.

Evidently, however, neither Lawford nor the other brigadiers of 7 Division were apprised of the lessons regarding trench location collected earlier in the campaign. This oversight is particularly significant in light of the fact that GHQ had solicited detailed reports in September for the specific purpose of informing newly arrived units of the unprecedented combat conditions of 1914. The failure to transmit this information to the brigades of 7 Division derived from several factors. First, Sir Henry Rawlinson's criticism of Lawford for the poor location of his trenches indicates that the IV Corps commander recognized the importance of locating trenches on rearward slopes to minimize exposure to enemy fire. Nevertheless, he apparently did not take the time to inform his subordinates of this necessity.

While Rawlinson was apparently negligent in this respect, this oversight was also a product of the origins of IV Corps, the optimism prevalent at GHQ in this period, and tensions between Rawlinson and Sir John French. IV Corps had assembled rapidly in early October with the intent of relieving Antwerp. At this point, there was neither a necessity nor an opportunity to inculcate in its units any of the defensive lessons acquired earlier in the campaign. Rawlinson's force then joined the BEF under the assumption that it would attack the German flank. Although the approach of considerable enemy forces cast doubt on the feasibility of the British offensive, French and his staff remained determined to advance. Consequently, GHQ did not consider the selection of defensive positions to be a particularly important issue before the beginning of the German counteroffensive.

Discord between the commander-in-chief and Sir Henry Rawlinson also contributed to the failure of GHQ to emphasize the defensive lessons of the 1914 campaign. From the attachment of IV Corps to the BEF on 9 October, Sir John French had viewed its commander with considerable suspicion. Rawlinson's apparent hesitancy on 18–19 October raised further doubts at GHQ regarding his determination to attack. In light of their determination to advance and their growing perception of Rawlinson as a timid commander, French and his staff had little interest in passing on information that might have encouraged him in his cautious behavior. Instead, GHQ continued to exhort IV Corps to advance even as German forces in its vicinity increased. Under considerable pressure to push forward, Rawlinson himself had little opportunity or inclination to emphasize the importance of selecting proper defensive positions. Nor did he benefit from an experienced staff that might have done so independently. Thus, when the counteroffensive began, the units of IV Corps were left exceedingly vulnerable to enemy attacks.

For Tommy Capper's 7 Division, the cost of this oversight was high. Holding exposed positions against concerted attacks, the infantry suffered heavily. Enemy shelling commenced at 7 am on 22 October. While German infantry attacks did not match the intensity of the previous day, Lawford's battered 22nd Brigade, which had incurred severe casualties since the beginning of the enemy offensive, was rapidly reaching the point of disintegration.[55] Lawford received badly needed support with the arrival of units of I Corps on his left during the afternoon. Bolstered by the infantry and artillery of 2 Division, the 22nd Brigade managed to hold its positions. This relief, however, came none too soon. As Rawlinson admitted in his diary: "[i]t is just as well that the I Corps have come up here for the Germans have massed large forces in these parts and had I to meet them alone I should have been overwhelmed and had to give up Ypres."[56]

The IV Corps commander proved to be correct, as incessant shell fire punctuated by infantry assaults prevailed throughout the night of the 22nd and into the day on the 23rd. Under such conditions, exhaustion was beginning to take its toll on 7 Division. As the IV Corps commander noted in his diary that day, Capper's division was "rather hard up for sleep."[57] Thus, while support provided by I Corps enabled the 22nd Brigade to hold its vulnerable positions on 23 October, the rest of 7 Division proved fragile under unremitting pressure. During the afternoon, the enemy again succeeded in breaking through the 21st Brigade, in the center of Capper's line. German troops took up positions in a wood behind the British line, enfilading the 2/Yorkshire Regiment. A counterattack by the reserve company of the Yorkshires succeeded in clearing the wood, but only at the price of 3 officers and "many men." Later in the day, an enemy force established itself in close proximity to the 1/Grenadier Guards of the 20th Brigade, and was only dislodged by an assault that night which cost the battalion four officers.[58]

As German attacks continued into the morning of 24 October, Sir Henry Rawlinson received the welcome news that 2 Division was shifting southward to take over the positions of the 22nd Brigade. This reduced the extended front of IV Corps from eight to approximately four miles, allowing the relief of Lawford's depleted force during the day, and thereby providing Capper with a significant reserve for the first time since the beginning of German attacks. Even with the strengthening of Capper's line, however, German pressure on 24 October proved overwhelming. Before 9 am, infantry attacks had compelled the commander of 7 Division to telephone Rawlinson requesting reinforcements. By 9:30, the enemy had broken through the 2/Wiltshire Regiment in Watts's 21st Brigade.[59] Fatigue was a key factor in the disintegration of the Wiltshires. Hugo Montgomery suggested in a postwar letter to Edmonds that the troops of the battalion "were probably all asleep, as they got no rest from the shelling, even after the march was over." Completely surprised by the German attack, three companies of the Wiltshires surrendered.[60]

Throughout the morning of the 24th, Capper's line remained in serious jeopardy. In expectation of its collapse, 7 Division headquarters was apparently preparing to make a last stand at 11 am. This proved premature, as the divisional commander reported his positions restored before noon. Nevertheless, the situation remained critical for the rest of the day. German forces mounted two more serious attacks during the afternoon, one of which broke through the front of Ruggles-Brice's 20th Brigade on the right of 7 Division. Determined counterattacks had largely restored the line by evening. Any successes, however, came at the cost of heavy casualties to the already depleted units of Capper's force. The task of retaking the positions captured from the Wiltshires in the morning fell to the 2/Royal Warwickshire Regiment of the battered 22nd Brigade, with support from the 2/Worcester Regiment on loan from 2 Division. Advancing under enemy shell fire, the two battalions dislodged the Germans and regained the trenches formerly occupied by the Wiltshires. In the process, the Warwicks lost 105 other ranks and several officers, including their commander,

Colonel Loring, allegedly shot while leading the attack in a pair of carpet slippers, after a German bullet had destroyed both his riding boot and his heel. The Worcesters suffered similar casualties, losing 6 officers and 106 other ranks.[61] While these courageous efforts reestablished the positions lost by the Wiltshires, they exacted a heavy toll on Capper's force. During 22–24 October alone, 7 Division lost over 120 officers and 2,700 other ranks. This high rate of officer casualties had a serious impact on the cohesion of the division. As Rawlinson remarked in his diary: "we are barely hanging on by our eyelids."[62]

The progressive deterioration of 7 Division was paralleled by a further decline in relations between the commander-in-chief and Sir Henry Rawlinson. On the morning of 24 October, both Sir John French and Henry Wilson remained confident regarding the prospects for a British advance. Any news that threatened to deflate their optimistic scenarios was thus not appreciated. This was particularly the case if such information came from Rawlinson. Since the failure of IV Corps to take Menin on 18–19 October, French in particular had viewed its commander as prone to anxiety without just cause. The crises afflicting 7 Division since the 20th had done little to change the commander-in-chief's perception. According to Price-Davies, an officer attuned to the climate of opinion at GHQ: "it became the fashion to say that 7th Div[ision] were running away and Sir John was always impatient with them."[63]

French's agitation with Rawlinson came to the fore on 24 October when he learned of the capture of the Wiltshires and the unhinging of the 7 Division line. Rather than arranging support for Capper's beleaguered force, GHQ brusquely informed IV Corps that its units would have to retake the lost ground by themselves. Sir Henry Rawlinson was certainly not the only corps commander to be treated in this fashion by Sir John French. Rawlinson, however, was apparently less daunted than Sir Horace Smith-Dorrien by the prospect of incurring the commander-in-chief's displeasure. Thus, frustrated by the unsympathetic response from GHQ, the IV Corps commander replied sharply: "it will be easier to hold a front of 8 miles when we have 2 Div[isions] in the IV Corps."[64]

Given the plight of 7 Division on 24 October, Rawlinson's annoyance is understandable. Nevertheless, his blunt response infuriated the commander-in-chief. Rather than allowing the news regarding the condition of 7 Division to moderate his optimism, French flew into a rage, refusing to see the IV Corps commander when Rawlinson visited GHQ on the evening of the 24th. French apparently even considered sacking his impudent subordinate. As Billy Lambton, the commander-in-chief's military secretary, informed Rawlinson the next day: "you will have to apologize and eat humble pie if you want to remain on in command."[65] A chastened Rawlinson penned the requisite apology and delivered it to GHQ on 25 October. Sufficiently mollified, the commander-in-chief responded with a saccharine letter of forgiveness, exclaiming unconvincingly: "[w]e have always been good friends—so let us remain so!"[66] This was hardly an accurate portrayal of the relationship between the two officers. French and Rawlinson had long viewed each other with suspicion, and the events of October

1914 had intensified their mutual dislike. Part of the commander-in-chief's anger, however, may have derived from the recognition that the condition of 7 Division threatened his plans to advance. According to Rawlinson, Archie Murray revealed to him on the 25th that his message "had given Sir J[ohn] a sleepless night because there was of course some truth in what I had said."[67]

Even if this was the case, French did not allow Rawlinson's revelations to spoil his plans to advance on 24 October. The extent to which the commander-in-chief and his staff had succumbed to cognitive closure in this period is evident in GHQ Operation Order No. 40, issued that evening. The order demonstrated absolutely no recognition of the plight of IV Corps, stating the intention of Sir John French "to advance tomorrow with the I, IV and Cavalry Corps and to contain the enemy with II and III Corps." To add insult to injury, it transferred Byng's division to Allenby's adjacent Cavalry Corps.[68] Placing 3 Cavalry Division under Allenby's control on 23 October was not entirely irrational, as it bolstered a relatively weak formation. Nonetheless, this transfer appears peculiar for two reasons. First, while Allenby's force had experienced intermittent enemy pressure since the 20th, its condition on the 24th was not nearly as serious as that of 7 Division. Indeed, the Germans made no serious attacks on the Cavalry Corps until 30 October. Secondly, Allenby had already received reinforcements on 22 October when his line was strengthened by the 7th Infantry Brigade of the Indian Corps.[69] The transfer of 3 Cavalry Division to the Cavalry Corps on the 25th thus appears unjustified, particularly in light of the heavy losses suffered by Capper's 7 Division since the 20th.

In the absence of any compelling reason to remove Byng's force from the already depleted IV Corps, it is plausible to argue that the transfer of 3 Cavalry Division derived in part from tension between Sir John French and Sir Henry Rawlinson. To contend that French removed Byng's division from IV Corps due to his annoyance with Rawlinson suggests rather unprofessional conduct on the part of the commander-in-chief. Given his mercurial temperament, however, and his outright refusal to speak with the IV Corps commander on the evening of 24 October, this assertion does not seem unreasonable. In any case, the content of Operation Order No. 40 indicates that Sir John French's opinion of Rawlinson contributed to his disregard of the plight of 7 Division on the 24th. While the commander-in-chief's determination to advance proved exceptionally resilient given the losses suffered by the BEF in late October, it is likely that he would have paid greater heed to Rawlinson's apprehensive reports had he held the IV Corps commander in greater esteem. Thus, friction between Sir John French and Henry Rawlinson compounded the effects of cognitive closure at GHQ. French's annoyance with the IV Corps commander encouraged him to ignore information that threatened his advance, and may even have compelled him to remove one of Rawlinson's divisions. This behavior did nothing to help Tommy Capper's embattled 7 Division as German attacks continued on subsequent days.

Predictably, Rawlinson's shrunken corps made little progress on 25 October. Fortunately for the exhausted troops of 7 Division, the attention of the enemy remained largely on Haig's I Corps for most of the day.[70] By late in the afternoon, however, German forces began to exert significant pressure on the 20th Brigade, holding the right of the 7 Division line around Kruiseke. The fate of this brigade, commanded by H.G. Ruggles-Brice, captured the imagination of contemporary writers. As Ernest Hamilton related in his account of the 1914 campaign:

The gradual annihilation of this splendid brigade—possibly the finest in the whole army—forms a story which is no less stirring than it is tragic. The tragedy is obvious, but it is relieved by the thought of the superb devotion of each of the battalions that formed the command of General Ruggles-Brice. Each battalion, in its own allotted sphere, fought to a finish. Each battalion in its turn furnished an example of unflinching heroism which is an epic in itself. They not only fought till there were no more left to fight, but they fought up to the very end with success.[71]

Significantly, no small part of this tragedy was due to continued misperceptions in the upper ranks of the BEF command structure. The failure of senior officers to acknowledge the intensity of the German counteroffensive and take measures to meet it left the 20th Brigade in exposed positions under heavy attacks for a full week. By the night of 25 October, the troops of Ruggles-Brice's force were exhausted and exceedingly vulnerable to enemy incursions. When German forces rushed the trenches of the 2/Scots Guards around 8:30 pm, two companies of British infantry were overwhelmed. The loss of a position was a blow to the dignity of any British regiment in 1914. To a battalion of Guards, however, such an affront was intolerable. According to Hamilton: "the Guards, like the Samurai, do not surrender while yet unwounded."[72] Thus, the two remaining companies of Scots Guards promptly moved forward in the dark to retake the lost trenches with little consideration for the feasibility of their objective. With no conception of which positions had been occupied by enemy troops and which remained in British hands, the Scots Guards faced a difficult task. While they retook the position in the early morning of 26 October, capturing over 200 prisoners in the process, the counterattack proved costly. The officer commanding the reserve companies was killed leading an unsuccessful bayonet charge on one of the occupied trenches. Eight other officers fell during the subsequent fighting.[73]

Nor were the Scots Guards able to retain the contested position the following day. Enemy artillery bombardments commenced at 9 am on the 26th, demolishing the trenches that the battalion had fought so hard to regain the previous night. By 2:30 pm, the neighboring 1/Grenadier Guards were forced to abandon Kruiseke as well, taking up positions on a hill west of the village. This location proved no safer, however, as German shells followed the retreating troops to their new positions, wreaking havoc on the entire brigade throughout the afternoon. After weathering enemy pressure for six days, the 20th Brigade proved unable to withstand the continued bombardment of the 26th. By 3 pm, Ruggles-Brice's force had largely disintegrated and its units began retiring in disorder. So hurried was the brigade's withdrawal that its commander neglected to inform either Capper or Lawford, whose 22nd Brigade was advancing in support. The relative inexperience of formation commanders and staff officers in 7 Division may have contributed to this oversight. Given that these officers had little opportunity to become accustomed to operating in a relatively large formation prior to the First Battle of Ypres, malfunctions in the command system of Capper's force were likely to occur under the considerable strain of the German counteroffensive. On 26 October, a lack of communication between commanders created confusion as the 20th Brigade fell back. As the commander of 7 Division informed Julian Byng at 3:20 pm: "[p]art of 20th Inf[antry] Bde is retiring but we do not know how much."[74]

The withdrawal of the 20th Brigade was less a tactical retreat than a rout. After learning from a member of his staff that several battalions of the brigade were retiring "in great disorder," Sir Douglas Haig ventured out from his headquarters during the afternoon to survey the situation himself. As the I Corps commander reported: "I rode out about 3pm to see what was going on, and was astounded at the terror-stricken men coming back." Haig's description was not simply an exaggeration aimed at slighting a rival officer. Sir Henry Rawlinson observed "some confusion and much shelling" when he visited 7 Division at dusk. As the IV Corps commander noted in his diary, Tommy Capper spent the entire night of 26–27 October reestablishing his line between Zandvoorde and Veldhoek.[75]

Given the disarray of 7 Division, Rawlinson reported unequivocally to GHQ at 9:50 pm on the 26th that his force was unable to participate in the next day's operations. The manifest collapse of the 20th Brigade finally convinced GHQ that 7 Division was no longer capable of holding its positions, let alone advancing. Beginning late on the 26th, units of Haig's I Corps began taking over Capper's line, thereby allowing the battered division to reorganize. The German counteroffensive had inflicted heavy casualties on 7 Division in a relatively short span of time. Between 19 and 27 October, Capper's force had lost 162 officers and 4,500 other ranks, more than one-third of its officers and 25 percent of its total strength.[76] These figures are particularly striking in light of the fact that the division had made no serious efforts to advance in this period.

The ability of 7 Division to maintain a semblance of cohesion despite such heavy casualties was due in no small part to the personal leadership of its commander. Numerous sources emphasize Tommy Capper's role in maintaining the resolve of his depleted units. According to John Charteris: "no one but Capper himself could, night after night, by the sheer force of his personality have reconstituted from the shattered fragments of his battalions a fighting line that could last through tomorrow."[77] Despite Capper's personal bravery, however, the operations of 7 Division in late October were apparently undermined by his poor relations with his subordinates. Price-Davies, who visited 7 Division headquarters on a daily basis in this period, observed a rift between Capper and his staff. In a letter to his wife, the liaison officer explained: "[h]is staff did not really play the game by him, they were I think rather disloyal & worked against him instead of with him." Price-Davies recognized that this problem was due in part to the peculiarities of the 7 Division commander. As he continued: "there were no doubt faults on both sides. Billy Drysdale says he [Capper] was mad. He says he used to come and tell him something, go away, and come back and tell him the same thing again. Well, you know his absent-minded way."[78]

Nor did Capper enjoy effective professional relationships with his brigade commanders in this period. Following the dispersal of IV Corps in late October, the 7 Division commander in fact attempted to sack all three of his brigadiers. He later reversed his decision and decided to retain the officers.[79] It is evident, however, that the operations of 7 Division were conducted in the context of strained relations between its commander and brigadiers. These tensions may have contributed to the poor communications between Capper and his brigades on the afternoon of 26 October. In any case, they did nothing to improve the fortunes of 7 Division as it clung to exposed positions in the face of sustained enemy attacks.

Unfortunately for the exhausted troops of Capper's Division, they were not long out of action. The units of the 22nd Brigade were not relieved until the 27th, by which time the other two brigades of the division had been reinserted into the line due to continuing German pressure. The commander of IV Corps, however, did not accompany them. On 27 October, GHQ placed 7 Division under Sir Douglas Haig. Without a force to command, Rawlinson and his staff returned to England, ostensibly to instruct 8 Division on the lessons of the 1914 campaign before it embarked on active operations in early November.[80] The dispatch of the IV Corps commander to England suggests that Sir John French now recognized the importance of instructing newly arriving units in the lessons of the 1914 campaign. It is nonetheless curious that GHQ deemed it necessary to assign a senior commander to such a task at the height of the First Battle of Ypres. While he stopped short of sacking Rawlinson, it is evident that Sir John French's frustration with the IV Corps commander lay behind his decision to remove him from active command in late October. Despite the apparent rapprochement of the two officers on 25 October, the commander-in-chief's rather arbitrary transfer of 3 Cavalry Division to Allenby the same day indicates his desire to limit Rawlinson's command responsibilities. The collapse of the 20th Brigade on the 26th provided French with an opportunity to place 7 Division under the more reliable Haig. The dispersal of his formation left the IV Corps commander under a cloud and without any significant duties. As Sir John French informed Kitchener on the 27th: "he [Rawlinson] is not really wanted here."[81]

Rawlinson would likely have spent the climax of the 1914 campaign on a leave of absence similar to that enjoyed by Sir Horace Smith-Dorrien if not for the suggestion of his friend, Henry Wilson. The sub-chief of Staff apparently proposed to Sir John French that Rawlinson return to England on the morning of the 27th.[82] Not only would this assignment serve the purpose of imparting to 8 Division valuable lessons of the campaign, but it would also alleviate tensions between French and the commander of IV Corps by reducing their proximity. Thus, while his divisions continued to fight under different commanders, Henry

Rawlinson remained in England during the height of the First Battle of Ypres, returning to active command on 12 November.[83]

CONCLUSION

Despite the formidable reputation of its component parts, IV Corps was ill-prepared for the First Battle of Ypres. Assembled and dispatched to Belgium in haste, Sir Henry Rawlinson's formation was deficient in numbers, equipment, and experience. This lack of preparedness was especially evident in the upper reaches of its command structure. The growing scarcity of trained staff officers in England left IV Corps and its divisions with inexperienced staffs that had little opportunity to absorb the lessons of the 1914 campaign before being thrown into active operations. This may explain some of the difficulties faced by IV Corps in October 1914, particularly the tendency of its units to locate themselves in dangerous positions on forward slopes. It seems that Rawlinson and his inexperienced staff failed to convey to these units the importance of shielding trenches from enemy fire. Significantly, staff officers within IV Corps were not unique in their inexperience. Even officers at GHQ had yet to master the task of controlling a force the size of the BEF, burdening IV Corps with ambiguous orders during the advance.

The oversights of unseasoned staff officers, however, were not the sole cause of the difficulties of IV Corps. Indeed, the consequences of such errors were intensified considerably by friction and rivalries among British officers. While the leadership of Tommy Capper undoubtedly helped maintain the morale of 7 Division, its problems were hardly alleviated by discord between Capper and his subordinates. More generally, the optimism prevalent at GHQ in October created unrealistic expectations for the advance of IV Corps. As a result, when the German offensive began, Rawlinson's force was left in possession of an extended salient that placed excessive demands on its limited manpower.

Rawlinson's failure to meet the lofty goals set by GHQ exacerbated tensions between himself and Sir John French just as enemy attacks began to fall heavily on IV Corps. French's frustration with Rawlinson not only left the commander-in-chief with little sympathy for the condition of IV Corps, but it also likely deterred GHQ from emphasizing lessons regarding trench location that the IV Corps commander and his staff had neglected to inculcate in their units. As a result, GHQ repeatedly ordered 3 Cavalry Division and particularly 7 Division to attack in spite of their mounting losses due to German attacks. The depletion of 7 Division, and Rawlinson's candor in pointing out the disadvantages it faced, further undermined the IV Corps commander's standing at GHQ. Frustrated with Rawlinson, Sir John French dispersed IV Corps, removing him from active command. As was the case with II Corps in this period, tensions between senior officers left the preservation of Rawlinson's line to the battalions of 7 Division. While the vaunted regiments of Capper's force accomplished this feat, they did so only through the personal bravery and leadership of junior officers, qualities that proved costly in 1914. The battalions of 7 Division held the British line in front of Ypres in October 1914, but only at an exorbitant price.

NOTES

1. Richard Holmes, *The Little Field-Marshal: Sir John French* (London: Jonathan Cape, 1981), 243; Anthony Farrar-Hockley, *Death of an Army* (New York: Morrow, 1968), 70, 80; Robin Prior and Trevor Wilson, *Command on the Western Front: The Military Career of Sir Henry Rawlinson, 1914–1918* (Cambridge: Blackwell, 1992), 13.

2. Rawlinson to Kitchener, 8 October 1914, Kitchener to French, 9 October 1914, WO 33/713; IV Corps War Diary, 8–9 October 1914, WO 95/706; Kitchener to French, 4 October 1914, WO 33/713, Public Record Office, Kew (PRO).

3. French to Rawlinson, 9 October 1914, WO 33/713; French to Rawlinson, 10 October 1914, IV Corps War Diary, WO 95/706; GHQ War Diary, 10 October 1914, WO 95/1, PRO.

4. Rawlinson Diary, 13 October 1914, Henry Rawlinson Papers, 1/1, Churchill College, Cambridge (CCC); IV Corps War Diary, 13 October 1914; Henry Wilson (under Murray's signature) to Rawlinson, "Situation, so far as is known, at nightfall, TUESDAY, October 13th, 1914," in IV Corps War Diary, WO 95/706; Rawlinson to GHQ, 12 October 1914, WO 33/713, PRO.

5. Rawlinson Diary, 15 October 1914, Rawlinson Papers, 1/1, CCC.

6. Sir Arthur Conan-Doyle, *The British Campaign in France and Flanders 1914* (London: Hodder and Stoughton, 1916), 233; Ernest Hamilton, *The First Seven Divisions* (New York: Dutton, 1916), 300; Tim Carew, *Wipers* (London: Hamish Hamilton, 1974), 66; A. Corbett-Smith, *The Marne—And After* (Toronto: Cassell, 1917), 257.

7. J.M. Craster, ed., *'Fifteen Rounds a Minute:' The Grenadiers at War, August to December 1914, Edited from the Diaries and Letters of Major 'Ma' Jeffreys and Others* (London: Macmillan, 1976), 2–3. See also J.G.W. Hyndson, *From Mons to the First Battle of Ypres* (London: Wyman, 1933), 42; Hamilton, *The First Seven Divisions*, 231; Carew, *Wipers*, 76–80; R.A.L. Haldane, *A Soldier's Saga* (Edinburgh: Blackwood, 1948), 297–298.

8. C.D. Baker-Carr, *From Chauffeur to Brigadier-General* (London: Ernest Benn, 1930), 49.

9. A. Rawlinson, *Adventures on the Western Front: August 1914–June 1915* (London: Andrew Melrose, 1925), 201.

10. Kitchener to French, 4 October 1914, WO 33/713, PRO; James Edmonds, *Military Operations: France and Belgium, 1914*, vol. 2 (London: Macmillan, 1925), 54; Rawlinson, *Adventures on the Western Front*, 147. While an infantry brigade comprised four regiments, its mounted equivalent contained only three.

11. Edmonds, *Military Operations: France and Belgium, 1914*, 49; Shelford Bidwell and Dominick Graham, *Fire-Power: British Army Weapons and Theories of War, 1904–1945* (London: Allen and Unwin, 1982), 95; Carew, *Wipers*, 94; Archibald Home, *A Diary of a World War I Cavalry Officer* (Tunbridge Wells: Costello, 1985), 45.

12. Hugo Montgomery to Edmonds, "7th Division, October 1914. (Note by Col. Montgomery, GSO1)," 4 February 1921, Edmonds 6/2, Edmonds Papers, Liddell Hart Centre for Military Archives, King's College, London (LHCMA). Also in 7 Division War Diary, WO 95/1627, PRO.

13. "Formation of 3rd Cavalry Division," 3 Cavalry Division War Diary, WO 95/1141, PRO.

14. Rawlinson to Clive Wigram, 17 October 1914, Rawlinson letter book, Henry Rawlinson Papers, 5201-33-17, National Army Museum (NAM), London. See also Hugo Montgomery to Edmonds, "7th Division, October 1914. (Note by Col. Montgomery, GSO1)," 4 February 1921, Edmonds Papers, 6/2, LHCMA.

15. Rawlinson Diary, 22 September–3 October 1914, Henry Rawlinson Papers, CCC. Rawlinson commanded 4 Division from 23 September–4 October.

16. Haig Diary, 18 October 1914, NLS; WO 256/2, PRO.

17. Rawlinson, *Adventures on the Western Front*, 162–163.

18. On Haig's relationship with Rawlinson, see Bidwell and Graham, *Fire-Power*, 81; Simkins, "Haig and the Army Commanders," 85. See also Liddell Hart, "Talk With Edmonds, 10/1/35," 11/1935/58, Liddell Hart Papers, LHCMA.

19. John Charteris, *At GHQ* (London: Cassell, 1931), 47.

20. Haig Diary, 20–21 October 1914, NLS; WO 256/1, PRO.

21. Holmes, *The Little Field-Marshal*, 127.

22. Holmes, *The Little Field-Marshal*, 243; Rawlinson Diary, 7 September 1914, Henry Rawlinson Papers, CCC.

23. Charles Callwell, *Experiences of a Dug-Out: 1914–1918* (London: Constable, 1920), 58. See also Kitchener to French, 12 October 1914, WO 33/713, PRO.

24. French to Rawlinson, 11 October 1914, WO 33/713; Kitchener to French, 12 October 1914, WO 33/713; IV Corps War Diary, 11 October 1914, WO 95/706, PRO; A. Rawlinson, *Adventures on the Western Front*, 162; Henry Rawlinson Diary, 12 October 1914, Henry Rawlinson Papers, CCC.

25. "7th Division, October 1914. (Note by Col. Montgomery, GSO1)," Edmonds 6/2, James Edmonds Papers, LHCMA; 3 Cavalry Division War Diary, 13–14 October 1914; 7 Division War Diary, 13–14 October 1914, WO 95/1627, PRO.

26. IV Corps War Diary, 15–17 October 1914, WO 95/706; GHQ Operation Order No. 36, 11:40 pm, 15 October 1914; GHQ Operation Order No. 36, 8:30 pm, 16 October 1914, GHQ War Diary, WO 95/1, PRO.

27. III Corps War Diary, 16 October 1914, WO 95/668; 3 Cavalry Division War Diary, 16 October 1914, WO 95/1141; 7 Division War Diary, 16–17 October 1914, WO 95/1627; IV Corps War Diary, 16–17 October 1914, WO 95/706, PRO.

28. GHQ Operation Order No. 38, 7:50 pm, 17 October 1914, WO 95/1, PRO; Henry Wilson Diary, 17 October 1914, Henry Wilson Papers, Imperial War Museum, London (IWM).

29. "Sir H. Rawlinson's Report on IV Corps, October 1914," IV Corps War Diary, WO 95/706; 7 Division War Diary, 18 October 1914, WO 95/1627, PRO.

30. GHQ Operation Order No. 36, 11:40 pm, 15 October 1914, WO 95/1, PRO.

31. GHQ Operation Order No. 38, 7:50 pm, 17 October 1914, GHQ War Diary, WO 95/1, PRO; Henry Rawlinson Diary, 18 October 1914, 5201-33-25, Henry Rawlinson Papers, NAM.

32. L.A.E. Price-Davies to Mrs. Price-Davies, 18 October 1914, Price-Davies Papers, IWM; 7 Division War Diary, 18 October 1914, WO 95/1627; Henry Rawlinson to Byng, 11 pm, 17 October 1914, IV Corps War Diary, WO 95/706, PRO.

33. 7 Division War Diary, 18 October 1914, WO 95/1627; IV Corps War Diary, 18 October 1914, WO 95/706, PRO; Haig Diary, 18 October 1914, NLS; WO 256/2, PRO.

34. Murray Diary, 18 October 1914, Archibald Murray Papers; Wilson Diary, 18

October 1914, Henry Wilson Papers, IWM.

35. Price-Davies to Mrs. Price-Davies, 18 October 1914, L.A.E. Price-Davies Papers, IWM.

36. 7 Division War Diary, 18 October 1914, WO 95/1627, PRO.

37. Macdonogh to Edmonds, 11 October 1922, CAB 45/141, PRO. See also Charteris, *At GHQ*, 50, 55.

38. GHQ to IV Corps, 8:30 pm, 18 October 1914; IV Corps War Diary, 18 October 1914, WO 95/706, PRO.

39. IV Corps War Diary, 19 October 1914, WO 95/706, PRO.

40. 3 Cavalry Division War Diary, 19 October 1914, WO 95/589; 7 Division War Diary, 19 October 1914, WO 95/1627; IV Corps War Diary, 19 October 1914; "General Rawlinson's Report on IV Corps, October, 1914," IV Corps War Diary, WO 95/706; Macdonogh to Edmonds, 11 October 1922, CAB 45/141, PRO.

41. "Sir H. Rawlinson's Report on IV Corps, October 1914"; IV Corps War Diary, 19 October 1914, WO 95/706; 3 Cavalry Division War Diary, 19 October 1914, WO 95/589; 7 Division War Diary, 19 October 1914, WO 95/1627, PRO.

42. French Diary 19 October 1914, Sir John French Papers, IWM; French to Kitchener, 20 October 1914, 10.20am, WO 33/713; GHQ to IV Corps, 9 pm, 9:05 pm, 19 October 1914, IV Corps War Diary, WO 95/706, PRO..

43. Hamilton, *The First Seven Divisions*, 172; Conan-Doyle, *The British Campaign in France and Flanders*, 234–237; Rawlinson, *Adventures on the Western Front*, 215.

44. IV Corps War Diary, 20 October 1914, WO 95/706; 7 Division War Diary, 20 October 1914, WO 95/1627; 3 Cavalry Division War Diary, 20· October 1914, WO 95/589 PRO.

45. GHQ Operation Order No. 39, 10:18 pm, 20 October 1914, GHQ War Diary, WO 95/1, PRO.

46. 7 Division War Diary, 21 October 1914, WO 95/1627; I Corps War Diary, 21 October 1914, WO 95/589; Macdonogh to Edmonds, 11 October 1922, CAB 45/141, PRO; Haig Diary, 21 October 1914, NLS, WO 256/2, PRO; Conan-Doyle, *The British Campaign in France and Flanders*, 239–241.

47. 3 Cavalry Division War Diary, 21 October 1914, WO 95/589; IV Corps War Diary, WO 95/706, PRO.

48. Hamilton, *The First Seven Divisions*, 178; 7 Division War Diary, 21 October 1914, WO 95/1627; IV Corps War Diary, 21 October 1914, WO 95/706, I Corps War Diary, WO 95/589, PRO.

49. IV Corps War Diary, WO 95/706, PRO.

50. Hamilton, *The First Seven Divisions*, 179. See also Conan-Doyle, *The British Campaign in France and Flanders*, 240.

51. Haig Diary, 22 October 1914, NLS; WO 256/2, PRO.

52. Rawlinson to Capper, 22 October 1914, Rawlinson letter book, 5201-33-17, Henry Rawlinson Papers, NAM.

53. Frederic Coleman, *From Mons to Ypres with French: A Personal Narrative* (Toronto: William Briggs, 1916), 267–268. See also I Corps War Diary, 7 November 1914, WO 95/589; 7 Division War Diary, 7 November 1914, WO 95/1627, PRO; Haig Diary, 7 November 1914, NLS; WO 256/2, PRO.

54. Conan-Doyle, *The British Campaign in France and Flanders*, 238. See also Henry Wilson to Henry Rawlinson, 27 October 1914, Henry Rawlinson Papers, CCC; French to Kitchener, 27 October 1914, 6:30 pm, WO 33/713, PRO.

55. 7 Division War Diary, WO 95/1627; IV Corps War Diary, WO 95/706; GHQ War Diary, WO 95/1, PRO.

56. Rawlinson Diary, 23 October 1914, Henry Rawlinson Papers, CCC; 2 Division War Diary, 22 October 1914, WO 95/589, PRO; Haig Diary, 22 October 1914, NLS, WO 256/2, PRO; Mowbray Diary, 22 October 1914, J.L. Mowbray Papers, IWM.

57. Rawlinson Diary, 23 October 1914, Henry Rawlinson Papers, CCC; IV Corps War Diary, 23 October 1914, WO 95/706, PRO.

58. 7 Division War Diary, 23 October 1914, WO 95/1627, PRO.

59. 7 Division War Diary, 24 October 1914, WO 95/1627; IV Corps War Diary, 24 October 1914, WO 95/706; GHQ War Diary, WO 95/1, PRO; Conan-Doyle, *The British Campaign in France and Flanders*, 242–243; Hamilton, *The First Seven Divisions*, 217.

60. GHQ War Diary, 24 October 1914, WO 95/1; "Sir H. Rawlinson's Report on IV Corps, October 1914," IV Corps War Diary, WO 95/706; 7th Division War Diary, WO 95/1627, PRO; Hugo Montgomery to Edmonds, "7th Division, October 1914," 4 February 1921, 6/2, Edmonds Papers, LHCMA

61. Carew, *Wipers*, 72–73; 7 Division War Diary, WO 95/1627, PRO; Conan-Doyle, *The British Campaign in France and Flanders*, 242–243; Hamilton, *The First Seven Divisions*, 219–220.

62. Rawlinson Diary, 25 October 1914, 1/1, Henry Rawlinson Papers, CCC.

63. L.A.E. Price-Davies to Mrs. Price-Davies, 13 November 1914, Price-Davies Papers, IWM.

64. IV Corps War Diary, 24 October 1914, WO 95/706, PRO; Rawlinson Diary, 25 October 1914; Billy Lambton to Rawlinson, 25 October 1914, 1/1 Henry Rawlinson Papers, CCC.

65. Lambton to Rawlinson, 25 October 1914; Rawlinson Diary, 25 October 1914, 1/1 Henry Rawlinson Papers, CCC.

66. Rawlinson Diary, 25 October 1914, 5201-33-25, Henry Rawlinson Papers, NAM; Rawlinson Diary, 25 October 1914; French to Rawlinson, 25 October 1914, 1/1 Henry Rawlinson Papers, CCC.

67. Rawlinson Diary, 25 October 1914, 1/1 Henry Rawlinson Papers, CCC.

68. GHQ Operation Order No.40, 24 October 1914, WO 95/1, 3 Cavalry Division War Diary, WO 95/589, PRO.

69. Hubert Gough, *The Fifth Army* (London: Hodder and Stoughton, 1931), 58; Cavalry Corps War Diary, 20–24 October 1914, WO 95/572; 1 Cavalry Division War Diary, 20–24 October 1914, WO 95/1096; 2 Cavalry Division War Diary, 20–24 October, WO 95/1141, PRO.

70. 7 Division War Diary, 25 October 1914, WO 95/1627, PRO.

71. Hamilton, *The First Seven Divisions*, 234.

72. Hamilton, *The First Seven Divisions*, 226–228, 231; 7 Division War Diary, 26 October 1914, WO 95/1627, PRO.

73. Hamilton, *The First Seven Divisions*, 227–230; IV Corps War Diary, 26 October 1914, WO 95/706; GHQ War Diary, WO 95/1, PRO.

74. 7 Division to 3 Cavalry Division, 3:20 pm, 26 October 1914, 3 Cavalry Division War Diary, WO 95/1141, PRO. See also 7 Division to 3 Cavalry Division, 2:25 pm, 26 October 1914, 3 Cavalry Division War Diary, WO 95/1141; 7 Division War Diary, 26 Oct 1914, Hugo Montgomery to 20th, 21st and 22nd Brigades, 28 October 1914, 7 Division War Diary, WO 95/1627, PRO; Haig Diary, 26 October 1914, NLS, WO 256/2, PRO.

75. Rawlinson Diary, 27 October 1914, 1/1 Henry Rawlinson Papers, CCC; Haig Diary, 26 October 1914, NLS; WO 256/2, PRO. See also GHQ War Diary, 26 October 1914, WO 95/1, PRO.

76. "Sir H. Rawlinson's Report on IV Corps, October 1914," IV Corps War Diary, WO 95/706; I Corps War Diary, 26–27 October, WO 95/589; IV Corps War Diary, WO 95/706, PRO; Haig Diary, 26–27 October 1914, NLS; WO 256/2, PRO; Rawlinson Diary, 27 October 1914, 1/1/ Henry Rawlinson Papers, CCC.

77. Charteris quoted in Keith Simpson, "Capper and the Offensive Spirit," *Journal of the Royal United Services Institute*, 118:2 (June 1973), 55. See also Baker-Carr, *From Chauffeur to Brigadier-General*, 50.

78. Price-Davies to Mrs. Price-Davies, 13 November 1914. See also Price-Davies to Mrs. Price-Davies, 10 November 1914, L.A.E. Price-Davies Papers, IWM.

79. Rawlinson Diary, 6–8 November; Henry Wilson to Henry Rawlinson, 30 October 1914, 31 October 1914, 1/1, Rawlinson Papers, CCC.

80. Henry Wilson to Henry Rawlinson, 27 October 1914; Rawlinson Diary, 27 October 1914, 1/1, Henry Rawlinson Papers, CCC; Wilson Diary, 28 October 1914, Henry Wilson Papers, IWM; Price-Davies Diary, 28 October 1914, L.A.E. Price-Davies Papers, IWM; 7 Division War Diary, 27 October 1914, WO 95/1627; IV Corps War Diary, 27 October 1914, WO 95/706, PRO.

81. French to Kitchener, 27 October 1914, WO 33/713, PRO.

82. Henry Wilson to Henry Rawlinson, 27 October 1914, 1/1, Henry Rawlinson Papers, CCC.

83. IV Corps War Diary, 12 November 1914, WO 95/706, PRO.

6

A Hazardous Experiment: Command and the Indian Corps in the First Battle of Ypres

Sir James Willcocks's Indian Corps joined the BEF at a critical juncture in the 1914 campaign. After landing at Marseilles in late September, elements of the corps began arriving in the British area of operations just as the enemy took the offensive on 20 October. Units of the Indian Corps reinforced British positions during the last ten days of the month. On the 31st, the formation, comprising the Lahore and Meerut Divisions, took over the entire line of Smith-Dorrien's exhausted and depleted II Corps, holding it until mid-November. While the arrival of Willcocks's force was fortuitous for the embattled BEF, Indian units encountered considerable difficulties adjusting to the conditions of the 1914 campaign. In late October and early November, the reputation of the corps suffered due to disciplinary problems and the apparent tendency of Indian soldiers to abandon their positions while adjacent British forces stood fast. Despite its important role holding the allied line during First Ypres, Willcocks's force was widely perceived to be inferior to British formations of comparable size.

In comparison to the rest of the BEF, the experiences of the Indian Corps during the First Battle of Ypres have received an abundance of scholarly attention. Gordon Corrigan's recent study, *Sepoys in the Trenches*, provides a detailed account of the operations of the Indian Corps on the Western Front, emphasizing the positive contributions of Indian units in 1914 and 1915.[1] Previous studies by two other historians, however, have illuminated significant problems faced by the corps, particularly during the fall of 1914. In a series of articles, Jeffrey Greenhut has advanced several related arguments regarding the nature of the prewar Indian Army and the performance of the Indian Corps on the Western Front. Greenhut argues that the policy of recruiting "martial races" rendered the Indian troops highly dependent on their British officers.[2] In 1914, this dependency was heightened due to the fact that officers served as "interpreters" of European warfare. The loss of these officers in battle thus exposed Indian units to profound operational "culture shock."[3] Poor equipment, mediocre commanders, and the prohibition of contact between Indian soldiers and European women, combined with heavy officer casualties to deplete the morale of Indian troops. Deprived of leadership in an unfamiliar and hostile environment, sepoys resorted to self-inflicted wounds to escape their plight.[4] In his study of the Indian Army from 1860 to 1940, David Omissi downplays the dependency of sepoys on their British officers in 1914, attributing the high incidence of self-inflicted wounds among Indian troops to homesickness, unfamiliarity with the conditions of the 1914 campaign, and disaffection due to the British policy of returning wounded troops to active service following their recovery.[5]

In spite of their differences of interpretation, Corrigan, Greenhut, and Omissi have all provided useful insights into the experiences of the Indian Corps in 1914. Nonetheless, their analyses overlook two issues that shaped these experiences during the First Battle of Ypres. First, while all three authors explore the relationship between sepoys and British officers, none attributes a great deal of importance to the coercion inherent in this relationship in 1914. Second, and more significantly, given the theme of this study, existing studies do not examine the broader command structure in which the Indian Corps operated. As a component of the BEF, Sir James Willcocks's corps served under GHQ throughout the First Battle of Ypres. In addition, Indian units employed independently in the line were subordinated to formation commanders of the British Army. The decisions of commanders outside of Willcocks's corps therefore had a profound influence on the force in this period.

This chapter will examine the impact of command on the operations of the Indian Corps, focusing in particular on the period from 25 October to 2 November, when German pressure fell most heavily upon Indian units. It will begin by identifying the potential strains inherent in the relationship between sepoys and officers at the battalion level in 1914. It will then examine command above the regimental level, arguing that the senior officers of the corps remained isolated from the modernizing trends that influenced the "hybrid" officers in the upper ranks of the BEF. This situation, combined with material and manpower deficiencies, left the Indian Corps poorly prepared for the campaign of 1914. Upon its introduction to active operations, the prejudices of British commanders and the shortcomings of Indian Corps officers led to the careless employment of Indian units. The resulting losses to these units rapidly produced a crisis, as sepoys resorted to self-mutilation in an effort to gain their discharge.

SEPOY-OFFICER RELATIONS IN 1914

In order to understand the impact of command on the operations of the Indian Corps, it is necessary to examine the relationship between Indian soldiers and their British officers. Upon the formation of the Indian Corps in 1914, each of its six brigades contained one British and three Indian infantry battalions. British Army battalions serving in India had a fighting strength of 28 officers and 816 other ranks, all of European descent. Their Indian Army counterparts, however, contained only 723 other ranks, all of Indian descent, commanded by a mixture of 17 Indian and 13 British officers.[6] Relations between soldiers and officers in Indian units were shaped by the British preference in this period for recruiting "martial races," primarily from the north and northwest of India. Beginning in the early 1880s, the focus of recruiting for the Indian Army had gravitated steadily northward, particularly toward Nepal, the Punjab, and the North West Frontier of India. By 1914, troops from Nepal, the Punjab, and the North West Frontier Province provided the army with 80 percent of its strength.[7]

Proponents of martial race theories expressed their arguments in Social Darwinist language. Descriptions of preferred groups extolled their inherent "manly virtues," such as the "dash" of the Pathan, "strong physique" of the Sikh, or the "great endurance" of the Garhwali.[8] Regardless of the qualities attributed to individual groups, however, they were largely of rural background or low caste, which made them particularly useful to the British for the task of maintaining colonial rule. The origins of "martial" groups left them poorly educated and ignorant of Western notions of self-government. Consequently, as Jeffrey Greenhut has observed: "their loyalty was assured."[9] The reliability of Indian soldiers had been of paramount concern to colonial authorities since the Indian Mutiny, and the allegiance of Sikhs, Jats, and other northern groups in 1857 enhanced their reputations in the eyes of the British in subsequent years. Thus, arguments regarding the inherent superiority of recruits from the martial races of the north, as well as practical concerns for the loyalty of Indian units, exerted a significant influence on the makeup of the Indian Army.

The tendency to recruit from groups of rural origins and low caste had important consequences for the distribution of authority in Indian Army regiments. As a result of their background, soldiers recruited from martial races tended to rely heavily on their officers for leadership. For several reasons, the bulk of this reliance was directed toward British officers. Due to the British practice of choosing Indian officers from the ranks, these officers were largely of the same origins as the other ranks. Thus, they often lacked basic literacy, let alone the relatively advanced military knowledge necessary to carry out the duties expected of their British counterparts.[10] In addition, since Indian officers were selected and subsequently promoted primarily on the basis of seniority, sepoys could serve for decades before attaining even the junior leadership position of *naik*, roughly equivalent to the rank of corporal in the British Army. Securing commissioned ranks, such as *jemadar*, *subedar*, and *subedar-major*, necessitated even greater perseverance. As David Omissi has observed, the relatively few sepoys who reached the rank of *jemadar*, equivalent to a lieutenant, were usually in their fifties by the time they did so.[11] Thus, during active operations, when officers were expected to interpret written orders and lead their troops in battle, the age and minimal education of Indian officers resulted in the concentration of authority in the hands of British officers. This situation likely reduced the danger that Indian officers would lead their troops effectively against colonial authorities in the event of a mutiny. Nonetheless, it also resulted in the dependency of sepoys and Indian officers alike on a relatively small number of British officers.

Whatever the implications of this dependency during active operations, contemporary European observers described the bond between sepoys and their British officers in glowing terms, often likening it to the relationship between parent and child.[12] The disciplinary regulations applied to Indian soldiers in 1914, however, were considerably more stringent than those governing the conduct of their British counterparts, let alone that of children. A memorandum issued by Sir James Willcocks in October 1914 detailed the disciplinary regime governing the conduct of Indian troops on the Western Front. Notably, Indian soldiers were subject to corporal punishment, in the form of flogging, for an assortment of offences. These included "housebreaking or plunder," "serious offences against the person or property of inhabitants of the country," and "disgraceful conduct." While the latter transgression apparently included a variety of infractions, Willcocks later specified drunkenness "on, or in the vicinity of the battlefield" as one punishable manifestation.[13]

British authorities were not oblivious to the dignity of the Indian troops. Disciplinary regulations thus directed that corporal punishment be administered in the absence of European soldiers or civilians. Although it was not inflicted in public, flogging was clearly used as a means of enforcing discipline in the Indian Corps in 1914. On 10 November, five sepoys previously awarded one year in prison for drunkenness had their sentences commuted to lashes by Sir James Willcocks.[14] This case appears to have warranted mention in the corps war diary because of the personal intervention of the corps commander. Officers commanding Indian battalions also employed corporal punishment, however, without reference to higher authorities. H.M. Alexander, a captain in the 1st Indian Mule Corps, recorded the following case in his diary on 24 September. As Alexander related: "Had one of my men flogged for leaving his post as sentry without leave. Sgt. Kendall did executioner most efficiently & I hope this will have a good effect."[15]

Admittedly, evidence of flogging in the Indian Corps in 1914 is relatively sparse. Nevertheless, the fact that it was administered as punishment for the varied infractions described above suggests that it comprised a reasonably important ingredient in the exercise of authority in Indian battalions. It is therefore unlikely that the relationship between sepoys and British officers consisted solely of mutual devotion. Rather, it would seem that any bond that existed between them was shaped significantly by coercion. Given that flogging had prevailed in the Indian Army before 1914, it is apparent that sepoys accepted this form of coercion as a component of their contractual relationship with the command structure above them. Upon the arrival of the Indian Corps in France, however, senior officers began to alter the terms of this relationship by tightening disciplinary regulations and increasing the use of corporal punishment. Of particular concern to British authorities was the prevention of sexual relations between Indian soldiers and European women. As Greenhut has observed, service in France provided the Indians with unprecedented contact with women of European descent. The prospect of intimacy between the two groups offended the racist sensibilities of the British. In addition, colonial authorities feared that sexual contact with European women would undermine the esteem in which Indian soldiers ostensibly held British women in India, thereby threatening the foundations of colonial rule.[16]

Consequently, the commanders of the Indian Corps applied unprecedented restrictions to the behavior of the Indian soldiers upon their arrival at Marseilles in late September. Officers imposed an 11 pm curfew on the troops camped near the city. Violators were assumed to be "seeking romance" and threatened with a dozen lashes. Greenhut contends that this punishment was seldom inflicted.[17]

Such leniency, however, did not prevail for long. As the fall of 1914 progressed, Sir James Willcocks grew increasingly concerned with preventing sexual contact between his Indian soldiers and European women. In circulars distributed to subordinate officers in October 1914, the corps commander repeatedly urged the severe punishment of Indians convicted of rape "in this country." Moreover, Willcocks altered disciplinary regulations to allow corporal punishment of troops found absent without leave, "when there is reason to believe that the offence was due to immoral relations, actual or intended, with a European woman."[18]

These policies resulted in harsh penalties for Indian troops. On 1 December, R.D. Jeune, a lieutenant in 1 Indian Cavalry Division, related the punishment of a soldier convicted of propositioning a local woman. As Jeune related:

A Sowar, Hazura Singh, of the 6th [Native Cavalry] was publicly flogged before the 4 native regiments for making indecent overtures to a French girl in Olivet. After a careful inquiry & court martial he was let off with the mild sentence of 20 lashes. However, these were well administered by a sturdy corporal in the 17th, a former sailor & well versed in the art of flogging. We all wished the fellow had got more, but he will have plenty of bare-back riding and fatigue duty for the future to remind him to behave better in Europe.[19]

Such severe restrictions contrasted with regulations regarding contact between soldiers and native women in India. Consequently, Indian troops reacted negatively to their lack of freedom in France. According to Jeffrey Greenhut, troops camped at Marseilles, "complained bitterly about this treatment, writing home that they were being kept in jail."[20] Restrictive British policies did not incite overt resistance among the troops. Clearly, however, attempts to prevent sexual contact with European women added an element of tension to relations between British officers and their Indian subordinates. Thus, as Sir James Willcocks's force embarked on active operations, command relationships within

Indian battalions bore considerably greater strain than those within regiments of the British Army.

THE COMMANDERS OF THE INDIAN CORPS

To young British officers at the outset of their military careers, the Indian Army offered a variety of enticements. For individuals without the financial means necessary to support the lifestyle of an officer in Britain, service in India offered an affordable alternative. In fact, the availability of cheap labor, combined with the elevated status of the British in Indian society, afforded officers a "quasi-aristocratic status no longer possible in Britain."[21] In addition, the Indian Army provided greater opportunities for action, and therefore promotion, than did service at home. As a result of these attractions, the Indian Army remained the preferred career choice for many talented young officers in the years prior to the First World War. In 1913, twenty of the top twenty-five graduates of the Royal Military Academy at Sandhurst opted for service in India.[22]

The intellectual and professional development of these officers usually atrophied, however, following their departure from Sandhurst. British soldiers in India were largely removed from the rest of the British Army as well as from British society in general. Jeffrey Greenhut has suggested that this isolation produced an intense conservatism among the officers. In addition, it afforded these officers little opportunity to obtain advanced military education. As was the case throughout the British Army, regimental traditions often discouraged officers stationed in India from seeking staff training. Even if they were not hindered by such considerations, opportunities to acquire the p.s.c. qualification were hardly abundant. Prior to the establishment of the Staff College at Quetta in 1907, British officers in the Indian Army could only obtain staff training at Camberley. This opportunity, however, was available to just five officers every two years. Furthermore, it proved exceedingly costly for most individuals, as they were forced to cover their own expenses for the duration of the two-year course, while forfeiting their pay in India. Nor was the p.s.c. particularly useful in obtaining staff appointments in the Indian Army without additional training in the languages spoken by Indian troops. Combined with the danger of missing a campaign on the subcontinent while at Camberley, the expense and limited employment value of the Staff College course deterred many officers from attending.[23]

The establishment of an Indian Staff College by Lord Kitchener provided a more attractive alternative. At a temporary location in Deolali beginning in 1905, and at Quetta from 1907, officers had the opportunity to obtain staff training in relatively close proximity to their own regiments. By the beginning of the First World War, 218 officers had attained p.s.c. status through the new institution.[24] It is reasonable to assume that many of these Quetta graduates remained in the Indian Army in 1914, along with a limited number of officers who had completed the staff course at Camberley. Thus, there existed at the outset of the war a nucleus of trained officers to fill staff positions. It is doubtful, however, that this group was sufficient to meet the numerous demands placed on the army in this period. Even before the Indian Army mobilized for war, it lost the services of a significant proportion of its officers. Of the approximately 2,500 members of the Indian officer corps in August 1914, 257 were on leave in Britain. The secretary of state for war promptly enlisted this group to assist in training the New Armies.[25] It is impossible to determine the proportion of these officers that possessed p.s.c. status. Nevertheless, Kitchener's retention of them undoubtedly depleted the pool of available staff officers in India. A very rough estimate would suggest that this remaining cadre amounted to approximately 200 officers at the beginning of the war.

These officers were utilized in a variety of roles in 1914. Most significantly, the routine administration of the Indian Army employed approximately 250 officers in various staff positions. In addition, Sir James Willcocks's corps, containing approximately 500 officers, was not the only force dispatched from India in 1914. Over 400 officers accompanied the British expedition against German East Africa.[26] All three of these functions required the services of trained staff officers. It is likely that the Indian Corps, destined for operations on the Western Front, contained a relatively high proportion of officers with p.s.c. credentials, particularly if Quetta graduates responded as enthusiastically as their Camberley counterparts to the prospect of active service in Europe. Nevertheless, the other demands for the services of trained staff officers in 1914 undoubtedly diminished the number available to the Indian Corps. It therefore seems likely that Willcocks's force contained less than 100 officers with formal staff training.

Certainly, some senior staff officers in the Indian Corps possessed impressive qualifications. For example, C.J. Sackville-West, GSO1 of the corps in 1914, had served as an instructor at Camberley prior to the war.[27] The vast majority of trained staff officers in Willcocks's force, however, had likely received only two years of training at Quetta. The value of this course in preparing officers for the campaign of 1914 is questionable. While officers followed a similar curriculum to that at Camberley, they also focused on issues of particular import to operations in India, conducting staff rides and patrol over the terrain of the North West Frontier. According to George Barrow, an instructor at Quetta prior to the war: "Kitchener's leading idea in deciding where to build the new college was that proximity to ground suitable for training in mountain warfare was the most important consideration."[28] Thus, while the training at Quetta undoubtedly provided officers with some grounding in the rudiments of staff duties, it offered only limited exposure to the difficulties of operating against a European enemy. As Sir James Willcocks related in his memoir of the war: "[s]taff work in India was only beginning to emerge from the bow and arrow days."[29]

Moreover, the curriculum at the Staff College at Quetta between 1907 and 1911 bore the mark of its first commandant, Tommy Capper. At both Camberley and Quetta, Capper had an enormous impact on staff training in the Edwardian army. His ideals, however, were not always attuned to the realities of modern warfare. While Capper stressed the importance of courage and self-sacrifice on the part of staff officers throughout his career, his advocacy of such notions intensified at Quetta. According to Barrow: "he carried some of his principles to an extreme stage where they became unworkable. He maintained that, for example, it was the duty of a staff officer to be killed in battle."[30] The extent to which students at Quetta absorbed such immoderate precepts is questionable. Nonetheless, Tommy Capper's emphasis on self-sacrifice provided students at the new Staff College with a rather dubious model on which to base their conduct in the face of modern weaponry. Nor did the component of the Quetta curriculum devoted to frontier operations prepare Indian officers for a campaign in Europe. Thus, while the course at Quetta may have trained some officers of Sir James Willcocks's force in the procedures of staff work, it provided an incomplete and even dangerous preparation for the campaign of 1914.

Whatever the limitations of the course at Quetta, it furnished staff officers of the Indian Corps with a more advanced military education than that possessed by most of their superiors. Above the regimental level, commanders in the Indian Army in this period were appointed from both the British and Indian armies. Collectively, they were significantly older than their counterparts in the rest of the BEF. The advanced age of these officers stemmed from several factors. First, as Greenhut has noted, the British Army often used command posts in India "as a place where less capable senior officers could be put out to pasture as a reward for long and faithful service."[31] Those commanders who had risen through the ranks in India were also older than officers holding equivalent posts in Britain due to the promotion policies of the Indian Army. As officers were chosen on the basis of seniority, even obtaining command of a brigade usually required a lengthy term of service. Once officers had attained senior command posts, however, they often occupied them to an advanced age for economic reasons. As Willcocks commented in his memoirs, the retention of ageing officers, "kept down the pension lists, and when money could be saved on anything connected with the Army, there was no doubt it would be done readily."[32]

The age of formation commanders in the Indian Corps also reflected the fact that officers stationed in India for prolonged periods did not benefit from the informal promotion channels that existed in Britain. Numerous high-ranking officers in the British Army in 1914 had served in India. Their service abroad, however, had been interspersed with appointments in England that enabled them to build social connections and maintain contact with mentors. The career of Sir James Willcocks provides a useful illustration of the difficulties encountered by an officer who did not possess influential ties in Britain. After joining the relatively unfashionable Leinster Regiment in 1878, Willcocks participated in numerous campaigns in Africa and Asia. According to J.W.B. Merewether and Sir Frederick Smith: "No man in the British Army had more decorations on his breast for active service than James Willcocks."[33]

Nevertheless, Willcocks possessed neither an influential patron, nor any association with the prevailing "rings" in the prewar British Army. In the words of Merewether and Smith, the Indian Corps commander "had carved out a career for himself without the aid of patronage, and in complete indifference to social and political influences."[34] Without connections in Britain, his rise to prominence suffered significant setbacks. As recently as April 1914, colonial authorities had overlooked Willcocks in selecting a new commander-in-chief of the Indian Army, choosing instead Sir Beauchamp Duff, a protégé of Lord Kitchener. As Willcocks reflected in his memoirs: "Commands of Armies were altitudes too dizzy to be reached by a soldier who had lived in khaki, it is true, but had worn it in far-away portions of the Empire, and had seldom been seen on the Downs of Salisbury or in the purlieus of Pall Mall or Whitehall."[35]

At 57, Willcocks was the oldest corps commander in the British Army in 1914. Like the Indian Corps commander, the formation commanders below him were older than the vast majority of their counterparts in the rest of the BEF. H.B.B. Watkis, commanding the Lahore Division, and Charles Anderson, commanding the Meerut Division, were 54 and 57 years old, respectively. The brigade commanders in the Indian Corps ranged from 54 to 60 years of age. By contrast, formation commanders in the original contingent of the BEF tended overwhelmingly to be in their early 50s or younger Among them, only Sir John French, Sir Horace Smith-Dorrien and Thomas Snow of 4 Division were older than 53.[36] While the age difference between the two groups of officers may seem slight, it suggests that the formation commanders of the Indian Corps were officers whose careers had lost momentum due to a lack of ambition, connections, or competence.

The age of these officers may also have contributed to their minimal staff training in comparison to their counterparts in the BEF. H.B.B. Watkis was the only commander in the Indian Corps in 1914 who had attended the Staff College at Camberley. In light of their age, remote postings and lack of advanced military education, it seems unlikely that the commanders of the Indian Corps in this period were affected by the modernizing trends that influenced the "hybrid" officers in the upper ranks of the BEF. Not surprisingly, senior commanders in the Indian Corps favored traditional approaches to command. Charles Anderson, for example, emphasized personal contact with his troops during active operations. According to Willcocks: "[Anderson's] chief amusement was to visit the trenches, and if you wanted to find him you could do no better than make for the front line closest to the Germans. I do not believe that there was a single General in the Expeditionary Force who so often visited his men in the trenches."[37]

In addition to their isolation from modernizing trends affecting the British officer corps, the senior officers of the Indian Corps possessed little or no practical experience relevant to commanding large formations in a European theater. During his tenure as commander-in-chief between 1902 and 1909, Lord Kitchener had attempted to convert the Indian Army from a frontier defense force to a regular army capable of operating against a European opponent. In this endeavor, he had created permanent brigades and divisions with fixed establishments. Budgetary restrictions, however, prevented Kitchener's successors from sustaining his initiative. By 1914, there still did not exist sufficient accommodation to house the units of the new formations in close proximity to one another. Consequently, the commanders of the brigades and divisions of the Indian Corps had no opportunity to gain experience organizing and directing their formations on maneuvers, let alone on active operations.[38]

Thus, in 1914, Sir James Willcocks and his subordinates at the divisional and brigade levels suffered due to the inability of the Indian Army to consider the organizational, operational and tactical realities of a campaign in Europe. Given that the primary concern of British colonial authorities was the maintenance of control over India itself, it is not surprising that they were unwilling to allocate resources to other tasks. Nevertheless, combined with the scant military education of commanders in the Indian Corps, this lack of preparation for war outside of India left these officers poorly equipped to exercise command in Europe in 1914.

These shortcomings were certainly evident in the commanders of the Indian Expeditionary Force dispatched to East Africa in 1914. Richard Meinertzhagen, a divisional staff officer with the contingent, unkindly described his commanders as "nearer to fossils than active, energetic leaders of men." According to Meinertzhagen, his initial commander, General Aitken, "lacked all the qualities which go to make a successful commander." Aitken's leadership of the British attack on the port of Tanga in November 1914 confirmed this assessment. As Meinertzhagen related: "not only Aitken but the whole of his staff were up in the front line or a very few yards behind....As a matter of fact, Aitken never influenced the fight from the word 'go,' for he had no reserves." Shortly afterward, the unfortunate Aitken was sacked and replaced by General Wapshare, "a kindly old gentleman, nervous, physically unfit, and devoid of military knowledge." Wapshare was succeeded in turn by General Tighe, a more capable officer who nonetheless "failed because he allowed alcohol to ruin his health."[39]

It is likely that the senior commanders of the Indian Corps in 1914 were more efficient than those whom Meinertzhagen described. Nonetheless, available evidence suggests that the opening campaign of the First World War proved overwhelming for many of them. After the war, Claud Jacob, a staff officer in the Meerut Division in 1914, related to Sir Basil Liddell Hart that the three brigadiers of his formation "were so bad that they violated 'all the principles of war' at once."[40] Similar difficulties existed at the divisional level. In December 1914, Captain Millward, a liaison officer, commented in his diary that Watkis envisioned an attack with his entire Lahore Division in the line. Watkis's potentially costly plan never reached fruition. At the beginning of January 1915, Sir James Willcocks sacked him along with four of the six brigadiers of the Indian Corps. As Greenhut has commented: "A more severe criticism of the prewar promotion and command selection process of the Indian Army would be hard to find."[41]

The limitations of the commanders of the Indian Corps in 1914 were considerable in themselves. To make matters worse, however, Sir James Willcocks's force operated under British officers who often proved indifferent and even disdainful toward the Indian Army. Despite the apparent preference of Sandhurst graduates for service in India, it is evident that there also existed in the British officer corps a general perception of the Indian Army as a force inferior to its British counterpart. At its root, this belief stemmed from prevailing attitudes toward Indian troops. As David Omissi has observed, British officers viewed the Indian army "as the home of the 'second rate soldier.' "[42] The dependency of Indian troops on their officers, a consequence of recruiting "martial races," undoubtedly supported this opinion. Racism contributed as well. British Army officers before and during the First World War referred to Indian battalions as "Niggar regiments." Individual soldiers were described by a variety of derogatory epithets. In his diary on 29 October 1914, Billy Congreve, a staff officer in 3 Division, described Indian soldiers attacking Neuve Chapelle as "great khaki slugs." Richard Meinertzhagen likened sepoys in East Africa to "jibbering monkeys," shooting two in an effort to prevent their retirement at Tanga in November 1914.[43]

Association with such soldiers reflected poorly on their officers. In 1881, L.R. Ashburner, a colonial administrator in Bombay, observed the contempt of British Army officers for their Indian counterparts, commenting: "I have known officers commanding British regiments [to] discourage, if not prohibit all social intercourse with officers of Native regiments." This attitude did not disappear prior to the First World War. John Masters reflected in his memoirs on the lingering prejudices against Indian Army officers in the interwar period. "Some British regiments," Masters recalled, "treated their attached Indian Army subalterns like dirt." A more general scorn for the Indian Army apparently accompanied disdain for its officers. At the Staff College at Quetta, Meinhertzhagen encountered an officer of a British regiment that regularly toasted "damnation to the Indian Army" at mess.[44]

The poor reputation of the Indian Army likely encouraged British military authorities to treat it as a repository for mediocre commanders without social and political connections. This tendency further tainted British perceptions of the force, and undermined relations between commanders in the BEF and the Indian Corps in 1914. With their low opinion of the Indian Army diminished further by the social obscurity and lackluster reputation of its senior commanders, British officers were less likely to treat commanders of the Indian Corps with the same professional respect that prevailed within the BEF itself. If the friction between Sir John French and his corps commanders in 1914 is any indication, this professional respect was limited even among officers of the British Army. Nonetheless, the commander-in-chief's treatment of his subordinates in the BEF was moderated by their political connections within the army. The case of Sir

Henry Rawlinson provides a useful example. In spite of his strained relationship with Rawlinson prior to the war, the ostensibly poor performance of IV Corps in October 1914, and Rawlinson's perceived impertinence during the same period, Sir John French did not formally relieve him of his command. The resiliency of the IV Corps commander in 1914 likely stemmed in part from his close relationships with both Henry Wilson and Lord Kitchener, both of whom exerted considerable sway over the decisions of the commander-in-chief.

Sir James Willcocks did not possess such powerful allies. Consequently, his relationship with the commander-in-chief in 1914 was not moderated by political considerations. Nor did any of Willcocks's subordinates have influential protectors within the British Army. Given Sir John French's temperament, and the critical condition of the BEF upon the arrival of the Indian Corps in France, the status of its senior officers as relative nonentities within the ranks of the British officer corps did not bode well for the treatment of their formations. Thus, in addition to the limitations of its own commanders, the Indian Corps suffered from the poor reputation and relative obscurity of these commanders among senior officers of the BEF.

MANPOWER AND FIREPOWER IN THE INDIAN CORPS IN 1914

As the preceding discussion has demonstrated, the purpose of the Indian Army and the composition of its units directly influenced the exercise of command in the Indian Corps. In addition, these characteristics left Sir James Willcocks's force poorly prepared to meet the human and material demands placed on it during the campaign of 1914. Deficiencies in manpower and weaponry would in turn place further stress on command relations within the corps. As was the case with Rawlinson's IV Corps, the Indian Corps contained considerably fewer troops than the other formations of the BEF in 1914. Willcocks's force left India with six full brigades. Upon its arrival in Egypt, however, army authorities directed the corps commander to detach the Sirhind Brigade of Watkis's Lahore Division to guard the Suez Canal. In addition, the five remaining brigades that arrived in France were composed predominantly of Indian battalions smaller than those in British formations. Thus, upon its arrival in France, the entire Indian Corps boasted a total strength of only 15,700 all ranks.[45]

Nor were these troops easy to replenish. Indeed, the Indian Corps faced a shortage of reinforcements before it even entered combat. The lack of immediately available replacement troops stemmed from the unfamiliarity of Indian Army authorities with the casualty rates of the 1914 campaign. Although the corps arrived in France with a reserve amounting to 10 percent of its total strength, the replacement of sepoys deemed unfit for service depleted this reserve before the force even reached the theater of operations.[46] Once the Indian Corps became involved in active engagements, the remaining reinforcements in France proved woefully inadequate to offset the heavy casualties suffered by

Indian units. The BEF had encountered similar difficulties by September 1914. While it was possible to reinforce British units relatively easily, however, the distance of the Indian subcontinent and the nature of Indian society compounded the problems involved in reconstituting sepoy battalions. Due to the difficulty of combining troops of different caste, faith, and linguistic background in the same unit, sepoys were divided into companies, or even regiments, of similar ethnic and religious traditions. Of the 136 battalions in the Indian Army in 1914, 84 contained separate "class companies," while the remainder consisted of homogeneous "class regiments." In practice, soldiers in particular class companies or regiments would often be recruited from the same community. Once these units began suffering casualties, it was extremely difficult to provide sufficient reinforcements.[47] British officers proved equally difficult to replace due to their specialized language skills. Particularly in Gurkha units, where troops generally spoke neither Urdu nor Hindi, a shortage of replacement officers loomed as Willcocks's force commenced active operations.

In addition to a lack of reinforcements, the Indian Corps faced serious deficiencies in weaponry. The weapons with which the force left India reflected the same British concerns regarding an Indian uprising that contributed to the recruitment of "martial races." Since the Mutiny of 1857, British military authorities in India had deliberately equipped native troops with inferior rifles and machine guns. Against the German Army, however, these weapons were clearly inadequate. They thus had to be replaced upon the arrival of the corps in France. Significantly, however, the British army did not possess sufficient machine guns to replace those captured by the enemy or destroyed in action during October and November 1914. Thus, upon the loss of the Vickers machine guns received upon the arrival of the corps in France, Indian units were forced to rely on the MH 450 guns that they had brought from India. As the commander of the Lahore Division complained in late November, these weapons were heavy, prone to malfunction, and generally useless in the field.[48]

The intended purpose of the Indian Corps as a frontier defense force contributed to deficiencies in its artillery in October 1914. Consequently, Willcocks's corps was supplied with heavy guns as well as smaller weapons upon its arrival at Marseilles. This supplement of artillery, however, did not provide the Indian contingent with firepower equivalent to that of a British corps. According to Sir James Edmonds, the guns allotted to the force did not include howitzers. Like Rawlinson's IV Corps, Willcocks's corps had to rely on the less effective 4.7-inch naval guns. The force was evidently deficient in field guns as well. When the Indian Corps replaced II Corps in the British line in late October, Sir Horace Smith-Dorrien left behind most of his artillery to support Willcocks's units.[49] Thus, the Indian Corps suffered significant deficiencies in manpower and weaponry as it entered the First Battle of Ypres. Combined with the limitations of its senior commanders and the indifference and disdain of the BEF command structure, these shortcomings threatened to undermine the effectiveness of the force in October and November 1914. Similar to the cases of

II Corps and IV Corps in the same period, such difficulties placed additional stress on the battalions of the Indian Corps. As Sir James Willcocks's force commenced active operations, however, command relations within these units remained much more fragile than in battalions of the British Army. The First Battle of Ypres would subject the already delicate relationship between officer and sepoy to overwhelming pressure.

THE ARRIVAL OF THE INDIAN CORPS ON THE WESTERN FRONT, OCTOBER–NOVEMBER 1914

The Indian Corps arrived on the Western Front at a crucial point in the 1914 campaign. On 21 October, the second day of German counteroffensives against allied positions, the two brigades of Watkis's Lahore Division began to arrive in the British theater of operations. Sir John French wasted little time in deploying them. Upon the arrival of the first units of the Lahore Division on the evening of the 21st, the commander-in-chief ordered two battalions of the Ferozopore Brigade to support Allenby's Cavalry Corps. The piecemeal employment of Indian battalions continued on subsequent days. On 24 October, three battalions of the Jullundur Brigade replaced exhausted French cavalry on the left of II Corps.[50]

With the loss of Neuve Chapelle by II Corps on 26 October, the deployment of Indian units intensified. That evening, the 9th Bhopal Infantry of the Ferozopore Brigade, previously attached to the Cavalry Corps, was placed at Smith-Dorrien's disposal, along with half of the 47th Sikhs of the Jullundur Brigade. The next day, the Lahore Division sent the remainder of its available troops to II Corps, including three squadrons of its divisional cavalry, and the division's detachment of engineers, the 20th and 21st Companies of Sappers and Miners. None of these troops participated in the abortive counterattacks on Neuve Chapelle by British and French troops on the 27th. They thus remained intact that evening when renewed German artillery bombardments broke the frail British positions around Neuve Chapelle, nullifying any gains made during the day. In an effort to repair his crumbling line, Colin Mackenzie, commanding 3 Division, directed the Indian units at his disposal to take over trenches in the front of McCracken's depleted 7th Brigade. Accordingly, the half battalion of 47th Sikhs, two companies of Sappers and Miners, and the entire 9th Bhopals occupied positions from left to right in the 3 Division line on the night of 27–28 October.[51]

Responding to pressure from Smith-Dorrien, Colin Mackenzie ordered the 7th Brigade to attack Neuve Chapelle again on the morning of the 28th. With the newly arrived units in the front trenches, and the battered battalions of the 7th Brigade in no condition to mount an offensive, McCracken ordered the Indians to spearhead the attack. Heavy fog delayed the assault until 11 am. After a twenty-minute artillery bombardment, the Indian troops moved forward. Despite the lateness of the attack and the brevity of the barrage, they made significant progress. Although the 9th Bhopals on the right faltered and retired, the Sappers and Miners and 47th Sikhs advanced enthusiastically into Neuve Chapelle.[52]

Upon entering the village, however, the Indian units became disorganized as they attempted to dislodge enemy troops from individual houses. Moreover, the absence of support from the 9th Bhopals on the right and British and French units on the left exposed them to heavy fire from German positions to the north and east. As casualties mounted, the units began to lose cohesion.[53] Subsequent efforts by the 3 Division staff to enlist the support of British units in reserve were ineffective. Exhausted and depleted by German attacks since 20 October, the British troops refused to advance in the face of heavy fire. With no support forthcoming, the Indian soldiers began retiring in disorder at approximately 1 pm, sustaining losses as they withdrew under the sights of German artillery and machine guns. The Sappers and Miners suffered particularly heavily in the abortive attack. One-hundred eleven of the 300 troops participating in the attacks were killed or wounded. Of the eight officers leading the two companies, four were killed, while the remainder suffered wounds of varying severity.[54]

The losses sustained by the Sappers and Miners caused considerable consternation among officers of the Indian Corps. As Sir James Willcocks related in his memoirs: "To those who know the Indian Army, it will at once be evident that to employ such highly trained technical troops as Sappers and Miners as ordinary infantry was to extract the very marrow from a Division engaged in this sort of siege warfare."[55] Consequently, in the aftermath of the ill-fated attack, GHQ launched an inquiry into the demise of the engineers, eliciting reports from Sir Horace Smith-Dorrien as well as other commanders involved. All of the officers agreed that in light of the weakened condition of British units, the use of the Indian engineers was unavoidable. The adjustment of the British line in the dark following enemy counterattacks on the evening of 27 October left a breach between the 9th Bhopals and 47th Sikhs. As the only reserve available to the 7th Brigade, the Sappers and Miners were ordered by General McCracken to fill the gap. The following day, the Indian units, still relatively unscathed, were the only available troops in any condition to mount an attack. Moreover, the 3 Division line had barely been reestablished on the morning of the 28th. It was therefore exceedingly difficult for McCracken to identify the positions of units under his command, much less alter them for his impending assault on Neuve Chapelle. As Smith-Dorrien explained: "The difficulty of coordinating such an attack under such circumstances was very great, and even if it had struck General McCracken that he had better not use the Sappers and Miners for the attack, it would have been impossible for him to have replaced them in the position in which they were with other troops."[56]

Nevertheless, the involvement of the engineers in the attack on 28 October also reflected a lack of regard for the different skills of Indian soldiers. Indeed, the use of the Sappers and Miners in the counterattack on the 28th appears to have resulted in part from a case of mistaken identity. The previous morning, H.B.B. Watkis had placed the Lahore Division's last reserves, consisting of the two companies of Sappers and Miners as well as three squadrons of cavalry, at the disposal of 3 Division. During the afternoon on 27 October, pressure on the Jullundur Brigade compelled its commander, P.M. Carnegy, to request the return of some of these troops. Mackenzie agreed to send back the Sappers and Miners. According to Smith-Dorrien, however, "owing to misunderstanding, the 15th Lancers were sent to General Carnegy, and the two Companies, Sappers and Miners, were retained at General Mackenzie's disposal."[57]

The circumstances surrounding this error remain obscure. Certainly the confusion and anxiety that prevailed in II Corps in late October 1914 compounded the likelihood of mistakes. Even so, it is difficult to imagine officers confusing British cavalry and engineers. Thus, it appears that the failure of British officers to differentiate between Indian troops contributed to the misuse of the Sappers and Miners. The loss of the engineers not only hindered the effectiveness of Willcocks's force, it also had a significant impact on its morale. After the war, John Headlam asserted to Sir James Edmonds that the use of the two companies as "storm troops" was "bitterly resented by the Indian Corps."[58]

Despite the demise of the Sappers and Miners, the responsibilities of Indian units expanded considerably at the end of October. Detachments of Indian troops had reinforced II Corps and Allenby's cavalry since 22 October. The exhaustion and depletion of Smith-Dorrien's force late in the month, however, necessitated its replacement by the entire Indian Corps. Beginning on 29 October, Willcocks's force, bolstered by the arrival of the Meerut Division, began taking over the II Corps line. Their new positions provided Indian troops with an inhospitable introduction to trench warfare. Poor weather and the high water table in Flanders combined to make trenches extremely wet. Officers in Gurkha units also complained that the diminutive stature of their troops left them unable to see over the parapets of their trenches. In addition, the eight-mile line occupied by the Indian Corps did not allow Sir James Willcocks the luxury of retaining ample reserves, despite the fact that Smith-Dorrien left behind 2 1/2 infantry brigades to bolster the Indian position.[59]

By 29 October, the focus of German attacks on the British line had begun to move northwards to the vicinity of Ypres. Nevertheless, units taking over the II Corps line soon suffered from German attacks of an intensity unfamiliar to both Indian troops and their commanders. On the night of the 29th, as the 2/8th Gurkhas of the Bareilly Brigade took over British trenches, they were greeted by an enemy bombardment that continued throughout the night and into the next morning, punctuated after daybreak by intermittent infantry attacks. In the face of these attacks, the inexperienced Gurkhas quickly consumed their available munitions. As the battalion commander, G.M. Morris, explained in an after-action report: "About noon I began to be anxious about ammunition."[60] Morris's apprehension proved timely, as German infantry launched a determined attack at approximately 1 pm. The commander of the Gurkhas deployed the entire battalion in his front trenches to repel the attack, but this simply exposed more of his troops to the continuing enemy artillery bombardment. By 3:30 pm, the troops on the right of the battalion had abandoned their positions. The rest of the 2/8th Gurkhas retired behind the adjacent Devonshire Regiment, a battered remnant of II Corps. Significantly, the Devons remained steady despite suffering from similar attacks on the 29th and 30th.[61]

The German infantry made no effort to exploit the breach in the Indian Corps line after dislodging the Gurkhas. Nonetheless, the enemy forces proved exceedingly difficult to evict from their new positions. While a counterattack on 31 October by the 58th Rifles of the Bareilly Brigade recaptured the Gurkhas' support trenches, their advanced trenches remained in enemy hands. Both the German attacks on the Gurkhas and the counterattacks by the 58th Rifles exacted a heavy toll, particularly on the vital cadre of British officers in both battalions. The 58th Rifles lost three British officers, including the battalion commander, as well as 4 Indian officers and 84 other ranks killed and wounded. The 2/8th Gurkhas suffered even more severely. In addition to 207 other ranks killed, wounded, or missing, the battalion lost five Gurkha officers and nine of its 12 British officers.[62] Such losses would have a dramatic impact on the effectiveness of the unit during subsequent operations.

Indian troops supporting Allenby's Cavalry Corps demonstrated similar fragility under fire on 31 October. Early on the morning of the 31st, at least nine German battalions launched an attack on the positions of De Lisle's 1 Cavalry Division around Messines. This portion of the line was occupied by dismounted British units, bolstered by the 57th Rifles of the Ferozopore Brigade, the only Indian battalion remaining with Allenby's corps. The cavalry stood fast against the enemy onslaught. The 57th Rifles, however, gave way, producing a gap in the British line. While an immediate counterattack by the 57th Rifles and the neighboring 5th Dragoon Guards was partially successful in regaining the lost trenches, it proved costly to the Indian battalion. As an after-action report in the 1 Cavalry Division War Diary explained: "All the European officers of the 57th Rifles being killed as well as a large proportion of the men, the regiment could not be rallied." The disintegration of the 57th Rifles had adverse consequences for the position of 1 Cavalry Division. At 9:50 am, according to the divisional war diary: "A message was sent to the Corps stating that we were unable to hold the whole of MESSINES, a gap having occurred owing to the 57th Rifles having fallen back."[63]

Sepoys in the vicinity of Neuve Chapelle encountered similar difficulties on the morning of 2 November, when the 2/2nd Gurkhas of the Dehra Dun Brigade were attacked. The Gurkhas had replaced units of II Corps in the British line less than three days earlier, and the position that they had inherited left much to be desired. Located just north of Neuve Chapelle, it formed a salient in the British line. In addition, the trenches occupied by the 2/2nd Gurkhas were cut off from behind by forest and threatened in front by the presence of German trenches as little as 40 yards away. During the morning of the 2nd, the enemy attacked the precarious position, inundating the Gurkha trenches with artillery fire. By 11 am, troops in the right portion of the trenches had given way, while those in the left took shelter with the adjacent Connaught Rangers, a British battalion of the Indian Army.[64]

Officers of the 2/2nd Gurkhas quickly launched counterattacks in hopes of regaining the lost position. These initiatives, however, proved both costly and ineffectual. Although the Germans eventually abandoned the position, it remained exceedingly vulnerable to enemy artillery fire, and consequently the Indian Corps was forced to adjust its line westward. In the abortive attempts by the 2/2nd Gurkhas to retake their trenches, seven of the battalion's 12 British officers were killed, and one officer was wounded. In addition, four Gurkha officers and 31 sepoys were killed, and three Gurkha officers and 101 other ranks wounded. The remainder of the unit was dispersed and demoralized. Following the failed attack, Roly Grimshaw, an officer of the Poona Horse, attempted to collect the remnants of the attacking force. As he recorded in his diary: "I found 2nd Gurkha men in all kinds of places. Ditches, ruins, and even under the culverts."[65] Similar to the 2/8th Gurkhas and 57th Rifles, the 2/2nd Gurkhas had been rendered largely ineffective less than ten days after commencing active operations.

Indian battalions were certainly not the only units in the British line to suffer heavily during the First Battle of Ypres. Nor were they alone in abandoning their trenches. After 20 October, exhaustion combined with the heavy losses incurred over the course of the 1914 campaign left the regiments of II Corps and IV Corps increasingly prone to flight in the face of German attack. Given the relatively recent arrival of the Indian Corps, however, it is apparent that the explanation for their fragility under fire lies elsewhere. Significantly, Indian units arrived at the front with little preparation for the realities of trench warfare. Archibald Home, a staff officer in the Cavalry Corps in 1914, commented in his diary on the reaction of Indian troops upon their introduction to active service in the British line. According to Home: "they don't understand trench work yet, all they wanted to know was why they were not going forward."[66] More specifically, sepoys displayed a lack of comprehension of the dangers of modern weaponry, exposing themselves quite carelessly to enemy fire. Sir Horace Smith-Dorrien noted this tendency after visiting Indian units in their newly acquired positions on 24 October. As the II Corps commander related in his diary:

It appears that the Indians were walking about in the most unconcerned way with an absolute disregard of shell fire, in fact rather enjoying it than otherwise, and I have had to point out to their General that although I have great admiration for their bravery, I must ask them to remember that concealment of our positions is one of the most important matters to be considered in this war.[67]

Indian troops demonstrated equally hazardous habits while attacking at night. In particular, sepoys conducting night raids in November 1914 repeatedly announced their approach to the enemy by cheering in unison as they left their own trenches. Commenting on a trench raid on the night of 9–10 November, Harry Keary, commanding the Garhwal Brigade of the Meerut Division, remarked: "It is to be regretted...[that] the men made the mistake of cheering which warned the enemy in the main trenches sooner than was necessary."[68] In addition to exposing the attacking troops to enemy fire, such behavior clearly diminished the effectiveness of night attacks. Nevertheless, it proved difficult to suppress. A similar attack by the 2/3rd Gurkha Rifles of the Garhwal Brigade four nights later was again preceded by cheering, despite the remonstrances of the brigadier. As an exasperated Keary explained to his superior, Charles Anderson: "I think I made it perfectly clear that the assault was to be a surprise one, men creeping forward as soon as ready to get into or close to [the] enemy's trench before any gun fire gave the alarm to the enemy."[69] The vocal disclosure of the assault had unfortunate effects on the attacking unit. According to an after-action report by its commander, the Gurkhas' cheer attracted heavy enemy fire, which hit all of their British officers and all but one Indian officer. Consequently, the attacking party lost momentum and fell back.[70]

Evidently, Indian troops entered the campaign of 1914 unfamiliar with such basic rules of conduct as seeking cover under fire and maintaining silence at night. The consequences of this dearth of experience were exacerbated, however, by the fact that their officers lacked sufficient knowledge regarding the proper deployment of troops under fire. Indeed, throughout late October 1914, it is evident that officers in the Indian Corps consistently overloaded the front trenches of their positions. In a postwar conversation with Liddell Hart, Claud Jacob, a staff officer in the Indian Corps in 1914, maintained that the brigadiers of the force "crowded all their men in exposed front trenches, tiring [them] out and exposing [them] to shell-fire, and kept no reserve."[71]

Jacob's claims are supported by evidence in the Indian Corps and divisional war diaries. Accounts of the demise of the 2/8th Gurkhas on 30 October reveal the presence of the entire battalion in the firing line immediately prior to its disintegration. By deploying all of his troops forward, the commander of the 2/8th Gurkhas, G.M. Morris, left no reserve to respond to a German breakthrough. Moreover, he exposed the whole unit to the heavy shell fire that inundated the front trenches, thereby compounding its losses. It is not clear whether Morris's decision was sanctioned by the commander of the Bareilly Brigade, F. Macbean. Nevertheless, the overloading of front trenches was apparently a recurring problem in other brigades of the corps during October 1914. On the 30th, H.B.B. Watkis dispatched two battalions to reinforce Carnegy's Jullundur Brigade. Along with the two units, the commander of the Lahore Division sent Carnegy the following rather stern directive:

As regards the two relieving battalions, I wish again to impress on you that *whole battalions are not to be placed in the front line of trenches.* By day, the front line should only be thinly occupied. In other portions of the British line, the front line is occupied by 1 man to every 8 or 10 yards—the remainder being kept in well-protected trenches or shelters in rear communicating with the front trenches. It is scarcely necessary to point out to you that in preliminary artillery bombardment with which the enemy always prefaces his attacks, the fewer men in the front line of trenches, the fewer will be casualties in those trenches.[72]

Thus, it is apparent that the often shaky performance of Indian units in the British line resulted from the unfamiliarity of sepoys and officers alike with the realities of warfare in 1914. Among the other ranks, such basic precepts as seeking cover from enemy fire and maintaining silence were only learned through experience. In addition, officers at the battalion and brigade levels were evidently unaware of the most efficient methods of deploying troops under fire. The fact that it required reminders from senior commanders to inculcate these methods raises questions about the proficiency of these officers. Their inability to adapt quickly to the conditions of the 1914 campaign compounded losses among their troops and increased the fragility of Indian battalions under fire.

The substandard performance of these units, however, did not stem solely from inexperience or incompetence within the Indian Corps. Indeed, it is evident that British staff at GHQ were not particularly thorough in apprising Sir James Willcocks's force of the lessons derived by British units in the initial stages of the war. The Indian Corps and its two divisions received copies of the "tactical notes" compiled in late September from the reports submitted by the staffs of the British corps. These documents contained valuable recommendations, particularly regarding the siting of trenches and artillery. Given that Indian units generally occupied existing British positions, however, the utility of such information was limited.

More significant for the purposes of Willcocks's corps, and absent from the "tactical notes," were guidelines for the conduct and deployment of units during active operations. Watkis's letter to Carnegy, quoted above, indicates that by 30 October, the commander of the Lahore Division was aware of the danger inherent in deploying excessive numbers of troops in advanced trenches. The fact that Indian brigade and battalion commanders retained this habit, however, suggests that they were not properly informed of the tactical conditions of the 1914 campaign before embarking on active operations. This may simply have resulted from an oversight on the part of GHQ. Nevertheless, it suggests a general disregard for the Indian Corps similar to that which led to the destruction of the Sappers and Miners of the Lahore Division. Thus, it seems that while Indian units entered the First Battle of Ypres unfamiliar with the tactical necessities of the 1914 campaign, some indifference on the part of senior British staff contributed to this lack of preparedness.

CASUALTIES IN THE INDIAN CORPS AND THE RESPONSE OF INDIAN SOLDIERS TO THE 1914 CAMPAIGN

As a result of their negligent deployment and nonchalant behavior under fire, Indian units suffered heavy casualties during the First Battle of Ypres. Such severe losses, particularly to British officers, seriously undermined the cohesion of these units. On 3 November, only twelve days after the first Indian units took up positions in the British line, the force recorded the following casualty totals:

	killed	wounded	missing
British officers	18	28	8
Indian officers	6	22	3
British, other ranks	25	63	6
Indian, other ranks	133	1,342	333
Total	182	1,455	352

Amounting to less than 13 percent of the total strength of the Indian Corps, these losses were hardly catastrophic. [73] Nor were they comparable to casualties incurred by British formations earlier in 1914. At the battle of Le Cateau alone, Smith-Dorrien's II Corps had lost over 7,800 all ranks. Viewed in this context, Sir James Willcocks's losses do not seem particularly severe. Nevertheless, German pressure on the section of the British line occupied by Willcocks's force eased just as Indian units began relieving the battalions of II Corps. Consequently, the Indian Corps occupied a relatively quiet zone of the front in this period. In addition, aside from the 28 October assault on Neuve Chapelle, Indian units were not required to launch any concerted attacks in this period. Given the relative inactivity of the force, these casualty totals are worthy of analysis. In addition to demonstrating the extent of the losses suffered by the Indian Corps during the First Battle of Ypres, they illuminate the response of officers and sepoys alike to the conditions of the 1914 campaign.

In examining the losses incurred among the commissioned ranks of the Indian Corps, it is apparent that British officers suffered much more heavily than did their Indian counterparts. While casualties among British officers amounted to 54, with at least 18 of these killed, Indian officers suffered only 31 casualties, with at least six killed. In light of the fact that Indians comprised the majority of officers in Indian Army battalions, this disparity is even more profound. Some of the losses of British officers represented in the figures above may have occurred in British battalions of the Indian Corps. Significantly, however, casualty figures for the Lahore Division in this period suggest that this was not the case. By 30 October, Watkis's division had incurred 1,315 of the 1,989 casualties suffered by the Indian Corps up to 3 November. While the losses of the Lahore Division included 25 British officers, none of these served in British battalions. Moreover, casualties among British officers outnumbered those among Indian officers even in the Indian battalions of the division.[74] The fragmentary nature of available data prevents precise conclusions. Nevertheless, these casualty figures indicate that even within Indian battalions, British officers incurred a much higher rate of casualties than Indian officers. There is no scarcity of anecdotal evidence to support this contention. H.M. Alexander, a supply officer in the Lahore Division, commented repeatedly on the incidence of officer casualties in his diary. On 28 October, he remarked: "we cannot go on at this rate; out of 70 officers here, nearly 20 have been hit in five days." By 3 November, the situation had deteriorated further. As Alexander observed: "The question of officers of Indian Regts is getting very acute indeed. I should think the percentage of killed & wounded must be quite 50% of the total."[75]

These heavy casualties undoubtedly reflected the heavy burden of command shouldered by British officers in Indian battalions. Given the limited authority delegated to officers recruited from the "martial races" of India, British officers remained largely responsible for the leadership of Indian troops during active operations. Not surprisingly, losses to the cadre of British officers in Indian battalions had a detrimental impact on their cohesion. As the Adjutant-General of the BEF, Neville Macready, observed in his 5 November wire to the War Office: "regiments that have lost many [British officers] are useless." Accounts by commanders and staff officers in the Indian Corps concur. G.A. Jamieson, commanding the 9th Bhopals, remarked on the instability of his unit under artillery fire in early November, commenting: "natives without British officers do not stand it like Britishers."[76]

Similarly, an account of a counterattack launched by the 57th Rifles upon their eviction from positions in Messines reveals the collapse of the unit following the loss of its British officers. According to Major E.L. Swifte, a senior officer in the battalion, the attack of the 57th Rifles lost momentum as six of the seven British officers involved became casualties. Without sufficient leadership, the troops retired in disorder. Nor could the cohesion of Indian units be easily repaired following the loss of their British officers. The difficulty of rebuilding depleted Indian battalions stemmed from two factors. First, given the limited reinforcements that had accompanied the corps to France, there simply were not sufficient officers with Indian language training available to replace the high number of casualties. A telegram sent from Nevil Macready to the War Office on 1 November illustrates the specific requirements of Indian units. As Macready related: "Gurkha battalion has lost 10 out of 13 British officers. Can you send at once any Gurkha officers in England? Owing to language Gurkha British officers only are of any use."[77]

Second, even if replacements could be found, they did not inspire the same trust in the troops as the original officers. Jeffrey Greenhut had characterized the bond between sepoys and their officers as a "multiplex" relationship. As he explains: "the British officer became a combination of military leader, teacher, father substitute, and general adviser to his men. As such, the Indian soldier's relationship was with the man inside the uniform, not with the uniform itself." Therefore, Indian troops preferred to serve under officers with whom they were familiar. Indeed, as David Omissi has observed: "The widespread appointment of new and unfamiliar officers made the men uneasy."[78] It thus seems clear that the loss of British officers had a serious and enduring effect on the performance of Indian battalions.

Given the abundant evidence indicating the deterioration of Indian units upon the loss of their original cadre of British officers, it is tempting to accept Tim Carew's description of these battalions as "a leaderless and purposeless rabble."[79] The high casualty rates among Indian soldiers in late October and early November appear to demonstrate the consequences of disorganization under fire. Of the 1,989 casualties in the Indian Corps by 3 November, 1,808 were incurred by Indian troops. British troops, who comprised 25 percent of the fighting strength of the force, suffered only 94.[80] Certainly, such figures suggest the dependency of sepoys on their British officers. The heavy casualties suffered by these officers apparently produced even greater losses among the Indian troops. Nevertheless, the image conveyed by Carew of Indian troops rendered helpless and vulnerable by the demise of their officers is not entirely accurate. Indeed, a closer examination of losses in the Indian Corps suggests a rather different process at work. Significantly, Indian soldiers who became casualties during the First Battle of Ypres were far more likely to be wounded than killed. While 1,342 Indian troops incurred nonfatal wounds or sicknesses up to 3 November, only 133 were killed. The overall casualty levels of British units in the Indian Corps were much lower. A considerably higher proportion of British soldiers, however, were killed in action. While just 63 troops in British battalions were wounded in the same period, the same group suffered 25 fatalities. Casualties in the Lahore Division up to 30 October show a similar distribution. In British units, 13 troops were killed and 19 wounded. In contrast, in Indian units, 64 troops were killed and 963 wounded.[81]

The significance of this disparity becomes evident when the nature of these wounds is examined. Numerous sources suggest that Indian troops demonstrated a high incidence of wounds in the left hand or arm in this period. In early November, Frederic Coleman observed "a score of wounded Wild's [57th] Rifles, almost to a man shot in the left hand or arm." An officer of the Indian battalion informed Coleman that the wounds stemmed from "the peculiar way the Indians shield their head with the left arm while firing."[82] The chauffeur made no further comment on this phenomenon. This explanation seems unlikely, however, as it is difficult to believe that the hands and arms of Indian soldiers were sufficient to stop bullets or shrapnel destined for their heads. Nonetheless, Coleman was not alone in attributing these wounds to the sepoys' exposure of their left hands to enemy fire. Twice in late October 1914, the staff of the Lahore Division instructed subordinate commanders to warn their troops "not to needlessly expose their hands when firing from trenches."[83]

By the beginning of November, however, commanders in the Indian Corps had arrived at a much more unsettling conclusion. As the assistant adjutant-general of the corps explained: "it has been ascertained without any doubt [that] many of the wounds received by Indian soldiers have been self-inflicted."[84] This practice was apparently widespread among Indian battalions. On 2 November, Henry Wilson remarked in his diary that as many as 65 percent of wounds to Indian soldiers were self-inflicted. Citing a 9 November inquiry by the Indian Corps, Jeffrey Greenhut has suggested a slightly lower figure of 57 percent.[85] Notwithstanding the disparity between these two figures, it seems evident that self-inflicted wounds comprised a large proportion of the nonfatal injuries suffered by Indian soldiers during their first two weeks of active operations.

The wounds appear to be a response to the unfamiliar and exceedingly unpleasant conditions experienced by Indian troops upon commencing active operations. As Greenhut has observed: "certain battalions, particularly those that had borne the first shock of combat, had far more than their share." Furthermore, he notes: "over half of the hand wounds suffered by Indian soldiers in the first year of combat were inflicted in the first two weeks."[86] These statistics suggest that self-inflicted wounds resulted from the collapse of the contractual relationship between sepoys and the commanders of the Indian Corps shortly after the force commenced active operations. Thrown into action with little regard for their skills and training, led by inexperienced commanders, and rapidly deprived of the officers on whom they depended, Indian troops resorted to self-inflicted wounds in hopes of escaping active service. Previous accounts have depicted self-mutilation as an act resulting from profound bewilderment and despair.[87] While such sentiments were undoubtedly present among sepoys in this period, it is apparent that this phenomenon also stemmed from a calculated and quite rational choice on the part of the Indian soldiers. Indeed, despite the apparent desperation involved in such an act, self-mutilation offered these soldiers their most plausible means of gaining a discharge. For sepoys in France, desertion was not a particularly attractive option, given their distance from India. Significantly, however, as David Omissi has noted, Indian Army policy prior to the First World War had dictated that wounded troops be granted leave, rather than be immediately returned to active service. There is evidence to indicate that this practice prevailed, at least in principle, during the First Battle of Ypres. On 14 November, in the wake of the discovery of self-mutilation in Indian units, Sir James Willcocks issued an order directing that: "[a]ll men wounded in the hands, or other slight wounds, will not now be invalided to India, but kept in France until they are fit to rejoin the ranks."[88]

Given the profound lack of Indian reinforcements in France in 1914, it is difficult to believe that troops with hand wounds were sent home. Nonetheless, the corps commander's directive suggests that even if this policy no longer prevailed, sepoys remained under the impression that a wound of any sort would result in their return to India. Evidence collected by the chief censor of the Indian Corps, E.B. Howell, supports this assertion. In February 1915, Howell commented to his superior: "Indian opinion regards the man who has been into the trenches & there been wounded as having very amply discharged his duty &

there can be no doubt that in the majority of cases the prospect of a return to the firing line appears to be regarded with something approaching dismay."[89]

Thus, it seems that self-mutilation represented a calculated effort by Indian troops to escape the conditions of service that they faced in France in late October and early November 1914. In the context of a tightened disciplinary regimen designed to prevent contact with European women, relations between Indian soldiers and the British command structure were strained as the Indian Corps commenced active operations. These relations deteriorated further as Indian units were thrown into active service by British commanders indifferent to their training and abilities. Faced in the midst of these difficulties with the loss of the officers on whom they depended for leadership, Indian troops undoubtedly recognized the high probability of their own demise in the event of their continued service. Consequently, they collectively demurred.

The discovery of widespread self-mutilation in Indian units, combined with their increasing fragility under fire, provoked a crisis in the upper ranks of the Indian Corps. On 2 November, Sir James Willcocks arrived at GHQ, where he explained the extent of self-inflicted wounds among his Indian troops and warned of the imminent collapse of his formation. According to G.S. Clive, a British liaison officer with the French Army, Willcocks informed Sir John French that his force "might go at any moment," and requested the addition of two British brigades to the Indian Corps. The commander-in-chief demonstrated little sympathy for Willcocks's plight. As Clive related in his diary: "Sir J answered that if they must go, they could go—into the sea, or to h-ll, & that he would not send more than 2 battalions."[90]

Sir John French's response likely reflected his own mercurial temperament, particularly on 2 November, when German pressure on British forces to the north of the Indian Corps remained acute. It is difficult, however, to imagine him dismissing the plight of a British corps so swiftly. While the commander-in-chief had responded brusquely to similar revelations by Sir Horace Smith-Dorrien during October, he had nonetheless bolstered II Corps with additional troops and artillery. That French dismissed the plight of the Indian Corps so rapidly indicates the disregard in which he and other British commanders continued to hold both Willcocks and his force. Left to maintain his line without the aid of further British reinforcements, Sir James Willcocks responded harshly to disaffection in the Indian Corps. On 2 November, he apparently had two soldiers executed to deter further cases of self-mutilation.[91] In addition, he announced on 14 November that Indian troops with hand wounds would be henceforth be returned to active service. Thus, rather than simply threatening Indian troops with severe punishment for sedition, Willcocks attempted to quell disaffection by removing the means by which Indian troops could escape active operations.

The efforts of the Indian Corps commander seem to have achieved their intent. As Greenhut has noted, the incidence of self-inflicted wounds in Indian units diminished after early November 1914. It is evident, however, that the performance of the Indian Corps did not show great improvement after the First

Battle of Ypres subsided. Relatively modest efforts by the Germans drove Indian units from their trenches on the night of 22 November and during the period 18–21 December. The continued frailty of Indian units under fire did not impress their commander. Informed in late November that the king of England wished to award a Victoria Cross to an Indian soldier or officer, Willcocks replied sourly that "there is no one deserving of such a high honour."[92] Evidently, the closure of escape routes for Indian troops did not lead to their willing acceptance of the terms of their service in Europe.

The commander of the Indian Corps took further measures to improve the performance of his unit in subsequent months. In January 1915, he replaced H.B.B. Watkis and four of the six brigade commanders of the Indian Corps. The only officers to survive the purge were Charles Anderson, who retained command of the Meerut Divison, R.M. Egerton, who remained at the head of the Ferozopore Brigade, and Harry Keary, who was promoted to command the Lahore Division.[93] Despite these changes, however, the record of the Indian Corps in France remained undistinguished. The fact that morale had not improved in Indian battalions was demonstrated in March 1915, when an Indian officer and 24 sepoys deserted to the enemy. As the year progressed, mounting losses combined with inadequate reinforcements to diminish the effectiveness of the force even further. Thus, in early November 1915, the Indian Corps left the Western Front. After the last troops had reembarked at Marseilles in early September, the corps ceased to exist as a component of the British Expeditionary Force.

CONCLUSION

In a rather uncritical account of the Indian Corps in France, J.W.B. Merewether and Frederick Smith characterized the introduction of Indian troops into European warfare as a "hazardous experiment." While the authors did not discuss many of the negative consequences of this experiment, their description remains apt. The nature of command relationships within Indian units, as well as the promotion policies and historical purpose of the Indian army, left Sir James Willcocks's force poorly prepared for the campaign of 1914. The practice of recruiting from designated "martial races" contributed to the dependency of Indian troops upon the small cadre of British officers in these units. Above the regimental level, appointment and promotion policies encumbered the Indian Corps with formation commanders who were largely isolated from modernizing trends in the prewar British officer corps. As a result, Sir James Willcocks and his subordinates faced even greater challenges than the "hybrid" officers of the British Army in adjusting to the scale and intensity of the 1914 campaign. The traditional orientation of the Indian Army toward frontier warfare complicated this process for the Indian Corps as a whole, as the force arrived in France with inadequate weaponry and no experience operating in large formations. The introduction of the Indian Corps into active operations at the height of the First Battle of Ypres thus proved to be a hazardous endeavor indeed.

Once Willcocks's force arrived at the front, the apparent disregard of British commanders compounded its problems. Stemming from racist attitudes and their general indifference toward Willcocks and his subordinates, this attitude led to the careless employment of Indian battalions. As was the case in Smith-Dorrien's II Corps and Rawlinson's IV Corps in this period, the oversights and errors of senior commanders placed additional stress on the component parts of the Indian Corps. Unlike the British regiments of II Corps and IV Corps, however, Indian battalions proved unable to withstand the strain of a new and unaccustomed type of warfare. The indifferent deployment of these units produced heavy casualties among their British officers, which in turn undermined the cohesion of the other ranks. These circumstances led Indian troops to reconsider their commitment to service in Europe, particularly in light of the tightened disciplinary regulations implemented upon the arrival of the corps in France. Thus, upon the loss of the officers on whom they relied for leadership in unprecedented and exceedingly unpleasant conditions, Indian troops opted to escape service in Europe through self-inflicted wounds.

By removing the Indian soldiers' primary means of escape, Sir James Willcocks and his staff reduced the incidence of self-mutilation. Nevertheless, Indian troops did not accept the terms of their service in Europe in the aftermath of the First Battle of Ypres. As further losses diminished the cohesion of Indian units, the troops remained fragile under fire, ultimately compelling their removal from the European theater. Overall, while the Indian Corps played an important role in maintaining the British line at the height of the First Battle of Ypres, the nature of command relationships within Indian battalions left them ill-prepared for the campaign of 1914. The shortcomings of senior commanders in the Indian Corps and the seeming indifference of the British command structure placed unsustainable pressures on these units, leading to a crisis in November 1914, and ultimately to the chronic ineffectiveness of Sir James Willcocks's force.

NOTES

1. Gordon Corrigan, *Sepoys in the Trenches: The Indian Corps on the Western Front, 1914–1915* (Staplehurst: Spellmount, 1999).

2. Jeffrey Greenhut, "Sahib and Sepoy: An Inquiry into the Relationship between the British Officers and Native Soldiers of the British Indian Army," *Military Affairs*, 48:1 (January 1984), 15–18.

3. Greenhut, "The 'Imperial Reserve': The Indian Corps on the Western Front, 1914–1915," *Journal of Commonwealth and Imperial History*, 12:1 (October 1983), 54–73.

4. Greenhut, "Race, Sex and War: The Impact of Race and Sex on Morale and Health Services for the Indian Corps on the Western Front," *Military Affairs*, 45:2 (April 1981), 71–74.

5. David Omissi, *The Sepoy and the Raj: The Indian Army, 1860–1914* (London:

Macmillan, 1994), ch. 4. See also Omissi, ed., *Indian Voices of the Great War: Soldiers' Letters, 1914–1918* (London: Macmillan, 1999).

6. J.W.B. Merewether and Frederick Smith, *The Indian Corps in France* (London: John Murray, 1919), 460. See also T.A. Heathcote, *The Military in British India: The Development of British Land Forces in South Asia, 1600–1947* (London: Manchester University Press, 1995), 178.

7. For a discussion of this policy, see Greenhut, "The 'Imperial Reserve,' " and "Sahib and Sepoy"; Omissi, *The Sepoy and the Raj*, 10–11, and " 'Martial Races': Ethnicity and Security in Colonial India, 1858–1939," *War & Society*, 9 (1991), 1–27; T.A. Heathcote, "The Army of British India," in David Chandler and Ian Beckett, eds., *The Oxford History of the British Army* (Oxford: Oxford University Press, 1994), 377; Chandar S. Sundaram, " 'Martial' Indian Aristocrats and the Military System of the Raj: The Imperial Cadet Corps, 1900–14," *Journal of Imperial and Commonwealth History*, 25:3 (September 1997), 416. In the late nineteenth century, the groups in Indian society designated as "martial" were Rajputs, Sikhs, Pathans, Punjabi Muslims and Gurkhas.

8 .See, for example, Merewether and Smith, *The Indian Corps in France*, Appendix I, "Description of the Indian Army."

9.Greenhut, "Sahib and Sepoy," 16. See also Heathcote, "The Army of British India," 377; Omissi, *The Sepoy and the Raj*, 28.

10. Greenhut, "Sahib and Sepoy," 16; Omissi, *Indian Voices of the Great War*, 4.

11. Omissi, The Sepoy and the Raj, 156. See also Heathcote, *The Military in British India*, 61; Merewether and Smith, *The Indian Corps in France*, 490.

Indian ranks and their British equivalents:

Infantry: *subedar*-major—major; *subedar*—captain; *jemadar*—lieutenant; *havildar-major*—quartermaster-sergeant; *havildar*—sergeant; *naik*—corporal; *sepoy*—private.

Cavalry: *risaldar*-major—major; *risaldar*—captain; *jemadar*—lieutenant; *kot daffadar*—quartermaster-sergeant; *daffadar*—sergeant; *sowar*—trooper.

12. See, for example, Merewether and Smith, *The Indian Corps in France*, 110–111, 471; Tim Carew, *Wipers* (London: Hamish Hamilton, 1974), 127–31, 136; A. Corbett-Smith, *The Marne—and After* (Toronto: Cassell, 1917), 225–226.

13. Appendix IV, Appendix XX, "Memorandum for the Guidance of Officers of the Indian Army Corps," in "AG's Branch, A & Q Indian Army Corps, 15.9.14 to 31.10.14, Volume I," Indian Corps Adjutant-General and Quartermaster General (AG & QMG) War Diary, WO 95/1091, Public Record Office, Kew (PRO).

14. Indian Corps Adjutant-General and Quartermaster General (AG & QMG) War Diary 10 November 1914, WO 95/1091, PRO.

15. H.M. Alexander Diary, 24 September 1914, Lieutenant-Colonel H.M. Alexander Papers, Liddle Collection, Brotherton Library, University of Leeds. See also R.D. Jeune Diary, 1 December 1914, Lieutenant R.D. Jeune Papers, Liddle Collection.

16. Greenhut, "Race, Sex and War," 71–72; Omissi, *The Sepoy and the Raj*, 65. John Masters, *The Ravi Lancers* (London: Michael Joseph, 1972), addresses this issue in a the format of a historical novel.

17. Greenhut, "Race, Sex and War," 72.

18. Appendices IV and XX, "AG's Branch, A&Q Indian Army Corps, 15.9.14 to 31.10.14, Volume I," Indian Corps AG & QMG War Diary, WO 95/1091, PRO.

19. R.D Jeune Diary, 1 December 1914, R.D. Jeune Papers, Liddle Collection.

20. Greenhut, "Race, Sex and War," 72.

21. Greenhut, "Sahib and Sepoy," 15.

22. Greenhut, "Sahib and Sepoy," 15. See also Omissi, *The Sepoy and the Raj*, 104.

23. Brian Bond, *The Victorian Army and the Staff College, 1854–1914* (London: Eyre Methuen, 1972), 97, 199–200; Greenhut, "Sahib and Sepoy," 5.

24. Bond, The Victorian Army and the Staff College, 208.

25. Greenhut, "The 'Imperial Reserve,' " 55; Heathcote, *The Military in British India*, 201.

26. Heathcote, *The Military in British India*, 201.

27. Bond, *The Victorian Army and the Staff College*, 253; "Indian Expeditionary Force—Commanding Officers," Indian Corps War Diary, WO 95/1088, PRO.

28. George Barrow, *The Fire of Life* (London: Hutchinson, 1931), 203–204. See also Bond, *The Victorian Army and the Staff College*, 205–206.

29. James Willcocks, *With the Indians in France* (London: Constable, 1920), 97.

30. Barrow, The Fire of Life, 123. See also Bond, The Victorian Army and the Staff College, 208, 318.

31. Greenhut, "The 'Imperial Reserve,' " 55.

32. Willcocks, With the Indians in France, 13.

33. Merewether and Smith, *The Indian Corps in France*, 18. Among the British commanders who served in India were Sir John French, Sir Douglas Haig, Sir Horace Smith-Dorrien, Hubert Gough, Sir Ian Hamilton, and Lord Kitchener.

34. Merewether and Smith, *The Indian Corps in France*, 18.

35. Willcocks, With the Indians in France, 75.

36. *Who Was Who*, vols. 2–4 (London: Adam and Charles Black, 1929–1952); Tim Travers, *The Killing Ground:The British Army, the Western Front and the Emergence of Modern Warfare* (London: Routledge, 1993), 281–293.

37. Willcocks, With the Indians in France, 52.

38. Heathcote, "The Army of British India," 379–380; Willcocks, *With the Indians in France*, 3.

39. Richard Meinertzhagen, *Army Diary: 1899–1926* (London: Oliver and Boyd, 1960), 109, 176.

40. Liddell Hart, "Talk With F.M. Sir Claud Jacob, 16/11/32," 11/1932/45, Liddell Hart Papers, Liddell Hart Centre for Military Archives, King's College, London (LHCMA).

41. Greenhut, "The 'Imperial Reserve,' " 62; Liddell Hart, "Talk With F.M. Sir Claud Jacob: 16/11/32," 11/1932/45, Liddell Hart Papers, LHCMA; Merewether and Smith, *The Indian Corps in France*, 199–200; Millward Diary, 20 December 1914, Major-General Millward Papers, 6510-143-1, National Army Museum, London (NAM).

42. Omissi, The Sepoy and the Raj, 105.

43. Meinertzhagen, *Army Diary*, 90–92; Pamela Fraser and L.H. Thornton, *The Congreves: Father and Son, General Sir Walter Norris Congreve, V.C., Bt-Major William LaTouche Congreve, V.C.* (London: John Murray, 1930), 241; Heathcote, *The Military in British India*, 170.

44. Meintertzhagen, *Army Diary*, 70; John Masters, *Bugles and a Tiger: A Volume of Autobiography* (New York: Viking, 1956), 15; Heathcote, *The Military in British India*, 170.

45. Heathcote, *The Military in British India*, 201; Merewether and Smith, *The Indian Corps in France*, 14; Lahore Division War Diary, 15 September 1914, WO 95/3911,

PRO.

46. Merewether and Smith, *The Indian Corps in France*, 453–454.

47. Stephen Peter Rosen, *Societies and Military Power* (Ithaca: Cornell University Press, 1996), 195; Greenhut, "The 'Imperial Reserve,' " 54; Heathcote, *The Military in British India*, 226; Omissi, *The Sepoy and the Raj*, 88.

48. GOC Lahore Division to BGGS, Indian Corps, 27 November 1914, Lahore Division War Diary, WO 95/3911, PRO; Greenhut, "The 'Imperial Reserve,' " 55.

49. James Edmonds, *Military Operations: France and Belgium, 1914*, vol.2, (London: Macmillan, 1925), 92; Smith-Dorrien Diary, 30 October 1914, CAB 45/206, PRO; Greenhut, "The 'Imperial Reserve,' " 55.

50. II Corps War Diary, 24 October 1914, WO 95/629; Lahore Division War Diary, 21, 24 October 1914, WO 95/3911; GHQ War Diary, 21, 24 October 1914, WO 95/1; Cavalry Corps War Diary, 21 October 1914, WO 95/572, PRO.

51. Wing to II Corps, 31 October 1914; McCracken, "Report on Attack on Neuve Chapelle, 28th October 1914"; Smith-Dorrien to CGS, 30 October 1914, II Corps War Diary, WO 95/629; Lahore Division War Diary, 26 October 1914, WO 95/3911; GHQ War Diary, WO 95/1, PRO.

52. Merewether and Smith, *The Indian Corps in France*, 53–55; 3 Division War Diary, 28 October 1914, WO 95/1375; McCracken, "Report on Attack on Neuve Chapelle," II Corps War Diary, WO 95/629, PRO.

53. 3 Division War Diary, 28 October 1914, WO 95/1375; Wing to II Corps, 31 October 1914; Millward, "Account of Attempt to Capture Neuve Chapelle, 28/10/14," II Corps War Diary, WO 95/629, PRO; Fraser and Thornton, *The Congreves*, 244.

54. Merewether and Smith, *The Indian Corps in France*, 59–60; GHQ War Diary, 28 October 1914, WO 95/1; Smith-Dorrien Diary, 29 October 1914, CAB 45/206; "Attack on Neuve Chapelle, 28th Oct. (As seen and described by Lieut. Cornwall, R.A.)," II Corps War Diary, WO 95/629; 3 Division War Diary, WO 95/1375, PRO.

55. Willcocks, With the Indians in France, 67.

56. Smith-Dorrien to GHQ, 3 November 1914; Wing to II Corps, 31 October 1914; McCracken, "Report on Attack on Neuve Chapelle, 28th October 1914," II Corps War Diary, WO 95/629, PRO.

57. Smith-Dorrien to CGS, 30 October 1914, II Corps War Diary, WO 95/629, PRO.

58. Headlam to Edmonds, 2 April 1923, CAB 45/182, PRO. See also Alexander Diary, 29 October 1914, H.M. Alexander Papers, Liddle Collection.

59. Willcocks to CGS, 15 November 1914; "Statement by Lieut. Colonel G.M. Morris, Commanding 2nd Bn. 8th Gurkhas," Indian Corps War Diary, WO 95/1088, PRO; Merewether and Smith, *The Indian Corps in France*, 67–70

60. "Statement by Lieut. Colonel G.M. Morris"; "Digest of Information Received from 5th Division Headquarters, thro' Colonel Jacob, regarding the loss of trenches held by 2/8th Gurkha Rifles," Indian Corps War Diary, WO 95/1088; "Resume of Account of Loss of 3 Trenches by 2/8th Gurkha Rifles on 30th October 1914," Meerut Division War Diary, WO 95/3930, PRO.

61. Smith-Dorrien Diary, 30 October 1914, CAB 45/206; "Resume of Account of Loss of 3 Trenches by 2/8th Gurkha Rifles," Meerut Division War Diary, WO 95/3930; "Digest of Information Received from 5th Division Headquarters," Indian Corps War Diary, WO 95/1088, PRO.

62. Merewether and Smith, *The Indian Corps in France*, 74–76; "Resume of

Account of Loss of 3 Trenches by 2/8th Gurkha Rifles," Meerut Division War Diary, WO 95/3930, PRO.

63. "Report on the Action of the 1st Cavalry Division about MESSINES, October 22nd to November 3rd, inclusive," 1 Cavalry Division War Diary; 1 Cavalry Division War Diary, 31 October 1914, WO 95/1096; Lahore Division War Diary, 27 October 1914, WO 95/3911, PRO.

64. Indian Corps War Diary, Appendix XI, "Report by Lieut. Colonel C. Norie, commanding 2/2nd Gurkhas, 4 November 1914"; C. Johnson to GOC Meerut Division, 10 November 1914; C.A. Anderson to Indian Corps HQ, 12 November 1914, WO 95/1088; Meerut Division War Diary, 2 November 1914, WO 95/3930, PRO; Merewether and Smith, *The Indian Corps in France*, 77–78.

65. J.Wakefield and J.M. Whippert, eds., *Indian Cavalry Officer, 1914–1915: Captain Roly Grimshaw* (Tunbridge Wells: Costello, 1986), 31; Merewether and Smith, *The Indian Corps in France*, 78–83; Meerut Division War Diary, 2 November 1914, WO 95/3930; "Report by Lieut. Colonel Norie," Indian Corps War Diary, WO 95/1088, PRO.

66. Archibald Home, *A Diary of a World War I Cavalry Officer* (Tunbridge Wells: Costello, 1985), 32.

67. Smith-Dorrien Diary, 24 October 1914, CAB 45/206, PRO. See also Wakefield and Whippert, *Indian Cavalry Officer, 1914–1915*, 30; A.H. Habgood Diary, 28 October 1914, A.H. Habgood Papers, Imperial War Museum, London (IWM); Corbett-Smith, *The Marne—and After*, 219; Carew, *Wipers*, 131.

68. Keary to General Staff, Meerut Division, 11 November 1914, Indian Corps War Diary, WO 95/1088, PRO. See also "Report on Rushing of Enemy's Trenches by a Combined Force of 1st/39th Garhwal Rifles and 2nd/39th Garhwal Rifles on night of 9th/10th November 1914," Indian Corps War Diary, WO 95/1088, PRO.

69. Keary to General Staff, Meerut Division, 19 November 1914, Indian Corps War Diary, WO 95/1088, PRO.

70. "Copy of a Report by Lieut-Colonel W.R. Brakespear, 3rd Gurkha Rifles, to the Brigade Major, Garhwal Brigade," Indian Corps War Diary, WO 95/1088, PRO; Merewether and Smith, *The Indian Corps in France*, 97.

71. "Talk with F.M. Sir Claud Jacob, 16/11/32," 11/1932/45, Liddell Hart Papers, LHCMA.

72. GOC Lahore Division to Carnegy, 30 October 1914, Lahore Division War Diary, WO 95/3911;"Resume of Account of Loss of 3 Trenches by 2/8th Gurkha Rifles," Meerut Division War Diary, WO 95/3930; "Statement by Lieut. Colonel G.M. Morris," Indian Corps War Diary, WO 95/1088, PRO.

73. Merewether and Smith, *The Indian Corps in France*, 64.

74. Lahore Division, Casualty Return up to 6pm, 30 October 1914, Indian Corps AG & QMG War Diary, WO 95/1091, PRO.

Casualties in Lahore Division to 30 October:

	killed	wounded	missing
British units			
officers	0	0	0
other ranks	13	19	1
Indian units			

British officers	4	20	1
Indian officers	2	16	0
other ranks	64	963	213
total	83	1,018	215

75. Alexander Diary, 28 October, 3 November 1914; H.M. Alexander Papers, Liddle Collection. See also Harry Keary to brother, 4 November 1914, H. Keary Papers, IWM; AG, GHQ (Neville Macready) to WO, 5 November 1914; AG, GHQ to WO, 1 November 1914, 3:05 pm, WO 33/713, PRO. Merewether and Smith, *The Indian Corps in France*, 89.

76. Major G.A. Jamieson (9th Bhopals) to Brigade Major, 7th Indian Infantry Brigade, 7 November 1914, Lahore Division War Diary, WO 95/3911; AG, GHQ to WO, 5 November 1914, WO 33/713, PRO.

77. AG, GHQ to WO, 1 November 1914, WO 33/713; "Brief Report on the part taken by the 57th Rifles (F.F.) in the actions in and around WYTSCHAETE and MESSINES on the 29th, 30th, 31st Octr, and 1st November 1914, by Major E.L. Swifte, 57th Rifles," Lahore Division War Diary, WO 95/3911, PRO. For similar accounts of Indian troops losing cohesion without British officers, see Fraser and Thornton, *The Congreves*, 242; Frederic Coleman, *From Mons to Ypres with French: A Personal Narrative* (Toronto: William Briggs, 1916), 228; Count Edward Gleichen, *The Doings of the Fifteenth Infantry Brigade, August 1914 to March 1915* (London: Blackwood, 1917), 194.

78. Omissi, *The Sepoy and the Raj*, 106; Greenhut, "Sahib and Sepoy," 17.

79. Carew, *Wipers*, 144.

80. Merewether and Smith, *The Indian Corps in France*, 64.

81. Merewether and Smith, *The Indian Corps in France*, 64; Indian Corps AG & QMG War Diary, WO 95/1091, PRO.

82. Coleman, *From Mons to Ypres with French*, 230.

83. Lahore Division War Diary, 28, 29 October 1914, WO 95/3911, PRO.

84. AAG, Indian Corps to Lahore Division, 1 November 1914, 6:48 pm, Lahore Division War Diary, WO 95/3911; Indian Corps AG & QMG War Diary, 2 November 1914, WO 95/1091, PRO.

85. Greenhut, "The 'Imperial Reserve,' " 57; Wilson Diary, 2 November 1914, Henry Wilson Papers, IWM.

86. Greenhut, "The 'Imperial Reserve,' " 57.

87. See, for example, Greenhut, "The 'Imperial Reserve,' " 69; Omissi, *The Sepoy and the Raj*, 115.

88. W.E. O'Leary to Indian Corps, 14 November 1914, Indian Corps AG & QMG War Diary, WO 95/1091; Willcocks to Fitzgerald, 10 November 1914, Kitchener Papers, PRO 30/57/52, PRO; Omissi, *The Sepoy and the Raj*, 118.

89. E.B. Howell to General Sir E. Barrow, 15 February 1915, "Reports of Chief Censor," L/MIL/5/825, Oriental and India Office Collection, British Library.

90. Clive Diary, 4 November 1914, G.S. Clive Papers, LHCMA. See also Wilson Diary, 2 November 1914, Henry Wilson Papers; Murray Diary, 2 November 1914, Archibald Murray Papers, IWM.

91. Willcocks to Fitzgerald, 10 November 1914, Kitchener Papers, PRO 30/57/52;

Indian Corps AG & QMG War Diary, 2 November 1914, WO 95/1091, PRO. Wilson Diary, 2 November 1914, Henry Wilson Papers, IWM.

92. Kitchener to French, 19 November 1914, French to Kitchener, 28 November 1914, WO 33/713; Indian Corps War Diary, 23–24 November 1914, WO 95/1088; Lahore Division War Diary, 23–24 November 1914, WO 95/3911; Meerut Division War Diary, 23–24 November 1914, WO 95/3920, PRO; Wilson Diary, 23 November 1914, Henry Wilson Papers, IWM; Peter Scott, ed., "The View From GHQ: The Third Part of the War Diary of General Sir Charles Deedes, KCB, CMG, DSO," *Stand To!*, 12 (Winter 1984), 32; Greenhut, "The 'Imperial Reserve,' " 57.

93. Merewether and Smith, *The Indian Corps in France*, 199–200. See also Liddell Hart, "Talk With F.M. Sir Claud Jacob, 16/11/32," 11/1932/45, Liddell Hart Papers, LHCMA.

7

The Victors of First Ypres: Sir Douglas Haig and I Corps, 21 October–11 November

The First Battle of Ypres reached its climax in the final days of October 1914. Pressure on British positions had increased since the beginning of the enemy offensive on the 20th. From 29 to 31 October, Sir Douglas Haig's I Corps endured attacks of unprecedented weight as the German Army attempted to pierce the allied line in the vicinity of Ypres. While the onslaught began to diminish in early November, the British line remained tenuous as depleted units suffered from continued assaults. Fighting in close cooperation with French forces, I Corps successfully bore the weight of the German offensive until its abatement after the 11th. By mid-November, the battle had come to a close. Exhausted by three months of active campaigning, the belligerents on the Western Front replenished their ranks and pondered the complexities of an unaccustomed type of warfare.

Historical accounts written prior to the 1980s generally depict this period in epic terms, recounting the heroic demise of the prewar British Army in shattering an offensive directed by the kaiser himself. The individual credited with the successful defense of Ypres is the commander of I Corps, Sir Douglas Haig. In the opinion of Anthony Farrar-Hockley: "of all the commanders available in the British Expeditionary Force at that time [Haig] was probably the officer most suited—perhaps the only one—to direct operations in front of Ypres."[1] This suitability stemmed from his unwavering composure, which he maintained throughout the battle. According to E.K.G. Sixsmith: "On the moral side, he was a rock. He was always at hand where the strain was greatest."[2]

In the past two decades, however, this heroic portrayal has been subject to considerable scrutiny. Scholars such as Gerard De Groot, Richard Holmes, and Ian F.W. Beckett have suggested that Haig experienced considerable anxiety on 31 October, as the British line threatened to buckle under the weight of enemy attacks.[3] Denis Winter has gone to even greater lengths, alleging that the inspiring ride of the I Corps commander up the Menin Road on the 31st was in fact a myth constructed by Haig himself. John Hussey has countered these assertions, defending the authenticity of Haig's ride and arguing that accounts of his anxiety were concocted by the mischievous official historian, Sir James Edmonds.[4]

Clearly, the comportment of the I Corps commander on 31 October remains the subject of considerable controversy. In scrutinizing Haig's behavior, however, historians have generally overlooked the functioning of the British command structure at the height of the First Battle of Ypres. As a result, its role in the performance of I Corps in this period remains largely obscured. In an attempt to shed light on this role, this chapter will examine the impact of command on the operations of Sir Douglas Haig's force from its arrival in Flanders until the abatement of the German attacks on 12 November. It will argue that continued tensions at GHQ as well as Haig's peculiar relationship with Sir John French allowed the I Corps commander considerable operational freedom. In addition, the proximity of British and French troops limited the front occupied by Haig's corps and provided it with reinforcements throughout the battle. While Haig's resolve helped I Corps resist enemy pressure, he experienced many of the same difficulties as other senior officers in absorbing the implications of modern weaponry. The chapter will conclude with a brief examination of Haig's attempts to influence historical interpretations of First Ypres following the conclusion of the 1914 campaign. That Sir Douglas Haig emerged as the principal hero of the battle was due in part to his own machinations.

THE PARALYSIS OF THE HIGH COMMAND: RELATIONS BETWEEN GHQ AND I CORPS, OCTOBER–NOVEMBER 1914

The operations of I Corps in late October are only fully comprehensible in the context of relations in the upper ranks of the BEF. Since the retreat from Mons, Sir John French had retained legitimate concerns regarding the permanency of his post. French's insecurity in this period was particularly significant given his unusual relationship with Sir Douglas Haig. While the commander-in-chief's opinions of Sir James Willcocks, Sir Henry Rawlinson, and Sir Horace Smith-Dorrien ranged from indifference to antipathy, his attitude toward Haig was quite different. French had long held Haig's abilities in high regard and he continued to do so in 1914. In addition, the commander-in-chief was undoubtedly aware of Haig's formidable political ties, particularly with the king. As a result, he treated the well-connected commander of I Corps with a measure of respect that was absent from his relationships with his other subordinates. French's respect gave Haig the ability to function with relative independence from the dictates of GHQ, an attractive prospect given his diminished confidence in French and his staff since the retreat from Mons. Thus, due to Sir John French's concern for the safety of his post and Haig's lack of regard for the commander-in-chief, I Corps had the ability to operate with considerable autonomy from GHQ in October 1914.

Relations between I Corps and GHQ deteriorated following the arrival of Haig's force in Flanders. In mid-October, as I Corps vacated its positions on the Aisne and made its way northward, Sir John French and Henry Wilson remained dangerously optimistic regarding the ability of the BEF to advance eastward. The overconfidence of senior officers led them to ignore reports provided by George Macdonogh's Intelligence Section warning of the approach of 3 1/2 enemy corps. As discussed in Chapter 5, GHQ's orders to attack on 19 October nearly led to disaster for IV Corps. Only the arrival of air reconnaissance reports indicating the presence of at least three German corps prevented Henry Rawlinson's force from stumbling into the enemy unawares.

Disregarding these ominous portents, senior officers at GHQ remained determined to press the offensive. In a meeting with Douglas Haig on the 19th, Sir John French estimated the strength of enemy forces between Menin and the English Channel at only one corps. While Macdonogh's assessments suggested otherwise, they did little to alter the prevailing opinion at GHQ. Following its assembly west of Ypres on the 19th, I Corps was directed to begin advancing northeast the next morning with the ultimate intention of capturing Thorout, approximately eighteen miles from Ypres.[5] On 20 October, Haig's force moved into the allied line east of Ypres, with IV Corps on its right and French forces on its left. While Rawlinson's force faced heavy attacks during the day, GHQ remained undeterred. Operation Order No. 39, issued on the evening of the 20th, directed I Corps to continue advancing toward Thorout.[6]

In accordance with these orders, Haig's force pressed forward on the morning of the 21st. On the left of the corps, however, units of 1 Division reported heavy enemy artillery fire supplemented by infantry attacks.[7] As German pressure continued into the early afternoon, the French cavalry on the left of 1 Division began to retire unannounced. At almost the same time, units of Capper's 7 Division, on the right of 2 Division, were pressed back as well. In light of the danger to both of his flanks and the persistence of enemy attacks throughout the afternoon, Haig halted both divisions at approximately 3 pm.[8] The failure of the I Corps advance demonstrated clearly the misconceptions of Sir John French and Henry Wilson regarding the strength of enemy forces east of Ypres on 21 October. In a letter written on the 22nd, Wilfrid Smith, commander of the 2/Grenadier Guards of 2 Division, provided a more accurate assessment of the situation facing Haig's force, remarking, "it is all rot saying we have nothing in front of us. There are heaps of Germans, and, as an army they are very good, and their gunners are perfect."[9]

The manuscript version of Haig's diary contains surprisingly little criticism of French or his staff immediately following the events of 21 October. After the war, however, George Macdonogh suggested to Edmonds that the ill-advised attack soured relations between I Corps and GHQ. As the former intelligence chief related:

If Harper would tell you what Johnnie Gough said to him on the day II [Corps] appeared at Zandvoorde, an appearance of which I had a day previously warned the C in C & CGS & for doing which I was blackguarded by O as it was contrary to their preconceived views & which they refused to pass on to DH, you would get a good idea of the difficulties we suffered under.[10]

Further evidence of a growing rift between GHQ and I Corps in this period remains obscure. By the close of the 1914 campaign, however, relations between the two headquarters had clearly worsened. As Sir Henry Rawlinson observed in his diary on 4 December: "[t]he I Corps seems to have been getting themselves disliked by their insubordination. HW [Wilson] seems to think Sir John is afraid of Sir Douglas Haig and therefore does not dare put him and his corps in their place."[11]

Rawlinson's remarks provide no clues regarding the cause of this "insubordination." Nevertheless, it is evident that several factors conspired to increase the operational independence of Haig's corps during the First Battle of Ypres. Sir John French's concern for the security of his post, combined with his respect for Haig, discouraged the commander-in-chief from interfering in the operational realm of I Corps. Moreover, by mid-October, Sir Douglas Haig had little confidence in the abilities of his superior. The delusions of French and Henry Wilson regarding the strength of German opposition in Flanders further diminished Haig's opinion of GHQ. Thus, as the First Battle of Ypres reached its greatest intensity, I Corps exercised a degree of operational autonomy that may well have been interpreted as insubordination. In light of the misconceptions that prevailed at GHQ in this period, however, Haig's force likely benefited from this freedom.

THE STRENGTH OF I CORPS

In addition to his autonomy from GHQ, Sir Douglas Haig had at his disposal a larger and more experienced force than the other corps examined in this study. Furthermore, I Corps operated on a shorter front than either II Corps or IV Corps, and received significant substantial French and British reinforcements as the battle continued into November. The relative strength of I Corps itself in October 1914 can be illuminated through a comparison with Smith-Dorrien's II Corps. Like II Corps, Haig's force arrived in Flanders in far from optimal condition. While it had not suffered to the same extent during the retreat from Mons, a month of trench warfare on the Aisne had taken a heavy toll on both 1 and 2 Divisions. Despite these losses, however, I Corps remained significantly stronger than Smith-Dorrien's force even in mid-October. Upon its transfer to Belgium in early October, I Corps had suffered total casualties amounting to approximately 470 officers and 9,500 other ranks, in comparison to 520 officers and 12,900 other ranks lost by II Corps.[12] The fact that his formation retained 50 more of its original officers and 3,400 more other ranks than II Corps suggests that the tactical effectiveness of I Corps had eroded to a lesser extent than in Smith-Dorrien's force. The higher proportion of elite units in Haig's corps also helped counteract the effects of heavy losses. Notably, two of the six brigades of I Corps consisted entirely of Guards regiments. The fact that these units comprised one-third of the strength of Haig's force likely helped it retain a greater measure of its cohesion despite significant casualties.

The strength of I Corps in October and November 1914 was reinforced by the stability that prevailed in its upper ranks. Notwithstanding the wavering health of Johnnie Gough, the comparatively seasoned I Corps staff remained intact throughout this period.[13] Moreover, unlike II Corps, which experienced a significant turnover of divisional commanders in 1914, I Corps retained its original roster until Samuel Lomax was wounded on 31 October. Given Sir Douglas Haig's willingness to relieve apparently irresolute officers such as Ivor Maxse, his retention of Lomax, Charles Monro, and all of the I Corps staff indicates that he perceived these officers to be competent. It also suggests that relations between Haig and his subordinates were reasonably harmonious. The relative experience, competence and cohesiveness of the officers in the upper ranks of I Corps undoubtedly enhanced its effectiveness during the First Battle of Ypres.

The impact of losses on I Corps was also offset by the fact that it held a shorter front than the other British corps. From its arrival in Flanders until its condition deteriorated seriously after 25 October, Smith-Dorrien's depleted II Corps held a front approximately eight miles long, without a significant corps reserve.[14] During this period, it was reinforced by only two battalions and a cavalry regiment from the Indian Corps on the evening of 21 October. Rawlinson's IV Corps, an even weaker formation, also held a line of eight miles during the German counteroffensive that commenced on 20 October. In contrast, I Corps held a relatively compact front during the initial stages of its operations in Flanders. Moreover, when German attacks threw Haig's force on the defensive, the corps benefited from an abundance of reinforcements as well as the cooperation of adjacent French formations. This favorable situation was the unintentional result of the optimism of GHQ in mid-October 1914. When I Corps arrived in Flanders, the line occupied by the other British corps already extended twenty-five miles. According to Sir James Edmonds, this front "was wider than their strength warranted." Sir John French and his staff, however, retained the hope of advancing against the ostensibly weak German forces in Belgium. Consequently, rather than utilizing Haig's corps to bolster the existing British line, French directed I Corps to advance on the left flank of the BEF, driving the enemy on Ghent.[15]

Initially, this task entailed operations over a fairly wide front. During its first three days in Flanders, Haig's force covered a swathe of Belgium extending from the Yser canal, directly north of Ypres, south-eastward to the village of Zonnebeke, a distance of approximately eight miles.[16] Nonetheless, I Corps was aided significantly in this period by the presence of French forces in the vicinity.

As the events of 21 October demonstrated, cooperation between allied forces often left much to be desired. Two days later, however, nearby French forces assisted Edward Bulfin's 2nd Brigade in recapturing a position near Bixschoote that had been evacuated by British troops. As an attack by adjacent French forces on Passchendaele reduced enemy pressure on the British, Bulfin's assault on the Bixschoote position proved successful, capturing 600 prisoners and apparently killing up to 1,500 Germans. Nearby French troops supported the operation further by taking custody of the prisoners and enabling the 2nd Brigade to occupy the recaptured position.[17]

The formalization of operational boundaries with the French resulted in the compression of Haig's front on the night of 23–24 October. Afterward, I Corps occupied a line of less than four miles, from Zonnebeke south to the Menin-Ypres Road (henceforth Menin Road), where it connected with the left of Rawlinson's IV Corps. This position proved relatively comfortable. From 24 to 27 October, Haig was able to retain a full division in reserve. The addition of 7 Division to I Corps on the 27th extended Haig's front south of the Menin Road to the village of Zandvoorde. Although the I Corps line now extended approximately seven miles, three infantry divisions provided relatively ample personnel to occupy it. Haig was in fact able to relieve the shaken 7 Division on the night of 26–27 October, enabling it to reorganize. All three divisions occupied positions in the line from the night of the 27th onward. The I Corps commander nonetheless retained Bulfin's 2nd Brigade as a corps reserve, in addition to reserves held by each division.[18] As a result, Haig was relatively well prepared to face the determined enemy attacks that commenced early on 29 October.

As the German offensive persisted, I Corps would continue to benefit from the availability of reinforcements. On 31 October, Byng's 3 Cavalry Division, previously attached to Allenby's Cavalry Corps, joined Haig's force and served as his corps reserve thereafter. In addition, the withdrawal of Smith-Dorrien's corps on 30 October provided a sizeable, if depleted, reserve upon which Haig was able to draw in early November. Moreover, after German pressure reached critical levels on 31 October, French commanders proved increasingly willing to support the British line.[19] Thus, while I Corps endured the heaviest enemy pressure of any British formation during the First Battle of Ypres, it faced these attacks from a position of relative strength.

THE STAND OF I CORPS, 29–31 OCTOBER

The strength of I Corps proved fortunate for the BEF. In the final week of October, the German line east of Ypres had been bolstered by a force commanded by General von Fabeck, comprised of five fresh divisions, an additional reserve division, and 260 guns. The attack of "Army Group Fabeck" commenced on the 29th, as German forces attempted to capture the village of Gheluvelt on the Menin Road. After intercepting enemy radio transmissions the previous evening, GHQ had advised I Corps to expect an attack.[20] Despite this warning, however, heavy fog allowed the Germans to surprise British units at around 6 am on 29 October, as they slipped between the 1st Guards Brigade of 1 Division and the battered 20th Brigade of 7 Division along the Menin Road approximately one mile east of Gheluvelt. The resulting gap in the British line allowed the Germans to move up the Menin Road toward Gheluvelt, simultaneously subjecting the village to heavy artillery fire.[21]

As the morning progressed, I Corps began to regain its equilibrium. On either side of the breach in the line along the Menin Road, British units launched fierce counterattacks. By early afternoon, the individual efforts of British battalions were assisted by the arrival of substantial reinforcements. Divisional and corps reserves, consisting of units from the 2nd, 3rd and 4th Guards Brigades, participated in counterattacks during the afternoon, pushing the Germans back from Gheluvelt and restoring most of the ground lost in the morning. These counterattacks also allowed the weaker 7 Division to restore its line south of the Menin Road. By evening, I Corps had established a line just east of Gheluvelt, approximately five miles from Ypres. While this represented the loss of over half a mile of ground during the day, Haig's line remained relatively strong, with Bulfin's brigade again in reserve.[22]

GHQ orders for 30 October enjoined I Corps to advance alongside French forces on the left. In light of the events of the 29th, however, Sir Douglas Haig's own instructions to his force were rather more circumspect. His operation order issued that evening directed units to entrench, reorganize and await information regarding offensive movement "when the situation is clearer."[23] Haig's caution proved fortunate for his troops. Throughout the 30th, Army Group Fabeck subjected I Corps to a prolonged artillery bombardment. On the right of Haig's line, enemy attacks were particularly destructive. During the morning, heavy shelling dislodged units of 7 Division and the adjacent 3 Cavalry Division from positions around the village of Zandvoorde. This section of the front was exceedingly precarious, primarily due to the exposed positions of British trenches. According to Ernest Hamilton:

The particular section in the line of defence known as the Zandvoorde trenches had from first to last been a death trap, and had proved particularly expensive to the 3rd Cavalry Division, whose special privilege it had been to defend them. They curved round the southeast side of the village, following the contours of the ridge, and, being the most prominent feature of the entire Ypres salient, were particularly susceptible to shell fire from all quarters.[24]

Given the damage previously inflicted on the exposed trenches of IV Corps, the location of Byng's cavalry on 30 October is rather surprising. The commander of 3 Cavalry Division clearly recognized the danger of these positions. As the divisional war diary observed on the 27th, "[i]t would seem that trenches must be on reverse slopes—field of fire giving way to protect against hostile shell fire. This was not the case with our trenches." The adjustment of Byng's line, however, was prevented by the fact that adjacent units of 7 Division held similar positions. According to the war diary, "as any alteration would largely affect (and endanger) those [positions] of the 7th Division on our left, the idea of moving them back had to be given up for the time."[25]

An adjustment of the line by units in two different formations was a difficult undertaking, particularly under the enemy pressure that prevailed in late October. Prior to the disbanding of IV Corps on the 25th, however, Sir Douglas Haig had made disparaging comments in his diary regarding its poorly sited trenches. Given Haig's criticisms of Rawlinson's positions, the positions occupied by 7 Division after its attachment to I Corps ought to have been of greater concern to him. Nevertheless, Haig did not order the adjustment of the line held by 7 Division, even after allowing it to reorganize on the 27th. Indeed, the I Corps commander also allowed units of 1 and 2 Division to take up positions on forward slopes on 29 October.[26] Haig's criticisms of Henry Rawlinson demonstrate that he recognized the importance of locating trenches in concealed positions. Yet he committed the same oversight as the IV Corps commander in failing to emphasize this principle to his subordinates.

Haig's neglect had serious consequences for both 7 Division and Byng's cavalry on 30 October. Beginning early in the morning, heavy shelling compelled the 7th Cavalry Brigade, on Byng's left, to retire as early as 8:30 am.[27] This withdrawal exposed units of 7 Division on its left to enfilade fire as well as further shelling. On the right of Capper's line, the 1/Royal Welch Fusiliers were virtually annihilated, losing 11 officers and 350 of 450 of their remaining troops. On the immediate left of the Royal Welch Fusiliers, the 2/Royal Scots Fusiliers also suffered heavily from German artillery fire. The location of their position on a forward slope caused particular difficulties for the Scots. According to Farrar-Hockley: "Whenever they attempted to leave their trenches, the shrapnel descended; for the ground behind, across which they had to travel, was open and rising."[28]

By 11 am, German pressure forced the withdrawal of 3 Cavalry Division and the right of 7 Division from Zandvoorde. In the early afternoon, however, the I Corps commander again called upon his reserve to stabilize the situation. Realizing the danger posed by the retirement of his right, Haig placed Bulfin in command of a detachment consisting of two battalions of the 2nd Brigade and the entire 4th Guards Brigade. He then directed this force to reestablish the right of 7 Division and relieve the disorganized 3 Cavalry Division. Bulfin accomplished this task by late afternoon, extending the I Corps line to the Ypres-Comines Canal, where it connected with Hubert Gough's 2 Cavalry Division. Thus, on the evening of 30–31 October, the I Corps line consisted of: 2 Division, holding the left at Zonnebeke; 1 and 7 Divisions, in positions north and south of the Menin Road; and Bulfin's force, extending the line to the canal on the right. Haig's front now extended over seven miles. The positions of 1 and 2 Division, however, remained strong despite enemy shelling during the day. Furthermore, additional reinforcements arrived on the night of 30–31 October in the form of three French infantry battalions and a cavalry brigade under General Moussy, which bolstered the right of the I Corps line around the Ypres-Comines Canal. In addition, although it continued to receive orders from the Cavalry Corps, Byng's 3 Cavalry Division had regrouped behind the right of the I Corps line, forming a "mobile reserve."[29]

The morning of 31 October dawned relatively quietly on the front of I Corps. Combined efforts by Bulfin's and Moussy's detachments to push forward before 7 am were quickly halted by enemy shell fire. At the same time, 1 Division reported a flurry of infantry attacks that died down by 7 am. While German artillery continued to harass both 1 and 7 Division, Haig's front remained stable in the early morning. Given the intensity of German attacks over the previous two days, however, the commander of I Corps evidently felt considerable concern for the safety of his line. At 6:55 am, following the revelation of enemy attacks on 1 Division, Haig requested that Allenby direct 3 Cavalry Division northward, apparently to provide support for I Corps positions astride the Menin Road. With his own force under considerable enemy pressure, the commander of the Cavalry Corps declined.[30] Undeterred, Haig ignored Allenby's refusal, issuing direct orders to Byng to move to the vicinity of the Menin Road.

Evidence concerning the appropriation of Byng's force by I Corps remains murky. According to the 3 Cavalry Division war diary, however, its two brigades "were moved" northward at 8 am to the area indicated by Haig in his earlier request to Allenby. Orders for this relocation certainly did not originate at Cavalry Corps headquarters. Allenby's force had faced increasing pressure since dawn, and as 3 Cavalry Division moved towards the Menin Road, German forces broke through the line of Henry De Lisle's 1 Cavalry Division at Messines. At 8:35, Allenby thus ordered Byng's force to move southwards to support De Lisle. Nevertheless, in the words of the war diary, Byng's force "had now come under the orders of the GOC 1st Army Corps who did not consider the situation justified this, and ordered the division to remain as originally ordered."[31] There is no evidence to indicate that Haig consulted GHQ regarding the transfer of Byng's division from the Cavalry Corps to I Corps. While Haig was senior to Allenby in the BEF hierarchy, he was certainly not authorized to commandeer an entire division from another corps without permission from a superior authority. That he did so regardless is indicative of the autonomy with which Haig conducted operations during the First Battle of Ypres.

Haig's justification for his annexation of 3 Cavalry Division also sheds light on his mood on the morning of the 31st. The I Corps commander explained his actions to Allenby in a wire received by Cavalry Corps headquarters at 9:20 am. As Haig stated: "[t]he situation here is so serious and as there are no reserves in hand I have told General Byng to remain....If situation eases [I] will send Byng at once."[32] Despite this explanation, the predicament facing Haig at 9:20 am was hardly grave. On the left of the I Corps line, the front of 2 Division remained relatively quiet. 1 Division and 7 Division continued to report enemy shelling, but neither divisional war diary indicates serious difficulties until at least 9:30 am. While the two latter divisions began to face heavy enemy attacks at 9:30 or shortly thereafter, this information was not immediately relayed to corps headquarters. Indeed, the I Corps war diary characterized the situation along its front as "normal" until 10 am, when "the 1st Division reported the situation in the trenches south and southeast of GHELUVELT to be serious."[33]

Given the relative calm that prevailed along the I Corps front, the desperate situation portrayed in Haig's wire to Allenby was clearly an exaggeration. Thus, it is apparent that Haig's seizure of 3 Cavalry Division was not justified, particularly since Allenby had refused his initial request for support due to the much greater pressure on his own force. Significantly, however, Haig formally requested the use of Byng's cavalry when it was within his power simply to commandeer it. This would suggest that his intentions were not in fact malicious. Rather, Haig's embellishment of the plight of his force, and his annexation of 3 Cavalry Division, appear to have stemmed from a heightened sense of anxiety. Apprehensive after facing heavy German attacks for two days, the I Corps commander overestimated the threat to his line on the morning of 31 October.

Fortunately for the Cavalry Corps, friction intervened to diminish the impact of Haig's anxiety and compel a more equitable distribution of forces. On its way to occupy the position designated by I Corps, Kavanagh's 7th Cavalry Brigade received orders directly from Allenby instructing it to hasten to the aid of the Cavalry Corps. Without contrary orders from I Corps or 3 Cavalry Division, Kavanagh immediately turned southward. Consequently, as the 3 Cavalry Division War Diary recorded, the 7th Cavalry Brigade "was allowed to proceed," while 6th Brigade continued north to support I Corps.[34] After assisting Allenby on the 31st, however, Kavanagh's brigade rejoined the 6th Cavalry Brigade in support of I Corps. For over two weeks following 31 October, both brigades of 3 Cavalry Division operated under Haig's command. Given that enemy attacks on I Corps persisted well into November, this arrangement was undoubtedly justified. Nevertheless, it is evident that Haig's trepidation had begun to influence his judgment early on the morning of the 31st, as he denied reserves to Allenby in an effort to bolster his own line.

By late morning on 31 October, the situation of Haig's corps had grown more precarious. Before 10 am, German artillery and infantry attacks began to intensify, especially in the vicinity of the Menin Road, on the front occupied by 1 Division and 7 Division. Shortly after noon, units of Landon's 3rd Brigade began vacating their trenches around Gheluvelt. This forced the retirement of troops of 7 Division south of the road, and the abandonment of Gheluvelt to the Germans. Simultaneously, the right of Capper's Division and Bulfin's detachment began to give way. According to the commander of the 2nd Brigade, units of 7 Division remained in exposed positions even on the morning of the 31st. As Bulfin related in his diary: "[t]he 7th Division on my left got it bad as they were on [a] ridge. My troops got it less being on low ground and out of sight."[35] German attacks forced the retirement of 7 Division from its trenches around midday. Shortly thereafter, Bulfin's position grew increasingly untenable as the enemy exploited the gap left by the retreating units of 7 Division. As he recounted: "Streams of Germans in unending numbers kept pouring over the ridge. As far as I could see to my North, there were endless glinting of spikes of German helmets."[36]

The situation facing Haig's force became even more serious in the early afternoon. At approximately 1 pm, a German shell hit the headquarters of 2 Division in a chateau near the village of Hooge, just as a conference between the commanders of 1 and 2 Division was taking place inside of it. The shell devastated the command structure of both divisions, killing or wounding ten officers, including S.H. Lomax, the commander of 1 Division. While Charles Monro of 2 Division escaped largely unscathed, the explosion incapacitated him for much of the afternoon.[37] From the perspective of Sir Douglas Haig, the predicament of I Corps at 2 pm on the 31st appeared desperate indeed. Along the Menin Road, the enemy had occupied Gheluvelt while units of 1 and 7 Division continued to fall back towards Ypres. On his right, German forces had compelled the retirement of units of Capper's division and were pressing on Bulfin's detachment as well. To make matters worse, the chain of command had been severed by casualties to the staffs of 1 and 2 Division.

It was in this context that Sir John French arrived at I Corps headquarters at the White Chateau east of Ypres. Haig's demeanor during this meeting has been the subject of considerable controversy among historians. In a 1931 conversation with Liddell Hart, Sir James Edmonds suggested that the I Corps commander was gripped by an anxiety that affected his own decisions and influenced the impressionable commander-in-chief. Liddell Hart recorded Edmonds's account as follows:

When French came to Haig's HQs about 2 pm, things were at their blackest. Haig was actually suffering a "scare" similar to that of Landrecies. He had drawn up orders for a general retirement to the line of the ramparts and canal at Ypres. (This was recalled under the persuasion of one of his staff before it reached its recipients and the copies of it were afterwards destroyed). French came out of the talk looking "chalky-white." Rice galloped in with the news that Gheluvelt was retaken while Haig was still standing on the stoop after seeing French off and at once sent his ADC, Straker, after French. But how far the news was clear or how far French understood it or changed his impression is dubious. As his car drove through Ypres it nearly ran down the CRE of 7th Division and the ADC on the box was shouting "Make way for the Commander-in-Chief to escape."[38]

In his biography of Johnnie Gough, Ian Beckett has provided a description of Haig on 31 October based on this account. More recently, however, John Hussey has challenged this version of events, particularly the notion that Haig had prematurely ordered the general retirement of I Corps. "With great respect," he argues, "it must be nonsense."[39]

Hussey has reconstructed the events of 31 October in a degree of detail unsurpassed in any account with the exception of the *Official History*. Nonetheless, it is evident that considerable apprehension prevailed at I Corps headquarters on the 31st. The precarious state of the I Corps line did in fact oblige Haig to prepare plans for the retirement of his force during the afternoon. According to the I Corps war diary: "[t]he situation…appeared so serious that orders were issued that although every effort was to be made to hold on to the line originally given, if that should be impossible the line VERBRANDEN MOLEN-ZILLEBEKE-HALTE-POTIJZE was to be held to the last."[40]

Granted, this position remained approximately two kilometers east of Ypres. Furthermore, the language used by the war diary suggests that this retirement was conceived as a contingency plan, rather than an immediate necessity. Thus, Edmonds's allegation that Haig "had drawn up orders for a general retirement to the line of the ramparts and canal at Ypres," was an exaggeration.[41] The official historian's portrayal, however, is not entirely misleading. Indeed, there is evidence to indicate that Haig's plan to retire was the product of considerable consternation. His appropriation of Byng's cavalry that morning suggests that Haig was experiencing anxiety even before his front began to show signs of fragility. Moreover, descriptions of Haig on the afternoon of 31 October portray a rather grim corps commander. Sir John French arrived at I Corps headquarters around 2 pm. According to Richard Holmes: "[h]e found the commander of I Corps 'very white but quite calm.' 'They have broken us right in,' said Haig, 'and are pouring through the gap.' " The arrival of a message at 2:30 pm indicating that the Worcester regiment had retaken Gheluvelt did little to improve the mood of the I Corps commander. According to John Charteris, the I Corps staff was heartened by the news, "except DH who pulled at his mustache and then said he 'hoped it was not another false report.' "[42]

Sir John French's conduct following his visit to I Corps headquarters provides further evidence of Haig's anxiety. Given the malleable temperament of the commander-in-chief, as well as his high opinion of his protégé's abilities, it is likely that French was influenced by Haig's assessment of the situation. Significantly, sources indicate a rather distressed commander-in-chief following his visit to the White Chateau. According to Holmes, Sir John French met with Foch shortly afterward in the village of Vlamertinghe, west of Ypres. There, he "painted a gloomy picture of the battle on I Corps front," and requested reinforcements as soon as possible. As French explained to Foch: "The only men I have left are the sentries at my gates. I will take them with me to where the line is broken, and the last of the English will be killed fighting." After the war, Ferdinand Foch recalled a similarly agitated commander-in-chief. As he related in his *Memoirs*:

The Field-Marshal painted a particularly black picture of the state of the I Corps. The troops were in full retreat towards Ypres….It was the beginning of a defeat. With troops as exhausted as these men were, and who could not be collected and reformed, the British line was definitely broken. If they were asked to continue the battle, Sir John French said, there was nothing left for him to do but go up and get killed with the British I Corps.[43]

French's grim portrayal of the situation may have stemmed from his own perceptions of the battle. On his way to Ypres, he had ample opportunity to view the disorder that prevailed behind the I Corps line in the early afternoon of the 31st. Nevertheless, in light of French's respect for Haig's judgment, it is highly unlikely that he would have displayed such consternation had he encountered a confident I Corps commander at the White Chateau. Thus, even if Haig did not exhibit overt panic, it is evident that his apprehension of the morning of 31 October continued and perhaps even deepened as the situation of I Corps grew more precarious.

Haig's anxiety continued to influence his subsequent behavior. After the war, the I Corps commander related to Edmonds that upon learning of the recovery of Gheluvelt, he mounted his horse and rode up the Menin Road toward the front to "take personal command of the situation, if need be, about Hooge."[44] According to the *Official History*, this ride had a significant effect on the morale of his troops as they weathered continued German attacks. In recent years, however, Haig's famed ride up the Menin Road has been the subject of controversy equal to that surrounding his general demeanor on 31 October. Gerard De Groot has suggested that the initiative "was intentionally designed to be a dramatic ride through the crowds of frightened troops in headlong retreat on the Menin road." The news of the recapture of Gheluvelt removed the necessity of such a dramatic gesture. Nevertheless, De Groot comments: "[t]hough its purpose had evaporated, the ride went ahead, much to the delight of Haig's future biographers."[45] Thus, according to De Groot, the ride was more useful in enhancing Haig's reputation than in altering the course of the battle.

Denis Winter makes an even more serious allegation in his controversial *Haig's Command*, contending that: "discrepancies in the various versions of Haig's celebrated ride suggest that the whole story was first distorted, then blown up by Haig to advance his own career." Winter documents the inconsistencies in different accounts provided by the I Corps commander regarding the exact timing of the ride. Observing that Haig was normally "extraordinarily accurate" in recording his activities, he suggests that these discrepancies reflect Haig's attempts to increase his own renown. While in postwar correspondence, Haig portrayed the ride as taking place at the height of the battle, Winter argues that it actually occurred during the relative calm of the morning.[46]

Haig clearly demonstrated a concern for his reputation throughout the 1914 campaign. Nevertheless, a variety of sources contradict Winter's assertion. According to John Hussey, S.R. Rice, a member of Haig's staff, recalled that Haig rode up the Menin Road at approximately 2:40 pm. Hugh Jeudwine, another member of the I Corps staff, recorded finding the I Corps commander on the Menin road west of Ypres at around 3 pm. Sightings of Haig were not limited to members of his own staff. The 3 Cavalry Division War Diary relates that at 3:30 pm: "Sir Douglas Haig rode up and ordered the 6th Cavalry Brigade to support the infantry (who were again advancing) on their right flank, and clear the woods S[outh] of Veldhoek."[47]

Nor was Haig's ride simply an attempt to enhance his reputation. While it may have pleased his future biographers, it is unlikely that the ride was staged with the deliberate intent of portraying the I Corps commander as a determined leader. Contrary to De Groot's assertion, the news of the recapture of Gheluvelt hardly signaled a British victory. The front of I Corps remained precarious, particularly on its right, where the line was not reestablished until 10 pm. Moreover, both 1 and 2 Divisions remained crippled by the demise of their commanders and staffs. Given the danger to I Corps, as well as Haig's continued anxiety during the afternoon of the 31st, it is unlikely that he was in a state to conceive of a staged attempt to enhance his own reputation for posterity. Rather, Haig's ride up the Menin Road represented a genuine attempt by the I Corps commander to intervene personally in the battle at a critical moment. As Haig explained in his diary: "I...rode forward to be in closer touch with the situation and see if I could do anything to organize stragglers and push them forward to help in checking [the] enemy."[48] His personal orders to 3 Cavalry Division support this interpretation of the ride.

The wisdom of this venture, however, has escaped the scrutiny of most historians. John Terraine has noted the limited utility of Haig's ride for the purposes of gathering information, commenting: "He [Haig] could see the confusion for himself; he could not see much else."[49] Significantly, Terraine remains the only scholar to have cast doubt on the value of the ride. More recent biographers such as De Groot and Winter have viewed the incident with such suspicion that they have not questioned Haig's judgment in embarking on such an endeavor. In light of the situation of I Corps on the afternoon of 31 October, however, Haig's ride forward with his staff seems a rather dangerous venture of limited value to his corps. While the spectacle of the corps commander riding up the Menin Road likely provided some inspiration to those soldiers in the vicinity, the majority of units of I Corps were not even within sight of the road. Thus, the proportion of Haig's troops that actually saw him must have been small indeed. Other than for the purpose of enhancing morale, there was little to justify the ride. Neither the task of organizing stragglers, nor that of distributing orders required the personal intervention of a corps commander, even in the absence of effective leadership at the divisional level. Moreover, by venturing forward at the height of the battle, Haig placed himself and his staff at great risk at a time when the command structure of I Corps had already been disrupted.

Even if Haig did return safely on 31 October, he effectively removed himself and much of his staff from control of his corps at a pivotal moment in the battle. Before embarking on the ride, the I Corps commander apparently made no arrangements to ensure his timely reception of important messages. Consequently, staff officers such as Jeudwine were forced to venture down the

Menin Road in search of Haig after finding him absent from corps headquarters. Admittedly, Haig's ride up the Menin Road did not result in disaster for I Corps. It was nonetheless dangerous behavior for the commander of a large formation under the conditions of the 1914 campaign.[50]

While this attempt to influence the course of the battle appears incongruous with Haig's normally cautious demeanor, it was apparently the result of his heightened anxiety on the afternoon of 31 October. Haig's behavior earlier in the 1914 campaign suggests that rather than attempting to ensure the safety of his own force, his first response in crisis situations was to intervene personally. At Landrecies, on the evening of 25 August, Haig had neither fled the scene nor even ordered the immediate withdrawal of I Corps. On the contrary, he had spoken dramatically regarding the necessity of self-sacrifice and personally organized the defense of the town. While Haig demonstrated no lack of personal bravery at Landrecies, it is clear that his anxiety distorted his judgment. The I Corps commander behaved similarly on 31 October. With his front in danger of collapse and his chain of command severed, Haig's apprehension led him to embark on a potentially disastrous attempt to intervene personally in the battle.

Despite this effort, the tenacity of the I Corps line on 31 October did not result directly from Sir Douglas Haig's intervention. Indeed, at the most critical stages of the battle, the upper levels of the I Corps command structure were isolated from events at the front. The demise of the commanders and staffs of 1 and 2 Division early in the afternoon largely negated command and control capabilities at the divisional level. Moreover, the resulting gap between the corps and brigade levels seriously undermined the ability of Sir Douglas Haig and his staff to control the battle. Nor did Haig's venture down the Menin Road help in this respect. The efforts of staff officers such as Hugh Jeudwine maintained some semblance of communications between the I Corps commander and his subordinates at the front. Along most of Haig's line, however, operations on the 31st were conducted without guidance from I Corps headquarters. Significantly, none of the divisional war diaries record any contact with I Corps during the afternoon and evening of 31 October. While Jeudwine aided in securing crucial reinforcements for Edward Bulfin's force on the right of the line, the staff officer obtained many of these troops locally, without consulting Sir Douglas Haig. After Jeudwine located him on the Menin road, the I Corps commander directed 3 Cavalry Division to assist Bulfin, and according to the corps war diary, the cavalry "materially helped to restore the line."[51] Nonetheless, the extent of this assistance appears to have been only one dismounted regiment.

Given Haig's relative ineffectiveness and the collapse of the command structures of 1 and 2 Divisions, the individual brigades and regiments of I Corps were increasingly left to their own devices in checking the enemy advance on 31 October. Consequently, with the exception of Tommy Capper, who remained at the head of 7 Division, the burden of command in Haig's force fell to brigade commanders and regimental officers. Fortunately for I Corps, there was no shortage of capable leadership at these levels. In the aftermath of the First Battle of Ypres, Charles Deedes, a staff officer at GHQ, credited the brigade commanders of Haig's force with the preservation of the British line on the 31st. As Deedes reflected: "[p]arts of our line were driven back, but owing to the personal leadership displayed by individual Brigadiers, such as Cavan, Bulfin and Fitzclarence, the situation was saved by the narrowest of margins, and enormous losses were inflicted on the enemy."[52]

Evidence of such personal initiative is abundant. Along the Menin Road, the leadership of Charles Fitzclarence, commanding the 1st Guards Brigade, was pivotal in stemming the enemy advance toward Ypres. Shortly after noon, troops of 7 Division were shelled out of their trenches east of Gheluvelt, retiring into the village with German infantry in pursuit. By 1 pm, according to the 1 Division war diary, the British line was "completely broken" south of the Menin Road, and Gheluvelt was in German hands.[53] Recognizing the grave danger posed to his own position and ultimately to Ypres by the breach on the adjacent front of 7 Division, Fitzclarence summoned reinforcements. The only troops available at the time were three companies of the 2/Worcesters, technically under the command of 2 Division. While the commander of the Worcesters was initially reluctant to place his force at the disposal of an officer outside of 2 Division, Fitzclarence convinced him of the gravity of the situation, and directed him on Gheluvelt.

In perhaps the most famous counterattack of the 1914 campaign, the Worcesters chased the enemy from the west side of the village. Enemy shelling later compelled the retirement of the British line to the west of Gheluvelt. Nonetheless, the attack of the Worcesters prevented a potential disaster by restoring a breach at a crucial point in the line. As the commander of the Worcesters acknowledged afterward, Fitzclarence's initiative "saved the day."[54] Similar presence of mind on the part of Edward Bulfin was pivotal in saving the right of the I Corps line. Around noon, the retirement of units of 7 Division had exposed the left of Bulfin's force. By swinging back his left, the 2nd Brigade commander was able to prevent the fracturing of his line. Under continued German attacks, however, the position grew increasingly fragile as the afternoon progressed. While the arrival of reinforcements secured by Jeudwine allowed Bulfin to bolster his left, he determined that an offensive effort was still necessary to relieve continued enemy pressure. With additional British troops advancing, Bulfin instructed his force to prepare for a counterattack. Informing his units of the impending arrival of "big reinforcements," he ordered them to deliver a "mad minute" of rifle fire upon hearing the cheers of the approaching troops.[55]

When the reinforcements arrived, the 2nd Brigade commander discovered that "they consisted of about eight Gordon Highlanders under Captain Stansfield, the Adjutant." The weakness of the force was concealed, however, by the forest behind the British line. Undaunted by the size of the detachment, Bulfin directed its commander to "[f]ix bayonets. Then, when I raise my hand, advance in quick time and make every man cheer as hard as he can, so as to make it appear that a big counterattack is being made by large numbers."[56] To his own surprise, Bulfin's ruse was successful. The charge of the Gordons carried the depleted line of the 2nd Brigade with it. According to an after-action report: "The effect was beyond belief. The Germans were broken and hustled and driven back through the wood." Assisted by the recovery of 7 Division on his left, Bulfin was able to exploit the German disorientation. By 9 pm, the 2nd Brigade line had largely been restored to its position during the morning.[57]

While brigade commanders such as Fitzclarence and Bulfin were pivotal in restoring the I Corps line on 31 October, the success of their initiatives also stemmed from the leadership of regimental officers. As John Charteris reflected in early November, "it is to the splendid training and fighting of the battalions that we owe our success and even our existence."[58] Regimental pride contributed to the tenacity of these battalions. In his diary, George Jeffries of the 2/Grenadier Guards described an incident on the 30th that illustrates this quality. As Jeffries related: "As we were halted by the roadside, a number of Gordon Highlanders came dribbling back from the line, some wounded but not all. I stopped a Corporal, who with a man was escorting a slightly wounded man well able to walk, and asked him if that was the custom in the Gordons. He said 'No Sir' and turned round and walked back."[59]

Regimental officers demonstrated similar tenacity on 31 October. In his memoir of the war, F.A. Bolwell, a member of the 1/Loyal North Lancashires of Bulfin's 2nd Brigade, described an incident that took place at battalion headquarters in the midst of the German attacks. According to Bolwell:

We kept them off for an hour or two when the C.O. of the King's Royal Rifles consulted us, or rather our C.O., about retiring. I remember the two Officers having a heated argument over it, as they stood by a farmhouse immediately in rear of the line. I do not, however, know what their argument was, but heard afterwards that the King's Royal Rifles had got short of ammunition. The words I did hear from our C.O. were: 'It's the General's orders that we hold the position at all costs, and this I'll do if I lose the whole regiment'.[60]

At Gheluvelt, the stubborn defense of the 1/South Wales Borderers was pivotal in sustaining the I Corps line on the 31st. During the morning, the British battalions positioned east of Gheluvelt were subjected to a devastating artillery bombardment followed by infantry attacks. By 10 am, the 2/Welch Regiment to the right of the South Wales Borderers had been "wiped out" by the enemy onslaught. The destruction of the Welch enabled the Germans to enter Gheluvelt, a development that threatened to cut off the South Wales Borderers, still holding positions to the east. The situation of this battalion at midday on 31 October appeared grim. As an officer recalled in an after-action report: "with no reinforcements available, it appeared impossible to…stem the advance of the enemy." Nevertheless, in an effort to alleviate pressure on their line, the South Wales Borderers launched a counterattack against German forces in their front.

Notwithstanding some embellishment in its description, the attack was a success. Using the old numerical identification of the battalion, the after-action report described the effort as follows:

As has always been the case in the past when cries have arisen in battle, the Old Spirit of the 24th was equal to the occasion. There was no hesitating, no halting, only a dominating and fierce desire to take toll for the loss of so many gallant comrades and to restore the lost position. The same old regimental esprit which has stood the test of ages prevailed equally through all ranks. The enemy, who showed no desire for cold steel, bolted pell mell.[61]

Although the attack resulted in the loss of three officers, it relieved the pressure on the South Wales Borderers. Shortly afterward, the counterattack of the Worcesters restored the line on their right. While the line of 1 Division was withdrawn west of Gheluvelt that evening, the perseverance of the South Wales Borderers proved vital in the maintenance of the line during the day. All along the I Corps front on 31 October, regimental tenacity combined with the initiative of brigade commanders to repel the heaviest German offensive of the 1914 campaign. Counterattacks by Fitzclarence in the center and Bulfin on the right enabled Capper's exhausted 7 Division to move forward and reestablish links with 1 Division and Bulfin's force. According to the I Corps war diary: "by 10 pm the line as held in the morning had practically been reoccupied."[62]

THE ANTICLIMAX: 1–11 NOVEMBER 1914

The attacks of 31 October marked the climax of the German offensive against Ypres. While enemy initiatives continued well into November, these efforts never reached the intensity of the period 29–31 October. Given the condition of I Corps in early November, resisting even limited enemy pressure proved an exceedingly difficult task. The formidable resolve of Sir Douglas Haig undoubtedly contributed to its successful accomplishment. Haig was assisted, however, by the continued leadership of junior commanders and even more so by considerable support from the French. On the night of 31 October, I Corps benefited from Sir John French's distress that afternoon, as Foch sent reinforcements to Haig's aid. Units of the French XVI Corps arrived on the right of Bulfin's detachment, shortening the I Corps line. In addition, French units to the north and south of Haig's front took the offensive over the next three days. While these efforts met with little success, they coincided with a temporary lull in the enemy attacks, as the German armies prepared for a final offensive thrust. Thus, in the words of Sir Arthur Conan-Doyle, early November saw "a short period of comparative rest for Haig's men."[63]

This respite proved fortunate for I Corps. Despite its initial strength and the availability of reinforcements, German attacks since 21 October had inflicted significant damage on Haig's force. The shelling of Hooge Chateau on the 31st had weakened the command structures of 1 and 2 divisions considerably. It is difficult to measure the impact of the decimation of the two divisional staffs. It is safe to assume, however, that it diminished the effectiveness of both divisions on subsequent days. While new staff officers could be appointed, it took time for them to develop the efficiency of officers who had performed staff duties since the beginning of the 1914 campaign. The battle had also taken its toll on commanders within I Corps. Sir Douglas Haig lost perhaps his most capable divisional commander with the incapacitation and eventual death of S.H. Lomax. Haig's praise of Lomax in his diary attests to his high opinion of the 1 Division commander, particularly in light of his derisive tendencies toward other British officers. The corps had also lost some of its brigade commanders. On 1 November, Bulfin was wounded by a shell near his front line and sent back to England. The following day, H.G. Ruggles-Brice, commander of the 20th Brigade of 7 Division, was wounded as well.[64] Thus, by early November, the command structure of I Corps was becoming steadily weaker through the loss of many of its key members.

Equally serious were the heavy casualties suffered by the battalions of I Corps. On 1 November, J.G.W. Hyndson, a subaltern in the 1/Loyal North Lancs of Bulfin's 2nd Brigade, detailed the losses of his unit during the height of the German offensive. As Hyndson recorded: "during the last three days desperate fighting, the twenty-five officers and 900 men who went into action on the 30th are now reduced to five officers and 150 men, which practically means for the time being that we have ceased to exist as a battalion."[65] Other regiments in I Corps had sustained casualties on a similar scale. By 4 November, the entire 1st Guards Brigade could muster less than 1,000 rifles. On the same day, Sir Douglas Haig recorded the strength of 1 Division as 92 officers and 3,491 other ranks. Capper's 7 Division, involved in active operations in Flanders since mid-October, was in even more critical condition. On 1 November, George Jeffries of the 2/Grenadier Guards had encountered Capper behind the I Corps line. As he recalled in his diary: "[s]tanding near by with only an A.D.C. was Major-General Sir T. Capper, commanding 7th Division, but he gave me no orders. I said, 'I'm afraid your Division has had a bad time, Sir.' He replied, 'Yes, so bad that there's no Division left, so that I'm a curiosity—a Divisional Commander without a Division.' "[66] Capper's black humor aside, his assessment was reasonably accurate. The following day, the 7 Division war diary recorded its strength as 44 officers and 2,396 other ranks.[67]

Despite the relative calm that prevailed on the I Corps front, Sir Douglas Haig recognized the dangerous depletion of both 1 and 7 Division. On 4 November, he sent Johnnie Gough to GHQ to request their immediate relief. Gough encountered a receptive audience at GHQ. The German offensive of 29–31 October had finally quelled the optimism of Sir John French and much of his staff. In addition, as Haig's chief of staff, Johnnie Gough commanded a degree of respect at GHQ that most British commanders did not. Thus, rather than rebuking Gough as he had Smith-Dorrien, Rawlinson, and Sir James Willcocks,

Sir John French responded quickly to his suggestion. The next day, the commander-in-chief ordered Sir Horace Smith-Dorrien to send 3 Division, currently in reserve, to reinforce Haig's line. By 6 November, eleven battalions of II Corps had relieved the decimated 7 Division.[68]

These reinforcements were hardly formidable. After their own ordeal in late October, the combined strength of Smith-Dorrien's regiments amounted to only 3,500 rifles. Thus, the I Corps line remained relatively frail in early November. Comprised of the remnants of 1, 2, and 7 Divisions, 3 Cavalry Division, and the recently arrived detachment from II Corps, Haig's makeshift force contained approximately 16,000 fatigued troops on 6 November.[69] Moreover, its effectiveness was undermined by the loss of key officers in earlier stages of the battle. Despite the relative weakness of his force, however, Sir Douglas Haig's resolve remained unshaken. Indeed, in early November, it seems likely that the I Corps commander learned what has been characterized as his most important lesson of the 1914 campaign. As Bidwell and Graham have argued, First Ypres confirmed Haig's preexisting beliefs regarding the value of tenacity in warfare. The I Corps commander's November diary entries contain evidence of this conviction. As he exclaimed on the 5th: "Our troops have been in the trenches for the last ten days and have also had terrible losses! But we have to stick it!"[70]

The stubborn defense of I Corps, however, was not solely a manifestation of the resolve of its commander. Indeed, a variety of factors contributed to the maintenance of the British line in November 1914. Not least among these was the continued effective leadership of officers at the brigade level and below. Despite the loss of capable commanders such as Lomax and Bulfin, there remained in I Corps officers of immense personal bravery. Among these was General Lawford, commanding the 22nd Brigade of 7 Division. On 7 November, just one day after the relief of Capper's division, the loss of several trenches in the I Corps line compelled the recall of the 22nd Brigade. By this point in the campaign, Lawford's entire force comprised just 7 officers and 1,100 other ranks. Undaunted by the weakness of his force, Lawford led the attack himself, recapturing the lost trenches and restoring the line.[71]

Even more important than the personal leadership of British commanders, however, was the continued support of French forces in the vicinity. On 5, 6, 7, and 9 November, French units on either flank of Haig's corps launched attacks against opposing enemy forces. In addition, Foch was apparently willing and able to reinforce the British line if necessary. On the 6th, he placed a cavalry division at Haig's disposal. Two days later, he informed Henry Wilson that "he had sufficient forces to stop the Germans from taking Ypres," should I Corps falter.[72] Thus, French troops in the vicinity provided a cushion of reserves for I Corps in the event of a renewal of serious enemy attacks. In addition, the offensive efforts of adjacent French units discouraged the development of such attacks on the I Corps front. French initiatives seldom made headway against the considerable German forces opposite Ypres. Moreover, German assaults continued to inflict damage on the units of I Corps in early November.

Nonetheless, it is apparent that French support was instrumental in Haig's ability to maintain his depleted line around Ypres.

German forces attacked with renewed intensity on 11 November, as the Prussian Guards Corps attempted to break through the British line around Ypres. While this attack was preceded by the heaviest artillery bombardment of the campaign, the I Corps commander had readjusted and strengthened his line since 31 October. Thus, rather than attempting to take shelter in exposed trenches, British troops could fall back to a supporting line of "strong points" from which they subsequently launched counterattacks. As a result, while German forces made significant headway against British positions during the morning of the 11th, counterattacks launched in the afternoon were largely successful in restoring the line.[73]

As was the case on 31 October, Haig's role in this process was marginal. As John Charteris remarked: "We at Corps HQ had not much to do, for it was fought out by troops on the spot, and we had no reserves to put in." Nor did Haig attempt to influence the battle personally, as he had on the 31st. It was thus left to the initiative of commanders at the front line to organize the defense. Conspicuous among these officers was Fitzclarence of the 1st Guards Brigade. According to John Terraine: "General Fitzclarence was the soul of the defence, and set about organizing attacks with whatever came to hand." As the fate of numerous British commanders in 1914 had demonstrated, however, personal leadership under fire proved exceedingly hazardous. In leading one of these counterattacks, Fitzclarence was killed on the night of 11 November.[74]

The attack of the Prussian Guards was the last serious attempt by the Germans to break the I Corps position around Ypres. While the enemy continued to harass the British line throughout November, the First Battle of Ypres effectively drew to a close on the 12th. The relative calm that ensued finally enabled the relief of Haig's force beginning on 15 November. While precise casualty figures are difficult to determine, it is clear that the withdrawal of I Corps had become a necessity. Following its action on the 7th, Lawford's 22nd Brigade had been reduced to a strength of 3 officers and 700 men. This represented a casualty rate of 80 percent among its other ranks, and 97 percent among its officers. By nightfall on 11 November, Fitzclarence's 1st Guards Brigade mustered only 4 officers and 300 other ranks.[75] For all practical purposes, the original units of Haig's I Corps no longer existed.

THE MAKING OF A HERO: THE HAIG DIARIES, FIRST YPRES AND THE REPUTATION OF SIR DOUGLAS HAIG

Among other British officers in 1914, Sir Douglas Haig emerged from the First Battle of Ypres with his reputation intact and even enhanced. After visiting Ypres on 11 November, Archibald Home, a staff officer in the Cavalry Corps, expressed admiration for Haig's leadership in his diary. As Home reflected:

it is the *man* one must think of—Douglas Haig—who has taken all this responsibility—who when the French on his right and left retired held on, who ordered the counter attacks, who set his personal feelings aside and became a machine for the good of his country. This is *the man* who has done all this and no one knows the iron resolution and great personality required not only to give the orders but to inspire the confidence required by the men to fight like they have....to my mind no pen can write a tribute fitting the work of 1st Corps or its commander in the defence of Ypres. The Germans set their heart on it—the 1st Corps foiled them.[76]

Henry De Lisle, commanding 1 Cavalry Division, expressed similar sentiments on the 12th. As he recalled in his memoir of the war: "I remember writing home that day saying that during the 20 years I had known Haig, I had never realised how big a soldier he was."[77]

Haig's performance at First Ypres clearly earned the admiration of at least some of his contemporary officers. Nonetheless, in securing his reputation, the I Corps commander was not content to rely on the merit of his achievements. Indeed, shortly after the battle ended, Haig began to take measures to ensure his positive portrayal in historical accounts of the 1914 campaign. The principal tool in these efforts was his personal diary. Throughout 1914, Haig used the diary to influence the king's opinion of other officers. An opportunity for him to influence the broader public perception of his role in the war emerged in December, however, when the historian Sir Arthur Conan-Doyle approached Lady Haig regarding the possibility of gaining access to the I Corps commander's personal record of the campaign.

Haig proved willing to grant this request. He nonetheless instructed his wife to use her discretion in removing potentially damaging material from the diary before providing Conan-Doyle with a copy. As he related in a letter to Lady Haig on 17 December: "I am sorry that Sir Conan Doyle is bothering you. You must not let him do that. But of course give him whatever *you* think is wise. I have complete confidence in your judgement in this matter." Lady Haig's editorial efforts apparently required considerable alterations to the diary. The following day, Haig suggested: "Why not cut out of my originals any paras. [sic] you think should not appear, and give the remains to someone to type. You have my original book with you now so there is no object in your having *two* original copies is there?"[78]

The extent of these expurgations remains unclear. It is evident, however, that they were not conducted simply for the purposes of brevity. Rather, Haig was concerned with preventing his ample criticisms of other officers from becoming public knowledge. As he complimented his wife in a subsequent letter: "what a trouble you take about keeping my stupid gossip & stories secret!"[79] The efforts of the I Corps commander and his wife to cleanse the diary of such material likely stemmed from a concern for his reputation as a senior officer. Evidence of Haig's rather harsh opinions of many commanders would undoubtedly have undermined his relations with these officers and diminished his standing in the eyes of others. This would likely have hindered Haig's career aspirations. Thus, much like the copy of his diary that Haig sent to the king, it is evident that the version provided to Conan-Doyle reflected the I Corps commander's ambitions in 1914. While George V's copy contained criticisms of other commanders, Lady Haig removed these comments from the version prepared for Conan-Doyle, thereby concealing them from a broader readership, including the officers he criticized. Haig's efforts to portray himself as the most capable commander in the BEF thus reached only a small, but influential audience in England.

An examination of the typescript version of Haig's diary also suggests that he retained a concern for his reputation as a commander in 1914 even after the end of the war. As discussed in Chapter 3, the typescript diary contains several additions to Haig's original entries in September 1914 that emphasize the failings of other officers. Haig made similar additions to his diary entries for the period of the First Battle of Ypres, particularly regarding his rival, Smith-Dorrien. Rather than deprecating the II Corps commander directly, Haig underlined the consequences of Smith-Dorrien's decision to face the Germans at Le Cateau. For example, in the manuscript version of the diary, Haig's entry on 27 October notes the difficulties facing II Corps with the following matter-of-fact description: "two nights ago S-Dorrien arrived at 11.30 at St. Omer to ask for help. Sir John had no reserves to give him, but luckily enemy did not attack." In the typescript, this statement is followed by Haig's comment: "again we see the ill effect on II Corps of having fought without good reason at Le Cateau."[80]

The typescript also contains more general criticisms of other British commanders. The manuscript entry for 5 November contains a rather dull description of a meeting between Sir John French and the British corps commanders. As it states:

I motored to Bailleul to see Sir John French and lunched with him. The table was laid in a room at the back of the chemist's shop. The Corps Commanders were present at the meeting, viz. Smith-Dorrien, Pulteney, Sir James Willcocks and Allenby. The II Corps...is to relieve my I Corps as soon as possible, so that my Divisions may have a rest in which to refit.

Immediately after this statement in the typescript, Haig elaborates on the proceedings of the meeting, exclaiming: "I was very astonished to find that the point which attracted most interest was 'winter leave' for the Army! Personally my one thought was how soon I could get my battle-worn troops relieved and given a few days rest out of the trenches and shell fire!"[81]

The typescript also includes numerous insertions that serve merely to add context or provide factual information regarding the operations of I Corps. Nonetheless, it is evident that in creating the typescript version of his diary, Sir Douglas Haig went to considerable effort to portray other senior officers in a negative light, particularly Smith-Dorrien, whose decision to fight at Le Cateau raised uncomfortable questions about Haig's own command in 1914. Given that he had provided Conan-Doyle with access to his diary as early as 1914, Haig was undoubtedly aware that the document would become fodder for future generations of historians. In an effort to secure his reputation for posterity, he took pains in creating the typescript to portray himself as the most capable of British commanders in 1914.

Overall, Haig's performance in 1914 did not necessarily distinguish him as the most capable commander in the BEF. While he demonstrated considerable resolve in early November, he did so from a position of relative strength in comparison to other British corps commanders in 1914. His behavior during the crises at Landrecies on 25 August and Ypres on 31 October demonstrates his susceptibility to anxiety under pressure. Moreover, his desire to intervene personally in both cases indicates that he had yet to grasp fully the scale of the 1914 campaign. In contrast, Sir Horace Smith-Dorrien had maintained his composure at Le Cateau, a situation as critical as any faced by Haig. In addition, he did not show Haig's tendency to forego his managerial responsibilities in the heat of battle. Smith-Dorrien's judgment in concealing the condition of his force in October is highly questionable. Significantly, however, he faced pressure from Sir John French in this period from which Haig was exempt. Indeed, much of Haig's success in 1914 and the acclaim he received afterward can be attributed to his connections and his skill in crafting his own reputation.

CONCLUSION

Of the British formations that participated in the First Battle of Ypres, I Corps is most closely associated with the ultimate repulse of the German offensive. The apparent success of Haig's force in comparison to other British formations, however, did not stem solely from the inherent superiority of its troops or the leadership of its commander. Rather, a variety of factors contributed to the tenacity of I Corps in late October and early November 1914. Sir John French's respect for Haig allowed the I Corps commander a degree of operational freedom from the misperceptions of GHQ that other corps commanders did not enjoy. I Corps also operated from a position of relative strength. Haig's force benefited from a competent, experienced and cohesive group of officers in the upper ranks of its command structure, as well as a manageable front, available reinforcements, and French support.

These factors largely offset any shortcomings in Haig's leadership during the First Battle of Ypres. While his command in this period featured no major errors, Haig was not immune to the mistakes committed by other commanders as they struggled to absorb the complexities of warfare in 1914. Like Henry Rawlinson, Haig initially failed to inculcate in his subordinates the necessity of concealing trenches. Moreover, the anxiety of the I Corps commander on 31 October brought to the fore his penchant for personal leadership on the battlefield. Haig's resolve did help to inspire his tired troops on the 31st and afterward. More important to the tenacity of I Corps, however, was the leadership provided by officers at lower levels of its command structure. At the brigade and regimental levels, the emphasis on personal leadership that distracted Haig from his responsibilities as corps commander proved effective, if costly, in maintaining the line. Moreover, as Haig's line deteriorated in November, it was above all the continued support of the French that enabled I Corps to survive until the German offensive faltered on the 11th. Rather than simply a triumph for the BEF, the First Battle of Ypres was wholly an allied victory. In the British Army, however, success at First Ypres was afterward attributed to the tenacity of Sir Douglas Haig and I Corps. Haig's manipulations of his diaries during and after the war suggest that he played a role in constructing this memory of the battle. Whatever its source, the lessons derived from this interpretation of the battle were not particularly helpful. Stubbornness and tenacity were not the only qualities that would expedite victory against an equally determined foe.

NOTES

1. Anthony Farrar-Hockley, *Death of an Army* (New York: Morrow, 1968), 18.

2. E.K.G. Sixsmith, *Douglas Haig* (London: Weidenfeld and Nicholson, 1976), 83.

3. Ian F. W. Beckett, *Johnnie Gough, V.C.* (London: Tom Donovan, 1989), 193; Gerard DeGroot, *Douglas Haig: 1861–1928* (Unwin Hyman, 1988), 165; Richard Holmes, *The Little Field-Marshal: Sir John French* (London: Jonathan Cape, 1981), 251.

4. John Hussey, "A Hard Day at First Ypres, The Allied Generals and Their Problems: 31st October 1914," *British Army Review*, 107 (August 1994), 88; Denis Winter, *Haig's Command: A Reassessment* (London: Viking, 1991), 36.

5. I Corps War Diary, 19 October 1914, WO 95/588, PRO; Haig Diary, 19 October 1914, Haig Papers, National Library of Scotland (NLS), WO 256/2, PRO; John Charteris, *At GHQ* (London: Cassell, 1931), 48.

6. GHQ Operation Order No. 39, 20 October 1914, 9:30 pm, GHQ War Diary, WO 95/1. See also Haig Diary, 20–21 October 1914, NLS, WO 256/2, PRO.

7. Haig Diary, 21 October 1914, NLS, WO 256/2, PRO; 1 Division War Diary, 21 October 1914, WO 95/1227; I Corps War Diary, 21 October 1914, WO 95/589, PRO.

8. 2 Division War Diary, 21 October 1914, WO 95/589; I Corps War Diary, 21 October 1914, WO 95/588, PRO; Haig Diary, 21 October 1914, NLS; WO 256/2, PRO.

9. Smith quoted in J.M. Craster, ed. *'Fifteen Rounds a Minute': the Grenadiers at War, August to December 1914* (London: Macmillan, 1976), 111; 2 Division War Diary, 21 October 1914, WO 95/589; I Corps War Diary, 21 October 1914, WO 95/588, PRO; Haig Diary, 21–22 October 1914, NLS; WO 256/2, PRO.

10. Macdonogh to Edmonds, 11 October 1922, CAB 45/141, PRO.

11. Rawlinson Diary, 4 December 1914. See also Rawlinson Diary, 6 December 1914, Lord Rawlinson Papers 1/1, CCC.

12. See chapter 4 for a discussion of British casualties in August and September 1914.

13. On Gough's health, see Beckett, *Johnnie Gough*; Charteris, *At GHQ*, 37.

14. "General Smith-Dorrien's Report on Operations of II Corps, 11th October to 18th November 1914," II Corps War Diary, WO 95/630, PRO.

15. I Corps War Diary, 19 October 1914, WO 95/588, PRO; Haig Diary, 20 October 1914, WO 256/2, PRO; James Edmonds, *Military Operations: France and Belgium, 1914*, vol.2 (London: Macmillan, 1925), 136.

16. Ernest Hamilton, *The First Seven Divisions: Being a Detailed Account of the Fighting from Mons to Ypres* (New York: Dutton, 1916), 217. See also GHQ War Diary, 21 October 1914, WO 95/1; I Corps War Diary, 21 October 1914, WO 95/588, PRO.

17. Bulfin Diary, 23 October 1914, CAB 45/140; 1 Division War Diary, 23 October 1914, WO 95/1227; I Corps War Diary, 22 October 1914, WO 95/588, PRO. On German casualties see GHQ War Diary, 23 October 1914, WO 95/1, PRO; Wilson Diary, 24 October 1914, Henry Wilson Papers, IWM; Hamilton, *The First Seven Divisions*, 215.

18. I Corps Operation Order No. 22, 24 October 1914, 11 pm; I Corps Operation Order No. 23, 25 October 1914, 9:50 pm; I Corps War Diary, 27 October 1914, WO 95/588; 1 Division War Diary, 25–29 October 1914 WO 95/589; GHQ War Diary, 23–24 October 1914, WO 95/1; E.S. Bulfin Diary, 25, 29 October 1914, CAB 45/140, PRO.

19. GHQ War Diary, 2–11 November 1914; WO 95/1, PRO.

20. 2 Division War Diary, 28 October 1914; 1 Division War Diary, 28 October 1914, WO 95/589, PRO; Hussey, "A Hard Day at First Ypres," 77; Farrar-Hockley, *Death of an Army*, 125–127.

21. Craster, *'Fifteen Rounds a Minute,'* 119; Haig Diary, 29 October 1914, NLS, WO 256/2, PRO.

22. G. de la P. Pakenham, "Unofficial Account of the Doings of 3rd Brigade between 29th October to date"; C. Fitzclarence, "Report on Actions between October 27th and November 2nd by the 1st Infantry Brigade," 1 Division War Diary, WO 95/1227; 1 Division War Diary, 29 October 1914, 2 Division War Diary, 29 October, WO 95/589; I Corps War Diary, WO 95/589, PRO.

23. I Corps Operation Order No.27, 29 October 1914, 5:50 pm, I Corps War Diary, WO 95/588, PRO; Farrar-Hockley, *Death of an Army*, 138.

24. Hamilton, *The First Seven Divisions*, 257.

25. 3 Cavalry Division War Diary, 27 October 1914, WO 95/589, PRO.

26. Haig Diary, 26 October 1914, NLS, WO 256/2, PRO.

27. Byng to Cavalry Corps, 30 October 1914, 8:30 am, 3 Cavalry Division War Diary, appendices, WO 95/1142, PRO. See also 3 Cavalry Division War Diary, 30 October 1914, WO 95/589, PRO.

28. Farrar-Hockley, *Death of an Army*, 142–143; 7 Division War Diary, 30 October 1914, WO 95/1627, PRO.

29. I Corps War Diary, 30 October 1914, WO 95/588; Bulfin Diary, 30 October 1914, CAB 45/140; 1 Division War Diary, 30 October 1914; 3 Cavalry Division War Diary, 30 October 1914, WO 95/589, PRO.

30. Cavalry Corps War Diary, 31 October 1914, WO 95/572, PRO.

31. 3 Cavalry Division War Diary, 31 October 1914, WO 95/589; Cavalry Corps War Diary, 31 October 1914, WO 95/572, PRO.

32. I Corps to Cavalry Corps, 31 October 1914, 9:20 am, "11 Messages Issued by I Corps, August–November 1914," Miscellaneous File No. 43, IWM. See also Cavalry Corps War Diary, 31 October 1914, WO 95/572, PRO.

33. I Corps War Diary, 31 October 1914, WO 95/588; 1 Division War Diary, 31 October 1914, WO 95/1227; 7 Division War Diary, 31 October 1914, WO 95/1627; 2 Division War Diary, 31 October 1914, WO 95/589, PRO.

34. 3 Cavalry Division War Diary, 31 October 1914, WO 95/589; Cavalry Corps War Diary, 31 October 1914, WO 95/572, PRO.

35. Bulfin Diary, 31 October 1914, CAB 45/140; I Corps War Diary, 31 October 1914, WO 95/588; 1 Division War Diary, 31 October 1914, WO 95/1227; 7 Division War Diary, 31 October 1914, WO 95/1627, PRO.

36. Bulfin Diary, 31 October 1914, CAB 45/140, PRO. See also 1 Division War Diary, 31 October 1914, WO 95/1227; 7 Division War Diary, 31 October 1914, WO 95/1627, PRO.

37. 2 Division War Diary, 31 October 1914, WO 95/589; Haig Diary, 31 October 1914, NLS; WO 256/2, PRO; 1 Division War Diary, 31 October 1914, WO 95/1227, PRO.

38. "The Inner Truth of 31st October 1914 at Ypres (as told to me by General Edmonds): 17.2.31," 11/1931/4, Liddell Hart Papers, LHCMA.

39. Hussey, "A Hard Day at First Ypres," 83; Beckett, *Johnnie Gough*, 193.

40. I Corps War Diary, 31 October 1914, WO 95/588, PRO.

41. On the relationship between Edmonds and Liddell Hart, see John J. Mearsheimer, *Liddell Hart and the Weight of History* (Ithaca: Cornell University Press, 1988), 58.

42. Charteris cited in John Terraine, *The Ordeal of Victory* (Philadelphia: Lippincott, 1963), 114; Holmes, *The Little Field-Marshal*, 251.

43. Foch cited in Terraine, *The Ordeal of Victory*, 114–115; Holmes, *The Little Field-Marshal*, 252.

44. Haig's comments on *Official History*, CAB 45/183, PRO. See also Haig Diary, 31 October 1914, NLS, WO 256/2, PRO.

45. De Groot, *Douglas Haig*, 165–166; Edmonds, *Military Operations: France and Belgium, 1914*, 325.

46. Winter, *Haig's Command*, 36–37.

47. 3 Cavalry Division War Diary, 31 October 1914, WO 95/589; "Personal Narrative of Major General Sir Hugh Jeudwine, KCB (then Colonel, GSO1, I Corps), Events on Right Flank of I Corps, Which Came under His Personal Observation on 31st October 1914," I Corps War Diary, WO 95/588, PRO; Hussey, "A Hard Day at First Ypres," 85.

48. Haig Diary, 31 October 1914, NLS, WO 256/2, PRO; Bulfin Diary, 31 October 1914, CAB 45/140; I Corps War Diary, 31 October 1914, WO 95/588; 7 Division War Diary, 31 October 1914, WO 95/1227, PRO.

49. Terraine, *The Ordeal of Victory*, 113.

50. "Personal Narrative of Major-General Sir Hugh Jeudwine," I Corps War Diary, WO 95/588, PRO.

51. I Corps War Diary, 31 October 1914, WO 95/588; 3 Cavalry Division War Diary, 31 October 1914, WO 95/589; Bulfin Diary, 31 October 1914, CAB 45/140; 7 Division War Diary, 31 October, WO 95/1627; 1 Division War Diary, 31 October 1914, WO 95/1227; 2 Division War Diary, 31 October 1914, WO 95/589; "Personal Narrative of Major-General Sir Hugh Jeudwine," WO 95/588, PRO.

52. Scott, ed., "The View from GHQ: The Third Part of the War Diary of General Sir Charles Deedes," 30.

53. 1 Division War Diary, 31 October 1914; Fitzclarence, "Report on Actions between Oct 27th & Nov 2nd by 1st Infantry Brigade," WO 95/1227, PRO.

54. "Statement by Lieutenant Colonel Hankey"; "Statement by Captain Thorne"; I

Corps War Diary, WO 95/588, PRO.

55. "Information about the Counter-attack of the 2nd Infantry Brigade," Bulfin Diary, CAB 45/140, PRO; 1 Division War Diary, 31 October 1914, WO 95/1227, PRO.

56. "Information about the Counter-attack of the 2nd Infantry Brigade," Bulfin Diary, CAB 45/140, PRO.

57. Bulfin to 1 Division Headquarters, November 1914, 1 Division War Diary, WO 95/1227; "Information about the Counter-attack of the 2nd Infantry Brigade," Bulfin Diary, CAB 45/140, PRO.

58. Charteris, *At GHQ*, 58.

59. Jeffries Diary, 30 October 1914, in Craster, *'Fifteen Rounds a Minute,'* 121.

60. F.A. Bolwell, *With a Reservist in France* (London: Routledge, 1916), 88.

61. "The Events as They Affected the 1st Battalion South Wales Borderers, of the 27th October–31st October 1914, during the 1st Battle of Ypres, the Now Acknowledged Most Critical Period of the Battle," CAB 45/140, PRO.

62. I Corps War Diary, 31 October 1914, WO 95/588; 1 Division War Diary, WO 95/1227, PRO; Haig Diary, 31 October 1914, NLS, WO 256/2, PRO.

63. Arthur Conan-Doyle, *The British Campaign in France and Flanders, 1914* (London: Hodder and Stoughton, 1916), 275. Haig Diary 1–2 November 1914; NLS, WO 256/2; I Corps War Diary, 1–3 November 1914, WO 95/589; 1 Division War Diary, 1–3 November 1914, WO 95/1227; 2 Division War Diary, 1–3 November 1914, WO 95/589, 3 Cavalry Division War Diary, 2 November 1914, WO 95/1141; GHQ War Diary, 1–3 November 1914, WO 95/1; PRO.

64. Farrar-Hockley, *Death of an Army*, 170; Bulfin Diary, 1 November 1914, CAB 45/140, PRO; Haig Diary 14 September 1914, NLS, WO 256/1, PRO. See also Charteris, *At GHQ*, 50–51.

65. J.G.W. Hyndson, *From Mons to the First Battle of Ypres* (London: Wyman, 1933), 97.

66. Jeffries Diary, 1 November 1914, in Craster, *'Fifteen Rounds a Minute,'* 125–126; Captain Allan J. Cameron Diary, 4 November 1914, E. Craig-Brown Papers, IWM; Haig Diary, 4 November 1914, NLS, WO 256/2, PRO.

67. 7 Division War Diary, 2 November 1914, WO 95/1627, PRO.

68. I Corps War Diary, 5–6 November 1914, WO 95/589; GHQ War Diary, 4–6 November 1914, WO 95/1; Smith-Dorrien Diary, 5–6 November 1914, CAB 45/206; Haig Diary, 4 November 1914, NLS; WO 256/2, PRO; Murray Diary, 4 November 1914, Archibald Murray Papers, IWM.

69. 7 Division War Diary, 2 November 1914, WO 95/1627, PRO; Haig Diary, 4 November 1914, NLS; WO 256/2, PRO; Conan-Doyle, *The British Campaign in France and Flanders*, 291.

70. Haig Diary, 5 November 1914. See also 7, 14 November 1914, NLS; WO 256/2, PRO. Shelford Bidwell and Dominick Graham, *Fire-Power: British Army Weapons and Theories of War, 1904–1945* (London: Allen and Unwin, 1982), 69.

71. Conan-Doyle, *The British Campaign in France and Flanders*, 294; 7 Division War Diary, 7 November 1914, WO 95/1627, PRO.

72. Wilson Diary, 8 November 1914, Henry Wilson Papers, IWM; I Corps War Diary, 7 November 1914, WO 95/589; GHQ War Diary, 5–9 November 1914, WO 95/1; Smith-Dorrien Diary, 7–9 November 1914, CAB 45/206, PRO.

73. I Corps War Diary, 11 November 1914, WO 95/588; GHQ War Diary, 11

November 1914, WO 95/1, PRO; Farrar-Hockley, *Death of an Army*, 175; Terraine, *Ordeal of Victory*, 120.

74. Haig Diary, 12 November 1914, NLS; WO 256/2, PRO; GHQ War Diary, 12 November 1914, WO 95/1, PRO; Terraine, *Ordeal of Victory*, 121.

75. I Corps War Diary, 11 November 1914, WO 95/589, PRO; Conan-Doyle, *The British Campaign in France and Flanders*, 294.

76. Archibald Home, *A Diary of a World War I Cavalry Officer* (Tunbridge Wells: Costello, 1985), 38.

77. Henry De Lisle, "My Narrative of the Great War," De Lisle Papers, LHCMA.

78. Haig to Lady Haig, 17, 18 December 1914, Haig Papers, NLS.

79. Haig to Lady Haig, 23 December 1914, Haig Papers, NLS.

80. Haig Diary, 27 October 1914. See also 7 November 1914, NLS; WO 256/2, PRO.

81. Haig Diary, 5 November 1914, NLS; WO 256/2, PRO.

Conclusion: The Nature of Command in 1914

On the British front, the climactic engagements of late October and early November were followed by a lull in operations. While skirmishes between British and German forces continued into December, it was not until the following spring that either side made a serious effort to break the stalemate that prevailed on the Western Front. Thus, for the BEF, the end of the First Battle of Ypres signaled the close of the 1914 campaign. How did British officers exercise command during this campaign? This study will conclude by advancing four arguments in response to this question. These arguments lead to a broader conclusion regarding the conduct of the 1914 campaign by British officers. They also raise significant questions about command in the BEF and other European armies throughout the First World War.

First, it is clear that the inexperience of the British Army in conducting large-scale operations against a well organized adversary had an important impact on the exercise of command. This institutional inexperience was manifested in a shortage of trained staff officers and a lack of clearly established procedures for the distribution of information. These problems hampered the control of the army by GHQ during the retreat from Mons and the coordination of the subsequent advance to the Aisne. Inexperience also contributed to the difficulties of British formations during the First Battle of Ypres, particularly the newly established IV Corps, which had little opportunity to prepare before commencing operations against considerable opposition.

Within the context of this inexperience, British officers displayed three distinct traits in their exercise of command. At the regimental level, officers placed a strong emphasis on personal leadership in battle. This leadership was a component of the paternalism common to British officers in this period. Such conduct elicited the loyalty of their subordinates, thereby enhancing the cohesion of British battalions in 1914. Casualties to the original cadre of officers in the

BEF and their gradual replacement with individuals unfamiliar to the other ranks undoubtedly weakened these battalions. Indeed, during the First Battle of Ypres, incidences of soldiers abandoning their positions became more prevalent. Nevertheless, even in October and November 1914, the personal leadership of both original and replacement officers was a key ingredient in the extraordinary tenacity of British battalions. The fact that Indian soldiers often proved less resolute than their British counterparts reflects the more fragile relationship that existed between British officers and sepoys in 1914. In the context of tightened disciplinary regulations and the alien conditions of warfare in Europe, the loss of familiar officers with the linguistic skills necessary to lead Indian soldiers compelled many sepoys to reconsider their commitment to service. The self-inflicted wounds that ensued in battalions of the Indian Corps, however, did not occur on any discernible scale in other formations of the BEF. Overall, it seems reasonable to argue that the courage and self-sacrifice of junior officers enabled the BEF to survive the 1914 campaign.

The third thesis to emerge from this study concerns the mixture of qualities displayed by officers in the upper ranks of the BEF. As Chapter 1 has demonstrated, the "hybrid" officers who filled senior command and staff positions in 1914 were influenced by modernizing trends in the army prior to the war, while retaining traditional qualities possessed by regimental officers. At the divisional level and above, the vast majority of British commanders and staff officers in August 1914 had formal staff training. Several had actually commanded the Staff Colleges at Camberley and Quetta. Moreover, many of these officers had been involved in tactical debates that had arisen since the South African War. In addition, however, many of these individuals exhibited traits common among regimental officers. Among these attributes were a fondness for sport, an aversion to narrow intellectualism, and a penchant for personal leadership in battle. This latter quality proved particularly significant during the 1914 campaign. At the height of the First Battle of Ypres, brigade and divisional commanders led their troops by example, often placing themselves at great risk. Even senior officers such as Sir Douglas Haig and Sir John French attempted to intervene on the battlefield in critical situations.

The double-edged traits displayed by "hybrid" officers proved to be a mixed blessing for the BEF in 1914. During the First Battle of Ypres, the personal leadership of formation commanders undoubtedly contributed to the cohesion of the army. The indifference to danger shown by brigade and divisional commanders such as Lawford, Bulfin, Fitzclarence, Byng, and Capper provided a stirring example to their subordinates. This emphasis on personal leadership, however, was not without its costs and drawbacks. Indeed, the conspicuous bravery of "hybrid" officers during the First Battle of Ypres resulted in the loss of several competent and experienced commanders. Nor were these casualties always necessary. It is doubtful that the loss of Hubert Hamilton, for example, was required to encourage the advance of 3 Division on 14 October. In addition to exposing commanders to undue risks, this preference for personal leadership distracted "hybrid" officers from the managerial responsibilities of directing large formations. Sir Douglas Haig's celebrated ride up the Menin Road on 31 October, for example, left I Corps without its commander during a period when its command structure had already been weakened significantly by the loss of its divisional staffs. As noted in Chapter 1, Sir John French displayed a similar preference for personal involvement in battle over the more mundane tasks involved in planning and coordinating the operations of the army. Dennis Showalter has observed that German commanders such as Hindenberg and Ludendorff also demonstrated a desire to maintain "a sense of involvement" with events on the battlefield in 1914. This desire did not impede their command capabilities significantly, however, as they simply established their headquarters close to the front.[1] In the BEF, this tendency resulted in spontaneous attempts by senior commanders to observe and influence events at the front. While these attempts did not result in disaster in 1914, they nonetheless hampered the control of large formations during critical periods of the campaign.

This emphasis on personal leadership, and the courage that it required, also affected the response of the BEF to the largely unprecedented conditions of 1914. As demonstrated in chapter 3, while British officers introduced a variety of measures to improve the tactical effectiveness of the BEF, they also placed a high premium on personal bravery. As a result, "hybrid" officers encouraged dangerous and often costly practices such as trench raids and holding exposed positions for the purposes of morale. Such exploits diminished the value of tactical innovations designed to protect British soldiers. Moreover, commanders who displayed boldness and tenacity on the battlefield were often promoted, while those deemed to be hesitant were relieved of their posts. This practice excluded officers such as Ivor Maxse, who might have been of assistance in the process of adapting to the conditions of modern warfare. Thus, while the presence of "hybrid" officers in the upper ranks of the army enhanced the cohesion of the BEF, their double-edged qualities were not altogether attuned to the realities of the 1914 campaign.

The fourth thesis to emerge from this study focuses in particular on one of these double-edged traits. As noted in Chapter 1, officers in the upper ranks of the BEF were unusually ambitious in comparison to most of their contemporaries in the British officer corps. While this ambition spurred them to increase their professional expertise, it also produced rivalries and animosities between officers seeking to further their careers. Historians have noted the presence of tensions between individual commanders and staff officers during the opening months of the war. This study goes beyond such general observations, however, to argue that a system of "Social Darwinism" existed in the upper ranks of the BEF in 1914. In its traditional sense, this term refers to the use of Darwin's concept of struggle between natural organisms to explain competition in human society. Nonetheless, it also provides an apt description of the system through which British officers competed for rank, influence and prestige in an environment characterized by pervasive and often conflicting social networks.

How did "Social Darwinism" operate? An examination of command in 1914 reveals a consistent tendency on the part of senior officers to view their colleagues as competitors for rank, influence, and prestige. This produced friction and intrigue in the upper ranks of the BEF, as officers attempted to undermine those individuals they perceived as threats to their positions or obstacles to their ambitions. This perception influenced Sir Douglas Haig's attitude toward many of his colleagues. At GHQ, Henry Wilson clearly perceived Archie Murray as an obstacle to his own ambitions. In the cavalry, Hubert Gough viewed Sir Edmund Allenby in similar terms. This competition between officers took place within the context of the social networks that existed in the upper ranks of the officer corps. Historians have noted the prevalence of rival cliques in the British Army prior to the war, as officers associated themselves with patrons who could further their careers. In addition, certain individuals maintained ties with powerful figures, such as King George V, who could bring their influence to bear on promotions in the upper ranks of the army. These social connections shaped relations between commanders in two ways. First, in a general sense, members of competing cliques tended to view one another with considerable suspicion. In addition, ambitious officers actively used their connections to undermine their rivals and advance their own careers. The phenomenon of "Social Darwinism" had several profound and often detrimental consequences for the exercise of command in the BEF in 1914. First, rivalries between officers belonging to different cliques interfered with their relationships during active operations. Rather than suppressing these rivalries at the beginning of the war, officers continued to regard their prewar adversaries with distrust. Sir John French, for example, viewed Sir Horace Smith-Dorrien and Sir Henry Rawlinson with considerable suspicion, due to their association with different patrons as well as their status as rivals to Sir Douglas Haig. During the First Battle of Ypres, this suspicion undermined relations between French and the two corps commanders and indirectly compounded the losses of II and IV Corps.

Second, certain officers took advantage of their connections to operate with a surprising degree of autonomy throughout the 1914 campaign. This tendency proved particularly damaging during the retreat from Mons, when Sir Douglas Haig's close ties with Sir John French allowed him to abandon Smith-Dorrien, leaving II Corps to fight alone at Le Cateau on 26 August. Similarly, Hubert Gough used his friendship with Haig and French to detach his brigade from the Cavalry Division, further depriving Smith-Dorrien of support at Le Cateau. Only during the First Battle of Ypres did this autonomy have a positive impact, as Sir Douglas Haig took advantage of his relationships with Sir John French and the king to operate independently of GHQ and its unrealistic expectations in October and November 1914.

Third, the absence of influential allies resulted in the marginalization of certain officers in the upper ranks of the army. Archie Murray, for example, possessed neither allies within the BEF nor an influential patron in Britain. Consequently, his authority at GHQ was subverted by the charismatic Henry

Wilson, who possessed the loyalties of the Operations Section and, for most of the 1914 campaign, the respect of Sir John French. Wilson's resulting dominance left GHQ prone to the phenomenon of premature cognitive closure, which produced dangerous misperceptions on the part of the senior staff, particularly during the retreat from Mons and the First Battle of Ypres. In addition, the marginalization of Sir James Willcocks had a negative impact on the operations of the Indian Corps. The fact that Willcocks did not possess influential allies encouraged Sir John French and other British officers to treat the Indian Corps with considerable disregard.

Finally, senior officers concealed their own shortcomings and emphasized those of their rivals in order to safeguard their own reputations, protect their positions, and advance their careers. In October 1914, Sir John French consistently provided an optimistic portrayal of the British advance in order to reassure Lord Kitchener of his competence as commander-in-chief. Throughout the campaign, Sir Douglas Haig criticized Sir Horace Smith-Dorrien in his diary in an effort to divert attention from his own failings during the retreat and portray himself as the most capable commander in the BEF. Haig's concern for his reputation extended well beyond the conclusion of the 1914 campaign, as he altered subsequent versions of his diary in order to protect his reputation. Thus, the system of "Social Darwinism" that prevailed in the upper ranks of the BEF in 1914 had widespread and often negative effects.

The specific arguments that emerge from this thesis point to a general conclusion regarding command in the BEF in 1914. They suggest that as British officers entered the war against Germany, they did not conceive of it as a campaign that required fundamental changes in their behavior. As a result, officers at the regimental level and above continued to rely on methods of leadership that they had employed in previous conflicts. Granted, it would have been surprising if officers had abandoned entirely their preference for personal leadership in battle, and in the case of regimental officers, it was fortunate for the BEF that they did not. Even commanders of relatively large formations, however, retained a penchant for personal intervention on the battlefield, despite the unprecedented scale and intensity of the 1914 campaign. More significantly for the operations of the BEF, British officers did not see the outbreak of war as occasion to suppress prewar animosities. What is remarkable is that these rivalries intensified, as officers used the campaign as an arena to advance their own careers at the expense of their competitors. Thus, rather than a crisis necessitating changes in their approach to command, senior British officers viewed the 1914 campaign as an opportunity to gain influence and prestige.

THE LESSONS OF 1914

The impact of the 1914 campaign on the subsequent conduct of the war by British commanders has been largely overlooked. Given that many officers who participated in the campaign rose to senior posts on the Western Front and in other theaters, however, this is undoubtedly a topic that deserves greater exploration. While such an investigation exceeds the scope of this study, it is nonetheless worthwhile to conclude by speculating very briefly on the lessons, or lack thereof, derived by British officers from the 1914 campaign. The experiences of the BEF in this period revealed serious shortcomings at the upper levels of its command structure. Nevertheless, the performance of British battalions and the leadership of junior officers compensated for misperceptions, oversights, and conflict in the upper ranks of the army. Indeed, the tenacity of the regiments of the Regular Army during the First Battle of Ypres enabled victory in spite of the limitations of senior commanders and staff officers. Given the largely successful outcome of the campaign, senior officers did not seriously examine their approach to command in its aftermath.

The intrigues that plagued the upper ranks of the BEF in 1914 did not go completely unnoticed among senior British soldiers and politicians. Early 1915 saw significant changes at GHQ, as Archie Murray, Henry Wilson, and the vast majority of the Operations Section were replaced, apparently at the behest of Lord Kitchener.[2] While this initiative removed several contentious individuals from the BEF, however, it did little to alleviate the problems caused by competition among senior officers. Intrigue continued throughout 1915, resulting in the removal of Sir Horace Smith-Dorrien and Sir John French, and the ultimate ascendancy of Sir Douglas Haig as commander-in-chief.[3] Thus, it appears that the experiences of 1914 did not lead officers to overcome the system of rivalries that pervaded the upper ranks of the army.

While British officers apparently did not learn lessons regarding the negative consequences of their behavior, their conduct of the 1914 campaign may offer insights to historians of the British Army in the First World War. The impact of "Social Darwinism" on the operations of the BEF in 1914 suggests that its effect on subsequent campaigns should receive greater attention. An analysis of relations among Sir Douglas Haig, Herbert Plumer, and Hubert Gough, for example, might expand on the insights provided by recent studies of the Third Battle of Ypres.[4] In addition, a greater awareness of competition among senior officers may provide a more sophisticated understanding of the learning curve experienced by the British officer corps during the First World War. While recent scholarship has demonstrated the technological, tactical and administrative evolution of the BEF, the impact of interpersonal relations on this process has not been examined in depth. Rivalry among officers may have encouraged individuals to pursue innovation on their own initiative. It may also have impeded the dispersal of these innovations throughout the army. This may explain the slow transmission of tactical and operational knowledge between formations in 1917. As Prior and Wilson have observed: "It is a sorry comment on the dissemination of information by the higher commands on the Western Front that the methods used to achieve success by one army commander might be completely unknown to another."[5] Whether its impact was positive or negative, a greater understanding of "Social Darwinism" may provide significant new insights into the process of organizational learning that occurred as the BEF adapted to the unprecedented challenges of the First World War.

Beyond its implications for the history of the British Army, this study may also shed light on the experiences of other European armies at the beginning of the First World War. Existing studies of these armies in 1914 suggest that the command and control problems of the BEF were not unique. As Leonard Smith has observed, French commanders displayed a similar lack of control over subordinate formations during the chaotic retreat of August 1914. Moreover, Dennis Showalter has demonstrated that units of the German Eighth Army also suffered due to a lack of coordination between infantry and artillery as they advanced in East Prussia in late August.[6] Given these similarities, the other difficulties encountered by the BEF may offer insights into the challenges faced by its allies and enemies in 1914. While the prevalence of interpersonal rivalries in other European armies has not been examined in depth, it certainly had the potential to affect the operations of organizations divided by cliques and factions such as the French and Russian officer corps. Furthermore, the independence displayed in August 1914 by German field commanders such as von Kluck and Francois suggests a desire to accrue prestige similar to that shown by Hubert Gough in the same period.[7] The impact of such behavior warrants further examination. As this study of the BEF has demonstrated, it could have a significant impact on operations. Even if it was less prevalent in these other armies, its existence would suggest that the ambitions of individual officers, and competition between them, are important factors in explaining the conduct of the First World War.

NOTES

1. Dennis Showalter, "Even Generals Wet Their Pants: The First Three Weeks in East Prussia, August 1914," *War & Society*, 2:2 (September 1984), 81. In August 1914, Hindenburg and Ludendorff established tactical headquarters "behind key points at the front." According to Showalter, while this practice did not necessarily enhance their control over subordinate formations, "[i]ts real accomplishment was to create a sense of involvement, a sense, however illusory, of being in direct touch with events."

2. Brian Bond, *The Victorian Army and the Staff College, 1854–1914* (London: Eyre Methuen, 1972), 316. On Kitchener's involvement in this process, see Bernard Ash, *The Last Dictator* (London: Cassell, 1968), 175–179.

3. Tim Travers, *The Killing Ground: The British Army, the Western Front and the Emergence of Modern Warfare, 1900–1918* (London: Routledge, 1993), 15–19.

4. For recent studies of "Third Ypres," see, Robin Prior and Trevor Wilson, *Passchendaele: The Untold Story* (New Haven: Yale University Press, 1996); Andrew Wiest, "Haig, Gough and Passchendaele," in G.D. Sheffield, ed., *Leadership and Command: The Anglo-American Military Experience since 1861* (London: Brassey's, 1997), 77–92. Peter Simkins, "Haig and the Army Commanders," in Brian Bond and Nigel Cave, eds., *Haig: A Reappraisal 70 Years On* (London: Leo Cooper, 1999), provides some insightful analysis of the relationship between Haig and Gough in 1917.

5. Prior and Wilson, *Passchendaele*, 57.

6. See Leonard V. Smith, *Between Mutiny and Obedience: The Case of the French Fifth Infantry Division during World War I* (Princeton: Princeton University Press, 1994), ch. 3; Dennis Showalter, *Tannenberg: Clash of Empires* (Hamden, CT: Archon, 1991).

7. On the French Army, see Douglas Porch, *The March to the Marne: The French Army, 1871–1914* (London: Cambridge University Press, 1981). On the Russian Army, see William Fuller, Jr., *Civil-Military Conflict in Imperial Russia* (Princeton: Princeton University Press, 1985); On the German Army in 1914, see Holger Herwig, *The First World War: Germany and Austria-Hungary, 1914–1918* (New York: Arnold, 1997), ch. 3, and Showalter, *Tannenberg*.

Bibliography

PRIMARY SOURCES

Public Record Office, Kew

CAB 45/129: Correspondence Regarding the Retreat from Mons, including T. D'O. Snow's Account of the Retreat
CAB 45/140: E.S. Bulfin Diary
CAB 45/141, 182, 183: Comments on *Official History*
CAB 45/206: Sir Horace Smith-Dorrien Diary
PRO 30/57/52: Kitchener Papers
WO 33/713: War Office-GHQ Telegraphic Correspondence
WO 79/62: Smith-Dorrien-Murray Postwar Correspondence Regarding August 1914
WO 95: GHQ, Corps, Divisional and Brigade War Diaries
WO 256: Douglas Haig, Typescript Diary

Imperial War Museum, London

C.L. Brereton Papers
E. Craig-Brown Papers
G.T.G. Edwards Papers
John French Papers and Diaries
A.H. Habgood Papers
H. Keary Papers
Lord Loch Papers
Ivor Maxse Papers
miscellaneous file 154/2388
miscellaneous file 43
J.L. Mowbray Papers

Archibald Murray Papers
L.A.E. Price-Davies Papers
Horace Smith-Dorrien Papers
K.F.B. Tower Papers
Henry Wilson Papers and Diaries

Liddell Hart Centre for Military Archives, King's College, London

Edmund Allenby Papers
E.H. Beddington Papers
John Charteris Papers
Sydney Clive Papers
Henry De Lisle Papers
James Edmonds Papers
Basil Liddell Hart Papers
Frederick Maurice Papers
Archie Montgomery-Massingberd Papers
Edward Spears Papers

Liddle Collection, Brotherton Library, University of Leeds, Leeds

A.N. Acland Papers
H.M. Alexander Papers
R.D. Jeune Papers
Transcript of Tapes #225–226, Peter Liddle interview with Sir James Marshall-Cornwall, May 1974
Transcript of Tape #268, Peter Liddle interview with Lieutenant-General Floyer-Acland, August 1974

Churchill College, Cambridge

Lord Rawlinson Papers

British Library, London

Aylmer Hunter-Weston Papers
Shaw-Sparrow Papers
Oriental and India Office Collection, L/MIL/5/825, "Reports of Chief Censor"

Intelligence Corps Museum, Chicksands, Bedfordshire

Walter Kirke Papers

National Army Museum, London

Rawlinson Papers

National Library of Scotland, Edinburgh

Douglas Haig Manuscript Diary, August–November 1914

Contemporary Accounts and Memoirs

Baker-Carr, C.D. *From Chauffeur to Brigadier-General.* London: Ernest Benn, 1930.

Barrow, George. *The Fire of Life.* London: Hutchinson, 1931.

Beaumont, Harry. *Old Contemptible.* London: Hutchinson, 1933.

Bolwell, F.A. *With A Reservist in France: A Personal Account of all the Engagements in Which the 1st Division 1st Corps Took Part, Viz: Mons (Including the Retirement), the Marne, the Aisne, First Battle of Ypres, Neuve Chappelle, Festubert, and Loos.* London: Routledge, 1916.

Brett, Maurice V., ed. *Journals and Letters of Reginald Viscount Esher. vol. 3, 1910–1915.* London: Nicholson and Watson, 1938.

Bridges, Tom. *Alarms and Excursions: Reminiscences of a Soldier.* Toronto: Longmans, 1938.

Callwell, Charles. *Experiences of a Dug-Out, 1914–1918.* London: Constable, 1920.

Callwell, Charles. *The Life of Sir Stanley Maude, Lieutenant-General, KCB, CMG, DSO.* London: Constable, 1920.

"Casualty." *"Contemptible."* Philadelphia: Lippincott, 1916.

Charteris, John. *At GHQ.* London: Cassell, 1931.

Coleman, Frederic. *From Mons to Ypres with French: A Personal Narrative.* Toronto: William Briggs, 1916.

Conan-Doyle, Arthur. *The British Campaign in France and Flanders, 1914.* London: Hodder and Stoughton, 1916.

Corbett-Smith, A. *The Retreat from Mons, by One Who Shared in It.* London: Cassell, 1916.

Corbett-Smith, A. *The Marne—And After.* Toronto: Cassell, 1917.

Craster, J.M., ed. *'Fifteen Rounds a Minute': The Grenadiers at War, August to December 1914, Edited from the Diaries and Letters of Major 'Ma' Jeffreys and Others.* London: Macmillan, 1976.

Dunn, J.C., ed. *The War the Infantry Knew: 1914–1919.* London: Jane's, 1987.

Fraser, Pamela, and L.H. Thornton. *The Congreves: Father and Son, General Sir Walter Norris Congreve, V.C., Bt-Major William LaTouche Congreve, V.C.* London: John Murray, 1930.

Fuller, J.F.C. *The Army in My Time.* London: 1933.

Fuller, J.F.C. *Memoirs of an Unconventional Soldier.* London: 1936.

Gleichen, Count Edward. *The Doings of the Fifteenth Infantry Brigade, August 1914 to March 1915.* London: Blackwood, 1917.

Gleichen, Count Edward. *A Guardsman's Memories: A Book of Recollections.* London: Blackwood, 1932.

Gough, Hubert. *The Fifth Army.* London: Hodder and Stoughton, 1931.

Gough, Hubert. *Soldiering On.* London: Arthur Barker, 1954.

Haldane, R.A.L. *A Brigade of the Old Army.* London: Edward Arnold 1920.

Haldane, R.A.L. *A Soldier's Saga.* Edinburgh and London: Blackwood, 1948.

Hamilton, Ernest. *The First Seven Divisions: Being a Detailed Account of the Fighting from Mons to Ypres.* New York: Dutton, 1916.

Home, Archibald. *A Diary of a World War I Cavalry Officer.* Tunbridge Wells: Costello, 1985.

Hyndson, J.G.W. *From Mons to the First Battle of Ypres.* London: Wyman, 1933.

Lowry, Gerald. *From Mons to 1933.* London: Simkin Marshall, 1933.

Macready, Neville. *Annals of an Active Life. vol. 1.* London: Hutchinson, 1924.

Masters, John. *Bugles and a Tiger: A Volume of Autobiography.* New York: Viking, 1956.

Maurice, Frederick. *Forty Days in 1914.* London: Constable, 1921.

Meinertzhagen, Richard. *Army Diary: 1899–1926.* London: Oliver and Boyd, 1960.

Merewether, J.W.B., and Frederick Smith. *The Indian Corps in France.* London: John Murray, 1919.

Montgomery, Bernard. *The Memoirs of Field-Marshal the Viscount Montgomery of Alamein, K.G.* London: Collins, 1958.

Rawlinson, A. *Adventures on the Western Front, August 1914–June 1915.* London: Andrew Melrose, 1925.

Repington, Charles a Court. *The First World War.* Aldershot: Gregg Revivals, 1991.

Robertson, William. *Soldiers and Statesmen: 1914–1918.* Toronto: Cassell, 1926.

Scott, Peter, ed. "The View from GHQ: The Second Part of the Diary of General Sir Charles Deedes, KCB, CMG, DSO." *Stand To!.* 11 (Summer 1984), 8–17.

Scott, Peter, ed. "The View From GHQ: The Third Part of the Diary of General Sir Charles Deedes, KCB, CMG, DSO." *Stand To!.* 12 (Winter 1984), 27–33.

Seely, J.E.B. *Adventure.* London: Heinemann, 1930.

Spears, Edward. *Liaison—1914.* 2d ed. London: Eyre and Spottiswood, 1968.

Stewart, Herbert. *From Mons to Loos: Being the Diary of a Supply Officer.* Edinburgh: Blackwood, 1916.

Swinton, Ernest. *Eyewitness: Being Personal Reminiscences of Certain Phases of the Great War, Including the Genesis of the Tank.* 2d ed. New York: Arno, 1972.

Terraine, John, ed. *General Jack's Diary, 1914–1918: The Trench Diary of Brigadier-General J.L. Jack, DSO.* London: Eyre and Spottiswood, 1964.

Wakefield, J., and J.M. Wippert, eds.. *Indian Cavalry Officer, 1914-1915: Captain Roly Grimshaw.* Tunbridge Wells: Costello, 1986.

Willcocks, James. *With the Indians in France.* London: Constable, 1920.

SECONDARY SOURCES

Articles

Badsey, Stephen. "Cavalry and the Development of Breakthrough Doctrine," in Paddy Griffith, ed., *British Fighting Methods in the Great War.* London: Frank Cass, 1996, 138–174.

Beckett, Ian. "Command in the Late Victorian Army," in Gary Sheffield, ed., *Leadership and Command: The Anglo-American Military Experience Since 1861.* London: Brassey's, 1997. 37–56.

Beckett, Ian. "George V and His Generals," in Matthew Hughes and Matthew Seligmann, eds., *Leadership in Conflict: 1914-1918.* London: Leo Cooper, 2000.

Best, Geoffrey. "Militarism and the Victorian Public School," in Brian Simon and Ian Bradley, eds., *The Victorian Public School: Studies in the Development of an Educational Institution.* London: Gill and Macmillan, 1975.

Ferris, John. "The British Army and Signals Intelligence in the Field during the First World War." *Intelligence and National Security.* 3:4 (October 1988), 23–48.

Ferris, John and Uri Bar-Joseph. "Getting Marlowe to Hold His Tongue: The Conservative Party, the Intelligence Services and the Zinoviev Letter." *Intelligence and National Security.* 8:4 (October 1993), 100–137.

French, David. "Sir James Edmonds and the Official History: France and Belgium," in Brian Bond, ed., *The First World War and British Military History.* Oxford: Clarendon, 1996.

Gardner, Nikolas. "Command in Crisis: The British Expeditionary Force and the Forest of Mormal, August 1914." *War & Society.* 16:2 (October 1998), 13–32.

Gardner, Nikolas. "Command and Control in the 'Great Retreat' of 1914: The Disintegration of the British Cavalry Division." *The Journal of Military History.* 63:1 (January 1999), 29–54.

Greenhut, Jeffrey. "Race, Sex and War: The Impact of Race and Sex on Morale and Health Services for the Indian Corps on the Western Front." *Military Affairs.* 45:2 (April 1981), 71–74.

Greenhut, Jeffrey. "The 'Imperial Reserve': The Indian Corps on the Western Front, 1914–1915." *Journal of Commonwealth and Imperial History.* 12:1 (October 1983), 54–73.

Greenhut, Jeffrey. "Sahib and Sepoy: An Inquiry into the Relationship between the British Officers and Native Soldiers of the British Indian Army." *Military Affairs.* 48:1 (January 1984), 15–18.

Harrison, Richard. "Samsonov and the Battle of Tannenberg, 1914," in Brian Bond, ed., *Fallen Stars: Eleven Studies of Twentieth Century Military Disasters.* London: Brassey's, 1991.

Heathcote, T.A. "The Army of British India," in Ian Beckett and David Chandler, eds., *The Oxford History of the British Army.* Oxford: Oxford University Press, 1994.

Hussey, John. "A Hard Day at First Ypres: The Allied Generals and Their Problems, 31st October 1914." *British Army Review.* 107 (August 1994), 75–89.

Hussey, John. "A Contemporary Record or Post-War Fabrication? The Authenticity of the Haig Diaries for 1914." *Stand To!.* 42 (January 1995), 29–31.

Hussey, John. "Sir Douglas Haig's Diary and Dispatches: Dating and Censorship." *Stand To!.* 47 (September 1996), 19–20.

Luvaas, Jay. "The First British Official Historians." *Military Affairs.* 26 (Summer 1962), 54–58.

Omissi, David. " 'Martial Races': Ethnicity and Security in Colonial India, 1858–1939." *War & Society.* 9 (1991), 1–27.

Phillips, Gervase. "The Obsolescence of the Arme Blanche and Technological Determinism in British Military History." *War in History.* 9:1 (January 2002), 39–56.

Sheffield, Gary. "Officer-Man Relations, Discipline and Morale in the British Army of the Great War," in Hugh Cecil and Peter Liddle, eds., *Facing Armageddon: The First World War Experienced.* London: Leo Cooper, 1996.

Showalter, Dennis. "Even Generals Wet Their Pants: The First Three Weeks in East Prussia, August 1914." *War & Society.* 2:2 (September 1984), 61–86.

Simpson, Keith. "Capper and the Offensive Spirit." *Journal of the Royal United Services*

Institute. 118:2 (June 1973).

Spiers, Edward M. "The British Cavalry, 1902–1914." *Journal of the Society for Army Historical Research*. 57:230 (Summer 1979), 71–79.

Spiers, Edward M. "The Late Victorian Army, 1868–1914," in Ian Beckett and David Chandler, eds., *The Oxford History of the British Army*. Oxford: Oxford University Press, 1994. 187–210.

Thackray, Arnold. "Natural Knowledge in Cultural Context: The Manchester Model." *American Historical Review*. 79:3 (June 1974), 674–706.

Travers, Tim. "The Army and the Challenge of War, 1914–1918," in Beckett and Chandler, eds., *The Oxford History of the British Army*. Oxford: Oxford University Press, 1994. 211–234.

Travers, Tim. "Learning the Art of War: Junior Officer Training in the British Army from the Eighteenth Century to 1914," in Elliott Converse III, ed., *Forging the Sword: Selecting, Educating and Training Cadets and Junior Officers in the Modern World*. Chicago: Imprint, 1998.

Books

Anglesey, The Marquess of. *A History of the British Cavalry, 1816 to 1919, Vol. IV, 1899–1913*. London: Leo Cooper, 1986.

Ascoli, David. *The Mons Star: The British Expeditionary Force, 5th August–22nd November 1914*. London: Harrap, 1981.

Ash, Bernard. *The Last Dictator*. London: Cassell, 1968.

Asprey, Robert. *The First Battle of the Marne*. New York: Lippincott, 1962.

Barnes, R. Money. *The British Army of 1914*. London: Seely, 1968.

Baynes, John. *Morale: A Study of Men and Courage: The Second Scottish Rifles at the Battle of Neuve Chapelle, 1915*. New York: Praeger, 1967.

Baynes, John. *Far From a Donkey: The Life of General Sir Ivor Maxse*. London: Brassey's, 1995.

Beckett, Ian F.W. *The Army and the Curragh Incident, 1914*. London: Army Records Society, 1986.

Beckett, Ian F.W. *Johnnie Gough, V.C.* London: Tom Donovan, 1989.

Beckett, Ian F.W. *The Judgment of History: Sir Horace Smith-Dorrien, Lord French and 1914*. London: Tom Donovan, 1993.

Bidwell, Shelford and Dominick Graham. *Fire-Power: British Army Weapons and Theories of War, 1904–1945*. London: Allen and Unwin, 1982.

Bond, Brian. *The Victorian Army and the Staff College, 1854–1914*. London: Eyre Methuen, 1972.

Bond, Brian, ed. *'Look to Your Front': Studies in the First World War by the British Commission for Military History*. Kent: Spellmount, 1999.

Bond, Brian, and Nigel Cave, eds. *Haig: A Reappraisal 70 Years On*. London: Leo Cooper, 1999.

Bonham-Carter, Victor. *The Strategy of Victory, 1914–1918: The Life and Times of the Master Strategist of World War I: Field-Marshal Sir William Robertson*. New York: Holt, Rinehart and Winston, 1963.

Bourne, J.M. *Britain and the Great War, 1914–1918*. London: Arnold, 1989.

Brown, Ian Malcolm. *British Logistics on the Western Front: 1914–1919*. Westport, CT: Praeger, 1998.

Carew, Tim. *Wipers*. London: Hamish Hamilton, 1974.

DeGroot, Gerard. *Douglas Haig: 1861-1928*. London: Unwin Hyman, 1988.

Edmonds, James. *Military Operations: France and Belgium, 1914* 2 vols. London: Macmillan, 1922 and 1925.

Farrar-Hockley, Anthony. *Death of an Army*. New York: Morrow, 1968.

Fussell, Paul. *The Great War and Modern Memory*. New York: Oxford University Press, 1975.

Griffith, Paddy. *Battle Tactics of the Western Front: The British Army's Art of Attack, 1916–1918*. New Haven: Yale University Press, 1994.

Griffith, Paddy, ed. *British Fighting Methods in the Great War*. London: Frank Cass, 1996.

Harris, J.P., and Niall Barr. *Amiens to the Armistice: The BEF in the Hundred Days' Campaign, 8 August–11 November 1918*, London: Brassey's, 1998.

Heathcote, T.A. *The Military in British India: The Development of British Land Forces in South Asia, 1600–1947*. London: Manchester University Press, 1995.

Herrmann, David. *The Arming of Europe and the Making of the First World War*. Princeton, NJ: Princeton University Press, 1996.

Herwig, Holger. *The First World War: Germany and Austria-Hungary, 1914–1918*. New York and London: Arnold, 1997.

Holmes, Richard. *The Little Field-Marshal: Sir John French*. London: Jonathan Cape, 1981.

Hughes, Matthew, and Matthew Seligmann, *Leadership in Conflict: 1914–1918*. London: Leo Cooper, 2000.

Huntington, Samuel. *The Soldier and the State*. Cambridge, MA: Harvard University Press, 1959.

Jervis, Robert. *Perception and Misperception in International Politics*. Princeton: Princeton University Press, 1976.

Jervis, Robert. *System Effects: Complexity in Political and Social Life*. Princeton: Princeton University Press, 1997.

Lebow, Richard Ned. *Between Peace and War: The Nature of International Crises*. Baltimore: Johns Hopkins University Press, 1981.

Macdonald, Lyn. *1914*. London: Michael Joseph, 1987.

Mearsheimer, John. *Liddell Hart and the Weight of History*. Ithaca: Cornell University Press, 1988.

Omissi, David. *The Sepoy and the Raj: The Indian Army, 1860–1914*. London: Macmillan, 1994.

Omissi, David, ed. *Indian Voices of the Great War: Soldiers' Letters, 1914–1918*. London: Macmillan, 1999.

Palazzo, Albert. *Seeking Victory on the Western Front: The British Army and Chemical Warfare in World War One*. Lincoln: Nebraska University Press, 2000.

Porch, Douglas. *The March to the Marne: The French Army, 1871–1914*. London: Cambridge University Press, 1981.

Preston, Adrian. *In Relief of Gordon: Lord Wolseley's Campaign Journal of the Khartoum Relief Expedition, 1884–1885*. London: Hutchinson, 1967.

Prior, Robin, and Trevor Wilson. *Command on the Western Front: The Military Career of Sir Henry Rawlinson, 1914–1918*. Oxford: Blackwell, 1992.

Prior, Robin, and Trevor Wilson. *Passchendaele: The Untold Story*. New Haven: Yale University Press, 1996.

Rosen, Stephen Peter. *Societies and Military Power*, Ithaca: Cornell University Press,

1996.

Samuels, Martin. *Command or Control? Command, Training and Tactics in the British and German Armies, 1888–1918.* London: Frank Cass, 1995.

Searle, G.R. *The Quest for National Efficiency: A Study in British Politics and Political Thought, 1899–1914.* London: Ashfield, 1990.

Sheffield, G.D., ed. *Leadership and Command: The Anglo-American Military Experience Since 1861.* London: Brassey's, 1997.

Sheffield, Gary. *Leadership in the Trenches: Officer-Man Relations, Morale and Discipline in the British Army in the Era of the First World War.* London: Macmillan, 2000.

Sheffield, Gary. *Forgotten Victory: The First World War—Myths and Realities* London: Headline, 2001.

Showalter, Dennis. *Tannenberg: Clash of Empires.* Hamden, CT: Archon, 1991.

Sixsmith, E.K.G. *British Generalship in the Twentieth Century.* London: Arms and Armour Press, 1970.

Sixsmith, E.K.G. *Douglas Haig.* London: Weidenfeld and Nicholson, 1976.

Smith, Leonard V. *Between Mutiny and Obedience: The Case of the French Fifth Infantry Division during World War I.* Princeton: Princeton University Press, 1994.

Smithers, A.J. *The Man Who Disobeyed: Sir Horace Smith-Dorrien and His Enemies.* London: Leo Cooper, 1970.

Smithers, A.J. *Toby: A Real-Life Ripping Yarn.* London: Gordon and Cremonesi, 1978.

Strachan, Hew. *The First World War, Volume 1: To Arms.* Oxford: Oxford University Press, 2001.

Terraine, John. *The Ordeal of Victory.* Philadelphia: Lippincott, 1963.

Terraine, John. *Mons: The Retreat to Victory.* 2d ed. London: Leo Cooper, 1991.

Travers, Tim. *How the War Was Won: Command and Technology in the British Army on the Western Front, 1917–1918.* London: Routledge, 1992.

Travers, Tim. *The Killing Ground: The British Army, the Western Front and the Emergence of Modern Warfare, 1900–1918.* London: Routledge, 1993.

Van Creveld, Martin. *Command in War.* Cambridge MA: Harvard University Press, 1985.

Winter, Denis. *Haig's Command: A Reassessment.* London: Viking, 1991.

Index

3 Division, 34, 43–45; during retreat
from Mons, 48–49, 54, 56, 61;
during advance to the Aisne, 74, 80–
83, 85, 87, 91, 93, 97, 99–100;
during First Battle of Ypres, 117,
121–35, 183, 186–88, 226, 238
4 Division, 14, 18, 37, 150, 181, ;
during retreat from Mons, 54–58,
61–62; during advance to the Aisne,
78, 80, 83, 87, 93
5 Division, 34, 43–44; during retreat
from Mons, 48–49, 54, 56–57, 60;
during advance to the Aisne, 74, 80,
83, 85, 87–88, 93, 97; during First
Battle of Ypres, 117–23, 125, 127–
31, 133–34
6 Division, 90
7 Division, 15–16, 145–46, 148–50;
during First Battle of Ypres, 152–66,
209, 212–17, 221–26
8 Division, 145, 165, 168
18 Division, 96–97
Cavalry Division, 34, 37–38, 42–43,
45–46; during retreat from Mons, 54,
62–63; during advance to the Aisne,
77, 83, 87, 95
1 Cavalry Division, 96, 149, 189,
215, 228
2 Cavalry Division, 19, 78, 96, 149,
157, 214
3 Cavalry Division, 145–46, 148–49,
152–57, 162, 165–66, 212–16, 220–
21, 226
Divisions, Indian: Lahore Division,
181, 184, 186–87, 191–93, 195, 198;
Meerut Division, 181–82, 188, 191,
198
Drysdale, Billy, 165
Duff, Sir Beauchamp, 181

Edmonds, Sir James, xiii, 40, 89, 109,
117, 129, 160, 185, 188, 209, 211;
assessments of senior officers, 4–5,
8–12, 16; as chief staff officer of 4
Division, 37, 62; allegations
regarding retreat from Mons, 56, 58;
allegations regarding First Battle of
Ypres, 208, 217–19
Egerton, R.M., 198

Falkenhayn, Erich von, 125

Fergusson, Charles, 43, 49, 74, 83, 88;
during First Battle of Ypres, 118,
121, 122–26, 137
Festubert, 136
Fitzclarence, Charles, 222–24, 227, 237
Foch, Ferdinand, 114, 153, 218–219,
224, 226
Forestier-Walker, George, 46, 48–50,
130–31, 133
Fournes, 127–28
French, Sir John, xiv, 39, 42–45, 201
n.33, 238–42; ideas and personality,
2–7, 10–15, 17, 19–24; and Curragh
incident, 3–4, 7, 12, 19–20; during
retreat from Mons, 49–50, 52, 54–
65; during advance to the Aisne, 76–
79, 81–83, 86, 88–89, 91, 95–102;
during First Battle of Ypres, 110–11,
113–15, 120–26, 130–37, 145–50,
208–10, 217–19, 224–26, 229–30.
See also Kitchener, Lord
Fuller, J.F.C., 24

General Headquarters (GHQ), 2–5, 7–
9, 15, 21–22, 28 n.3, 33–35, 38–45,
240–42; during retreat from Mons,
46–49, 51–65; during advance to the
Aisne, 74–77, 79–83, 85–89, 92, 98–
102; during First Battle of Ypres,
109–11, 114–17, 119, 123–26, 130,
132, 134, 137, 145–46, 152–59, 161–
66, 174, 187, 192, 208–13, 230. *See
also* Murray, Sir Archibald;
premature cognitive closure; Wilson,
Henry
George V, King, 12, 99–100, 228–29,
240
Gheluvelt, 115, 212–13
Ghent, 152
Givenchy, 119, 125, 136
Gleichen, Count Edward (15th
Brigade), 6, 96, 118–21, 125–26,
128–29, 136
Gough, Hubert, 6, 11, 15–16, 201 n.33,
240, 242–43; and Curragh incident,
3, 7; ideas and personality, 19–20,
23–24; during retreat from Mons,
56–57, 63; during advance to the
Aisne, 78, 82, 95; during First Battle
of Ypres, 157, 214

About the Author

NIKOLAS GARDNER is currently lecturer in Military History at the University of Salford in the United Kingdom. After receiving his Ph.D. in History from the University of Calgary, he taught European and Military History at the University of Calgary and Mount Royal College.